Positive Learning in the Age of Information

Olga Zlatkin-Troitschanskaia
Gabriel Wittum · Andreas Dengel
Editors

Positive Learning in the Age of Information

A Blessing or a Curse?

Springer VS

Editors
Olga Zlatkin-Troitschanskaia
Mainz, Germany

Andreas Dengel
Kaiserslautern, Germany

Gabriel Wittum
Frankfurt am Main, Germany

ISBN 978-3-658-19566-3   ISBN 978-3-658-19567-0   (eBook)
https://doi.org/10.1007/978-3-658-19567-0

Library of Congress Control Number: 2017963358

Springer VS

Printed on acid-free paper

This Springer VS imprint is published by Springer Nature
The registered company is Springer Fachmedien Wiesbaden GmbH
The registered company address is: Abraham-Lincoln-Str. 46, 65189 Wiesbaden, Germany

Contents

**PART IV
Learning with Ethics and Morality**

Part V
Learning with Information and Communication Technology:
Impact and Risk Evaluation

Editorial – About a ‚PLATO‘

Olga Zlatkin-Troitschanskaia, Gabriel Wittum,
and Andreas Dengel

While learning has constantly been an object of research in manifold disciplines and fields, it has generally been understood in a positive sense. In the Age of Information, we are witnessing an increasing number of phenomena in the context of knowledge construction and accumulation that we describe as "negative learning". This includes, for example, the deliberate circulation of counterfactual knowledge leading to negative learning outcomes, i.e., deficient decision-making and acting, like medical errors.

On the one hand, the age of Internet imposes difficulties in fully avoiding this phenomenon, although new technologies could reduce it. On the other hand, following classical-humanist ideals, we assume to transform negative learning into positive learning, in both formal and informal education, by using new digital and artificial intelligence technologies. These will aim for positive learning outcomes, i.e., correct domain-specific knowledge. However, realizing such a transformation successfully relies on a specific ability to learn in the context of new and constantly changing learning environments of the current Age of Information. Thus, we propose these skills to be a fundamental educational objective in the digital age, purposefully imparted and fostered in the context of formal education.

This objective can only be achieved through multidisciplinary work and comprehensive research. Up to now, too little empirical evidence is available on human learning processes in the Age of Information. Furthermore, traditional learning theories cannot explain the phenomena of positive and negative learning in a differentiated and sophisticated manner. Therefore, a substantial amount of theoretical-conceptual, methodological, and empirical work is necessary on this long research journey. To provide a thorough documentation on the state of research of this newly established international, collaborative research project PLATO („Positive Learning in the Age of Information"), to consolidate the currently rather fragmented research and to provide a common basis for further work, we have published this volume.

The first section of the volume focuses on illustrating theoretical-conceptual fundamentals of positive learning in the Age of Information. *Howard Gardner* reminds us about the three fundamental facets of education in the 21st century, being curriculum, character and context, to accomplish PLATO's educational ideal and research goals. *Stephen Kosslyn* particularly focusses on the specific role and value of humanities, and emphasizes the ideal of the PLATO program, according to which the imparted knowledge and skills are transferable and thus enable the crucial ability to learn in the Age of Information. The first section closes with the chapter of *Zlatkin-Troitschanskaia, Schmidt, Molerov, Shavelson, and Berliner* presenting the conceptual foundations of the newly established terms "positive" and "negative learning". These are also the basis for the subsequent articles that deal with the diverse fundamentals of learning on various levels.

The second part of this volume particularly focuses on primarily neuronal and cognitive fundamentals of learning, as well as their interplay with different information structures and their various representations. By means of videos showing actors speaking a foreign language, in an fMRI-study, *Nagels, Kelly, Kircher, and Straube* demonstrate that hand gesture alert auditory cortices have possible learning impacts on foreign language processing.

In the chapter by *Klein, Dengel, and Kuhn*, the focus is on the importance of information representation for learning. In an eye-tracking study about solving multiple representation problems in upper-division physics, remarkable differences in students' visual attention are demonstrated which essentially influence information processing and learning.

In the third article of the second section, *Markus Knauff* discusses Supporting and Hindering Effects on Rational Reasoning. Based on findings from many experimental studies it is particularly illustrated how people deal with (un)trustworthy information and to what extent this can influence learning.

Whereas the first three chapters mainly deal with the learner's behavior, the focus in the following three essays of this first part is on information structures that serve as learning sources and on their connection to learning outcomes. The chapter by *Wittum, Jabs, Hoffer, Nägel, Bisang, and Zlatkin-Troitschanskaia* deals with the question of how national and mathematical languages are connected, using a computational modeling concept for a quantitative comparison of mathematical and natural language and investigating its effect on learning.

Focusing on cross-linguistic analysis, *Walter Bisang* investigates knowledge representation and cognitive skills in problem solving from the perspective of linguistic typology. By comparing linguistic structures of the Japanese and English versions of a knowledge assessment test he analyses how differences in languages can explain differences in students' test performance.

In the paper from *Mehler, Zlatkin-Troitschanskaia, Hemati, Molerov, Lücking, and Schmidt*, student learning in higher education is explored by integrating computational linguistic analysis of multilingual learning data and educational measurement approaches. In particular, the study illustrated which different language features and text types influence the student performance in the content knowledge test, including cross-linguistic differences between German and English.

The third section of this volume focuses on learning as an interaction and communication process in formal and informal learning environments, which may either foster or inhibit positive learning. The focus is twofold: the first three contributions deal with learning in mass and social media; the two following focus on learning in formal higher education.

In the second paper of this section, *Wineburg, Breakstone, McGrew, and Ortega* present a newly developed assessment of civic online reasoning that measures the ability to judge the credibility of online information. The findings indicate, for example, that students often fell victim to easily manipulated website features. In the next paper of this section, *Maurer, Quiring, and Schemer* illustrate the research from different studies about unintentional learning in, for example, political communication processes, and demonstrate how (mis)represented information influence knowledge acquisition, indicating that media effects positive and negative learning. In the contribution from *Oeberst, de Vreeze, and Cress*, Wikipedia and the extreme right-wing Metapedia were compared in terms of the norm of neutrality, and different analyses demonstrate biases in collaboratively constructed knowledge. In the next chapter of the third section, *Daniel Koretz* critically discusses the approaches to the study on negative learning, in particular in mass and social media, and he emphasizes the importance to distinguish between two different attributes of negative learning, namely factually incorrect knowledge and social undesirable beliefs.

The other three papers in this section deal with learning in formal higher education from the perspective of teaching. *Meyer, Imhof, Coyle, and Banerjee* present a model of deeper learning in higher education and discuss how deeper learning might pertain to the notion of positive learning that promotes the development of disciplinary literacies and transferable knowledge.

Hansen-Schirra, Hofmann, and Nitzke focus on the acquisition of generic competencies through authentic project simulation in translation studies and discuss it as a teaching approach to enhance a development of generic skills in higher education. The third section is closed by *Richard Shavelson* with critical remarks reminding us that education alone cannot overcome negative learning opportunities, and underlining that not only human support is needed to get rid of negative learning but also artificial technologies and intelligent environments that are trained and/or constructed for interaction and communication processes fostering positive learning.

In the fourth section of this volume, the contributions focus in particular on beliefs and attitudes from the perspective of ethics and morality as crucial aspects of positive learning. In the first chapter of this section, drawing on work on the Ethics of Belief and Bayesian Inference, *Wanja Wiese* questions what "positive learning" means in the first place by discussing some conceptual and empirical obstacles in teaching the ability for positive learning, particularly under the umbrella of epistemic norms and the philosophy of mind. In the next chapter from *Dormann, Demerouti, and Bakker*, the focus is on the relation between learning demands and resources, learning engagement, critical thinking, and fake news detection. They contrast negative and positive learning by indicating that motivation can significantly foster while stress can hinder positive learning. Positive learning is not only meant to follow epistemic norms and to foster learning engagement and motivation but also to reconcile morality and rationality. This is dealt with in particular in the contribution from *Gerhard Minnameier*, who discusses positive learning in the moral domain from a decision-theoretic as well as from a game-theoretic point of view. This part is finished by the critical discussion from *Fritz Oser*. Based on the concept of Negative Knowledge he highlights the positive value of negative learning and proposes a transformational model of positive learning.

In the Age of Information, learning takes place with the use of information technology. The fifth and last section of this volume deals with the technological impact and evaluates the opportunities and risks of learning with information and communication technologies. In the first paper from *Koichi Kise*, the focus is on deeply sensing learners for better assistance by going towards the distribution of learning experiences. He claims that not only learners' performance such as the level of knowledge should be taken into account in (dynamical and interactive) e-learning systems, but data from bio-sensors assessed by, for example, eye-tracking, should also be simultaneously measured to get better insights into how positive learning can be promoted.

In an eye-tracking study, *Ishimaru, Bukhari, Heisel, Großmann, Klein, Kuhn, and Dengel* investigate augmented learning on anticipating digital textbooks that display contents dynamically based on students' interests to foster student understanding and learning.

The risks and opportunities of the new information and communication technologies and particularly the Internet regarding its potential to support learning and training in the digital age is discussed by *Kravcik, Ullrich, and Igel* in the third chapter of section five. They consider how augmented reality and educational big data can support the development of artificial intelligent agents that promote learning and teaching in the Age of Information. However, taking into account all aspects of the construct of positive learning, these new technologies not only come with benefits but also with challenges.

The last contribution of section five by *Giovanni Ciampaglia* focuses on the digital misinformation pipeline. Particular attention is paid to the fact that risks that arise not only as a result of biased information (e.g., "fake news") but also due to rumors, hoaxes, propaganda etc. on social media need to be detected and adequately dealt with. The author presents an outlook for further research perspectives in the field of learning with the new information and communication technologies.

Overall, the articles in this volume illustrate the breadth and depth of envisioned research, and present preliminary findings of the PLATO program. As a whole, this volume offer a broad overview of a newly established international field of research, which is of great significance for higher education in particular. More in-depth and extensive work in this field is necessary for exploring the phenomena of positive and negative learning und developing appropriate and effective teaching-and-learning approaches in the 21st century. Along with other recent publications and with leading international studies in this field of research cited in these papers, this volume offers a valuable foundation for further development of this emerging field.

The PLATO research program as well as this volume, which contains documentation on the current state of research, would not have been possible without the excellent collaboration of several universities, research institutes, teams of researchers and experts from various disciplines und research fields. It was the national and international dialog during the preparations for the PLATO program that allowed for valuable insights into current, in part not yet published, research projects and developments. At this point, we would especially like to thank among others *Daphné Bavelier, David Berliner, Giovanni Ciampaglia, Kai Cortina, Luciano Floridi, Angela Friederici, Howard Gardner, Daniel Koretz, Koichi Kise, Stephen Kosslyn, Susanne Lajoe, Richard Nisbett, Fritz Oser, James Pellegrino, Roy Pea, Michael Posner, Richard Shavelson, and Sam Wineburg* for their active contribution to the PLATO project. Of course, not all colleagues and experts were able to contribute to this volume, however, we are very grateful for the collaboration with the ones named above and many more experts and research institutes since they have made a significant contribution to PLATO.

Overall, we thank all advisors and authors, who have supported us with their excellent contributions and thus made this volume possible. In particular, we thank our graduate students at the University of Mainz participating in the PLATO project for providing continuous support in preparing this volume, namely *Carolin Bahm, Alina Dietrich, Mirco Kunz, Sophia Völker and Benedikt Lauterbach*. We also thank *Katja Kirmizakis, Barbara Oppermann, Emily Wattison and Annika Weibell* for proofreading the papers. Finally, we would like to thank the university administration of the JGU Mainz for supporting the PLATO project as well as this volume with constructive advice and finances.

September 2017

PART I
Theoretical Fundamentals
of Positive Learning

Higher Education: A Platonic Ideal[1]

Howard Gardner

Abstract

What form should a non vocational, liberal arts education take in the 21st century? Three facets stand out. Curriculum should foreground those ways of thinking that young adults are capable of: philosophical and semiotic reflection, interdisciplinary connecting, synthesizing and systemic thinking. Character should help to form the kinds of professional workers and citizens which are needed at the local as well as the global level. Context should model and epitomize the kinds of institutions that are worthy of admiration and encourage students to seek and to foster such contexts for the rest of their lives and for posterity. The key components of such an education should be valorized around the world, even as, consistent with the goals of the PLATO Project, it should be perennially adapted to changing conditions. While it is especially appropriate for young adults, it can and should be pursued across the life span.

1 Acknowledgment: I am grateful to Ann Blair, Susan Engel, Wendy Fischman, Jin Li, John Rosenberg, Kathryn Webber, and Ellen Winner for their careful reading of earlier drafts of this essay. I also want to thank the generous funders of the project on "Liberal Arts and Sciences in the 21st Century"—this essay draws heavily on the work that they have supported.

Keywords

Liberal Arts; Curriculum; Institutions; Character; Ethics; Professions; Synthesis; Citizen; Adolescence; Philosophy; Semiotics; Interdisciplinarity.

1   Introduction

As one scans the globe, or even makes comparisons within the United States or Western Europe, the differences across institutions of higher education loom vast. Many are professionally oriented or, at the least, pre-professional; some value a curriculum of choice, others a structured program in the liberal arts and sciences, or deep immersion in a particular subject matter; some emphasize teaching, while others are focused on research and the training of future researchers. These institutions also cater to many different kinds of students, ranging from those whose families are wealthy and highly educated to those who are the first in their families to matriculate beyond secondary school. Ages of the students may vary considerably; and many pay little or no tuition and live at home, while others confront huge fees and may accrue sizeable debt – a debt that may limit their life choices after graduation.

While acknowledging these sizeable and sometimes consequential differences, in this essay I deliberately put them aside. I contemplate the kind of higher education that I would like *all* young people—or at least the vast majority of youth—to have, indeed, to participate in actively. In a few fortunate cases, the students in question will already have achieved such an education by the latter years of adolescence—probably because of the high quality of their primary and secondary educations, possibly because they grew up in a remarkable household or exerted herculean efforts on their own behalf. In many cases, the students may not receive such an education in their late teens or early 20s—but particularly in this era where lifelong learning in increasingly valorized, they should eventually experience it; and both the students themselves and the communities in which they live will be likely beneficiaries.

My focus on late adolescence and early adulthood is deliberate. Adolescents and young adults—roughly 16-25 years of age—are capable of cognitive feats that are beyond the ken of most younger children. At this stage of life, young people are most open to cognitive broadening, least likely to be burdened by other commitments (full time work, taking care of their own household, starting a family).

The education that I describe in these pages is both timeless and timely. Timeless in the sense that it goes back to Socrates, Plato and the period of the Greek city states—and may well have had antecedents or parallels in other traditions with which I have less familiarity (cf. Jaeger 1945). Timely in the sense that it seeks to address the challenges and opportunities of today and, if my intuitions are credible, of tomorrow as well.

Consistent with the organizing principles of the PLATO Project (cf. Zlatkin-Troitschanskaia et al. 2017), I discuss in turn three issues: *Curriculum* (or course of study); *Character* (the kinds of human beings that we hope to nurture); and *Context* (the educational environments conducive to these curricular and character goals).

2   Three facets of teaching and learning in higher education

2.1   Curriculum

Broadly speaking, school curricula in our time should achieve two fundamental goals: Inculcate students in the major ways of knowing that scholars have developed over the past centuries so that the students themselves can employ them and perhaps extend them; and give students the skills to communicate effectively—in writing, in speaking and conversing, in person and online. More specifically, these curricula should introduce mathematical, scientific, humanistic, and artistic ways of thinking and knowing (Gardner 1999). As they are introduced to these ways of thinking, students should learn about the methods that are used by the respective disciplines; which findings (or truths) have been widely accepted and why; which issues are in sharp dispute and likely to remain so; and how one can progress toward consensus, where that seems imminent or possible.

My assumption is that much of this introductory work can be done in primary and secondary education. Obviously, if it has not taken place or has been poorly modelled and/or insufficiently supported, these omissions become additional challenges for formal higher education or for self-education over the course of life.

Accordingly, higher education should introduce students to three broad forms of knowledge with which they are less likely to have familiarity and less able to employ readily:

1. Philosophical thinking

At least since the time of Socrates and Plato, human beings have pondered the deepest and most significant issues of human existence: who we are as human beings, what does it mean to lead a virtuous life; what is truth and how do we establish it; why do we have society (and societies) and how should they be ordered, led, regulated, maintained or changed? Implicitly, we encounter such questions much earlier in life—for example, through stories, works of art, revealing or problematic personal experiences—ranging from residing or travelling in different societies to experiencing the death of loved ones. But most young people do not follow up on these questions in a systematic way; they are unaware of the centuries-long conversation within and across societies on these and other enigmas; they do not explore the links between questions that they themselves are pondering (e.g., Who am I? What is love?), and the many powerful ways in which these questions have been and continue to be pondered by wise women and men.

As one example, consider issues of personal identity—what does it mean to be a person, who am I, why am I the way I am, do others have distinct identities, how do they resemble or differ from my own and how could I tell? Virtually every conscious human being reflects on these issues in one way or another—from the time that we recognize ourselves in a mirror to the time when we contemplate the loss of a loved one or our own death. But our ability to reflect intelligently and broadly on these questions is enormously enhanced if we learn about how thoughtful members of our species have conceived of existence, identity, the self, will, and self-consciousness; how these issues are approached in art and humanistic scholarship, on the one hand, and in studies of other organisms, other entities (like robots), and our own developing brains and minds. As a result of this immersion, we can think more deeply about these issues and communicate our thoughts more effectively to others.

2. Semiotics or modes of symbolization

Like 'philosophy', the polysyllabic word 'semiotics' may be off-putting; but the ideas of semiotics are exciting, and many young people resonate to them (Eco 1986; Goodman 1968; Langer 1942). All of us recognize that we communicate with oral and written language; but we also communicate, knowingly or unknowingly, by means of many other symbol systems—digital, mathematical, computer programs, facial and bodily expressions, works of art, signaling codes, even deliberate omissions and hesitations etc. Each symbol system turns out to be more suitable for addressing certain questions and communicating certain messages than for addressing or communicating others. Each of these semiotic forms works more effectively in certain media—print, film, photography, computer code, hypermedia, two dimension depiction, sculpture, architecture, musical performance—than in others. Coming to understand the means of communication available to us and to others, how they work, what their strengths and limitations are, which sensory systems they engage, which ones we favor and why, turns out to be interesting, enabling, enlarging.

We can carry out semiotic analyses on any kind of message, ranging from our thoughts about our personal identity to our convictions and uncertainties about global warming to our evaluation of the ideas in this essay. As an example familiar to almost everyone, consider what happens when one spends some time in a culture—or even a household—that is quite different from the ones with which we are already familiar. We need to be able to represent this experience to ourselves and, not infrequently, to others—nowadays, most persons would take photographs and post them, though I myself prefer to muse and write (and occasionally dream) about them. The choice of medium is just the beginning: Does one craft a factually objective account in language; compose a story or a poem; make drawings, caricatures, designs, sculptures; devise a website; or choose some other medium of communication? As a parallel exercise, does one look at how others have represented such experiences for themselves and for others—in semiotic terms, which symbol systems do they employ; how and why do they employ them; and with what effect?

3. Synthesizing knowledge

Even those individuals who have mastered specific subjects or disciplines have little experience in combining knowledge, insights, quandaries from these sources of knowledge in ways that are illuminating, or that point up unsuspected problems or unanticipated possibilities and insights. After all, unless you understand a particular way of thinking, or a particular concept, reasonably well, you will not have the requisite distance to judge how it fits, or fails to fit, into ways of thinking or concepts that have arisen in another discipline (or for that matter, in a radically different symbol system). And you may also have difficulty initiating the kind of higher order 'systemic' thinking that allows one to compare one system—whether it be Marxist vs capitalist vs anarchistic views of society; or genetic vs epigenetic vs cultural explanations of behavior—with one another.

Nobel Prize physicist Murray Gell-Mann once remarked that, in our time, the most important mind is the synthesizing mind (Gardner 2005). All of us are now deluged with copious information and misinformation, much of it undigested, much of it difficult to understand, let alone evaluate. No longer can a person simply study one area of knowledge without being exposed to others; the boundaries between areas of knowledge and expertise are increasingly porous. To be sure, various programs and 'apps" may help the individual sift, sort, and synthesize the information that may arise in specific disciplines and be expressed in specific symbol systems—to nudge us toward Positive Learning. But in the end, each of us needs syntheses, interdisciplinary amalgams that fulfil our own needs, our own curiosity, our own rigid as well as flexible views of the world. Similarly, we need bridges between those disciplines about which we are knowledgeable, and those on the border of—or well beyond—our own expertise. While there are formal courses in philosophy and semiotics, the field of personal or computational synthesis is still young. In my own case, I've learned from studying the works of great synthesizers, like biologist Jared Diamond (1999) and geologist Stephen Jay Gould (2002), and by soliciting feedback on my own more modest attempts.

2.2   Character

In most societies, over the centuries, education has had two primary goals: to introduce the major forms of literacy (the traditional 'three R's,) and to nurture individuals of admirable character. When schools were religious in origin and Scripture effectively constituted the curricula, the precepts and desiderata of the religion-in-question determined the character; when schools became public or national rather than dedicatedly religious, the form of character-to-be-achieved was that of a good citizen. And indeed, in many societies today, the national curriculum has embodied within it—implicitly if not explicitly—the traits and traces of patriotism most admired in the ambient society.

Still, at a time when competition among nations is fierce, and national tests focus on disciplines (and particularly performance on tests of Science, Technology, Engineering, and Mathematics (STEM) knowledge), the classical goal of the formation of good character often recedes in importance. Sometimes, there is a focus on what we may term 'performance character'—what it takes to get ahead personally. This focus ignores those traits that are important if we are to serve others than ourselves (Weissbourd and Gardner 2017). And all too often, the formation of character is ignored altogether. This is unfortunate, to say the least. The result is not the absence of character, but rather the encouragement, by default, of less attractive features of character, ranging from selfishness to arrogance to bullying.

On my analysis, growing out of decades of study of good work and good citizenship, it is helpful to distinguish two developmentally arrayed forms of character (Gardner 2010; Gardner 2011; Gardner et al. 2001).

The first is the development of *neighborly morality*. Here I refer to the traits, behaviors, and dispositions that we are expected to develop and exhibit with reference to the people with whom we grow up and regularly interact—family, friends, classmates. Its tenets are familiar to everyone and for the most part uncontroversial: the Golden Rule (do unto others ...) and the Ten Commandments (honor thy parents—and thy God—and refrain from lying, swearing, stealing, killing, and committing adultery). One hopes that as part of growing up in society, one not only knows these tenets but endeavors to follow them; if not, then higher education has a lot of remediation to accomplish.

Much less appreciated, but of great importance in any complex society, are the *ethics of roles* (cf. Weber 1958). In invoking the term 'roles', I refer to the behaviors, attitudes, and expectations that we associate with certain positions (technically, certain statuses) within that complex society. Associated with most roles in such a society is the acknowledgement that difficult issues will arise; by definition, these will not have clear and simple solutions: to resolve these dilemmas, one needs to draw on past knowledge and models, consult regularly with knowledgeable peers, reflect intensively and extensively, make the best decision that time permits; and then, recognizing that one will not always be successful, reflect on what went wrong and how one might do better next time.

In contemporary society, the ethics of roles is constantly tested in two realms: the work of the professional, and the work of the citizen.

For the professional—be one a teacher, lawyer, nurse, or engineer—vexed questions arise almost daily. Whom should one serve? In what way? What to do when there are conflicting demands on one's time, or when one's expertise pulls in different directions? How to balance personal needs and pressures with the code, the ethos, of the profession and of the professional? How to make amends when one has fallen short of the ideals and values of the professions? What are the consequences when one consistently violates precepts of the code? And what happens when long-established norms and practices are no longer viable—as happens all too frequently in a digital age (cf. Susskind and Susskind 2016)?

For the citizen a raft of analogous dilemmas arise. How does one inform oneself with respect to issues of the day? How does one know whom or what to trust and what to ignore? Should one personally run for office or join a governing body? And if not, in what other ways can one contribute to the welfare of the communities in which one lives? How should one vote—especially when there is tension between one's personal wellbeing and the needs and demands of the broader community? And beyond casting a ballot, are there other viable ways to practice good citizenship (petitioning, attending meetings, participating on websites or social media concerned with civic issues)?

I do not wish to suggest that there exists consensus on good work and good citizenship across or even within societies. (Indeed, the concept of 'the good' raises both philosophical and semiotic issues). But I feel confident in asserting that it is best to put forth one's own position publicly; to listen carefully and discuss openly areas of disagreement; to attempt to reach consensus or at least 'agree to disagree'; and to remain open to eventual 'meeting of the minds'.

As is the case with the curriculum that I've outlined, it's important to keep in mind which issues of character can and should be addressed in the first years of schooling—and that is where 'neighborly morality' should be at a premium. In primary and middle grades, kindness toward others and awareness of their needs and desires are key. As one goes to secondary school and to higher education, these facets of neighborly morality should certainly be continued and, indeed, reinforced—and in the best of circumstances, they have been solidified and internalized. But in addition, the educational system needs to prepare young people for the important roles of worker and citizen—because, rest assured, one cannot count on other societal institutions to take on such formidable educational challenges.

Even for young adults who have had a fine education and are primed to master the curricula that I have described and to construct the character that is desirable, the challenges for our time are formidable. Three, even four years may not suffice. But here is where our third factor—the context—can be of signal help.

2.3   Context

The institutions in which higher education takes place have the potential to aid, or to hinder, attainment of the curricular and character goals that I have outlined. Whether they live up to their positive potential—constituting a healthy learning environment—may well determine whether these curricular and characterological desiderata are achieved, or are even broached.

Here I am reminded of a well-known discussion in Gilbert Ryle's philosophical treatise *The Concept of Mind* (1949). In explicating the nature of certain complex concepts, Ryle discourages us from trying to locate them in a particular time or place—he terms this 'the fallacy of misplaced concreteness". As a convenient and apt example, he chooses "The University". Ryle points out that the university does not exist specifically in the buildings or the textbooks, or even the particular subject areas and persons. Rather it is an omnibus concept—one that allows us to continue our conversations about an institution distributed in time and place, even though we may lack a common concrete instantiation. Indeed, 'university' is the kind of concept that young persons may have difficulties in thinking about, because, as primarily concrete thinkers, they are particularly susceptible to the aforementioned fallacy.

But whatever the college or university is, or is not, we may think of it as a set of experiences with certain rough temporal and spatial characteristics. How those experiences play out— particularly at times of crisis or opportunity—constitute powerful learning experiences and especially so when the education is residential and takes place over several years.

An example from my own university: In 2012, a significant proportion of students taking a course at Harvard College cheated. (By a curious coincidence, the course was Government 1310—"Introduction to Congress"!). A scandal ensued and many students were punished. Monitoring the behavior of senior administrators, I was distraught that initially they said so little publicly about the incident—its possible causes, consequences, and implications for future policy. Eventually leaders did take appropriate actions—but at the time I commented that 'the silence at the top' constituted the loudest message of all. In the absence of any explanation or comments from designated leaders, students as well as outside observers were left with a raft of questions: What happened? Why did it happen? Could it have been prevented? What processes were used to adjudicate the cases of accused students and with what effect? What did the events reveal about the College? What change in messages and policy might ensue? And how could one determine whether such changes were effective? Indeed, what does 'effective' mean in such cases? Different attitudes, enhanced understandings, or simply different actions?

The cheating example is just one of the numerous troubling incidents that occur regularly in colleges and universities. Some occur at quite specific times and places: a sexual assault; a fraternity party that results in damage to persons or property; the hiring or firing of a controversial professor; dispute about whether to invite a controversial speaker; and, nowadays, leaks of inappropriate or controversial messages sent through social media. Others are policy issues that are less time-bound but equally serious: On what bases are faculty and senior administrators hired and promoted? Which subjects and topics should be valorized or avoided? Should certain groups (athletes, legacies) get favorable admission or on-campus treatment? And, a question dating back to the time of Wilhelm von Humboldt—Who is responsible for the articulation, monitoring, and adjustment of overall goals—designated leaders, faculty, students, or the demands and priorities of the wider society?

Students will spend an enormous amount of time at the college or university—a time of life when they are highly impressionable and as free from obligations as they will ever be. Drawing on a large scale research project in American colleges and universities in which I am involved, I can conceptualize two very different kinds of institutional contexts:

On campus A there is a clear sense of mission, developed and fine-tuned over a considerable period of time. This mission is well known. Students are informed about it before they matriculate; reminded of it when they come to campus; and observe older students, faculty, and administrators refer to the mission and embody it in their own actions and interactions. Indeed, the full range of staff know and seek to realize the mission; and when alumni return to the campus, they are eager for signs that the mission endures, and they become concerned if the mission seems to have been forgotten, or has become attenuated, or suddenly or subtly changed. Most important, those members of the community who fail to honor the mission are informed that they are undermining its effective operation. If they don't mend their ways, they are to be severed from the community; and there is consensus that the right decision has been made in the longer term interests of the institution and its mission.

On campus B, there is also a stated mission and on paper it sounds good. But the mission is seldom mentioned on tours of the campus; it's not an important part of student experience on the initial days and weeks on campus; and indeed, many members of the community do not remember, or even know, the stated mission. An anthropologist ignorant of the mission would infer the school has *no* dedicated educational mission. Instead, such a mythical observer would conclude that what is valued on the campus are big time athletics, weekend binge drinking, and lavish expenditure on buildings and galas. Special privileges are afforded to successful athletes, while students with large bank accounts exhibit their wealth ostentatiously. When alumni return to the school, they seek to recreate the athletic victories, the parties, and the drinking of their earlier times.

In publications that evaluate institutions of higher education, the two schools may get similar ratings—because the ratings may be based on the selectivity of admission or on reports of student satisfaction or on increase in endowment, but no observer would confuse Campus A with Campus B.

Obviously, these two portraits are exaggerations. Social scientists would call them 'ideal types'—the rest of us might call them 'caricatures.' Campus A may become unduly smug; Campus B may seek to invigorate its stated mission. But anyone knowledgeable about the educational scene in the United States at this time would recognize the difference; and I suspect there would be high agreement on which campuses (far fewer) are closer to prototype A and which are closer to prototype B.

At issue here are the contexts of institutions (Heclo 2011). These contexts take decades to build and achieve so that they actually constitute the DNA of the time- and at- the-place. Alas, the caliber of the institutions can more readily be undermined—one or more ill equipped leaders, crises or scandals not anticipated and not dealt with adequately, can bring about a quick and possibly long-lasting decline or even demise.

Contexts are powerful—be they primary school classrooms, college or universities, religious institutions, or residential neighborhoods. I would submit, that at least in the United States and possible elsewhere, the contexts of institutions of higher education exert powerful, long-term and possibly lifelong effects on the minds and mores of students who matriculate there for several years.

With reference to our themes, educational contexts are powerful and perhaps even determinant of curricula and character. Whether or not the institution (in its mission) pays lip service to the liberal arts, the importance of Socratic discussion or Platonic dialogues, the development of critical and creative thinking, students will notice whether their classes, their clubs, their professors, and others on the campus, are actually and regularly posing big questions, reflecting thoughtfully on possible answers, and sharing the wisdom of the past and its applicability—as well as its possible irrelevance—to contemporary and future concerns. By the same token, students will notice how individuals *ordinarily* treat one another in class, hallways, dining halls, in strolls across campus, at cultural and athletic events; and they will notice equally what gets said and done—and what does NOT get said and what does NOT get done—when something extraordinary happens (as it surely will!) and what consequences ensue in successive days, months, years.

To underscore: Both neighborly morality and the ethics of roles are at stake. Context counts a lot; it can even be determinant!

3   Conclusion

In this essay I've covered a lot of territory. I have allotted considerable space to my own views and, it should be conceded, my own prejudices. I could offer ratio-nales and rationalizations for this decision; but suffice it to say that it is sometimes important to step back, to survey a broad horizon, and to try to make sense of it as best one can—secure in the knowledge that one cannot have it all right and that others will step in and edit or erase as merited (cf. Rosenberg 2017).

This essay is also a response to a specific context: the launching of the am-bitious PLATO Project (cf. Zlatkin-Troitschanskaia et al. 2017). This timely and worthwhile endeavor seeks to lay out, in more specific terms, the higher education that is needed and wanted in our time and how that might be achieved. In my remarks, I have sought to be Platonic in two senses: going back to the roots of education as we know it in the West (Jaeger 1945) and in the sense of an ideal (Platonic) form. Without presuming to appropriate the language of the PLATO Project, I have sought to describe one instance of Positive Learning: curriculum that includes three higher forms of thought (philosophical, semiotic, interdisciplin-ary); character that begins in early life with neighborly morality and then adds a focus on the ethics of civic and professional roles; and the institutional context that is most likely to yield learning which we can valorize and cherish. Both the selection of foci, and my particular 'take' can be debated, and I welcome such debate.

Without doubt, the picture I've sketched is quite American—indeed, representative of that slice of the United States that still values a broad education in the liberal arts, and that recognizes that morality and ethics cannot be assumed, they must be nurtured. Clearly, a fuller picture would need to include systems of higher education that are more focused on particular professions and occupations, that are nationally funded, and that honor international standards, such as the Bologna protocol. Yet, I would regret if readers from other cultural backgrounds were to dismiss as parochial the portrait that I have fashioned here. While the specifics doubtless matter, the broad points about curriculum, character, and context should have global relevance and significance.

But to evoke the terms 'global' or 'universal' reminds us that we live in a rapidly changing and largely unpredictable world (Goldstein 2015; Harari 2017). Architects of the PLATO Project are well aware of this, and so they are appropriately cognizant of developments in brain sciences (and other scientific and humanistic disciplines) as well as breakthrough in technologies, software, hardware, new platforms, new media. It will take individuals far more knowledgeable, far wiser than I am, to judge which aspects of my prescription are timeless and which are, perhaps hopelessly, time-bound—and hence subject to the disruptive forces of our era, ranging from the proliferation of digital and social media to the resurgence of nationalism and xenophobia and propaganda, now lexicalized as 'alternative reality''. Yet, should the time come when much (or even all) of humanity is replaced, by neuro-electric transmission, genetic manipulation, computer programs that are smarter than we are and robots that are more agile than we ever can be, there still remains the haunting question—for what end? And it is to that question that my words have been directed.

Bibliography

Diamond, J. (1999). *Guns, germs, and steel*. New York, NY: Norton.

Eco, U. (1986). *Semiotics and the philosophy of language*. Bloomington: Indiana University Press.

Gardner, H. (1999). *The disciplined mind*. New York, NY: Penguin Books.

Gardner, H. (2005). *Five minds for the future*. Boston, MA: Harvard Business School Press.

Gardner, H. (Ed.) (2010). *Good Work: Theory and practice*. http://thegoodproject.org/pdf/GoodWork-Theory_and_Practice-with_covers.pdf. Accessed: 12 August 2017.

Gardner, H. (2011). *Truth beauty and goodness reframed*. New York, NY: Basic Books.

Gardner, H. (2012, September 23). *Reinventing ethics*. New York Times. https://opinionator. blogs.nytimes.com/2012/09/23/reinventing-ethics/. Accessed: 12 August 2017.

Gardner, H., Csikszentmihalyi, M., & Damon, W. (2001). *Good work: When excellence and ethics meet*. New York, NY: Basic Books.

Gardner, H., & Shulman, L. (Eds.) (2005). On professions and professionals. *Daedalus*, 134(3).

Goldstein, R. (2015). *Plato in the googleplex: Why philosophy won't go away*. New York, NY: Vintage.

Goodman, N. (1968). *Languages of art*. Indianapolis, IN: Bobbs-Merrill.

Gould, S. J. (2002). *The structure of evolutionary theory*. Cambridge, MA: Harvard University Press.

Harari, Y. (2017). *Homo deus*. New York, NY: HarperCollins.

Heclo, H. (2011). *On thinking institutionally*. New York, NY: Oxford University Press.

Jaeger, W. (1945). *Paideia: The ideals of Greek Culture*. Oxford, England: Oxford University Press.

Langer, S. (1942). *Philosophy in a new key*. Cambridge, MA: Harvard University Press.

Rosenberg, J. (2017). An educated core: Rethinking what liberal-arts undergraduates ought to learn, and how. *Harvard Magazine*, July-August, 2017, 47–55.

Ryle, G. (1949; reprinted 2002). *The concept of mind*. Chicago, IL: University of Chicago Press.

Susskind, R., & Susskind, D. (2016). *The future of the professions*. Oxford, England: Oxford University Press.

Weber, M. (1958). *From Max Weber: Essays in sociology*. In H. Gerth and C. W. Mills (Eds.). New York, NY: Oxford University Press.

Weissbourd, R., & Gardner, H. (2017). Beyond performance character: From 'me' to 'we'. (Unpublished manuscript).

Zlatkin-Troitschanskaia et al. (2017). *Positive Learning in the Age of Information*. Draft Proposal Cluster of Excellence. Johannes Gutenberg University Mainz (Unpublished Manuscript).

Why We Should Teach the Humanities

An Outsider's Perspective

Stephen M. Kosslyn

Abstract

The humanities currently are under attack in many quarters. This brief chapter offers a perspective on why they are valuable to teach. Rather than emphasizing their role in illuminating what it means to be human or the like, this chapter underlines their utility in teaching skills and types of knowledge. In particular, it summarizes the role of different aspects of the humanities in interpretation, vicarious learning, understanding human nature, acquiring values, and enhancing experience. The chapter ends with an observation that these skills and knowledge are only useful if they transfer beyond the original context, so that students can use them in their daily lives.

Keywords

Humanities; Vicarious Learning; Human Values; Human Nature; Human Experience; Far Transfer.

1   Introduction

I do not work in the humanities. Nevertheless, I am appalled to see the resurgence of negativity about the humanities and want to provide a perspective on why we should include them in any twenty-first century curriculum—at all grade levels, from K through university.

But first, why is it necessary to defend the humanities? We need to do this because some have tried to treat the humanities as unnecessary luxury items, of interest only to the elites. We are told by their advocates that the humanities lead us to appreciate what it is to be human, but some have questioned what this means and whether it matters. We've lately heard arguments that considering what it is to be human doesn't put bread on the table or help working people get through the day.

But such views miss a crucial point: the humanities are the best way to learn some important skills and knowledge. Yes, they help us to appreciate what it is to be human and to live full and complete lives, but they also serve much more utilitarian, quotidian purposes—and that's what I want to focus on here.

To understand the utility of the humanities, we must begin by appreciating that they are not "one thing," and different aspects of the humanities have utility in different ways. The humanities include literature, languages, history, philosophy, religion, cultural studies, law and politics, visual arts and music. But it's not just the subject matter and approaches that distinguish these fields: They also differ in terms of what we learn from studying and engaging in them.

In what follows I briefly consider the benefits of learning specific aspects of the humanities, with different fields often conferring overlapping benefits. I conclude with a cautionary tale, noting what it will take to realize the full potential of the humanities viewed from this perspective.

2   Five types of benefits

The humanities seem well suited for teaching five different skills and types of knowledge: Interpretation, vicarious learning, understanding human nature, acquiring values, and enhancing experience.

Interpretation

Literature, history (including art history), philosophy and other aspects of the humanities require students to learn "close reading." These disciplines focus on interpretation, on extracting and creating meaning (cf. Mintz 2017). To the extent that alternative interpretations are entertained, this activity strikes to the heart of one type of critical thinking. Students can easily learn to create numerous possible interpretations—and then to consider how best to use evidence to sort among them. Such critical thinking is important in daily life, for everything from evaluating news reports to interacting effectively with other people.

Vicarious learning

Much of literature and representational art has value by putting us in another person's shoes and leading us vicariously to experience different worlds. Later, if we find ourselves in a comparable situation, we have a leg up—having already experienced something about how to interpret and respond to such situations.

More generally, literature—and some representational art—exercises our capacity to see things from novel perspectives. We humans can learn by mentally simulating the world—which often involves visualizing specific scenarios—and by imitating what others do; we don't learn just through brute trial and error (think of what learning to drive would be like if trial-and-error were the only way we could learn!). In fact, a recent study showed that reading literature (but not popular genres) actually increases the reader's empathy (Chiaet 2013; Kidd and Castano 2013). It's easy to argue that one measure of the quality of a piece of literature is the ease with which one can emphasize with the characters and gain new insights and knowledge by accompanying them on their journeys. Such knowledge has obvious utility in human interactions of all sorts.

Understanding human nature

Studying history can teach us fundamental facts about "human nature," about how the environment can shape (and has shaped) what we are and can be. Each historical event is unique, and thus it is difficult to generalize to future events. However, all history involves human beings, and hence history can teach us how human nature can be pushed, bent and molded. For instance, just knowing that certain circumstances can lead people to behave like Nazis is useful when contemplating the possible impact of current and future events. History outlines the extent of the possible, the range of variation of human nature—and this is definitely worth knowing if one wants to understand politics, social interactions, and many other aspects of human behavior.

Acquiring values

Literature, philosophy, cultural studies, the law and politics can help us formulate our own values. Studying these fields is particularly powerful because they can "show, not tell." We can develop our own values by being forced to think through (and feel!) the consequences of possible situations and actions.

For example, think about the classic "trolley car problems" (introduced by the philosopher Phillipa Foot in 1967), where you have to decide whether you should violate a seemingly obvious moral principle (e.g., "don't kill an innocent person") to save even more lives; being in such hypothetical quandaries leads to types of personal growth that are very difficult to achieve in any other way. When done well, such experiences leave it to you, the reader, to decide; nobody is telling you what to think.

Enhancing experience

The utility of the humanities extends beyond learning valuable information. Studying art and music literally changes how we perceive the world—it makes us more sensitive to the world around us. Such sensitivity enhances the kinds of analytic skills that are developed when we in turn interpret what we see or hear.

As if this weren't enough, these sorts of experiences are not only useful and stimulating but also are often pleasurable—which should not count against them! We should not be blinded to the enormous utility of the humanities by the mere fact that we often enjoy them.

3   Making these benefits matter

"The notion that the humanities are essential to creating lives of purpose and meaning, appreciation of the fine arts, and understanding of diversity – is a view that has increasingly lost traction. The idea that the liberal arts have a special purchase on critical thinking, abstract reasoning, and effective communication is rejected by many." (Mintz 2017).

The above quote appears accurate, and there are reasons for this. Aside from issues surrounding political correctness, concerns about job preparation and the like (see Mintz 2017), there seems one other crucial factor: Often the humanities seem self-referential. Teaching in the humanities often does not invite ways to extend the skills and knowledge outside the narrow confines of the materials at hand. However, to be useful, skills one acquires in one context must generalize ("transfer") to others (e.g., see Barnett and Ceci 2002). For instance, learning about human nature by reading novels must in turn apply to real-life situations that share crucial underlying characteristics with the fictional situation. In general, in order accomplish such transfer, so that what is learned in class or via reading is readily applied in daily life, the learner needs both to understand the underlying principles that define when one instance is like another and needs to experience many examples so that it becomes evident how the surface characteristics may vary.

For the humanities, to promote transfer a teacher probably needs to focus on the form of the material, so that skills can be applied to anything of the same form. For example, teaching close reading in one context should then apply in all other contexts—one learns to unpack what one is reading, to draw inferences and evaluate them. These skills can be applied during all reading, and can be taught easily in courses on literature, philosophy, and history.

The utility of the humanities thus depends crucially on how they are taught. Changing teaching so that it promotes transfer will be difficult, but worth the effort—if only because of the way it further enriches the lives of students.

In short, the humanities have much to offer, and what they offer is not easily gained through other means. A person without any depth in the humanities has missed some of the best of what education, and life, has to offer.

Bibliography

Barnett, S. M., & Ceci, S. J. (2002). When and where do we apply what we learn? A taxonomy for far transfer. *Psychological Bulletin, 128*(4), 612–637.

Chiaet, J. (2013, October 4). Novel finding: Reading literary fiction improves empathy. *Scientific American*. Retrieved from https://www.scientificamerican.com/article/novel-finding-reading-literary-fiction-improves-empathy/

Foot, P. (1967). The problem of abortion and the doctrine of the double effect. *Oxford Review, 5*, 1–7.

Kidd, D. C., & Castano, E. (2013). Reading literary fiction improves Theory of Mind. *Science, 342*(6156), 377–380. doi: 10.1126/science.1239918

Mintz, S. (2017). Strategies for saving the liberal arts. *Higher Ed Gamma*: https://www.insidehighered.com/blogs/higher-ed-gamma/strategies-saving-liberal-arts

Conceptual Fundamentals for a Theoretical and Empirical Framework of Positive Learning

Olga Zlatkin-Troitschanskaia, Susanne Schmidt, Dimitri Molerov, Richard J. Shavelson, and David Berliner

Abstract

We present a short overview of the idea, genesis and developing process of PLATO (Positive Learning in the Age of InformaTiOn) as a new, complex, international, interdisciplinary program aimed at investigating the phenomena of positive and negative learning in the digital age. While the basic idea of PLATO originated in empirical educational research, many other very different disciplines have consequently been incorporated into this program, in order to expand learning research and to offer a comprehensive and multi-perspective explanation of learning in 21st century higher education. We draw upon and critically discuss previous research, highlighting implications for developing a theoretical and empirical framework for the new program.

Keywords

Positive learning; Negative Learning; Learning Outcomes; Information; Higher Education; Digital Age; Holistic Model.

1 Introduction and background

The new PLATO program (Positive Learning in the Age of Information) is based on research that has been conducted in the last decade in higher education. As initial reviews of the state of research demonstrated (e.g., Kuhn and Zlatkin-Troitschanskaia 2011), hardly any research had been conducted to enhance scientific knowledge, especially about student learning outcomes in higher education – neither at national nor international level. There had been international studies in the school sector, such as the famous Programme for International Student Assessment (PISA) study (OECD 2014); but higher education research was lacking both the theoretical models and assessment instruments to measure student learning and its outcomes in an objective, reliable, and valid way. In fact, there was hardly any empirical evidence of the knowledge and skills students acquire in higher education, the learning outcomes they achieve by the end of their studies, or the de-facto impact of teaching and learning in higher education.

This was the state of affairs despite significant deficits in students' learning outcomes documented in survey results from the economy and industry and studies on adult education (such as the Programme for the International Assessment of Adult Competencies (PIAAC), OECD 2016). These studies have not only underlined students' lack of domain-specific training, for example, domain-specific knowledge, but have also especially highlighted the inert knowledge (Gick and Holyoak 1980; Meyer and Land 2003; Renkl et al. 1996) or tacit knowledge (Polanay 1966; Schmidt and Hunter 1993) as well as noticeable deficits in so-called 21st century skills. In effect, too many students are unable to transfer the obtained knowledge and skills into real-life contexts. Formal education has not helped them develop some of the skills needed in real life, such as problem solving, analytical reasoning, critical thinking, perspective taking and responsibility for consequences of their own (professional) decisions and actions (Berliner 2013).

More recently, researchers have shown increased efforts internationally to study and assess learning and student learning outcomes (see Zlatkin-Troitschanskaia et al. 2015; 2016a, 2017c, for review). In Europe, and in particular in Germany the national research program, "Modeling and Measuring Competencies in Higher Education" (KoKoHs), was established to address these deficits.

The KoKoHs program contributed significantly to PLATO by establishing a new field of research on learning outcomes in higher education, bringing together the most renowned international researchers from more than 20 countries and 4 continents in an effective cooperation network and building a new community in empirical higher education research (Zlatkin-Troitschanskaia et al. 2017a, c).

Funded by the German Federal Ministry of Education and Research with approximately 25 million euros, KoKoHs comprised more than 70 research projects and 220 researchers. KoKoHs researchers began modeling and measuring both students' learning itself and the effects of college attendance on learning in an objective, reliable, and valid way and over time. They developed more than forty conceptual models and over two hundred test instruments for various study domains (e.g., engineering, economics, teacher education etc.) (Zlatkin-Troitschanskaia et al. 2017a).

A follow-up phase of the KoKoHs program is currently in progress (2016-2020) (Zlatkin-Troitschanskaia et al. 2017b). While models and test instruments for measuring students' domain-specific and generic knowledge and skills exist and innovative measurement methods are being developed in KoKoHs, one challenge currently being addressed are longitudinal models of change in learning and of learning effects (e.g., value-added models, Shavelson et al. 2016).

Most of the instruments have been validated and tested with several thousand students. Overall, KoKoHs has assessed over 50,000 students from over 230 universities in Germany in different study domains (Zlatkin-Troitschanskaia et al. 2017a). A few test instruments have also been adapted and used in international studies. For example, the translated and adapted versions of the same test instruments were used to assess economic knowledge in Germany as well as in America, Asia (Japan and South Korea) and in some European countries (Austria, Finland and Switzerland) (e.g., Brückner et al. 2015b; Förster et al. 2015; Zlatkin-Troitschanskaia et al. 2016b).

So far, the findings from KoKoHs empirical research are in parts very alarming: Students in various study disciplines showed lower competency levels than expected. For instance, the majority of students in teacher education in the field of German as a second language only met a minimum standard (e.g., Gültekin-Karakoç et al. 2016). OECD studies have shown further sobering findings, as well, indicating that students' skills do not necessarily increase with more years spent in formal education in schools and universities (OECD 2016). The international PIAAC study assessed basic adult skills (reading proficiency, everyday calculation skills, and technology-based problem solving) and showed in particular that a person's skill level does not necessarily correlate with the number of years spent in formal education and training, implying that more formal education does not guarantee the higher-level abilities needed in a globalized information society.

In fact, students' performance on the same content knowledge tests, for example in economics, over the years or compared between the first and the final year of studies showed evidence of a decrease in domain-specific knowledge not only at the individual level but also across institutions (e.g., Brückner et al. 2015b; Zlat-

kin-Troitschanskaia et al. 2016b). The results on study success showed extreme inter-individual differences in knowledge acquisition and learning outcomes among
students even within disciplines (e.g., in economics and engineering). Some studies
indicated systematic effects for students from specific socio-demographic groups
or learning paths and unfavorable entry conditions were hardly compensated for
over the course of studies (e.g., Happ et al. 2016a).

In general, a significant number of students displayed a decrease in domain-specific knowledge acquisition over the course of their studies (e.g., in economics,
Happ et al. 2016b). This could be interpreted as "negative" learning, in which the
intended acquisition of subject-specific concepts or generic abilities and skills that
are nonetheless crucial to solving subject-specific tasks was not achieved during
the course of studies (e.g., Brückner and Zlatkin-Troitschanskaia in press 2018). So
far, little is known about the causes of this phenomenon or as to whether and how
such undesirable effects could be alleviated through targeted teaching-and-learning opportunities and support in (formal and informal) education.

The term *negative learning* originates from this context describing the phenomenon of decreasing content knowledge among students in the course of their
(economics) studies (Walstad and Wagner 2016; Happ et al. 2016b). Walstad and
Wagner (2016) first introduced the term negative learning to describe change in
knowledge levels in a pre-posttest study: from correct responding on the pretest to
incorrect responding on the posttest.

We would like to stress that we do not consider effects of forgetting or generalization of knowledge as forms of negative learning. As PLATO advisor Daphné
Bavelier rightly argues, many studies on brain plasticity and learning indicate that
forgetting knowledge details or generalizing through and across learners' experiences is a fundamental and necessary part of constructing (new) knowledge (see
also Richards and Franklan 2017, for review). Bavelier suggests that especially
from a neuroscientific perspective forgetting details may be a key to the unique
way learners transfer and generalize knowledge (and for how inadequate deep networks are at this type of transfer, see, e.g., Momennejad et al. 2017)[1].

Measurement bias and errors may obviously occur due to the field testing
conditions when assessing students' learning, especially learning over time, and
a much more precise and in-depth analyses of the effects of forgetting, co-con-
struction, generalization, and transfer of knowledge are necessary. When explaining domain-specific learning, in particular, one can also argue that – following
established learning models such as "threshold concepts" (Meyer and Land

---

[1]   We are highly grateful to *Daphné Bavelier* for providing this extremely valuable
    comment.

2005; Davies 2012) – students need to reorganize prior knowledge around different topics or models in order to achieve higher thresholds (Brückner and Zlatkin-Troitschanskaia in press 2018). However, existing findings, for example, from examinations of knowledge acquired in classes attended or from analyses of distractors and response behavior (see section 2) indicate that, aside from the expected effects of forgetting, students also acquire factually wrong knowledge such as domain-specific misconceptions, which we consider a form of negative learning. Conceivable explanations of negative learning can be manifold: One explanatory factor may be the amount of freely accessible, reliable (or unreliable) information about a discipline or area of knowledge from credible (or untrustworthy) sources (e.g., Wineburg in this volume). Hence, when explaining negative learning, we expect to see differences between disciplines and study domains such as mathematics and economics. This and other assumptions need to be verified.

Bearing these and further possible concerns (see below) about the concept of negative learning in mind, a complementary concept is defined as a fundamental educational goal: As an initial conceptual approach, *positive learning* is characterized in contrast to negative learning as successful acquisition of subject-specific or generic concepts, abilities, and skills. However, there is much more. When looking beyond mere learning skills and processes within individual students at the sources of information used in learning, the learning environments, and social and societal contexts in which knowledge, skills and abilities are acquired, a broad field of potential influences opens that might explain learning. For instance, students may develop false disciplinary or interdisciplinary concepts (misconceptions or alternative conceptions) as well as attitudes and prejudices that impede learning and information processing according to common quality standards (e.g., introducing bias), or contradict universal societal values and norms, i.e., of the humanist ideal (see also Köhler 1938). Teaching positive learning, then, includes providing students and citizens with a capacity for warranted (factual and ethical) beliefs (see also Lind 2016). Thus, positive learning can be described as a state of development along the lines of moral behavior based on warranted knowledge and evidence as well as ethical beliefs.

What is more, research on learning needs to be contextualized within the realities of knowledge acquisition today, which include enormous changes in media and information landscapes due to digitalization and new information and communication technology (ICT) as a source and environment for learning and increasingly as a generator of information (e.g., artificial intelligence applications). While digitalization has been implemented more slowly in formal education than in some other areas of society it is an old truth in educational research that much of students' learning takes place outside of formal education environments, even in occasions when students may not be aware they are acquiring knowledge (e.g., when consuming mass or social media). Studies outside of formal education have been a desideratum for a long time, but have rarely been undertaken by educational researchers due to challenges of accessibility and privacy. This said, a holistic model of positive learning would need to include these different dimensions, which can be integrated within a large-scale fundamental interdisciplinary research program such as PLATO.

Having described the conceptual and empirical basis for PLATO we present now the most relevant studies and results bearing on this new initiative. We focus on both the findings from empirical learning research and existing conceptual approaches for describing student learning[2] (section 2). On this basis, we summarize implications for the development of a theoretical and empirical framework for PLATO[3] (section 3). Finally, we draw some overall conclusions for further research in PLATO (section 4).

2   Research on learning in educational and non-educational contexts

For a literature search using the combination "learning" and "education", Google scholar found more than 3.730.000 scientific papers in approx. 0.15 sec. Hence, at least quantitatively, one can hardly talk about research gaps. At the same time, there is consensus in the scientific community that the existing models and approaches cannot adequately explain learning processes or learning outcomes in the 21st century. As the PLATO advisor and cooperation partner, educational researcher James Pellegrino pointed out very fittingly:

> "Most current approaches to curriculum, instruction, and assessment are based on theories and models that have not kept pace with modern knowledge of how people learn. They have been designed on the basis of implicit and highly limited conceptions of learning [...] [that] tend to be fragmented, outdated, and poorly delineated for domains of subject-matter knowledge" (2006, p. 3).

---

2   A comprehensive overview of all relevant works would go far beyond the scope of this chapter. For a more detailed insight, see encyclopedias such as Weinert (1996); Fry et al. (2008); Secolsky & Dension (2017).

3   Acknowledgements: suggestions and recommendations by many PLATO advisers and cooperation partners were included in this chapter. In particular, we would like to thank *Daphné Bavelier, Klaus Beck, Angela Friederici, Howard Gardner, Stephen Kosslyn, Susanne Lajoe, Stefan Müller-Stach, Fritz Oser*, and *Michael Posner*.

This criticism refers to implicit and limited assumptions about learning in current research, which would lead to a perpetuation of fragmented and unclear ideas about teaching-and-learning structures and processes. As the traditional concept of learning is rather narrow, research has expanded its conceptualization, for example, as: deeper learning (Pellegrino and Hilton 2012), higher-order learning (Paas et al. 2003), insightful learning (Baumert et al. 2004), collaborative learning (Vygotsky 1978), conceptual learning (Gagné 1985), inferential learning (Minnameier 2016), self-regulated learning (Bandura 1979) and multimedia learning (Mayer 2005). While these and other existing concepts for describing and explaining learning in the context of traditional teaching-and-learning theories (e.g., Alexander 1997; Bandura 1979; Bruner 1966; Köhler 1947; Mayer 2002; Mislevy 1996; Pellegrino and Glaser 1982; Piaget 1972; Skinner 1953; Snow 1989; Tolman 1952; Vygotsky 1980; Weinert 2001) are significant and valuable, they are, however, pushed to their limits when attempting to explain learning in the age of information. In particular, current learning theories do not offer sophisticated explanations for the phenomena of negative and of positive learning in the digital age.

Other established theories, which have been in use for some time already, have not succeeded in explaining sufficiently the interindividual differences in student performance; such models have included the learning taxonomy by Bloom (1956) and by Anderson and Krathwohl (2001), conceptual threshold models (Meyer and Land 2005; Davies 2012), novice-expert models (Chi 1981; Alexander 2003) or the still relatively young concept of competence (Weinert 2001). All those theories have in common that they define learning or learning outcomes as consisting of different knowledge types, abilities and mental processes. However, neither the classification of knowledge and skills into different (cognitive) levels nor of the tasks into different degrees of difficulty has led to sophisticated explanations of the differences in student learning. For instance, research on expertise (e.g., Ericsson and Charness 1994) has yielded the insight that prior knowledge is more important in solving domain-specific tasks than general cognitive abilities such as intelligence (Chi 1981; Chi et al. 1981; for the multiple intelligence see Gardner 1999, 2011). However, this line of research has hardly considered any individual preconditions that could have thoroughly explained possible differences also on an expertise level.

Current competency research is aimed at investigating learning from a holistic perspective by including not only purely cognitive facets but also non-cognitive dispositions. Yet, even this approach lacks the consideration of fundamental structures of learning besides the typical psychological and pedagogical facets. Notably, most of the abovementioned learning concepts and models are based on theories that were developed before the digital age. The peculiarities that the new technology presents to learning have not been considered in most of these theories. For instance, Mayer (2009) pointed out that there is a lack of empirically founded insight and theoretical explanatory models that would enable evaluations of the effectiveness of various kinds of digitally supported learning.

The current analyses of decreasing content knowledge among university students indicate that this phenomenon goes far beyond explanations such as forgetting curves (Loftus 1985; Averell and Heathcote 2011) or testing effects such as guessing in multiple-choice questions (e.g., Happ et al. 2016a; Walstad et al. in press), and may also encompass the (unconscious) development of misconceptions during studies. For instance, as the studies by Brückner (2017) and Brückner and Zlatkin-Troitschanskaia (2018) indicate, using the example of misconceptions in learning economics, there are significant correlations between correct response rates on economics knowledge tests and student's perceived familiarity with an economic concept, i.e., familiarity with given content, which in turn influences the rate of correct responses significantly. The results indicate that the perception of information, which is also based on (non-cognitive) beliefs, plays a significant role during learning and acquisition of knowledge (see also Dormann et al. in this volume).

This is a remarkable finding that raises questions as to what causes the observed negative learning effects and whether and how one can increase the likelihood that college and university graduates become competent, responsible and autonomous citizens (equipped) with 21st century knowledge and skills (e.g., Lai and Viering 2012; Pellegrino and Hilton 2012). Even though we cannot compare learning outcomes today with learning outcomes prior to the age of information, we can recognize the influences many different sources of information and various teaching-and-learning media have on learning outcomes, without, however, being able to explain either the positively intentioned, the negative, unintentional effects or the underlying correlations.

The introduction of digital, interactive media has enabled new types of knowledge accumulation, teaching and learning as well as information consumption, which all take place on a global scale but have been insufficiently examined so far. The implementation of new media as teaching-and-learning resources with (possible) complex, diverse or even conflicting information correlate with unintended negative effects of education related to the acquisition of knowledge and skills in the sense of positive learning (e.g., Dormann et al in this volume). However, we do not yet have the necessary theory-based explanatory models to systematically differentiate media use and information processing of individuals and society that stimulate or inhibit positive learning (on media effects, see Mauer et al. in this volume; Oeberst et al. in this volume).

Many studies indicate that multiple representations of information (e.g., simultaneously presented verbal and visual modes) are not always an advantage for learning (e.g., Goldmann 2003). One possible negative effect is information overload, which refers to learners being unable to process and efficiently organize the available data and information, particularly when they are novices and the information is presented in unfamiliar representation formats and systems (e.g., Berka et al. 2007; for further effects in digital education see, e.g., Horz 2011). With cognitive overload or mental overexertion, learners may perceive the multitude of information and data as "stressors" in the learning process (see also Dormann et al. in this volume). However, if personal and situational conditions are favorable, numerous sources of information from various media can function as cognitive stimulators, tapping additional mental resources and supporting the intended knowledge acquisition.

Research projects in mathematics and physics education indicate that competent handling of multiple representations is linked with domain expertise and serves as a basis for gaining deep, robust and flexible conceptual understanding of the underlying content domain (e.g., in physics, see Kohl and Finkelstein 2005; 2006; Docktor and Mestre 2014; Meltzer 2005). While studies highlighted differences between problem-solving approaches of experts and novices, with some of these differences involving representation use (for, e.g., accidental representational effect see Zhang and Norman 1994), only a few studies have compared students' attention to representations of information while solving a problem in the domain.

In addition to limited understanding of the impact of individual differences among students on learning, we have limited knowledge of the impact on learning of fundamental linguistic, numeric-mathematical and spatial information representation structures (e.g., Mehler et al. in this volume) and the corresponding mental structures and processes they evoke in learners. Research on fundamental information structures and mental processing as well as recent linguistic and (neuro-)cognitive research have given multiple insights into the relationship between individual thought patterns and languages (e.g., Nagels et al. in this volume; Bisang in this volume), and particularly between language structures and numerical thinking. For instance, studies have repeatedly shown an impact of numerical data in test tasks, compared to tasks that contained no numerical data (e.g., Brückner et al. 2015b; Shavelson et al. in press). However, the relation between language and thinking is still under researched. Meanwhile, some theories suggest that the differences in thinking are not exclusively based on language but also occur in non-language-based learning tasks, for example, in figural and mathematical tasks (Waldmann 2008; Goldstone and Steyvers 2001; Spelke and Tsivkin 2001). The investigation of numerical or mathematical structures and their effects on learning is still underresearched, as well (e.g., Wittum et al. in this volume). For instance, current research, for the first time, is trying to describe neuro-cognitive processes in linguistic topologies (in the form of homotopy types) using mathematical models (Manin 2015)[4].

In summary, as noted, only a small number of studies have considered some contextual and individual factors impacting knowledge acquisition and student learning outcomes in higher education when examining the development of specific aspects of student knowledge and skills. Based on existing educational and learning theories and models alone we cannot adequately describe or explain the phenomena of positive and negative learning (see one example in Mehler et al. in this volume). To explain negative and positive learning, the concept and its explanation factors need to be described and operationalized through suitable modeling and measuring approaches (e.g., Mislevy 2016; Brückner and Pellegrino 2016; Shavelson et al. 2015). For instance, distinct classifications of information structures are necessary to differentiate positive from negative effects in different learning contexts. Hence, a key question for PLATO is: How can we build on existing research in order to achieve significant progress in learning research by explaining negative and positive learning in the age of information?

3   Implications for developing a PLATO framework

The program's title PLATO is not only an abbreviation of Positive Learning in the Age of Information, but also refers to the philosopher *Plato* who posited the axiom in his *"Allegory of the Cave"* which can be interpreted as follows: Learning occurs through the conscious or unconscious perception of information from the environment and through individual or social (co-)construction of knowledge when it is integrated with previously acquired information. The title is programmatic: One of the central research focuses in PLATO is on investigating information as a source and means of (positive and negative) learning and the underlying structures of information (e.g., linguistic), as well as, cognitive, and neuronal correlates.

When investigating and explaining learning in the age of information the current state of research highlights that it is no longer sufficient to consider learning exclusively from a formal educational research perspective. As learning is always embedded in a specific situational context, the associated cognitive and non-cognitive processes need to be explained in relation to the characteristics of the specific learning sources and means (such as tasks, teachers, books, social media, etc.).

---

4   We are highly grateful to *Stefan Müller-Stach* for providing this valuable comment.

So far, only separate, isolated perspectives have been examined; they need to be integrated into a holistic perspective in a comprehensive model. When looking to current research for a model, we found that learning processes and outcomes, particularly in higher education, have not yet been comprehensively evaluated or modeled – despite the existence of descriptive and explanatory approaches fragmented across various disciplines and research fields. Consequently, a task in PLATO is to combine these approaches in an integrative model. To explain learning in our time, among other PLATO advisors, educational measurement expert Robert Mislevy (2016), in his socio-cognitive approach, suggested to consider learning from multiple disciplinary perspectives, and on different layers, not only within individuals, but also in terms of regular patterns in interactions between learners, i.e., the inter-individual systems they create, including language, culture, etc. To this end, he has provided an integrative framework based on a confluence of ideas from different research areas (e.g., from educational sciences, learning research, teaching methodology, sociolinguistics, research on different types of literacy, computer sciences, anthropology as well as cognitive and situational socio- and neuropsychology). Mislevy's approach (2016) integrates inductive, empirically driven approaches (examining social and cultural patterns) and deductive, theoretically driven approaches (from, e.g., cognitive psychology and neuropsychology).

According to Mislevy's (2016) approach, human cognitive processes (as well as some neurological fundamentals), including corresponding mental operations, can be modeled as bridging interactions between the person's knowledge, skills, abilities, and other characteristics, and information represented in specific (e.g., computer-based) learning sources; learning/media environments can be interpreted as cognitive stimuli or activators for (but also as inhibitors of) learning. Consequently, each information characteristic can be connected to a person's corresponding information processing, which needs to be further specified; for instance, language abilities could be specified in terms of reading or listening comprehension, using a linguistic complexity coefficient based on, for example, syntax, lexis, ambiguity (Mislevy and Yin 2009; Mehler et al. in this volume; Kise in this volume).

Significant differences were found between students' test results depending on both the language of the test instruments and the students' language proficiency (e.g., Brückner et al. 2015a; Happ et al. 2016a); however, such language-related differences could not be explained from the educational research perspective alone, and needed expertise from linguistics. The specific expertise offered a deeper understanding of language issues, adaptations of test instruments, and their respective consequences for learning (e.g., Bisang in this volume; Mehler et al. in this volume).

Beside the linguistic differences, another remarkable finding were systematic differences in students' performance depending on mathematics-related test item components: Within the same content knowledge test in one study domain, for example, in the study domain of economics, student performance differed significantly between items that required students to carry out mathematical operations and items that required no use of mathematics (e.g., Brückner et al. 2015b; Shavelson et al. in press). The fact that different disciplines rely on mathematics to different extents is not new, but these findings indicate that content knowledge structures do not necessarily follow disciplinary layouts. Hence, the PLATO program needs to focus more closely on the fundamental structures that enable or support knowledge acquisition in various study domains.

Following the idea from linguistics and particularly language typology—that types of language structures can be traced across different languages (Bisang in this volume)—the question arises whether this idea of "typology" could also be transformed and adapted for mathematics. If so, the existence of regular mathematical structures in thought could be explored, in the sense of mathematical typologies.

This example indicates that much more fundamental and sophisticated research, an emergence and confluence of expertise from mathematics, linguistics, computer science, neuroscience and cognitive science, communication and media science etc. as well as several very different intersecting disciplines is required.

The first cornerstone (A) for collaborative research in PLATO was set with a focus on information structures and information processing (e.g., Wittum et al. in this volume; Mehler et al. in this volume). To explore the nature of negative and positive learning from the perspective of mental structures and cognitive and neuronal correlates of information structures, expertise from cognitive and neuroscience needed to be included in PLATO (e.g., Knauff in this volume; Nagels et al. in this volume).

Besides exploring fundamental mental structures, the question of positive and negative learning in the age of information is closely related to students' interaction with information itself, with its representation, sources, and with the environment. After all, mental structures are built up from and influenced by informational structures.

Current findings from media and communication sciences suggest that especially use of online (mass and social) media not only may play a key role in learning, but that negative learning in particular might be associated with online media use (e.g., Maurer et al. in this volume; Oeberst et al. in this volume).

As findings from empirical educational research indicate, only a small part of students' learning can be explained by their participation in formal learning opportunities (Zlatkin-Troitschanskaia et al. 2016a); the remaining variance may be due to informal and unintended learning. So far this is rarely studied empirically, and media consumption in particular is usually not classified as formal learning. Hence, in PLATO, informal and unintentional (knowledge and skill acquisition that students may not even recognize) learning also needs to be included, such as deliberate knowledge and skill acquisition in media environments, as well as unintended learning.

In different informal environments, students may acquire knowledge that could equally influence their learning in higher education. While the differences in learning under these conditions are hardly researched, one can expect, however, significant differences in students' attitudes and motivations but also in their critical stance and dedication to retaining content, and that these factors can influence learning. In this regard, PLATO places a special focus on self-regulated learning (Dabbagh and Kitsantas 2012; see also Dormann et al. in this volume). In order to understand the processes of unintentional learning and to enable students to develop personal abilities to filter information cognitively and morally and to, then, embed it in their existing network of knowledge, there needs to be more detailed insights on the interdependencies between learning materials from diverse sources (e.g., different Internet sources) and learning mechanisms.

To further and deeper explore this very large area of knowledge generation through interaction and communication in different learning environments, - that builds the second cornerstone (B) in PLATO - broad and various expertise from several areas of education, communication and media science, psychology, sociology, and intersectional disciplines such as educational psychology is included.

In the digital age, it is also becoming more and more important for students (and citizens more generally) to develop specific abilities and skills to deal with the abundance of information in environments inside and outside of formal higher education. Students should be able to not just take in any information they find online, but also to first evaluate its quality, for example, by judging the credibility of the source (e.g., Wineburg in this volume). The call for critical thought is an old one, although with new media, the demands for identifying credible sources have increased. As previous findings suggest the conditions of some new media environments are less favorable for positive learning than others (e.g., Oeberst et al. in this volume); or that some habits, behaviors or mental structures resulting from consistent use of specific media may leave students more or less predisposed to acquire new knowledge.

Certainly, today's fake news and alternative facts, which gained notoriety, for example, in the course of the US presidential election, have led to increasing concerns about possibly negative learning from media sources. These concerns include the political instrumentalization of information, attacks on the way knowledge is generated, disregard for long-established quality standards by some parts of society, or perhaps an indifference about how to use and accept knowledge generated by others (e.g., Koretz in this volume). One might argue that the PLATO program is especially topical for this reason alone. However, PLATO's idea and corresponding research go far beyond learning with "fake news", which could be a passing problem for which automatic detectors might exist in the near future (e.g., Ciampaglia in this volume). Hardly any artificial learning system can evaluate the moral and ethical value of information; let alone the fact that any automated program such as fake news detectors can also be manipulated or misused by its creators. Hence, PLATO includes not only analyses of biased and manipulated information by means of artificial intelligence but also goes beyond with a focus on morals and ethics as normative fundamentals of positive learning in the digital age –forming a third cornerstone in PLATO (C).

In the future, students (and citizens) will increasingly need to take responsibility for what they learn inside and especially outside of higher education institutions. Students need to acquire essential skills such as critically dealing with diverse media and a changing media landscape. Before they can be taught these abilities, it is first necessary to examine the conditions for distinguishing and acquiring quality information in depth. In this context, philosophy and ethics serve as linking disciplines which could help bridge findings from the abovementioned individual research areas in PLATO through overarching concepts that explain what we are justified to believe and at what point we can accept knowledge (e.g., Wiese in this volume).

The absence of a critical stance toward information can lead to disastrous decisions, and educators are fast to call for more critical thought. However, at the same time, too much deliberation (e.g., continuous doubting), especially of low quality or of little discipline, can be impractical and inhibit action. Hence, it is necessary to teach context-sensitive models of reasoning that lead to positive learning (Gardner in this volume; Shavelson in this volume).

Besides the Ethics of Belief from the field of philosophy (Wiese in this volume; Metzinger 2009), expertise from the field of theology is considered in PLATO, as well. Beliefs including epistemological and religious orientations determine how we approach, select, and process new information, and what moral and ethical standards we apply to it. Hence, morals and ethics play a crucial role in knowledge acquisition: new notions may conflict with previously acquired knowledge; and students then need to resolve these conflicts and dilemmas (e.g., Lind 2016; Minnameier in this volume). On the one hand, a strong ability to identify moral and ethical conflicts is important; for example, students in economics need to be able to spot when economic and social interests collide as a prerequisite for sustainable action. On the other hand, students also need to be able to resolve and cope with the conflicts they identify. There is little benefit if they identify conflicts in knowl-edge and experience but cannot process them adequately; then they may react, for example, by disengaging or rejecting new knowledge or evidence.

This example also illustrates the need for greater awareness of states of thought and emotion in learning, and creates a link to the areas of resilience, self-regula-tion, attitudes, and positive psychology (e.g., Dormann et al. in this volume); these are linked to a focus on values, ethics, and morals in information processing and formation of students' attitudes which influence the complex process of learning. Helping students guard against manipulation in learning in order to prevent neg-ative learning is half the rent, the other half is to help them to reach the states that enhance learning, and drive positive learning. There are many possible learn-ing/media environments that call for multidisciplinary examination in PLATO. Cognitive engagement, for example, is one of the stated key goals for learning opportunities and educators, though students can be equally engaged and to some extent informed by watching entertainment TV or YouTube videos, as well. Hence, questions arise such as: How should higher education as a completely different environment compete for students' attention? What cognitive and emotional states can educators offer that are more attractive? How do they function at the cognitive and neuronal level? How can students be taught to foster greater mental autonomy, responsibility, evidence-based rationality, ethical behavior etc.?

The fourth cornerstone (D) is represented by the research on risks and oppor-tunities of learning with new ICT, which combines expertise from the fields of mathematical modeling, artificial intelligence, educational psychology, sociology, and philosophy. Today, students are not alone in learning. Machines are learning, as well; and students are learning with machines. Machines allocate learning re-sources, track learning progress, and incorporate algorithms that direct students' attention (e.g., Ciampaglia in this volume). The combination of sensing learning environments, signal and behavioral cue data bases, and higher-level domain or generic learning models has enabled ICT-based adaptive learning support systems (e.g., Klein et al. in this volume). Based on these, personalized learning content can be delivered if (teachers' and learners') learning preferences and goals are speci-fied, while computer-based, mobile, virtual or augmented reality applications can offer new, more realistic, rich modes of experiencing, engagement, and learning. There are ample opportunities for the development of learning technology, while cognitive, reasoning-related, economic, infrastructural and other risks of a more ICT-dependent learning environment on the individual and societal level remain to be evaluated. Digitalization demonstrates all signs of increasing over the next decades. With new technologies disrupting industries at an ever-increasing pace, higher education cannot expect to retain its relevance and popularity in the long-term without innovation in teaching and learning (e.g., Gardner in this volume). Hence, PLATO focuses particularly on ICT-supported and fully ICT-based learning environments; the practical relevance and (long-term) application perspective of the fundamental research in PLATO reflect new challenges in learning to get a better understanding of the changes in learning that students and in fact all learners face. Thus, both development of new technologies and risk assessment of technology use are both research subfocuses of PLATO.

The PLATO approach encourages researchers to maintain an open mind, patience, and the willingness to extend beyond familiar domain boundaries and disciplinary perspectives, keeping in mind that the points of friction can lead to the most productive innovations. A few years ago, researchers would not have dreamed of undertaking such a complex program, examining many different perspectives in a holistic approach to learning fundamentals – and mean it. Indeed, PLATO's is a quite an ambitious agenda, and single influences are not easily distinguished. PLATO, then, risks not instantly succeeding, and may take a decade or two in connecting the different individual research areas, including the investigation of opportunities and risks of learning with new ICT. However, recent advances in computing have brought comprehensive interdisciplinary measurement models of learning within reach (e.g., Kise in this volume). What would have been an impossible research program a few decades ago today is a massive, but feasible endeavor. We are convinced that the time is right to start collecting and linking the first pieces of the puzzle so that, over the years, PLATO can make progress towards a more complete picture of positive and negative learning in the age of information.

4   Conclusions

Even though the first four cornerstones (presented above) for the development of a holistic concept of learning in the Age of Information have been set, more than a decade of intensive, fundamental research is still necessary in order to reach the goals of PLATO: A holistic explanatory model is to be developed and established as a framework for the study of positive learning and negative learning in the age of information. The current sketch delineates key areas of research to make significant progress over the next years, including: (A) intra-individual cognitive and neuronal learning processes, as well as (reliable and unreliable) information structures in learning sources and materials; (B) individual, social, societal, and technological interactional and communicative practices in (formal and informal) learning contexts; (C) ethical and moral foundations for responsible and conscious learning at both individual and societal levels; and (D) development, opportunity and risk evaluation of technology-supported learning.

The initial PLATO consortium combines expertise in artificial intelligence, cognitive, communication, cultural, educational, ethical, information technology, linguistic, mathematical modeling, media, moral-theological, neural, philosophical, psychological, and sociological components as well as intersectional perspectives (e.g., from media ethics or computational linguistics).

To pick just one example, the findings by Mehler et al. (in this volume) not only substantiate empirically prior assumptions about the language-dependence of the score of a learning outcomes assessment, but the results indicate an explained variance in students' knowledge test scores of almost 50% for the most predictive item features. Should the findings be replicated and the methodology prove robust over time, this study alone would call for the establishment of a novel strand of computational linguistic research in educational assessment. Similar innovations can be expected for all PLATO research areas.

The goal for the modeling is to create through such interdisciplinary cooperations and advanced computational possibilities research design blueprints that can be integrated to form a holistic, multilayered, multiscaled, environment- and value-sensitive model of learning. It is meant to provide a robust basis for diverse applications (e.g., in educational technology), and be dynamic enough to enable inclusion of further findings and approaches from complementary disciplines. Once initial target research designs, approaches and computational models covering positive learning have been developed in PLATO, for example, linking an information source considered by a student to (1) the student's cognitive and neural processes, (2) their current or changing social and technological learning environment, (3) their personal ethical considerations, (4) and their learning outcomes and longitudinal development, further areas of influence are conceivable for integration, for example, from fields such as students' biological-medical preconditions, pre-tertiary educational experiences, or other areas of intelligence such as musical skills.

Bibliography

Alexander, P. A. (1997). Mapping the multidimensional nature of domain learning: The interplay of cognitive, motivational, and strategic forces. In M. L. Maehr & P. R. Pintrich (Eds.), *Advances in motivation and achievement* (Vol. 10, pp. 213–250). Greenwich, CT: JAI Press.

Alexander, P. A. (2003). The development of expertise: The journey from acclimation to proficiency. *Educational Researcher, 32*(8), 10–14.

Anderson, L. W., & Krathwohl, D. R. (2001). *A taxonomy for learning, teaching, and assessing: A revision of Bloom's taxonomy of educational objectives*. New York: Longman.

Averell, L., & Heathcote, A. (2011). The form of the forgetting curve and the fate of memories. *Journal of Mathematical Psychology, 55*, 25–35. doi:10.1016/j.jmp.2010.08.009

Bandura, A. (1979). *Sozial-kognitive Lerntheorie*. Stuttgart: Klett-Cotta.

Baumert, J., Kunter, M., Brunner, M., Krauss, S., Blum, W., & Neubrand, M. (2004). Mathematikunterricht aus der Sicht der PISA-Schülerinnen und-Schüler und ihrer Lehrkräfte. In Deutsches PISA-Konsortium (Eds.), *PISA 2003: Der Bildungsstandard der Jugendlichen in Deutschland – Ergebnisse des zweiten internationalen Vergleichs* (pp. 314–354). Münster: Waxmann.

Berka, C., Levendowski, D. J., Lumicao, M. N., Yau, A., Davis, G., Zivkovic, V. T., & Craven, P. L. (2007). EEG correlates of task engagement and mental workload in vigilance, learning, and memory tasks. *Aviation, space, and environmental medicine, 78*(Supplement 1), B231–B244.

Berliner, D. (2013). Inequality, Poverty, and the Socialization of America's Youth for the Responsibilities of Citizenship. *Theory Into Practice, 52*(3), 203–209. doi:10.1080/00405841.2013.804314

Bloom, B. S., Engelhart, M. D., Furst, E. J., Hill, W. H., & Krathwohl, D. R. (1956). *Taxonomy of educational objectives: Handbook I: Cognitive domain* (Vol. 19). New York: Longmans, Green and Co.

Brückner, S. (2017). *Prozessbezogene Validierung anhand von mentalen Operationen bei der Bearbeitung wirtschaftswissenschaftlicher Testaufgaben*. Landau: Empirische Pädagogik.

Brückner, S., Förster, M., Zlatkin-Troitschanskaia, O., & Walstad, W. B. (2015a). Effects of prior economic education, native language, and gender on economic knowledge of first-year students in higher education. A comparative study between Germany and the USA. *Studies in Higher Education, 40*(3), 437–453.

Brückner, S., Förster, M., Zlatkin-Troitschanskaia, O., Happ, R., Walstad, W. B., Yamaoka, M., & Asano, T. (2015b). Gender Effects in Assessment of Economic Knowledge and Understanding: Differences among Undergraduate Business and Economics Students in Germany, Japan, and the United States. *Peabody Journal of Education, 90*(4), 503–518.

Brückner, S., & Pellegrino, J. W. (2016). Integrating the Analysis of Mental Operations into Multilevel Models to Validate an Assessment of Higher Education Students' Competency in Business and Economics. *Journal of Educational Measurement, 53*(3), 293–312.

Brückner, S., & Zlatkin-Troitschanskaia, O. (2018). Threshold concepts for modeling higher education students' understanding and learning in economics - implications for instruction and assessment. In O. Zlatkin-Troitschanskaia, H. A. Pant, M. Toepper, C. Lautenbach, & C. Kuhn (Eds.). *Assessment of Learning Outcomes in Higher Education – Cross National Comparisons and Perspectives*. Wiesbaden: Springer.

Bruner, J. S. (1966). *Toward a theory of instruction*. Cambridge, Mass: Belkapp Press.

Chi, M. T. (1981). Knowledge development and memory performance. In *Intelligence and learning* (pp. 221–229). New York: Plenum Press.

Chi, M. T., Feltovich, P. J., & Glaser, R. (1981). Categorization and representation of physics problems by experts and novices. *Cognitive science, 5*(2), 121–152.

Dabbagh, N., & Kitsantas, A. (2012). Personal Learning Environments, social media, and self-regulated learning: A natural formula for connecting formal and informal learning. *The Internet and higher education, 15*(1), 3–8.

Davies, P. (2012). Threshold concepts in economic education. In G. M. Hoyt & K. McGoldrick (Eds.), *International handbook on teaching and learning economics* (pp. 250–258). Cheltenham, UK, Northampton, Mass: Edward Elgar.

Docktor, J. L., & Mestre, J. P. (2014). Synthesis of discipline-based education research in physics. *Physical Review Special Topics - Physics Education Research, 10*(2). https://doi.org/10.1103/PhysRevSTPER.10.020119

Ericsson, K. A., & Charness, N. (1994). Expert performance: Its structure and acquisition. *American psychologist, 49*(8), 725–747.

Förster, M., Zlatkin-Troitschanskaia, O., Brückner, S., Happ, R., Hambleton, R. K., Walstad, W. B., Asano, T., & Yamaoka, M. (2015). Validating test score interpretations by comparing the results of students from the United States, Japan and Germany on a test of economic knowledge in higher education. *Zeitschrift für Psychologie, 223*(1), 14–23.

Fry, H., Ketteridge, S., & Marshall, S. (Eds.) (2008). *A handbook for teaching and learning in higher education: Enhancing academic practice* (3rd ed.). New York, London: Routledge.

Gagné, R. M. (1985). *The Conditions of Learning and Theory of Instruction.* New York: CBS College Publishing.

Gardner, H. (2011). *Frames of mind: The theory of multiple intelligences.* Basic books.

Gardner, H. (1999). *Intelligence reframed: Multiple intelligences for the 21st century.* Basic books.

Gick, M. L., & Holyoak, K. J. (1980). Analogical problem solving. *Cognitive psychology, 12*(3), 306–355.

Goldman, S. R. (2003). Learning in complex domains: When and why do multiple representations help? *Learning and Instruction, 13*(2), 239–244. doi: https://doi.org/10.1016/S0959-4752(02)00023-3

Goldstone, R. L., & Styvers, M. (2001). The sensitization and differentiation of dimensions during category learning. *Journal of experimental psychology: General, 130*(1), 116–139.

Gültekin-Karakoç, N., Köker, A., Hirsch, D., Ehmke, T., Hammer, S., Koch-Priewe, B. & Ohm, U. (2016). Bestimmung von Standards und Stufen der Kompetenz angehender Lehrerinnen und Lehrer aller Fächer im Bereich Deutsch als Zweitsprache (DaZ). *Die Deutsche Schule. Beiheft 13, 132*–148.

Happ, R., Zlatkin-Troitschanskaia, O., Beck, K., & Förster, M. (2016a). Increasing Heterogeneity in Students' Prior Economic Content Knowledge – Impact on and Implications for Teaching in Higher Education. In E. Wuttke, J. Seifried, & S. Schumann (Eds.), *Economic Competence and Financial Literacy of Young Adults* (pp. 193–210). Opladen: Barbara Budrich Publishers.

Happ, R., Zlatkin-Troitschanskaia, O., & Schmidt, S. (2016b). An Analysis of Economic Learning Among Undergraduates in Introductory Economics Courses in Germany. *Journal of Economic Education, 47*(4), 300–310. doi:10.1080/00220485.2016.1213686

Horz, H. (2011). Lernen mit Medien. In H. Reinders, H. Ditton, C. Gräsel, B. Gniewosz (Eds.), *Empirische Bildungsforschung* (pp. 21–32). Wiesbaden: VS Verlag für Sozialwissenschaften.

Kohl, P. B., & Finkelstein, N. D. (2005). Student representational competence and self-assessment when solving physics problems. *Physical Review Special Topics – Physics Education Research, 1*(1). doi: https://doi.org/10.1103/PhysRevSTPER.1.010104

Kohl, P. B., & Finkelstein, N. D. (2006). Effects of representation on students solving physics problems: A fine-grained characterization. *Physical Review Special Topics - Physics Education Research, 2*(1). https://doi.org/10.1103/PhysRevSTPER.2.010106

Köhler, W. (1947). *Gestalt psychology: an introduction to new concepts in modern psychology.* New York: Liveright.

Köhler, W. (1938). *The place of value in a world of facts.* New York: Liveright.

Kuhn, C., & Zlatkin-Troitschanskaia, O. (2011). *Assessment of competencies among university students and graduates – Analyzing the state of research and perspectives* (Working Papers Chair of Business Education Issue No. 89). Mainz: Johannes Gutenberg University. Retrieved from http://www.wipaed.uni-mainz.de/ls/ArbeitspapiereWP/gr_Nr.59.pdf

Lai, E. R., & Viering, M. (2012). *Assessing 21st century skills: Integrating research findings.* Paper presented at the annual meeting of the National Council on Measurement in Education, Vancouver, B.C., Canada.

Lind, G. (2016). *How to teach morality - Promoting Deliberation and Discussion, Reducing Violence and Deceit.* Berlin: Logos.

Loftus, G. R. (1985). Evaluating forgetting curves. *Journal of Experimental Psychology, 11*(2), 397–406. doi:10.1037/0278-7393.11.2.397

Manin, Y. I. (2015). Neural Codes and Homotopy Types: Mathematical Models of Place Field Recognition. *Moscow Mathematical Journal, 15*(4), 741–748.

Mayer, R. E. (2005). Cognitive theory of multimedia learning. In R. E. Mayer (Ed.), *The Cambridge handbook of multimedia learning* (pp. 31–48). New York, NY: Cambridge University Press.

Mayer, R. E. (2009). *Multimedia Learning.* Cambridge University Press.

Meltzer, D. E. (2005). Relation between students' problem-solving performance and representational format. *American Journal of Physics, 73*(5), 463. https://doi.org/10.1119/1.1862636

Metzinger T. (2009). *The Ego Tunnel. The Science of the Mind and the Myth of the Self.* Basic Books: New York.

Meyer, J. H., & Land, R. (2003). *Threshold concepts and troublesome knowledge: Linkages to ways of thinking and practising within the disciplines* (pp. 412–424). Edinburgh: University of Edinburgh.

Meyer, J. H., & Land, R. (2005). Threshold concepts and troublesome knowledge (2): Epistemological considerations and a conceptual framework for teaching and learning. *Higher education, 49*(3), 373-388.

Minnameier, G. (2016). Forms of abduction and an inferential taxonomy. In L. Magnani & T. Bertolotti (Eds.), *Springer Handbook of Model-based Science* (pp. 169–189). Berlin, Heidelberg: Springer.

Mislevy, R. J. (2016). How developments in psychology and technology challenge validity arguments. *Journal of Educational Measurement, 53*(3), 265–292.

Mislevy, R. J. (1996). Test theory reconceived. *Journal of Educational Measurement, 33*, 379-416.

Mislevy, R. J., & Yin, C. (2009). If Language Is a Complex Adaptive System, What Is Language Assessment? *Language Learning, 59*, 249–267. cdoi.org/10.1111/j.1467-9922.2009.00543.x

Momennejad, I., Russek, E. M., Cheong, J. H., Botvinick, M. M., Daw, N., & Gershman, S. J. (2017). The successor representation in human reinforcement learning. *Nature Human Behaviour* 1, 680–692. https://doi:10.1038/s41562-017-0180-8

Organisation for Economic Cooperation and Development (OECD) (2014). *PISA 2012 Results: What Students Know und Can Do: Student Performance in Mathematics, Reading and Science.* Paris: OECD Publishing.

Organisation for Economic Cooperation and Development (OECD) (2016). *Skills Matter: Further Results from the Survey of Adult Skills* (OECD Skills Studies). Paris: OECD Publishing. doi:http://dx.doi.org/10.1787/9789264258051-en

Paas, F., Renkl, A., & Sweller, J. (2003). Cognitive Load Theory and Instructional Design: Recent Developments. *Educational Psychologist, 38*(1), 1–4. doi:10.1207/S15326985EP3801_1

Pellegrino, J. W. (2006). *Rethinking and redesigning curriculum, instruction and assessment: What contemporary research and theory suggests.* Commission on the Skills of the American Workforce, Chicago, 1–15.

Pellegrino, J. W., & Hilton, M. L. (2012). *Education for life and work: Developing transferable knowledge and skills in the 21st century.* Washington, DC: The National Academies Press.

Pellegrino, J. W., & Glaser, R. (1982). Analyzing aptitudes for learning: inductive reasoning. In R. Glasser (Ed.), *Advances in Instructional psychology* (pp. 269–345). Hillsdale, NJ: Erlbaum.

Piaget, J. (1972). *The psychology of the child.* New York: Basic Books.

Polanyi, M. (1966). *The Tacit Dimension.* London: Routledge & Kegan Paul.

Renkl, A., Mandl, H., & Gruber, H. (1996). Inert knowledge: Analyses and remedies. *Educational Psychologist, 31*(2), 115–121.

Richards, B. A. & Frankland, P. W. (2017). The persistence and transience of memory. *Neuron, 94*(6), 1071–1084. doi: http://dx.doi.org/10.1016/j.neuron.2017.04.037 |

Schmidt, F. L., & Hunter, J. E. (1993). Tacit knowledge, practical intelligence, general mental ability, and job knowledge. *Current Directions in Psychological Science, 2*(1), 8–9. doi:10.1111/1467-8721.ep10770456.

Secolsky, C., & Denison, D. B. (Eds.). (2017). *Handbook on measurement, assessment, and evaluation in higher education* (2nd ed.). New York: Routledge.

Shavelson, R. J. (2016). *On Sailing A Ship Without A Compass: The Role Of Assessment In Improving College Students' Learning.* Twenty-first Annual Boisi Lecture in Education and Public Policy.

Shavelson, R. J., Davey, T., Ferrara, S., Holland, P., Webb, N., & Wise, L. (2015). *Psychometric considerations for the next generation of performance assessment.* Princeton, NJ: Educational Testing Service.

Shavelson, R. J., Domingue, B. W., Mariño, J. P., Molina Mantilla, A., Morales Forero, A., & Wiley, E. E. (2016). On the practices and challenges of measuring higher education value added: the case of Colombia. *Assessment & Evaluation in Higher Education, 41*(5), 695–720.

Shavelson, R. J., Marino, J., Zlatkin-Troitschanskaia, O., & Schmidt, S. (in press). Reflections on the Assessment of Quantitative Reasoning. In B. L. Madison, & L. A. Steen (Eds.), *Calculation vs. context: Quantitative literacy and its implications for teacher education* (2nd ed.). Washington, DC: Mathematical Association of America.

Skinner, B. F. (1953). *Science and Human Behavior.* New York: MacMillan

Snow, R. E. (1989). Cognitive-conative aptitude interactions in learning. In R. Kanfer, P. L. Ackerman, & R. Cudeck (Eds.), *Abilities, motivation, and methodology* (pp. 435–474). Hillsdale, NJ: Lawrence Erlbaum Associates, Inc.

Spelke, E. S., & Tsivkin, S. (2001). Language and number: a bilingual training study. *Cognition, 78*, 45–88.

Tolman, E. C. (1952). A cognition motivation model. *Psychological Review, Vol 59(5)*, S.389-400.

Vygotsky, L. S. (1978). *Mind in society: The development of higher psychological processes.* Cambridge: Harvard University Press.

Waldmann, M. R. (2008). Kategorisierung und Wissenserwerb. In J. Müsseler (Ed.), *Allgemeine Psychologie* (2nd ed., pp. 377–427). Berlin, Heidelberg: Springer.

Walstad, W. B., Schmidt, S., & Zlatkin-Troitschanskaia, O. (in press). The Response Patterns in Difference Scores from Multiple Choice Tests: Insights and Implications for the Assessment of Student Learning.

Walstad, W. B., & Wagner, J. (2016). The disaggregation of value-added test scores to assess learning outcomes in economics courses. *Journal of Economic Education 47*(2), 121–131.

Weinert, F. E. (Ed.). (2001). *Leistungsmessungen in Schulen.* Weinheim und Basel: Beltz.

Zhang, J., & Norman, D. A. (1994). Representations in Distributed Cognitive Tasks. *Cognitive Science, 18*(1), 87–122.

Zlatkin-Troitschanskaia, O., Pant, H. A., Kuhn, C., Toepper, M., & Lautenbach, C. (2016a). *Messung akademischer Kompetenzen von Studierenden und Hochschulabsolventen. Ein Überblick zum nationalen und internationalen Forschungsstand.* Wiesbaden: Springer.

Zlatkin-Troitschanskaia, O., Pant, H. A., Lautenbach, C., Molerov, D., Toepper, M., & Brückner, S. (2017a). *Modeling and Measuring Competencies in Higher Education.* Wiesbaden: Springer VS.

Zlatkin-Troitschanskaia, O., Pant, H. A., Toepper, M., Lautenbach, C., & Molerov, D. (2017b). Valid Competency Assessment in Higher Education – Framework, Results, and Further Perspectives of the German Research Program KoKoHs. *AERA Open, special topic "Student Learning Outcomes in Higher Education".* doi:10.1177/2332858416686739

Zlatkin-Troitschanskaia, O., Schmidt, S., Brückner, S., Förster, M., Yamaoka, M., & Asano, T. (2016b). Macroeconomic knowledge of higher education students in Germany and Japan – a multilevel analysis of contextual and personal effects. *Assessment & Evaluation in Higher Education, 41*(5), 787–801.

Zlatkin-Troitschanskaia, O., Shavelson, R. J., & Kuhn, C. (2015). The International state of research on measurement of competency in higher education. *Studies in Higher Education, 40*(3), 393–411. doi:10.1080/03075079.2015.1004241

Zlatkin-Troitschanskaia, O., Shavelson, R. J., & Pant, H. A. (2017c). Assessment of learning outcomes in higher education: International comparisons and perspectives. In C. Secolsky & D. B. Denison (Eds), *Handbook on measurement, assessment, and evaluation in higher education* (2nd ed., pp. 686-697). New York: Routledge.

PART II
Learning as an Interplay between Neuronal, Cognitive and Information Structures

Hand Gestures Alert Auditory Cortices

Possible Impacts of Learning on Foreign Language Processing

Arne Nagels, Spencer D. Kelly, Tilo Kircher, and Benjamin Straube

Abstract

When acquiring a foreign language, the first challenge is to break into the speech stream to identify basic linguistic units. The present study tested the hypothesis that hand gestures facilitate this process by alerting auditory cortices to attend to and identify meaningful phonemic information. During fMRI data acquisition, participants watched videos of an actor speaking in Russian under three conditions. Sentences were produced with just speech alone or were accompanied by two types of hand gestures: 1) metaphoric gesture and 2) free gesture. The main finding was that there was increased auditory cortex activation when both types of gestures accompanied speech compared to speech alone, but there were no differences between the two speech + gesture conditions (or gesture alone conditions). These results suggest that hand gestures may play a role in focusing attention to auditory processing to increase capacity when listening to novel speech in a foreign language.

Keywords

Language; Foreign Language; Learning; L2; Speech; Hand Gesture; Auditory Cortex; Metaphoric.

1   Introduction

The effect of hand and arm movements on language learning has not been directly addressed yet. In particular it is not clear, which neural circuits are involved when a foreign language (L2) is presented with co-verbal gestures. L2 learners face many challenges, but perhaps the greatest initial obstacle is learning to parse and break into a speech stream of novel sounds. The present study explores how nonverbal behavior— such as co-speech hand gestures—may influence auditory brain regions to help learners overcome this initial challenge.

Speech and gesture are theorized to form an integrated system in language production for one's native language (L1) (Clark 1996, McNeill 1992), and recent research has extended this theory to language comprehension (Kelly et al. 2010b). These claims have recently been strengthened by research in cognitive neuroscience using multiple methodologies (Holle and Gunter 2007, Ibáñez et al. 2010, Ibáñez et al. 2011, Kelly et al. 2004, Kelly et al. 2007, Ozyürek et al. 2007, Wu and Coulson 2005, Wu and Coulson 2007a, Wu and Coulson 2007b, Wu and Coulson 2010). In particular fMRI studies revealed that gestures generally activate "traditional language regions" (such as the left inferior frontal gyrus [IFG] and the superior temporal sulcus [STS]) (Dick et al. 2009, Green et al. 2009, Holle et al. 2008, Holle et al. 2010, Hubbard et al. 2009, Kircher et al. 2009, Skipper et al. 2007, Skipper et al. 2009, Straube et al. 2011a, Straube et al. 2009, Willems et al. 2007, Willems et al. 2009). Building on this work in the L1 domain, researchers have begun to explore the role of hand gestures in the neural processing of an L2 (Kelly et al. 2009, Macedonia et al. 2011). For example, Kelly and colleagues showed that not only do people learn and remember novel vocabulary items (in Japanese) better when they are instructed with iconic hand gestures (making a drinking gesture while saying, "Nomu means drink"), but words learned with iconic gestures produce a larger Late Positive Complex (an ERP component reflecting depth of imagistic encoding in memory) than words learned with just speech alone (Kelly et al. 2009). In a subsequent fMRI study, participants were taught words in an invented language accompanied by meaningful and meaningless hand gestures, and at test, words learned with meaningful gestures were remembered better and produced more activation in the premotor cortex than words learned with meaningless gestures (Macedonia et al. 2011). These studies show that hand gestures play a significant role in learning and neural processing of words in a foreign language.

One possible explanation for the effects of hand gestures on phonemic learning is that the visual information conveyed through gesture cross-modally primes information in the auditory modality (Calvert et al. 1999, Colin et al. 2002, Sams et al. 1991, Stein and Meredith 1993). That is, because gesture and speech are a tightly integrated system (McNeill 1992), learners "tune into" speech in focused ways when gestures accompany certain words, and this may help to the auditory system break into the novel speech stream.

The present study investigates whether hand gestures serve to increase auditory brain activity when processing novel speech in a foreign language. To test this, we had German speakers listen to sentences in Russian either with or without semantically related and unrelated hand gestures. We predicted that because gestures help people parse foreign speech (Gullberg et al. 2010), sentences containing any sort of gesture (related and unrelated to the semantic speech content) should increase activity in auditory brain regions relative to a speech only baseline.

2   Methods

2.1   Participants

Fourteen male, right-handed (Oldfield 1971) healthy volunteers, all native German speakers (mean age = 29 years, range: 23 to 38 years) without impairments of vision or hearing, participated in the study. The participants had no previous knowledge of or in-depth contact with Russian or any other Slavic language. None of the participants had any medical, neurological or psychiatric illness, past or present. All participants gave informed consent, and were paid 20€ for participation. The study was approved by the local ethics committee.

2.2   Stimulus construction

A set of 1296 (162 x 8) short video clips containing eight conditions were initially created (see Kircher et al. 2009). The current study focuses on a subset of 5 of these conditions: 1) Russian sentences in isolation (foreign speech only; FS); 2) Russian sentences and corresponding related, metaphoric gestures (foreign speech and related gesture; FS&RG); 3) Russian sentences and unrelated, free gestures (foreign speech and unrelated gestures; FS&UG); 4) "related," metaphoric gestures in isolation (RG); 5) "unrelated," free gestures in isolation (UG).

2.3   Experimental procedure

Participants were instructed to watch the videos and then to respond at the beginning of each by pressing one of two buttons with the left hand (index and middle finger) to indicate whether a spot displayed on the actor's sweater was dark or light (see Fig. 1, for a dark example). During fMRI each participant performed four runs with 64 video clips and the duration of approximately 11 minutes each. For further information see Kircher et al. (2009) and Straube et al. (2009).

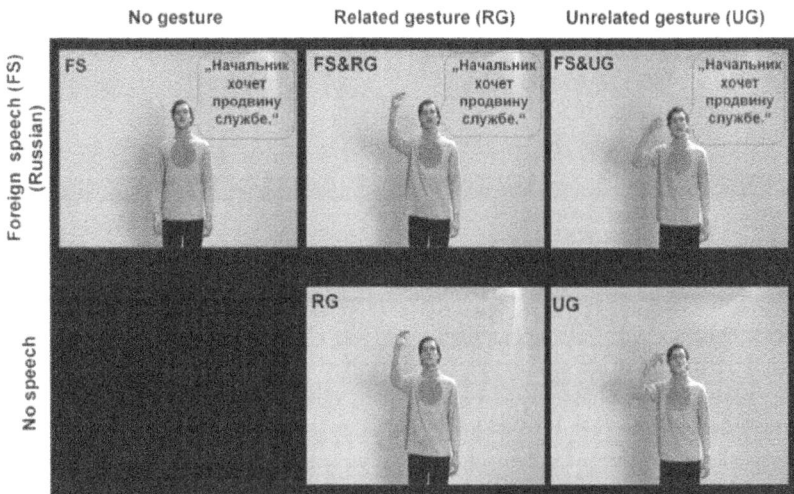

Fig. 1   Examples of the different speech and gesture video-clips

The stimulus material consisted of video clips of an actor uttering abstract, metaphorical sentences in a foreign language (at least to our German participants) with just speech alone (FS, top left) and together with related gestures ("RG") and unrelated gestures ("UG") (FS+RG and FS+UG; top middle and right, respectively). In addition, the actor produced the two types of gestures alone (bottom two panels). One screen shot of an example video is shown for each condition. The spoken

Russian sentences are written in Cyrillic into the speech bubble of each picture for illustration (unlike in the actual stimuli).

2.4   MRI data acquisition

MRI acquisition was performed on a Philips scanner (Philips MRT Achieva series) with 3-Tesla magnetic field strength. Functional data were acquired with echo planar images in 31 transversal slices (repetition time [TR] = 2000 ms; echo time [TE] = 30 ms; flip angle = 90; slice thickness = 3.5 mm; interslice gap = 0.35 mm; field of view [FoV] = 240 mm, voxel resolution = 3.5 x 3.5 mm). Slices were positioned to cover the participant's whole brain.

2.5   Data analysis

MR images were analyzed using Statistical Parametric Mapping (SPM; www.fil. ion.ucl.ac.uk) implemented in MATLAB (Mathworks Inc., Sherborn, MA). The identical single subject analyses of Kircher et al. (2009) were used for the new group analysis (flexible factorial analyses; SPM5). The resultant outputs of the single subject analyses performed in SPM2 (see Kircher et al. 2009) are comparable to and compatible with the newer SPM5-version that was used for the group analyses.

The expected hemodynamic response was defined at the time where speech and gesture co-occurred in the bimodal conditions. For each event-type the expected hemodynamic response was modeled by two response functions, a canonical hemodynamic response function (HRF; (Friston et al. 1998)) and its temporal derivative. The functions were convolved with the event sequence to create the stimulus conditions in a general linear model (Kircher et al. 2009). The group analysis was performed by entering contrast images into a flexible factorial analysis, in which participants are treated as random variables. The same significance threshold where applied as in the previous analyses of these data (Kircher et al. 2009). Thus, voxels with a significance level of $p < .05$ uncorrected belonging to clusters with at least 23 voxels are reported for all analyses. A Monte Carlo simulation of the brain volume was conducted to establish an appropriate voxel contiguity threshold (Slotnick et al. 2003). Assuming an individual voxel type I error of $p < .05$, a cluster extent of 23 contiguous re- sampled voxels was indicated as necessary to correct for multiple voxel comparisons at $p < .05$. The reported voxel coordinates of activation peaks refer to the MNI space.

2.6   Stimulus construction

Note that the only way that participants could determine whether the gestures were related or unrelated was if they understood the meaning of the Russian sentences (which none of our German participants did). Also note that the two gesture in isolation controls were not merely muted versions of the two Russian sentences + gesture conditions—rather, they were created separately with the actor not producing any accompanying speech.

All 1296 sentences had a length of 5 to 8 words, with an average duration of 2.47 seconds (SD = 0.4) and a similar grammatical form (subject – predicate – object). The stimuli were produced by the same male actor, performing them in a natural, spontaneous way, to illustrate the content of the sentences (Green et al. 2009, Kircher et al. 2009, Straube et al. 2011a, b, Straube et al. 2010, Straube et al. 2009). If one sentence was recorded in a natural way subsequently the control conditions were produced with the aim to hold all item characteristics constant (e.g., sentence duration or movement complexity), regardless of the gesture (metaphoric, free, no gesture). All video clips had the same length of 5 seconds with at least 0.5 seconds before and after the sentence onset and offset, respectively, where the actor neither speaks nor moves. With the purpose to keep the stimuli as natural as possible the head was not removed from the video.

Sets of 1024 video clips (128 abstract sentences with metaphoric gestures with their counterparts in the other seven conditions) were chosen from the total pool of stimuli for the fMRI experiment (see Kircher et al. 2009). Out of these 1024 videos four homogeneous sets were created with the aim that each participant was presented with 256 sentences during the scanning procedure. The videos were counterbalanced across the participants so that one subject did not see either gesture or speech repetitions of any single item. Across all participants each item occurred in each condition leading to an additional control for possible differences in stimulus characteristics.

2.7   Experimental design

During the fMRI scanning procedure, videos were presented via MR-compatible video goggles (stereoscopic display with up to 1024 x 768 pixel resolution; VisuaStim XGA ©, Resonance Technology, Inc.) and nonmagnetic headphones (audio presenting systems for stereophonic stimuli: Commander XG; Resonance Technology, Inc.), which also dampened scanner noise.

Thirty-two items of each of the eight original conditions (we focus on a subset of 5 of these) were presented in an event-related design, in a pseudo-randomized order and counterbalanced across participants, so that one subject did not see gesture or speech repetitions of any single item (Kircher et al. 2009). All videos were followed by a baseline condition (gray background with a fixation cross) with a variable duration of 3750 ms to 6750 ms (average: 5000 ms).

2.8   Contrasts of interest

To test the hypothesis that gestures enhance activity in the auditory cortex during processing of a foreign language we compared the bimodal "gesture-Russian" conditions with the isolated Russian condition [(FS&RG + FS&UG) > FS]. Because this contrast would also activate brain areas related to the processing of visual gesture information we excluded brain regions activated by gesture per se [exclusive mask (RG ∩ UG)]. Finally to restrict brain regions to those relevant to the processing of auditory information we restricted the analyses to brain regions activated in the isolated Russian condition (inclusive mask FS > baseline [fixation cross]).

To test if activation increases are independent of gesture type (RG vs. UG), we performed conjunction analyses between the separate contrasts of each gesture-Russian condition versus Russian alone [(FS&RG > FS) ∩ (FS&UG > FS). The same masking procedure was applied as in the previous analysis to restrict activations to region related to auditory processing. Exploratory contrasts with regard to effects of a foreign language on visual processing mechanisms were also conducted and described in the supplemental material (see Supplementary Fig. 1).

3   Results

For the general effect of gestures on the processing of a foreign language [(FS&RG + FS&UG) > FS], we found activation in the bilateral occipital, posterior temporal and inferior parietal brain regions (see Fig. 2A). Because we were not interested in activation related to pure visual gesture processing within this contrast, we calculated the conjunction of both isolated gesture conditions (RG ∩ UG) to exclusively mask the previous analyses. For this conjunction analyses we found a distributed network of predominantly bilateral occipital, parietal and frontal activations (see Fig. 2B).

The main contrast of interest compared the gesture conditions in language context with the speech only condition ([(FS&RG + FS&UG) > FS]; Fig. 2A). To identify those brain regions relevant for auditory processing we calculated the baseline contrast for the isolated Russian condition (FS > baseline; Fig. 2C) exclusively masked by activation revieald by gesture conditions (RG ∩ UG; Fig. 2B). Thus, for the effect of gestures on processing of a foreign language [(FS&RG + FS&UG) > FS] within arears relevant for auditory processing (i.e., exclusively masked for gesture processing (RG ∩ UG) and inclusively masked for foreign language processing (FS > baseline)), we found two significant activation cluster in the posterior temporal lobes (Left: MNI X, Y, Z: -56, -40, 16; t = 3.61, 57 voxels, cluster extend: BA22, BA42, BA37; Right: MNI X, Y, Z: 68, -32, 4; t = 3.57, 45 voxels, cluster extend: BA42, BA37; see Fig. 2D). Sectional slices and contrast estimates for corresponding activation clusters are illustrated in Figure 3.

Conjunction analyses [(FS&RG > FS) ∩ (FS&UG > FS)] reveald that increase of activation in the posterior temporal lobe is independent of gesture type (Left: MNI X, Y, Z: -56, -40, 16; t = 3.05, 35 voxels, cluster extend: BA22, BA42, BA37; Right: MNI X, Y, Z: 68, -32, 4; t = 3.10, 26 voxels; cluster extend BA42, BA37).

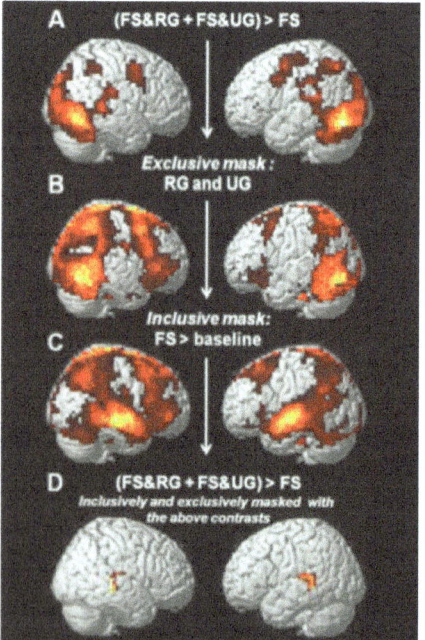

Fig. 2   The effect of gestures on the neural processing of a foreign language

Fig. 2 illustrates the general activation of gestures on the processing of a foreign language [A; (FS&RG + FS&UG) > FS], the exclusive mask of pure gesture processing [B; (RG ∩ UG), the inclusive mask of pure Russian processing (C; FS > baseline), and the first contrast (A) exclusively masked for gesture processing (B) and inclusively masked for speech processing (C; see D). FS: Russian sentences in isolation; FS&RG: Russian sentences and related gestures; FS&UG: Russian sentences and unrelated gestures; RG: related gestures in isolation; UG: unrelated gestures in isolation.

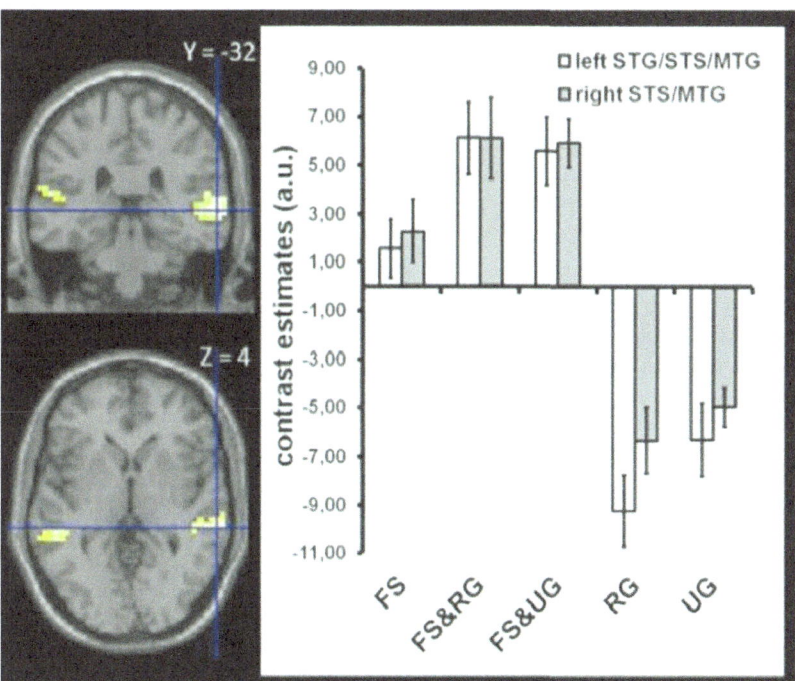

Fig. 3 Activation in the auditory cortices across the experimental conditions

Fig. 3 illustrates the activation in the auditory cortices across the experimental conditions. On the left of Fig. 3 the activation of the analyses reported in Fig. 2D is demonstrated on coronal and axial slices. Bar graphs on the right illustrate the contrast estimates (in arbitrary units; a.u.) for the left (light gray) and right (dark gray) activation cluster across all fife conditions. Compared to Russian speech alone (FS), gesture + speech (FS&RG and FS&UG) increased, whereas gesture alone (RG and UG) decreased, activation in both the left and right temporal lobes (BA22, BA42, BA37). Error bars represent the standard error of the mean. FS: Russian sentences in isolation; FS&RG: Russian sentences and related gestures; FS&UG: Russian sentences and unrelated gestures; RG: related gestures in isolation; UG: unrelated gestures in isolation; STG/S: superior temporal gyrus/sulcus; MTG: Middle temporal gyrus.

4   Discussion

The results support our predictions: Russian speech accompanied by related and unrelated gestures increased activity in auditory brain regions compared to a speech only baseline. We speculate, that when the meaning of speech is incomprehensible, gestures give cues to word boundaries or important acoustic features and this will ramp up, and require vigilance from, auditory brain regions. This could facilitate L2 learning.

Hand gestures have no clear meaning during language comprehension unless they accompany meaningful speech (Feyereisen et al. 1988, Habets et al. 2011, Kelly et al. 1999, Kelly et al. 2010a, McNeill 1992). Thus, the present results were not due to semantic aspects of speech and/or gesture, but rather, they most likely reflected lower-level perceptual processes. Accordingly, we found similar effects in the neural activation of auditory regions for the related and unrelated gesture conditions. Moreover, it is interesting that the two conditions presenting gestures in isolation (RG and UG) produced a significant *decrease* in auditory activity compared to when those gestures were accompanied by Russian speech. In fact, not only did gesture alone decrease auditory activity, but it also *increased* activity in visual cortices (see Supplementary Fig. 1). In this way, it appears that when gestures are presented in isolation, they are treated mostly as visual stimuli (MacSweeney et al. 2002), but when they are layered onto speech (even when it is incomprehensible), gesture becomes more tied to auditory processing. Indeed, when gestures are presented with Russian speech, they actually boost auditory activity relative to speech alone (for a similar effect in L1, see Hubbard et al. 2009). This provides strong neural evidence that gestures are tightly linked to speech during language processing (McNeill 1992).

What might be the function of gesture increasing activity in auditory cortices during L2 exposure? Although the present study is (to our knowledge) the first to explore this issue for online encoding of an L2 (cf. Kelly et al. 2009, Macedonia et al. 2011) for neural correlates *after* encoding), the L1 literature offers some clues. For example, Hubbard et al. (2009) showed that speech accompanied by beat gestures boosted activation in bi-lateral non- primary auditory cortex compared to speech alone (Hubbard et al. 2009). That finding was interpreted as evidence that neural regions traditionally assumed to process only speech are also recruited for multimodal sensory processing, which suggests that certain nonverbal behaviors, such as hand gestures, can help listeners parse and make sense of the accompanying speech stream. Similarly, for the present results, it is possible that hand gestures helped listeners make sense of the Russian sentences.

Although the present study did not have a behavioral measure that would allow us to test this conjecture directly, there is evidence to support such a claim. For example, Krahmer and Swerts (2007) showed that when beat gestures accompanied words in L1, listeners actually perceived those words to be louder than words not accompanied by gestures (Krahmer and Swerts 2007). In the context of an L2, Gullberg and colleagues (2010) found that exposure to a spoken weather forecast (in Mandarin Chinese) accompanied by deictic gestures facilitated native Dutch speakers' ability to identify words spoken in Mandarin (Gullberg et al. 2010). Our results highlight one possible mechanism for these previous results. The gestures in our study boosted activity in auditory cortices, and one function of this increase could be that participants paid more auditory attention to the novel speech stream.

In conclusion, the present study extends previous research showing that multimodal input—conveyed through speech, lips and hands—increases activity in auditory brain regions (Calvert et al. 1999, Colin et al. 2002, Hubbard et al. 2009, Sams et al. 1991). To our knowledge, this is the first study to explore this sort of neural activity—specifically, the processing of speech and hand gestures—in the context of listening to an unknown foreign language. Together, these studies highlight the importance of considering the whole range of tools that language learners have at their disposal and provide insights into improving ways in which languages can be taught and learned in more natural and embodied contexts.

Bibliography

Calvert, G. A., Brammer, M. J., Bullmore, E. T., Campbell, R., Iversen, S. D., & David, A. S. (1999). Response amplification in sensory-specific cortices during crossmodal binding. *Neuroreport 10*(12), 2619–2623.

Clark, H. H. (1996). *Using language*. Cambridge: University Press Cambridge.

Colin, C., Radeau, M., Soquet, A, Demolin, D., Colin, F., & Deltenre, P. (2002). Mismatch negativity evoked by the McGurk-MacDonald effect: A phonetic representation within short-term memory. *Clinical Neurophysiology 113*(4), 495–506.

Dick, A. S., Goldin-Meadow, S., Hasson, U., Skipper, J. I., & Small, S. L. (2009). Co-speech gestures influence neural activity in brain regions associated with processing semantic information. *Hum Brain Mapp 30*(11), 3509–3526.

Feyereisen, P., Van de Wiele, M., & Dubois, F. (1988). The meaning of gestures: What can be understood without speech? *Curr Psychol Cogn* 8, 3–25.

Friston, K. J., Fletcher, P., Josephs, O., Holmes, A., Rugg, M. D., & Turner, R. (1998). Event-related fMRI: Characterizing differential responses. *Neuroimage 7*(1), 30–40.

Green, A., Straube, B., Weis, S., Jansen, A., Willmes, K., Konrad, K., & Kircher, T. (2009). Neural integration of iconic and unrelated coverbal gestures: A functional MRI study. *Hum Brain Mapp 30*(10), 3309–3324.

Gullberg, M., Roberts, L., Dimroth, C., Veroude, K., & Indefrey, P. (2010). Adult language learning after minimal exposure to an unknown natural language. *Language Learning* 60, 5–24.

Habets, B., Kita, S., Shao, Z., Ozyurek, A., & Hagoort, P. (2011). The Role of Synchrony and Ambiguity in Speech-Gesture Integration during Comprehension. *J Cogn Neurosci 23*(8), 1845–1854.

Holle, H., & Gunter, T. C. (2007): The role of iconic gestures in speech disambiguation: ERP evidence. *J Cogn Neurosci 19*(7), 1175–1192.

Holle, H., Gunter, T. C., Rueschemeyer, S.-A., Hennenlotter, A, & Iacoboni, M. (2008). Neural correlates of the processing of co-speech gestures. *Neuroimage 39*(4), 2010–2024.

Holle, H., Obleser, J., Rueschemeyer, S.-A., Gunter, T. C. (2010). Integration of iconic gestures and speech in left superior temporal areas boosts speech comprehension under adverse listening conditions. *Neuroimage 49*(1), 875–884.

Hubbard, A. L., Wilson, S. M., Callan, D. E., Dapretto, M. (2009). Giving speech a hand: Gesture modulates activity in auditory cortex during speech perception. *Hum Brain Mapp 30*(3), 1028–1037.

Ibáñez A., Manes, F., Escobar, J., Trujillo, N., Andreucci, P., & Hurtado, E. (2010). Gesture influences the processing of figurative language in non-native speakers: ERP evidence. *Neurosci Lett 471*(1), 48–52.

Ibáñez, A., Toro, P., Cornejo, C., Urquina, H., Hurquina, H., Manes, F., Weisbrod, M., & Schröder, J. (2011). High contextual sensitivity of metaphorical expressions and gesture blending: A video event-related potential design. *Psychiatry Res 191*(1), 68–75.

Kelly, S. D., Barr, D. J., Church, R. B., & Lynch, K. (1999). Offering a Hand to Pragmatic Understanding: The Role of Speech and Gesture in Comprehension and Memory. *Journal of Memory and Language 40*, 577–592.

Kelly, S. D., Creigh, P., & Bartolotti, J. (2010a). Integrating speech and iconic gestures in a Stroop-like task: Evidence for automatic processing. *J Cogn Neurosci 22*(4), 683–694.

Kelly, S. D., Kravitz, C., & Hopkins, M. (2004). Neural correlates of bimodal speech and gesture comprehension. *Brain Lang 89*(1), 253–260.

Kelly, S. D., McDevitt, T., & Esch, M. (2009). Brief training with co-speech gesture lends a hand to word learning in a foreign language. *Language and cognitive processes 24*(2), 313–334.

Kelly, S. D., Ozyürek, A., & Maris, E. (2010b): Two sides of the same coin: Speech and gesture mutually interact to enhance comprehension. *Psychol Sci 21*(2), 260–267.

Kelly, S. D., Ward, S., Creigh, P., & Bartolotti, J. (2007). An intentional stance modulates the integration of gesture and speech during comprehension. *Brain Lang 101*(3), 222–233.

Kircher, T., Straube, B., Leube, D., Weis, S., Sachs, O., Willmes, K., Konrad, K., & Green, A. (2009). Neural interaction of speech and gesture: Differential activations of metaphoric co-verbal gestures. *Neuropsychologia 47*(1), 169-179.

Krahmer, E., & Swerts, M. (2007). The effects of visual beats on prosodic prominence: Acoustic analyses, auditory perception and visual perception. *Journal of Memory and Language 57*(3), 396–414.

Macedonia, M., Müller, K., & Friederici, A. D. (2011). The impact of iconic gestures on foreign language word learning and its neural substrate. *Hum Brain Mapp 32*(6), 982–998.

MacSweeney, M., Woll, B., Campbell, R., McGuire, P. K., David, A. S., Williams, S. C., Suckling, J., Calvert, G. A., & Brammer, M. J. (2002). Neural systems underlying British Sign Language and audio-visual English processing in native users. *Brain 125*(7), 1583–1593.

McNeill, D. (1992). *Hand and mind: What gestures reveal about thought.* Chicago: Univ. of Chicago Press.

Oldfield, R. C. (1971). The assessment and analysis of handedness: The Edinburgh inventory. *Neuropsychologia 9*(1), 97–113.

Ozyürek, A., Willems, R. M., Kita, S., & Hagoort, P. (2007). On-line integration of semantic information from speech and gesture: Insights from event-related brain potentials. *J Cogn Neurosci 19*(4), 605–616.

Sams, M., Aulanko, R., Hämäläinen, M., Hari, R., Lounasmaa, O. V., Lu, S. T., & Simola, J. (1991): Seeing speech: Visual information from lip movements modifies activity in the human auditory cortex. *Neurosci Lett 127*(1), 141–145.

Skipper, J. I., Goldin-Meadow, S., Nusbaum, H. C., & Small, S. L. (2007). Speech-associated gestures, Broca's area, and the human mirror system. *Brain Lang 101*(3), 260-277.

Skipper, J. I., Goldin-Meadow, S., Nusbaum, H. C., & Small, S. L. (2009). Gestures orchestrate brain networks for language understanding. *Curr Biol 19*(8), 661-667.

Slotnick, S. D., Moo, L. R., Segal, J. B., & Hart, J., Jr. (2003). Distinct prefrontal cortex activity associated with item memory and source memory for visual shapes. *Brain Res Cogn Brain Res 17*(1), 75–82.

Stein, B. E., & Meredith, M. A. (1993). *The merging of the senses.* Cambridge: MIT Press.

Straube, B., Green, A., Bromberger, B., & Kircher, T. (2011a). The differentiation of iconic and metaphoric gestures: Common and unique integration processes. *Hum Brain Mapp 32*(4), 520–533.

Straube, B., Green, A., Chatterjee, A., & Kircher, T. (2011b). Encoding social interactions: The neural correlates of true and false memories. *J Cogn Neurosci 23*(2), 306–324.

Straube, B., Green, A., Jansen, A., Chatterjee, A., & Kircher, T. (2010). Social cues, mentalizing and the neural processing of speech accompanied by gestures. *Neuropsychologia 48*(2), 382–393.

Straube, B., Green, A., Weis, S., Chatterjee, A., & Kircher, T. (2009). Memory effects of speech and gesture binding: Cortical and hippocampal activation in relation to subsequent memory performance. *J Cogn Neurosci 21*(4), 821–836.

Willems, R. M., Ozyurek, A., & Hagoort, P. (2007). When language meets action: the neural integration of gesture and speech. *Cereb Cortex 17*(10), 2322–2333.

Willems, R. M., Ozyurek, A., & Hagoort, P. (2009). Differential roles for left inferior frontal and superior temporal cortex in multimodal integration of action and language. *Neuroimage 47*(4), 1992–2004.

Wu, Y. C., Coulson, S. (2005). Meaningful gestures: Electrophysiological indices of iconic gesture comprehension. *Psychophysiology 42*(6), 654–667.

Wu, Y. C., & Coulson, S. (2007a). How iconic gestures enhance communication: An ERP study. *Brain Lang 101*(3), 234–245.

Wu, Y. C., & Coulson, S. (2007b). Iconic gestures prime related concepts: An ERP study. *Psychon Bull Rev 14*(1), 57–63.

Wu, Y. C., & Coulson, S. (2010). Gestures modulate speech processing early in utterances. *Neuroreport 21*(7), 522–526.

Students' Visual Attention While Solving Multiple Representation Problems in Upper-Division Physics

An Eye Tracking Study

Pascal Klein, Andreas Dengel, and Jochen Kuhn

Abstract

The famous physicist Feynman reminded us, that different representations of the same physical law can evoke varied mental pictures and thus assist in making new discoveries. In this study, we taught students two different (but yet equivalent) cognitive strategies to graphically interpret the physical meaning of divergence, a concept which is settled at the intersection between upper division mathematics and physics. Using eye-tracking, we studied students' understanding and cognitive processing of both strategies when they were engaged in graphical vector field representations and tried to integrate abstract mathematical equations for problem solving. Fixation patterns and relevant eye-tracking measures reveal that both visual strategies are cognitively processed differently, that different strategies result in different gaze patterns, and that both strategies may lead to different learning outcomes. We discuss implications for future research, for example, how positive learning can be fostered by computer-generated individual feedback based on gaze data, and for implementing findings into teaching.

Keywords

Multiple Representations; Eye Tracking; Vector Field Plots; Mathematization; Upper-division Physics; Problem Solving; Cognitive Processing; Teaching; Learning Outcomes.

1   Introduction

Representations are powerful learning tools because they can emphasize crucial conceptual aspects of the learning material (Ainsworth 2006). Physics education research has shown that competent and flexible use of representations (e.g., in the context of problem solving) is considered a key aspect of expertise in complex domains (Goldman 2003; Kohl and Finkelstein 2008). Specific representations of physical content may promote positive learning, while other representations may not suit the cognitive architecture of individual learners. In particular, representational competence and problem-solving skills are closely connected, i.e. students who are consistently competent in using different representations perform better at problem-solving tasks (Meltzer 2005; Nieminen et al. 2012). Even though lecturers and teachers may assume that students' representational competence (e.g., graph and formula interpretation skills) is adequately developed when enrolling at university, there is a lot of evidence that many students have difficulties with representations (e.g., McDermott et al. 1987; Kozma and Russell 1997; Klein et al. 2017). Due to these considerable difficulties on the one hand, and the essential role of representations on the other, physics educators and researchers advocate explicitly addressing them in physics instruction (Nieminen et al. 2012). If students are unable to learn *about* representations, that is, how representations depict information, they will not successfully learn *from* representations. Hence, positive learning of physical concepts requires a sound understanding of external representations.

As concepts become more complex, it can be beneficial to have multiple external representations (e.g., text, pictures or equations) that provide different views on these concepts (Schwonke et al. 2009). This point was made in a more general form by the physicist Richard Feynman. In his classic "The Character of Physical Law", Feynman (1967) placed a great emphasis on the importance of deriving different formulations for the same physical law, even if they are mathematically equivalent (e.g., Newton's law, the local field method, and the minimum principle). Different representations of a physical law, Feynman reminded us, can evoke varied mental pictures and thus assist in making new discoveries: "Psychologically they are different because they are completely unequivalent when you are trying to guess new laws" (p. 53). We agree with Feynman. The assertion that mathematically equivalent representations can make a difference to human understanding is the key to our analysis of vector field representations. In this paper, we investigate student's visual understanding of vector field plots, which are an important tool for learning theoretical physics and which occur in the introductory and upper-division university physics curricula. Prior research has shown that most students and even graduates fail to connect the concept of divergence to graphical vector field representations (Bollen et al. 2016; Pepper et al. 2012). As we will point out in the discipline-specific introduction (Section 3), there are two equivalent but yet different approaches to this problem, requiring different cognitive strategies: integral and differential approaches. To shed light on how learners use these mental representations during problem-solving, we use eye tracking. The analysis of eye movements has become a widely used approach to gain information of visual attention and information intake while learners are engaged with complex tasks (Rayner 1998). In particular, we use eye tracking to explore student's visual attention when they (try to) integrate the mathematical concept of divergence to the visual representation of a vector field, after providing them with two different cognitive strategies for doing so. By this means, we explore the effectiveness of each strategy, the visual processing of different representations (equations vs. diagrams), and on the same representation (equation or diagram) using different cognitive strategies.

2　Theoretical background

2.1　The role of (multiple) visual representations in learning physics

Research in a variety of domains has demonstrated that visual representations have the potential to substantially promote learning (e.g., Ainsworth et al. 1998; Rasch and Schnotz, 2009; Schnotz and Bannert 2003; Seufert 2003). Different representations emphasize complementary conceptual aspects of the learning material and have different effects on mental processing (Kozma et al. 2000; Schnotz and Bannert 2003). However, students' benefit from multiple representations depends on their ability to make connections between them (Ainsworth 2006; Bodemer and Faust 2006; Butcher 2006). For instance, learning about kinematics requires students connecting diagrams, equations and pictures of motion processes (Klein et al. 2017). Making connections between equations and graphical representations is a difficult task that students often do not engage in spontaneously, even though it is critical to their learning (Ainsworth et al. 2002; Rau et al. 2012). Hence, students need instructional support to make these connections, especially when concepts become more complex and sophisticated, as, for example, in upper-division physics.

As mentioned, prior research shows that learning of domain knowledge critically depends on the students' ability to make connections between multiple representations (Ainsworth 2006; Schwonke and Renkl 2010). In this paper, we distinguish between two types of representations: symbolic and graphical representations. This is a broad category of external representations, which can also be distinguished within a more specific category of representations. Symbolic representations, such as text or equations, are composed of features that have arbitrary relation to the real-world aspects they describe. According to Rau, Michaelis and Fay (2015, p. 461), symbolic representations "are interpreted based on their semantic meaning that we encode based on previously learned conventions (e.g., "1" stands for a quantity of one of something). Graphical representations are composed of perceptual features that have identifiable correspondence to the real-world aspects they depict. Therefore, graphical representations can be encoded based on their perceptual meaning."

As Rau (2016, p. 9) points out, "students' learning from visual representations requires that they have visual understanding of how a visual representation depicts information about domain-relevant concepts". She refers to the conditions of multimedia learning theories (Ainsworth 2006; 2014; Mayer 2005, 2009; Schnotz 2005) and concludes that visual understanding involves the ability to map visual representations to prior knowledge about the referent (i.e., to particular aspects of a domain-relevant concept they depict). These connections involve mapping internal representation to conceptual knowledge. Therefore, using graphical representations to learn about domain content, students need to learn which perceptual features of the graphical representations are relevant, how to interpret these features, and how to map these features to other representations such as equations in the case of diagrams. We apply this concept of visual understanding to our domain-specific content in Section 3.

2.2   Visual attention and eye tracking

As competent handling of representations is a prerequisite to develop scientific expertise, problem solving and understanding of physical concepts, it is important to discover how students read and use visual representations (van Gog and Scheiter 2010). Eye-Tracking is a non-intrusive method to obtain information about visual attention and cognitive processing while students solve problems, in particular if visual strategies are involved as in our research. A robust body of research has shown that eye-gaze may be considered an unbiased indicator of the focus of visual attention (Hoffmann and Subramaniam 1995; Itti et al. 1998; Salvucci and Anderson 2001), and that eye-tracking measures can be related to performance measures, particularly in the context of processing visual stimuli (Gegenfurtner et al. 2011). Therefore, we consider this non-intrusive method both useful and appropriate to gain insight into student cognitive processing of visual representations and how this connects to learning outcomes.

The most often used eye-tracking measures are derived from fixations and saccades. While fixations are relatively long periods usually lasting between 100 and 600 ms, in which the eye is almost still, saccades are very fast eye shifts between fixations lasting less than 100 ms. In our study, we consider three measures: fixation duration, number of fixations, and saccade length. Eye movement data are typically interpreted based on the *eye-mind assumption* (Just and Carpenter 1976), meaning that fixations reflect the attention and cognitive processing at specific locations, and are determined by the perceptual and cognitive analysis of the information at that location. Longer fixations indicate deeper processing or more difficult processing. This assumption is well in line with the theory of long-term working memory which connects fixation duration to information processing (Ericsson and Kintsch 1995). Within the same framework, the number of fixation in a certain area of interest also reflects cognitive effort to process information. Supported by the information-reduction hypothesis, the number of fixations reflects selective attentional allocation, with experts focussing on relevant areas to obtain information while negotiating irrelevant areas (Haider and Frensch 1999; Gegenfurtner et al. 2011). While doing so, experts also show extended visual span, i.e., greater saccade lengths. It can be assumed that eye movements are linked to attentional selection as proposed by the rubber band model of eye movements and attention (Henderson 1992). Experts can process parafoveal information which enables fast scanning over visual information, as supported by the holistic model of image perception (Kundel et al. 2007). In summary, these three measures can give reliable indications of task difficulty (in term of required cognitive effort) and student expertise.

3 Domain-specifics: Understanding divergence of vector field plots

3.1 Vector field representations and different representations of divergence

Divergence is a mathematical concept with many applications in physics. It appears, for example, in the differential form of Maxwell's equations,

$$\nabla \cdot \vec{E} = \frac{\rho}{\epsilon_0}, \nabla \cdot \vec{B} = 0, \qquad (EQ1)$$

with $\vec{E}, \vec{B}, \rho$ and ϵ_0 indicating the electric / magnetic field vector, charge distribution, and dielectrical constant, respectively. Divergence also appears in continuity equations describing the transport of some quantity.

In general, divergence of a vector field $\vec{f}$ is expressed by the scalar product of the differential operator "nabla" (∇) and the vector field, i.e.,

$$div \, \vec{f} = \nabla \cdot \vec{f}, \qquad (EQ2)$$

which can be expanded using two-dimensional Cartesian coordinates:

$$\nabla \cdot \vec{f} = \frac{\partial f_x}{\partial x} + \frac{\partial f_y}{\partial y}. \qquad (EQ3)$$

While this differential form can be evaluated at any specific point $\vec{r}$ where the vector field and its partial derivatives are defined, divergence can also be expressed in an integral form (in terms of a flux integral) referring to a finite region V (Gauss's theorem),

$$\int_V div \, \vec{f} \, dV = \int_{\partial V} \vec{f} \cdot d\vec{n}, \qquad (EQ4)$$

where $d\vec{n}$ denotes the (outer) surface normal of V and ∂V denotes the boundary of V.

These equations become better understood when a geometrical representation of a vector field is considered, see Figure 1.

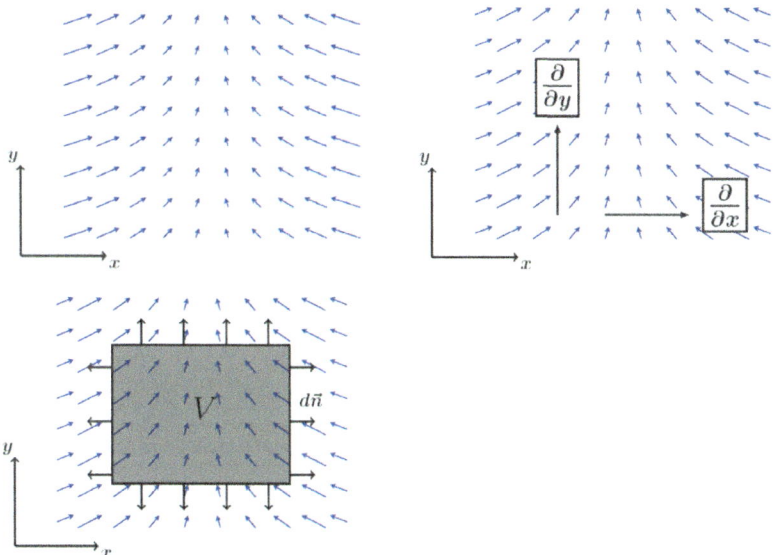

Fig. 1 Example of a graphical vector field representation (*left*) and two visual strategies for deciding whether the field is divergence-free or not

The field plot refers to the vector field

$$\vec{f}(x, y) = \begin{pmatrix} -x \\ 1 \end{pmatrix}. \ (EQ5)$$

As can easily be seen by applying the differential representation of divergence (Eq. 2) in Cartesian coordinates, i.e.,

$$div \, \vec{f}(x, y) = \frac{\partial f_x}{\partial x} + \frac{\partial f_y}{\partial y} = -1 + 0 = -1, (EQ6)$$

this vector field is not divergence free, i.e. $div \, \vec{f} \neq 0$ for every position in the field. While it is certainly possible that divergence is a local property of a vector field, i.e. $div \, \vec{f}$ is a function of x or y, we restrict our research to vector field plots which have either zero or non-zero divergence in every position of the field. However, without the mathematical expression of the vector field representation, making this conclusion is more difficult and requires visual strategies of inspecting the vector field plot.

First Visual strategy: Given a visual field representation, the differential form of divergence instructs looking for changes of the field components over the x- and y-direction (partial vector derivatives) starting in a certain point. Vividly speaking, the eye performs horizontal and vertical patterns over the vector field. If the x- and the y-component do not change in horizontal and vertical direction, respectively, or if changes cancel each other, the field is divergence free. If one or more field-component is zero, this task becomes straightforward. Cases in which changes of the field components in the x- and the y-direction cancel each other will not be considered in the following. As indicated in Fig. 1 (b), the y-component of the field is constant, and there is a significant change of the x-component in horizontal direction at any position. Hence, the field is not divergence-free. This result coincides with the analytical solution to the problem.

Second visual strategy: Divergence can also be evaluated using its integral representation given above. Given a visual field representation, one can estimate divergence with the flux through the boundary ∂V of a test-volume V in the field. Test volumes could take any form, but it is appropriate to make use of field's symmetry such that the outer surface normal $d\vec{n}$ is either parallel or perpendicular to the field vector $\vec{f}$. If the outer surface normal is perpendicular to the vector field arrow, for example, $d\vec{n} \cdot \vec{f} = 0$, then there is no flux coming in or out of the surface. Otherwise, if $d\vec{n} \cdot \vec{f} \neq 0$, one must balance positive and negative flux accounting for all boundaries of the test volume. A good test volume for the vector field example is given by a rectangle, as can be seen in Fig. 1 (c). For the upper and lower boundaries of V, the surface normal is in opposite directions to identical field vectors, hence there is no flux through these boundaries. Furthermore, vector arrows enter the field on the left side of the volume and on the right side; hence we can conclude that this vector field has non-zero divergence.

Both representations of divergence, differential and integral, find applications in many scientific disciplines (engineering, oceanography, gravimetry, atmospheric sciences, etc.). Therefore and because of the crucial role of representational competence for scientific expertise (see Section 2), it is important that students develop visual understanding of the mathematical concept to fully capture the physical relationships.

The *Visual Divergence Problem* (VDP), as defined by deciding graphical vector field representations either divergence-free or not, marks the starting point of our research. Along with either the integral or the differential prompt to apply divergence (equations 3 and 4), we investigate students visual processing of vector fields and the effectiveness of both visual strategies to solve the VDP.

3.2 Prior research concerning divergence of vector fields and research questions

Maths and physics education research showed that both, graduate and undergraduate students, have conceptually difficulties with divergence (Pepper et al. 2012; Baily et al. 2016; Singh and Maries 2013; Bollen et al. 2016). In particular, students believe that divergence indicates where field lines start or end or that divergence is a measure of how strong field lines spread apart or bend. These misunderstandings originate from lacking adequate visual representations of divergence, and show the need of representational support.

On the one hand, students are able to evaluate mathematical expressions by applying the nabla operator to vector fields, but they have no coherent picture about the meaning of divergence at all (Baily et al. 2016). As mentioned above, students fail to make correct assumptions about graphical representations of vector fields (Bollen et al. 2016; Singh and Maries 2013) such as those given in Figure 1.

So far, there has been no work concerning the conceptual differences of both representations of divergence (integral and differential). It remains unknown how they are processed cognitively, and which one promotes better visual understanding of the concept of divergence. As both representations appear in upper-division physics education and as both are important for both a local and global understanding of the nabla operator, we consider this work as valuable. Contributing to this line of research, and complementing it with attentional information, we conducted an instruction-based eye-tracking study under controlled conditions. Based on prior work and the considerations presented in Section 1 and 2, we formulate the following research questions:

RQ1: Which visual strategy promotes better learning, as revealed by performance scores on the visual divergence problem?

RQ2: Are both visual strategies cognitively processed differently?

2a. Does time on task differ between both strategies?

2b. Do eye-tracking measures related to the graphical vector field representations differ between both visual problem-solving strategies?

2c. Do eye-tracking measures related to algebraic equations differ between both visual problem-solving strategies?

2d. Do eye-tracking measures differ between the graphical vector field representation and the algebraic equation, independent of the visual problem-solving strategy?

4 Methods

4.1 Sample

Thirty-nine physics students (35 male) aged 19—24 (average 20.6 years, SD = 2.6 years) took part in the experiment. All participants were about to attend an introductory electromagnetism course (total enrolment: 72 students) and had successfully completed two mechanics lectures (calculus-based mechanics and experimental physics). Divergence has been introduced in both mechanics lectures, and has also been recapitulated in the electromagnetism course before the experiment was conducted. Participation was voluntary, took 30 min in total (survey and experiment), and was compensated with 10$.

4.2 Pre-instruction survey

Before students took part in the instruction-based experiment concerning the VDP, they conducted a survey assessing their prior knowledge and demographics. Three questions containing several true-false and open-response items aimed at prerequisite knowledge of differential and integral approaches to the VDP, and required students to express their response confidence on a rating scale.

The first question (Q1) required students to judge whether the x- or y- components of three given vector field representations (similar to the field represented in Fig. 1) are zero or non-zero, a prerequisite to evaluate vector derivatives, cf. Eq. (3).

During the second task (Q2), students visually compared the flux of a homogeneous vector field through different parts of the boundary ∂V of a regular octagon placed in the field. Finally, students were asked to make assumptions about the divergence of a vector field similar to those in Fig. 1. They should explain and justify their statements pre-testing took 15 minutes and was completed by all participants.

4.3 Study design and material

After completing the pre-instruction survey, students started the instruction-based experiment displayed on a computer screen. The sequence of the experiment is illustrated in Figure 2.

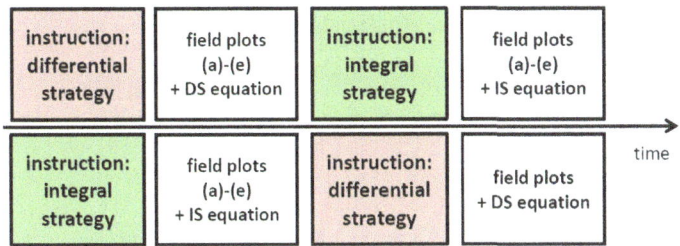

Fig. 2 Study design. Each student either completed the upper or lower sequence, consisting of 1 instructional slide and 5 problem-solving exercises on each strategy (12 slides in total)

Depending upon chance, each student either started with the first strategy (the derivative strategy, DS) or the second strategy (the integral strategy, IS). Both instructions, DS and IS, covered 250 words (one textbook page), respectively, and included a step-by-step description with visual cues about application of either strategy (worked-out example).

In each instruction period, students applied the prevailing strategy to five vector fields (V1—V5) which were presented one after another. There were no time constraints for answering the questions, but no student took longer than one minute for each exercise. The vector fields used in the study are presented in Figure 3 (right). Figure 3 (left) illustrates the slides of one problem (V3) which has to be solved using the differential strategy. Within one strategy and between tasks, the instruction text and the displayed equation remained the same, while the field changed from V1—V5. The equation changed between strategies, displaying Eq. (3) for the DS, and Eq. (4) for the IS, respectively.

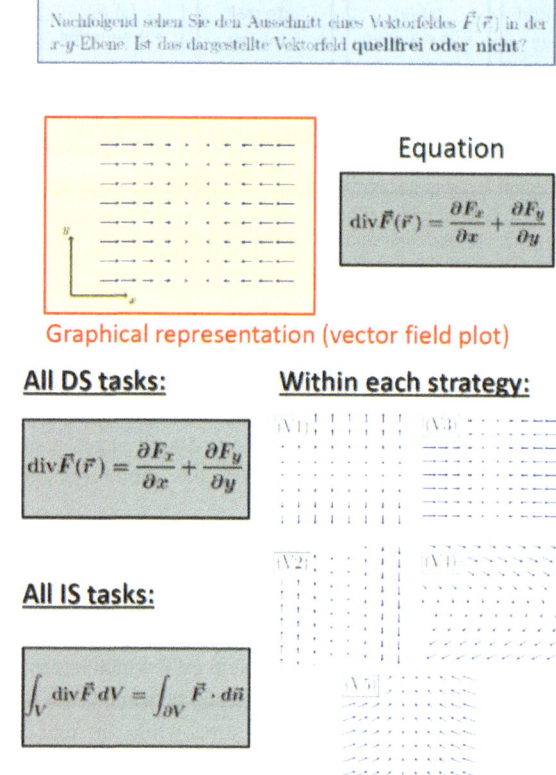

Fig. 3   Example of one slide showing text instruction, graphical vector field representation and equation (*left*)

During experiment, instruction remained the same but the vector field was exchanged (V1—V5, *right*). Depending upon the instrucational stragey, either the upper or lower equation was present which belong to the DS or IS, respectively.

Students did not receive any feedback after completing a visual divergence problem, and were unable to skip back to the instruction page. Each student completed both instruction periods in order to balance group effects. Students were told to apply only the current strategy.

4.4   Eye-tracking procedures and measures

We obtained gaze data for all 39 students using a Tobii X3-120 eye tracker installed on a 24" LCD screen as they worked with the VDP. All students had normal or correct-to-normal vision. The device has an accuracy of 0.4 degrees and allows a relatively high freedom of head movement. Its sampling frequency is 120 Hz. Gaze recording was accomplished using the Tobii Studio Pro software (version 3.4.8) able to detect saccades, fixations, and visualizations of data. Figure 4 shows sample heatmaps and gaze paths for one problem. From this data, we extracted the following measures for all students and every vector field 1—5 in each condition (DS, IS):

- Number of fixations; that is the number of all fixations within the graphical vector field representation (NFg) of each VDP and within the equation (NFe).
- Fixation duration; that is duration of each individual fixation within the graphical field plot (FDg) and within the equation (FDe).
- Saccade length; that is distance of eye movements between two fixations within the graphical vector field representation and the equation, respectively (SLg and SLe).

5   Results and conclusion

5.1   Pre-instruction survey

The first question (Q1) was answered correctly by most students (average performance score P=0.96, SD=0.16) with high confidence (average confidence index C=0.80, SD=0.25). From these results, we can conclude that students had little problems to identify x- and y-components of vector fields, and should be able to understand the differential strategy by instruction.

The second task was more difficult as performance measures (average P=0.85, SD=0.21) and confidence measures (C=0.65, SD=0.30) reveal, but as 85% of responses were correct in average, we can consider a good understanding of the flux concept prior to instruction.

However, only 3 out of 39 students (8%) gave a correct and complete solution to the third question, and 14 students (36%) were not able to make any reasonable assumption about divergence of the graphical vector field representation. The correct responses contained reasoning with vector derivatives as well as application of the flux concept "anything that comes in an arbitrary volume, also goes out [supported by a sketch]".

From these results, we can conclude that students only had some minor problems with the concept of flux through the boundary, and that only very few students (3 out of 39) were able to solve the VDP prior to instruction.

5.2   Students performance vs. strategy (after instruction, RQ1)

Results are shown in Table 1.

Tab. 1   Student performance scores on each VDP (cf. Fig. 3). Statistics refer to a two-tailed t-test (N=39)

Task	DS	IS	Total	p-value	Cohen's d
(V1)	0.85	0.51	0.68	0.001	0.75
(V2)	0.56	0.87	0.72	0.002	0.72
(V3)	0.79	0.77	0.78	0.79	--
(V4)	0.26	0.72	0.49	<10-4	1.02
(V5)	0.82	0.69	0.76	0.20	--
total	0.66	0.71	0.68	0.23	--

The derivative strategy yielded a correct response in 66% of cases, and the integral strategy in 71% of cases. There is no significant difference between these strategies in total meaning that they were equally effective in terms of total test score reached by students. Keeping in mind that the chance guessing correct is 50%, we conclude that even after instruction students' total performance on the VDP is mediocre (68%). When only the first instruction period is considered, total performance score is 0.60. Considering the overall score of 0.68, we can conclude that students slightly improved their reasoning in the second instruction period, independent from the specific instruction. This may be due to reconsidering the first strategy before given the final answer, disregarded students were told not to do so.

From the results depicted in Table 1, we further obtain evidence that the effectiveness of each strategy may depend upon the specific field (Cohen's d = 0.72-- 1.02). It is notable that the derivative strategy seems to fail when the vector field has no divergence (cases V2 and V4) but may be superior when divergence is non-zero (cases V1 and V5). In other words, students are more declined to accredit divergence to vector fields when using the derivative strategy (false positive). This may be due misinterpreting the partial vector derivative, cf. Eq. (3), and needs further investigation.

5.3   Time-on-task vs. strategy (RQ 2a)

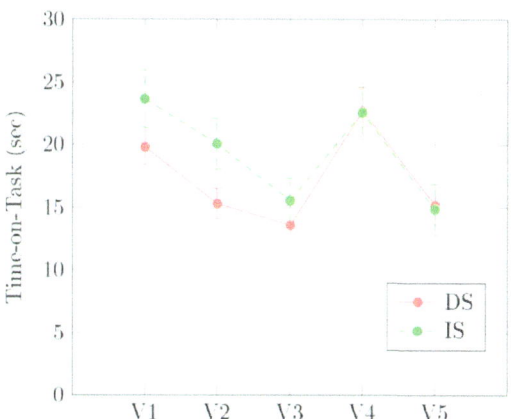

Fig. 4   Average time-on-task students spent on each VDP by strategy

Considering all five vector fields, the average time spent by students are 17.3 s (SD = 10 s) and 19.5 s (SD = 13 s) for the differential and the integral strategy, respectively. This difference is significant ($p=0.04$, $d = 0.20$). As can be seen in Figure 4, average time-on-task was significantly higher using the integral strategy considering the vector fields V1—V3 as compared to the differential strategy. There was no significant difference between vector fields V4 and V5. Considering the vector field representations given in Figure 3, it is notable that V1—V4 are one-dimensional vector fields, i.e., vector arrows possess only one directional component (x or y). Calculating partial vector derivatives is quite easy in this case because one does not have to decompose the field arrows. In contrast, V4 and V5 are two-dimensional fields which possess both, x- and y- directions. Decomposing the field arrows causes mental effort, therefore the time-on-tasks increases. From these data we can conclude that the differential strategy is more effective based on time-on-task considering one-dimensional vector fields as compared to the integral strategy. However, this result does not imply that the derivative strategy leads to better performance within this specific class of vector fields, as Section 5.2 has shown.

5.4   Eye-tracking measures vs. strategy (RQ 2b - 2d)

Heatmaps provide us with a qualitative impression how students' visual attention
was distributed when solving the VDP. Figure 5 indicates substantial differences
in visual attention (and hence cognitive processing) between both strategies (DS
and IS) considering three identical VDPs. Using the differential strategy, students
made more fixations on the coordinate system (see x-y- axis of Fig. 5), and on the
equation, as compared to using the integral strategy. The coordinate representation
of divergence, as given in Eq. (3), seems to establish a closer link between the explicit abstract representation and the vector field as compared to coordinate-free
the integral representation (EQ. 4). Referring to the field plot, students seemed
to focus on a smaller region when using the integral strategy as compared to the
differential strategy. This could be explained by the fact that students looked for
changes in the field plot when applying the DS, hence they followed the field lines
with longer saccades. This result could also be explained by systematic differences
between students when engaging in the field plot, resulting in a broader total distribution. In contrast, there were little differences between students during the IS
approach.

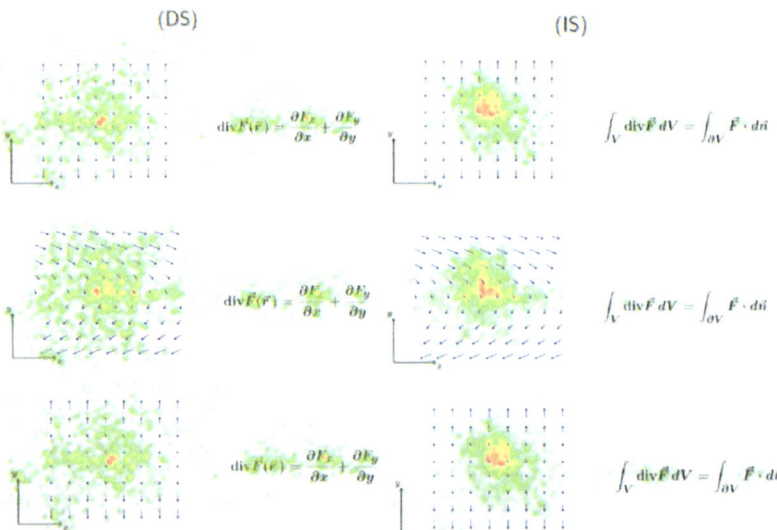

Fig. 5 Heatmap comparison of three identical VDPs when students applied the differential strategy (*left*) and the integral strategy (*right*). Note the different gaze distribution within the vector field and the different densities at the equations

The integral strategy required students to imagine a rectangle to balance positive and negative flux. While rectangles could theoretically be placed at any position and could take any size, the heatmaps indicate that students preferred placing them it at the centre with a small size, most likely in order to conserve mental resources. Upcoming studies with retrospective interviews can proof this hypothesis.

From heatmaps, we can conclude that both strategies provoke substantial differences in visual processing of vector fields. Analysing eye-tracking measures allows for a more quantitative approach to support our statements above. Table 2 shows the eye-tracking measures which have been introduced in Section 4.4.

Tab. 2 Eye-tracking measures (mean and standard error) considering different AOIs and strategies (NF = number of fixations, FD = fixation duration, SL = saccade length, DS/IS = differential / integral strategy)

	Graphical representation		Equation	
	DS	IS	DS	IS
NF	36.5 (0.3)	42.1 (0.4)	7.5 (0.08)	3.6 (0.04)
FD (s)	0.29 (0.01)	0.32 (0.01)	0.18 (0.01)	0.18 (0.01)
SL (°)	3.82 (0.16)	2.96 (0.14)	7.01 (0.23)	8.95 (0.25)

We found significant differences in number of fixations ($p<10^{-5}$, $d = 0.35$), fixation duration ($p=0.03$, $d = 0.23$) and saccade length ($p=0.003$, $d = 1.5$) between both visual strategies (DS and IS) considering the graphical vector field representation. This means that both strategies foster indeed a different visual behavior when students inspect the vector field plot (RQ 2b). When students apply the integral strategy, they made significantly more fixations on the visual representation as compared to using the derivative strategy. According to the information reduction hypothesis (cf. Section 2.2) this means that students need to attend to more information leading to a longer processing time. Differences between fixation durations are also marginal longer when the integral strategy is applied supporting the hypothesis that processing requires more cognitive effort. Indeed, students need to construct a mental representation of a test volume in order to balance the flux through its boundary which may cause cognitive load. In contrast, the derivative strategy does not require constructing an additional mental representation in all cases. For example, there is no vector decomposition some of the vector fields (cf. Fig. 3). We also found striking evidence for longer saccade lengths when students worked with the derivative strategy. According to the holistic model of image perception (cf. Section 2.2), students extract information from widely distanced and parafoveal regions. This occurs, for example, when students explore the change of the field across horizontal or vertical directions.

Furthermore, we found differences in number of fixations ($p<10^{-5}$, $d=0.52$) and saccade length ($p = 0.001$, $d = 1.72$) considering the equations belonging to DS or IS, respectively (RQ 2c). We can thus confirm that students used EQ (3) more often than EQ (4) as indicated by heatmaps (cf. Fig. 5), and that they tended to skim over the integral representation. Eye-tracking measures indicate that EQ (3) was more useful for students when trying to apply the cognitive strategy to solve the VDP. As stated above, there might be a more direct link between the coordinate representation of divergence and the two-dimensional field representation as compared to the integral representation and the flux concept. The integral strategy might be less abstract and presumably easier to apply without formalism for students.

Finally, we found differences between processing equations and graphical representation in terms of number of fixations ($p<10^{-9}$, $d = 1.8$), fixation duration ($p<10^{-9}$, $d = 1.5$), and saccade length ($p<10^{-9}$, $d>2$), independent from the cognitive strategy students used. These large effect sizes provide evidence in different mental processing of abstract symbols (equations) and graphical representations (e.g., vector fields).

6   Discussion

Results have shown that both strategies solving the visual divergence problem (VDP) complement each other: The effectiveness of either strategy fluctuates across specific VDPs, and eye-tracking measure revealed that both strategies imply different visual processing of the vector field plots. Hence, both strategies contribute to student's visual flexibility, a prerequisite of problem solving. We conclude that teaching both strategies enhances students' development of a coherent mental concept of divergence. In a next step, we explore correlations between performance scores and eye-tracking measures (saccade lengths, number of fixations), which can be useful to predict whether students need further instructional support (visual cues). This is giving great potential for future research, for example, technology-based diagnostics (cf. also Kise in this volume): We could study students' visual behavior while solving the VDP without specific instruction and compare eye-tracking measures with our specific findings to define thresholds for providing feedback and helping cues. We will also analyze reading behavior of both instructional strategies and look for possible correlations to student performance and take regressions between different visual stimuli into account.

Bibliography

Ainsworth, S. (2006). DeFT: a conceptual framework for considering learning with multiple representations. *Learning and Instruction, 16*(3), 183-198.

Ainsworth, S. (2014). The multiple representation principle in multimedia learning. In R. E. Mayer (Ed.), *The Cambridge handbook of multimedia learning* (2nd ed., pp. 464–486). New York, NY: Cambridge University Press.

Ainsworth, S. E., Bibby, P. A., & Wood, D. J. (1998). Analysing the costs and benefits of multi-representational learning environments. In M. W. van Someren, P. Reimann, H. P. A. Boshuizen, & T. de Jong (Eds.), *Learning with multiple representations*. Oxford, England: Pergamon.

Ainsworth, S., Bibby, P., & Wood, D. (2002). Examining the effects of different multiple representational systems in learning primary mathematics. *Journal of the Learning Sciences, 11*(1), 25-61.

Baily, C.R., Bollen, L., Pattie, A., van Kampen, P., & de Cock, M. (2016). Student thinking about the divergence and curl in mathematics and physics contexts. In A.D. Churukian, D. Jones & L. Ding (Eds.), *Physics Education Research Conference series* (pp. 51-54).

Bodemer, D., & Faust, U. (2006). External and mental referencing of multiple representations. *Computers in Human Behavior, 22*(1), 27-42.

Bollen, L., van Kampen, P., Baily, C.R., & de Cock, M. (2016). Qualitative investigation into students' use of divergence and curl in electromagnetism. *Physical Review Physics Education Research, 12*, 020134.

Butcher, K. R. (2006). Learning from text with diagrams: promoting mental model development and inference generation. *Journal of Educational Psychology, 98*(1), 182-197.

Ericsson, K. A., & Kintsch, W. (1995). Long-term working memory. *Psychological Review, 102*, 211-245.

Gegenfurtner, A., Lehtinen, E., & Säljö, R. (2011). Expertise differences in the comprehension of visualizations: A metaanalysis of eye-tracking research in professional domains. *Educational Psychology Review, 23*(4), 523–552.

Goldman, S. R. (2003). Learning in complex domains: when and why do multiple representations help? *Learning and Instruction, 13*(2), 239-244.

Feynman, R. (1967). *The character of physical law*. Cambridge, MA: MIT Press.

Haider, H., & Frensch, P. A. (1999). Eye movement during skill acquisition: More evidence for the information reduction hypothesis. *Journal of Experimental Psychology: Learning, Memory, & Cognition, 25*, 172–190.

Henderson, J. M. (1992). Visual attention and eye movement control during reading and picture viewing. In K. Rayner (Ed.), *Eye movements and visual cognition: scene perception and reading* (pp. 260-283). New York, NY: Springer.

Hoffman, J. E., & Subramaniam, B. (1995). The role of visual attention in saccadic eye movements. *Attention, Perception, & Psychophysics, 57*(6), 787-795.

Itti, L., Koch, C., & Niebur, E. (1998). A model of saliency-based visual attention for rapid scene analysis. *IEEE Transactions on pattern analysis and machine intelligence, 20*(11), 1254-1259.

Just, M. A., & Carpenter, P. A. (1976). Eye fixations and cognitive processes. *Cognitive Psychology, 8*, 441-480.

Klein, P., Müller, A., & Kuhn, J. (2017). Assessment of representational competence in kinematics. *Physics Education Research, 13*, 010132.

Kohl, P. B., & Finkelstein, N. D. (2008). Patterns of multiple representation use by experts and novices during physics problem solving. *Physical Review Special Topics – Physics Education Research,* 4(010111). doi:10.1103/PhysRevSTPER.4.010111

Kozma, R. B., & Russell, J. (1997). Multimedia and understanding: expert and novice responses to different representations of chemical phenomena. *Journal of Research in Science Teaching, 34*(9), 949–968.

Kozma, R., Chin, E., Russell, J., & Marx, N. (2000). The roles of representations and tools in the chemistry laboratory and their implications for chemistry learning. *The Journal of the Learning Sciences, 9*(2), 105-143.

Kundel, H. L., Nodine, C. F., Conant, E. F., & Weinstein, S. P. (2007). Holistic component of image perception in mammogram interpretation: Gaze-tracking study. *Radiology, 242,* 396–402.

Mayer, R. E. (2005). Cognitive theory of multimedia learning. In R. E. Mayer (Ed.), *The Cambridge handbook of multimedia learning* (pp. 31–48). New York, NY: Cambridge University Press.

Mayer, R. E. (2009). *Multimedia Learning*. Cambridge University Press.

McDermott, L.C., Rosenquist, M., & van Zee, E. (1987). Student difficulties in connecting graphs and physics: Examples from kinematics. *American Journal of Physics, 55,* 503.

Meltzer, D. E. (2005). Relation between students' problemsolving performance and representational format. *American Journal of Physics, 73,* 463.

Nieminen, P., Savinainen, A., & Viiri, J. (2012). Relations between representational consistency, conceptual understanding of the force concept, and scientific reasoning. *Physical Review Special Topics – Physics Education Research, 8*, 010123.

Pepper, R.E., Chasteen, S.V., Pollock, S.J., & Perkins, K.K. (2012). Observations on student difficulties with mathematics in upperdivision electricity and magnetism. *Physical Review Physics Education Research, 8*, 010111.

Rasch, T., & Schnotz, W. (2009). Interactive and non-interactive pictures in multimedia learning environments: effects on learning outcomes and learning efficiency. *Learning and Instruction, 19*(5), 411-422.

Rau, M.A. (2016). Conditions for the Effectiveness of Multiple Visual Representations in Enhancing STEM Learning. *Educational Psychology Review,* 1-45. doi:10.1007/s10648-016-9365-3

Rau, M. A., Aleven, V., Rummel, N., & Rohrbach, S. (2012). Sense making alone doesn't do it: fluency matters too! ITS support for robust learning with multiple representations. In S. Cerri, W. Clancey, G. Papadourakis & K. Panourgia (Eds.), *Intelligent tutoring systems* (Vol. 7315, pp. 174-184). Berlin/Heidelberg, Germany: Springer.

Rau, M. A., Michaelis, J. E., & Fay, N. (2015). Connection making between multiple graphical representations: A multi-methods approach for domain-specific grounding of an intelligent tutoring system for chemistry. *Computers & Education 82*, 460-485.

Rayner, K. (1998). Eye movements in reading and information processing: 20 years of research. *Psychological Bulletin, 3,* 372–422.

Salvucci, D. D., & Anderson, J. R. (2001). Automated eye-movement protocol analysis, *Human-Computer Interaction, 16*(1), 39–86.

Schnotz, W. (2005). An integrated model of text and picture comprehension. In R. E. Mayer (Ed.), *The Cambridge handbook of multimedia learning* (1st ed., pp. 49–69). New York, NY: Cambridge University Press.

Schnotz, W., & Bannert, M. (2003). Construction and interference in learning from multiple representation. *Learning and Instruction, 13*(2), 141-156.

Schwonke, R., Berthold, K., & Renkl, A. (2009). How multiple external representations are used and how they can be made more useful. *Applied Cognitive Psychology, 23*, 1227–1243.

Schwonke, R., & Renkl, A. (2010). *How do proficient learners construct mental representations of different but related external representations?* Paper presented at the EARLI SIG2, Tuebingen, Germany.

Seufert, T. (2003). Supporting coherence formation in learning from multiple representations. *Learning and Instruction, 13*(2), 227-237.

Singh, C., & Maries, A. (2013). Core graduate courses: A missed learning opportunity? *AIP Conference Proceedings, 1513*(1), 382. doi:10.1063/1.4789732

Van Gog, T., & Scheiter, K. (2010). Eye tracking as a tool to study and enhance multimedia learning. *Learning and Instruction, 20*, 95-99.

Supporting and Hindering Effects on Rational Reasoning

A Slightly Unbalanced Survey

Markus Knauff

Abstract

Rational reasoning is a core competence of human beings. We are often good at making rational inferences and coming to justified conclusions. However, sometimes people deviate from the norms of rationality. Here I report experimental findings from my group on five different topics: (1) how people reason with problems which are easy or difficult to visualize, (2) how people deal with problems for which more than one possible solution exists, (3) how the trustworthiness of the information sources affects mental reasoning processes, (4) how cognitive reasoning interacts with moral values, and (5) how highly emotional content affects rational reasoning. I close with some thoughts on the connection between rationality and learning and describe some implications for education, legal reasoning, computer science, and social media.

Keywords

Cognition; Rationality; Reasoning; Logical Thinking; Knowledge; Visual Imagery; Mental Models; Spatial Reasoning; Legal Reasoning; Beliefs; Preference; Belief Biases; Content Effects.

1   Some views on human rationality

What makes people mentally competent to reason rationally? Why is actual human reasoning sometimes error-prone? How do mental reasoning mechanisms interact with knowledge, beliefs, and other cognitive and non-cognitive psychological processes? These are the *three big questions* of the cognitive science of human reasoning.

The first question is still an issue of many debates. Some theories claim that humans are equipped with mental inference rules and reason by syntactic language-based mental proofs of derivation. The key idea of the theory is a repertoire of inference rules represented in long-term-memory (LTM). These rules are derived from general knowledge and refer to sentential connectives such as "if" and "then" and quantifiers like "all" and "some". The language-based rules are used to solve inference problems by introducing and eliminating sentential connectives. This process is carried out by transferring the inference rules into working memory (WM) and applying them to the given premises, which are also represented in a language-like format. The result is a language-based conclusion (e.g., Rips 1994).

Other theories assume that humans use subjective probabilities to reason rationally (e.g., Oaksford and Chater 2007). It can be argued that this is another version of the rule-based approach, although the mental rules are now concerned with the computation of subjective probabilities. Some information about the probabilities of events is given, and people use this information to compute other probabilities. An important rule in several of these theories is the *Bayes rule*, which many readers may know from statistics (Oaksford and Chater 2007). Another way to compute the subjective probabilities is the *Ramsey Test*, which is technically the subjective probability of q given p (Ramsey 1990; Evans and Over 2004).

Yet other theories adopt the position that people use *mental simulations* to draw rational inferences. These *mental models* capture possibilities of how the world is or could be under certain conditions (e.g., Johnson-Laird 1983; Johnson-Laird and Byrne 1991; Knauff 2013). The key assumption of mental model theories is that reasoning does not rely on syntactic operations like in rule-based approaches, but on the construction and manipulation of mental models. Mental models represent a possible "state of affairs" described in the premises of an inference problem. The common assumption of most mental model accounts (Johnson-Laird 1983; Johnson-Laird and Byrne 1991) is the conception of reasoning as a cognitive process, in which spatially organized or iconic models of the given premises are constructed, and then alternative models are sequentially generated and inspected. A conclusion is true if it holds in all models that agree with the premises. For model theorists, people often come to rational inferences in this way (Johnson-Laird 1999, 2006, 2010).

The second question—as to why human reasoning is sometimes error-prone—is also a matter of many controversies. Some theorists believe that humans are fundamentally irrational. In most cases, people do not use their rational reasoning competences, but simple heuristics that systematically deviate from the norms of rational reasoning. These heuristics result in cognitive biases and faulty inferences (Kahneman and Tversky 1974). Other theories are more positive. These accounts assume that humans have – in theory – the competence to think and act rationally, but that this competence – in practice – is limited by many internal and external conditions: incomplete knowledge, uncertain and unreliable information sources, limited cognitive capacities, and so on (Evans et al. 1993). Yet other theories say that the matter is empirically undecidable or take over positions between the two extremes (Cohen 1981; Evans 2012; Stupple and Ball 2014).

This chapter focuses on the third question—the interplay between mental reasoning and other cognitive and non-cognitive processes. One reason for this is that the *formal* structure and the *content* of an inference interact in many interesting ways, and that these interactions also help to understand how the rational – or irrational – mind works. The second reason is that the interaction of reasoning, knowledge, beliefs, and other factors is highly relevant for many questions of recent times. For instance, the Internet is full of knowledge and pseudo-knowledge, beliefs, prejudice, and more or less reliable information. How do people's background knowledge and their prior beliefs affect how they learn by selecting and evaluating information from the Internet and social media? The third reason is that this research field is also related to the *format* in which information is presented – as pictures, texts, or diagrams. This is an important matter for the useful presentation of information on the Internet or in many learning contexts (Mayer 2009; see also Kravcik et al. in this volume). I now summarize experimental findings on five different topics: (1) how people reason with problems which are easy or difficult to visualize; (2) how people deal with problems for which more than one possible solution exists; (3) how the trustworthiness of information sources affects mental reasoning processes; (4) how cognitive reasoning interacts with moral values; and (5) how highly emotional content affects rational reasoning. My intention is not to give a comprehensive review, but instead to raise some new questions and to answer these questions with some (more or less) unexpected results. In the last section, I draw some general conclusions on the role of visualisation and preferences in learning. Finally, I discuss how these findings can help practitioners in education, computer science, and social media to facilitate rational reasoning and learning.

2   How people reason with problems that are easy or difficult to visualize

People often report to experience their thinking as "seeing with their inner eye" or as inspecting a "picture-like" mental image. Various sorts of experimental evidence are compatible with this subjective experience, including the well-known studies of the mental rotation and the mental scanning of images (Kosslyn 1980; Shepard and Cooper 1982). However, my group and others reported several experiments drawing an opposite picture of what laypeople and even experts in the psychology of reasoning often believe: Visual mental images can impede reasoning and hinder the process of inference. If the content of a reasoning process is easy to imagine visually, people need more time and make more errors than with less visual problems (Knauff 2013). In Knauff and Johnson-Laird (2002), we empirically identified four sorts of reasoning problems: (1) visuo-spatial problems that are easy to envisage visually and spatially, (2) visual problems that are easy to envisage visually but hard to envisage spatially, (3) spatial problems that are hard to envisage visually but easy to envisage spatially, and (4) abstract problems that are hard to envisage either visually or spatially. We then asked our participants to solve these four sorts of reasoning problems and measured the error rates and how much time they needed to perform the inference. A theory based on visual mental images would predict an advantage of visual and probably visuo-spatial problems. Our prediction, however, was that problems that elicit visual images containing details that are irrelevant to an inference should impede the process of reasoning. Our findings supported these predictions: in several experiments, we found that problems that are easy to visualize impaired reasoning. Reasoners were significantly slower with these problems than with the other sorts of problems. In other experiments, we also found that visualization results in lower reasoning accuracy; people make more errors with visual problems than with the other sorts of problems (Knauff and May 2006; Knauff 2009). We call this the *visual-impedance effect* (Knauff and Johnson-Laird 2002; Knauff 2013).

Why is that so? To answer this question, we performed a brain imaging study using the same sorts of problems. The results are presented in Figure 1. Interestingly, all four types of reasoning problems evoked activity in the parietal cortices, a region that is typically involved in the representation and processing of spatial information. In Knauff (2013), I argued – very simply put – that this seems to be a "default mode" of brain functioning during reasoning. Individuals might have the facility to construct spatially organized mental models from all sorts of problems. However, only the visual problems also activate areas of the visual cortices. Yet, these images are too concrete and thus side-track the reasoner from the information that is actually relevant to the rational inference. The main message from these results is that visual images are often overrated and can actually be a nuisance for people's thinking (see also Klein et al. in this volume). I return to this in the general discussion (Section 7).

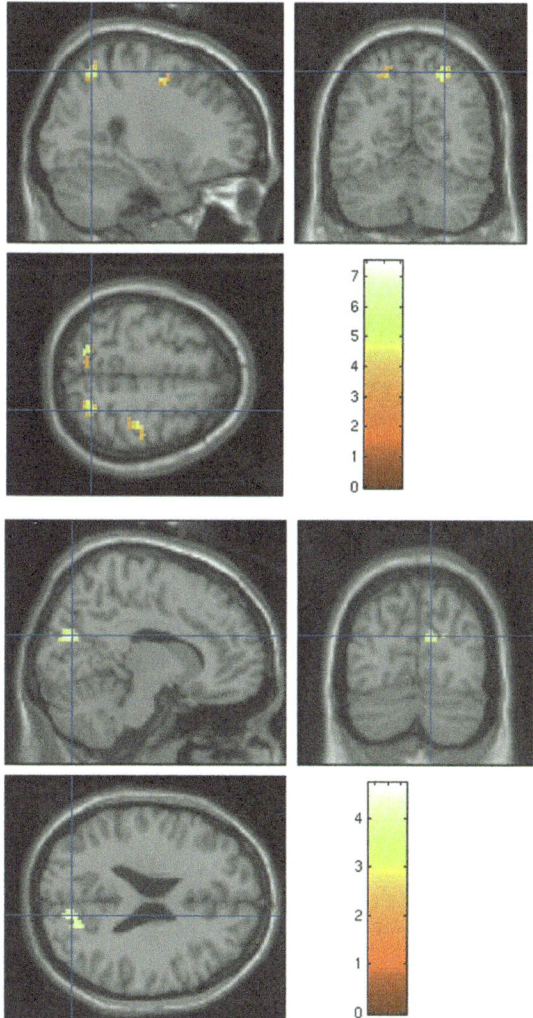

Fig. 1   Images representing differentially activated brain areas during reasoning

The brain is presented from three different perspectives: from the side (as if vertically cut through at about the position of the eyes), transverse (as if vertically cut through in parallel to the axis between the ears), and horizontal (as if horizontally cut through in parallel to the axis of the eyebrows). The three upper images show the foci of activation resulting from reasoning with all four sorts of problems (visual, visuo-spatial, spatial, abstract). The highlighted areas are located in the parietal cortices, a region that is typically involved in the representation and processing of spatial information. The three lower images show the additional activity during reasoning with the visual problems. The highlighted areas are located in the occipital cortex, a region that is involved in the representation and processing of visual information. This region is typically active when people experience visual mental images (from: Knauff et al. 2003, p. 15-16; see text for details; cf. also Nagels et al. in this volume).

3   How people deal with problems for which more than one possible solution exists

In daily life, people are often confronted with problems for which more than one possible solution exists. Or we can interpret the given problem in more than one way. Reasoning researchers often call such problems *indeterminate problems* or *multiple-models problems*. My group extensively investigated such problems in the domain of spatial thinking. Imagine you get the following information about the location of different geometrical shapes in a design task of a graphics editor software:

The square is to the left of the circle.
The rectangle is to the right of the circle.
The circle is to the left of the ellipse.
The ellipse is to the left of the cross.

Now please say whether the circle is to the left of the cross. If you think about it, you will realize that three arrangements are possible:

Square	Circle	Rectangle	Ellipse	Cross
Square	Circle	Ellipse	Rectangle	Cross
Square	Circle	Ellipse	Cross	Rectangle.

In all three arrangements, the correct answer should be "Yes, the circle is to the left of the cross." However, if you ask people which arrangement they had in mind, almost all consider only the first arrangement but neglect the other possibilities. We call this mentally preferably constructed arrangement the *preferred mental model*. And we could show that this model guides the further process of thinking. It saves cognitive resources but sometimes also results in illusory inferences and erroneous conclusions (Jahn et al. 2007; Knauff 1999; Knauff et al. 2004; Rauh et al. 2005).

In Ragni and Knauff (2013), we developed a detailed theory and an executable computational model of spatial reasoning with preferred mental models that explains and reconstructs such findings. The PRISM Model relies on seven basic cognitive principles (Ragni and Knauff 2013, p. 564).

1. When individuals are confronted with indeterminate reasoning problems, they are likely to construct just a single, simple, and typical model, even when a description is compatible with several alternative models. This model that first comes to the reasoner's mind is the preferred mental model.
2. Preferred mental models of spatial descriptions are those constructed according to the principle that new objects are added to a model without disturbing the arrangement of those tokens already represented in the model.
3. Reasoning with indeterminate premises is biased toward preferred mental models. Thus, inferences about relations conforming to a preferred model are easier than inferences about relations that hold only in alternative models.
4. The difficulty of an inference does not depend on the number of logically possible models but on the difficulty of mentally constructing preferred and alternative mental models of the circumstances the premises describe.
5. People search for alternative interpretations of the premises only if this is explicitly required. If a search for alternative models is required, it always starts with the preferred model. Alternative models are constructed by local transformations, and the process follows the principle of minimal changes.
6. Alternative models that require a longer sequence of local transformations are more likely to be neglected than models that are only minor variations of the preferred model. Therefore, the danger of missing a particular alternative model increases with its distance from the preferred model.
7. Logical errors and illusory inferences result from omitting models in which the conclusion from the preferred model does not hold.

Please also note that I could have used pictorial icons for the geometrical shapes in the example. However, this would have been misleading given the results reported in Section 2 (visual impedance effect). In fact, our approach does not rely on visual images that represent shape, texture, size, and the like, but on more abstract spatial layout models. These spatial layout models only capture the relevant spatial relations, but do not require any specific assumptions about how the objects or any other entities are represented in the model. In Knauff (2013), I suggest a *"space to reason theory"* that unifies my thoughts on the role of visual and spatial representations in rational reasoning with the concept of preferred mental models (see also Krumnack et al. 2011; Ragni et al. 2006; Ragni et al. 2016). Again, I return to this in the general discussion (Section 7).

4   How the trustworthiness of information sources affects mental reasoning and belief revision

An important question for psychologists and the public is: How do people change their opinion over time or in the light of new information that does not agree with their current beliefs? Psychologists have done some research on this matter by choosing an experimental paradigm in which participants are confronted with conditional sentences (premises) that posit that if proposition p is true then proposition q is true. The work in this paradigm shows that human belief revision is affected by many factors, including asymmetries between particular facts and general laws (Revlis 1975; Revlis et al. 1971), conditional and categorical premises (Dieussaert et al. 2000; Elio and Pelletier 1997; Girotto et al. 2000; Revlin et al. 2001), and major and minor premises (Politzer and Carles 2001). An important finding in the field is that people prefer to withdraw those pieces of information that they cannot explain. Typically, people try to find explanations for inconsistences in a set of premises, and they retain those premises that they can more easily integrate into a plausible explanation (Khemlani and Johnson-Laird 2011).

Knauff, Bucher, Krumnack, and Nejasmic (2013) were the first who explored how people change their mind about the location of objects in space. The participants received statements that described the spatial relations between a set of objects. From these premises, they drew a conclusion, which then, in the next step, was contradicted by a new, irrefutable fact. The participants' task was to decide which of the objects to relocate and which one to leave at its initial position. We predicted that the revision process is affected by the functional asymmetry between reference objects (RO) and the located objects (LO) of spatial relations. The distinction is standard in psycholinguistics and spatial language research, where researchers agree on the assumption that a spatial locational description refers to the position of an object (LO) relative to another object or area (RO) (e.g., Hayward & Tarr 1995). The results from two experiments corroborate this hypothesis. We found that individuals have a strong preference to relocate the LO of the premises, but avoid relocating the RO.

However, much more work on belief revision was conducted in artificial intelligence (AI) and formal philosophy (Gärdenfors 1988, 1992; Harman 1986; Nebel 1990). Here, Gärdenfors (1992) defined belief revision as "A new sentence that is inconsistent with a belief system K is added, but, in order to maintain consistency in the resulting belief system, some of the old sentences in K are deleted" (p. 3). Theorists in artificial intelligence as well as logicians and philosophers constructed several theories of belief revision, of which the most well-known are *minimal change* (Harman 1986) and *epistemic entrenchment* (Gärdenfors 1988). According to the principle of minimal change, the belief that will be rejected is the one that causes the least amount of change in the existing belief set. The notion of epistemic entrenchment, on the other hand, suggests that when forced to choose between two beliefs, people prefer to give up the less entrenched one. Probably the best-known system of belief revision in AI are *AGM-postulates* developed by Alchourrón, Gärdenfors, and Makinson (1985). Recently, Spohn (2012) developed a *ranking theory*, which provides a normative account of the dynamics of beliefs and a promising alternative to probabilistic approaches. Skovgaard-Olsen (2016) showed that this approach is also useful to model descriptive results from human belief revision.

Psychologists have paid less attention to the theoretical difference between different belief revision theories, but more on the cognitive factors that might influence belief revision. One of these factors is how people take into account from which *external source* the new information comes. Imagine you hear:

If Karl sells a damaged car, then he offers the car for a reduced price.
Karl sells a damaged car.
But: Karl does not offer the car for a reduced price.

In Wolf, Rieger, and Knauff (2012) we varied the person who uttered the first two sentences (premises). For instance, sentence 1 could come from a police officer and sentence 2 from a used car dealer, or the other way around. The third sentence was defined as irrefutable fact. We conducted several norming studies how trustworthy different groups of people are. The question then was how often people believe in the different premises when they were uttered by more or less trustworthy persons? Furthermore, we used easy and difficult reasoning problems. We found the following: The more trustworthy the person was the more often the statement was believed and therefore the other premise was rejected. This effect was even stronger for more difficult tasks (Wolf et al. 2012). Our interpretation is that in particular if the inference is difficult, people rely more on the trustworthiness of the source. They use the trustworthiness as heuristic to decide which belief they retain or reject. It is easy to see that this result is highly relevant for reasoning in daily life. Whom do you believe more about the reasons for the ongoing climate change? The CEO of a large industrial concern or a renowned climate scientist? Whom does Trump believe?

5   How cognitive reasoning interacts with moral values

Logically valid conclusions are rationally justified. Yet, people often are not willing to follow the principles of formal logic. Image you hear the following:

If a child eats a lot of candy, it gets cavities.
Ann eats a lot of candy.
Therefore, Ann gets cavities.

This is a logically valid inference and rationally justified. Nothing can now happen that make this inference wrong. This is called the monotonicity of classical logic. However, in real life the situation is different, which is the reason why people often do not draw this logical inference and are therefore often mistakenly considered irrational (Evans 2012). In real life, we know that many *exceptions* from the rule exist. For instance: Ann only eats sugar-free candy. Ann brushes her teeth regularly. Ann often goes to the dentist. Several experiments show that this is one core reason why people often infer that Ann will not get cavities although this is wrong according to classical logic. The reason is that people retrieve *counterexamples* or *exceptions* from LTM that overwrite the logical inference. Many studies show that the more exceptions people have in mind, the more likely they are to withdraw the logically valid conclusion (Cummins 1995; De Neys et al. 2003a, b). This is called *defeasible reasoning*. This research field is closely related to belief revision, but does not focus so much on the change of epistemic states, but rather on the principles of inferential reasoning with inconsistent premises.

But what happens if the structure of the inference leads to a conclusion that does not agree with the reasoners' beliefs or values? Are people willing to consider counterexamples and exceptions even if that would lead to an inference that they perceive as unpleasant, unjust, or immoral? In several experiments, we investigated how people consider exculpatory circumstances when reasoning with legal conditionals such as "If a person kills another human, then this person should be punished for manslaughter". We presented these legal rules together with exculpatory circumstances as counterexamples. The participants' task was to decide whether they would adhere to the legal conditional rule and punish the offender or defeat the rule and thus do not punish the transgressor (Gazzo Castañeda and Knauff 2016a, b). We showed that people are willing to accept exceptions in the form of exculpatory circumstances (self-defence, psychological illness, etc.) for mildly morally outraging crimes (e.g., shop-lifting), but not for highly morally outraging crimes (e.g., sexual abuse of children). We explained these results with the theory of moral outrage and peoples' desires to punish offenders (Darley 2009). Furthermore, our studies in this field show that this effect is weaker in lawyers (luckily), but even stronger in highly religious people, or in people who live in a country with low trust in the legal system (Gazzo Castañeda and Knauff 2014). In a recent German textbook, we related these findings to the often surprisingly irrational opinions of the public to spectacular court cases reported in the media (Knauff and Knoblich 2016).

6   How highly emotional content affects rational reasoning

We all know that emotions can have a significant effect on the way we think, decide, and solve problems. Experimental psychologists and also empirically working clinical psychologists have thus not surprisingly drawn much attention to interactions between emotions and rational reasoning (Blanchette 2014; Beck 1995). Our group is not an exception.

One of our projects was on defeasible reasoning and emotions. Our research question was how the conclusions drawn from conditionals describing emotionally positive or negative situations can be defeated by subsequent emotionally negative or positive information, respectively. Consider the following problem:

> If my mother dies, then I am sad.
> My mother dies.
> I get my dream job.
> Am I sad?

Would you conclude being sad even though you get your dream job? Here is yet another problem:

> If I get my dream job, then I am happy.
> I get my dream job.

My mother dies.
Am I happy?

How would you answer now? Would you conclude to be happy, even though your mother died? Our results show that negative information defeats positively charged conclusions more strongly (second example) than positive information defeats negatively charged conclusions (first example). We call this a "negativity bias" (Gazzo Castañeda et al. 2016).

In another set of experiments, different groups of participants first had to pass a manipulated intelligence test. Their emotional state was altered by giving them manipulated feedback, i.e. that they performed excellent, poor or on average. Then they completed a set of logical inference problems. Problem content also had either a positive, negative or neutral emotional value. Our results showed a clear effect of affective state on reasoning performance. Participants in negative mood performed worse than participants in positive mood, but both groups were outperformed by the neutral mood reasoners. Problem content also had an effect on reasoning performance (Jung et al. 2014).

Many psychologists have suggested theories about how reasoning and emotions interact. One theory says that emotion has a detrimental effect on reasoning performance because working memory resources are otherwise allocated and not available to solve the task (Oaksford et al. 1996). Other theories assume that the allocation of attentional processes is of major relevance in this context. The idea is that emotional processing requires attentional resources, which are therefore not available for reasoning (Gable and Harmon-Jones 2013). By that as it may, the interaction of rationality and emotion lies in the heart of our picture of human beings and has preoccupied man for thousands of years (see Kirman et al. 2010). However, this topic goes far beyond the scope of this chapter.

7   General discussion and conclusions

Some colleagues from reasoning research might not like the "ideology" of this article. They probably argue that the distinction between the *form* and *content* of reasoning problems is misleading, because human reasoning is intrinsically knowledge-driven, in particular when it comes to reasoning in everyday life. Thus, talking about "content effects" is principally wrong, as it implies that we can distinguish between inference and knowledge (Elqayam 2011). Another critique might be that I use logic to define what a valid and invalid inference is. Some researchers argue that psychologists should not use logic or any other normative standards but just describe how people reason (Elqayam and Evans 2011). I made my (sceptical) position on those matters clear in the last chapter of Knauff (2013). Here I want to close with some messages for the areas of multi-media learning, education, legal reasoning, and visualization on the Internet.

Take, for instance, the *visual impedance effect*. It is easy to see that this effect is important for people working in education or software development. I agree with Mayer (2009), who reported empirical studies showing that people learn better, when extraneous pictures are excluded from a multi-media-system rather than included. In many cases, visual overload can hinder learning effectiveness. Stenning (2002) showed that students with inferior reasoning performance are those who translate logical problems into visual images. Conversely, the students with better logical performance are exactly those students who do not use visual diagrams but rather abstract spatial strategies. Notably, especially highly "visual" students are the ones who learn best when they avoid overly visual representations (Stenning 2002). The main message from such results is that visual images are often overrated and can actually be a nuisance for people's learning and thinking. This also provides an argument against the excessive use of visual decoration in textbooks, multi-media learning, mass media, and all kinds of Internet applications and social media.

Another example are *preferences* in reasoning. Preferences save WM resources, having lower construction and processing costs. Inferences conforming to these preferred models are easier than inferences that are valid for alternatives. However, normally, I think, people do not even search for such alternative models. Certainly, from a logical point of view, a conclusion is only true if no model exists, that refutes the conclusion (in this respect my terminology to talk about multiple "solutions" was not entirely correct but intuitively appealing). However, I do not think that people follow this logical understanding of validity. Rather, in most problems, they are perfectly satisfied with the conclusion that follows from a single model—the preferred one—and do not search for counterexamples. People and problems may differ in this respect (Knauff 2013), but the question of how rational we are has much to do with how many alternatives we construct for problems with multiple possible models. This aspect of the theory is for two reasons also important from an applied point of view: First, in our daily life, inferences and preferences about them give rise to different actions and result in certain beliefs, desires, prejudices, and attitudes toward sets of objects or events, typically reflected in an implicit or explicit decision or choice. In fact, they are important for many areas of complex cognition (Knauff and Wolf 2010). Second, the preferred models can also explain why people often have difficulties to come to "unusual" solutions, which are more far away from the "standard solution" provided by the preferred model. Finding innovative solutions requires people to go beyond the preferred solutions. But it seems to be very hard to revise our preferred solution so radically that we consider an entirely new answer to a problem. This might be related to the well-known "insight problems" in which a solution seems to arrive out of nowhere (Kaplan and Simon 1990; Kounios and Jung-Beeman 2009) and to questions of creativity (Csikszentmihalyi 2013) and technical innovation (Gilbert et al. 2001; Voss et al. 1994).

A third example comes from the area of belief revision and defeasible reasoning. Our results show that in particular if the inference is difficult, people rely more on the trustworthiness of the source (see also Dormann et al. in this volume). They use the trustworthiness as heuristic to come to the judgement. These results have important consequences in the context of "post-truth politics" and "fake news" in social media. Which sources do Internet users consider trustworthy? And how trustworthy are they actually? How can we identify deliberately wrong information and unreliable source of information?

In our projects, we also collaborated with lawyers and legal theorists. In law and legal theory, defeasible reasoning is important in several ways (cf. Bäcker 2010; Prakken and Sartor 2004). For instance, during police investigations, new evidence can "defeat" previous insights, during trials attorneys and prosecutors can defeat each other's arguments, and legal rules are sometimes not applied in light of exculpatory evidence. The most prominent domain of defeasible reasoning is reasoning with fundamental rights. The best-known examples are right to dignity, liberty, freedom of thought and of expression, or right of property. However, there are instances where such fundamental rights are in conflict, for instance when the right to information conflicts with right to property. Therefore, judges in the federal court have to decide which of the rights deserves more importance, although both are theoretically equally important. Alexy (2003) calls this weighting of fundamental rights "*balancing*". Gazzo Castañeda and I recently published a paper on this legal reasoning by balancing. What do people decide if, for instance, the law to property conflicts with law to information? Can one of these rights be "defeated" by the other? Our results show that people with no professional expertise in law decide between two conflicting fundamental rights in a case-by-case fashion. Typically, participants protected the fundamental right whose violation evoked the highest moral outrage or whose violation was considered more serious. In our paper, we discuss the implications of our findings for law theory and psychology, and we argue that paradigms from cognitive psychology are useful to investigate questions from other fields, in this case from legal theory (Gazzo Castañeda et al. 2017).

Overall, we can say that people are often able to draw rationally justified inferences just based on the formal structure of the arguments (Knauff 2007, 2009, 2013). However, in daily life such formally valid inferences can also be complemented, biased, or even overwritten by what we know or believe to know about the area of discourse. In these cases, we might have good reasons not to believe in what is formally correct. This does not make us irrational. Having good reasons for something is a key concept of most theories of rationality. This also leads back to the first two questions of the introduction (competence and errors). However, we must be very careful. Our system of beliefs can often be full of inconsistencies, unjustified assumptions, prejudices, stereotypes, and groundless attitudes. Fake news, post-truth politics, and many misinformation strategies on the Internet and in social media build exactly on such risky thinking strategies. An important issue for future cognitive research therefore is to go outside the lab and to study how we can facilitate "good" reasoning and learning in everyday life and the Internet to benefit the society.

Acknowledgements

This research was supported by DFG grant KN 465/10-2 within the Priority Program "New Frameworks of Rationality" (SPP 1516). I thank the editors for their helpful suggestions and comments on this paper.

Bibliography

Alchourrón, C. E., Gärdenfors, P., & Makinson, D. (1985). On the logic of theory change: Partial meet contraction and revision functions. *Journal of Symbolic Logic,* 50, 510–530.

Alexy, R. (2003). Die Gewichtsformel. In J. v. Jickeli, P. Kreutz, & D. Reuter (Eds.), *Gedächtnisschrift für Jürgen Sonnenschein* (pp.69–78). Berlin: De Gruyter Recht.

Bäcker, C. (2010). Rules, principles, and defeasibility. In M. Borowski (Ed.), *On the nature of legal principles,* ARSP-Beiheft 119 (pp. 79–91). Stuttgart: Steiner.

Beck, J. (1995). *Cognitive Therapy: Basics and Beyond.* New York, NY: Guilford.

Blanchette, I. (Ed.). (2014). *Emotion and Reasoning.* New York, NY: Psychology Press.

Cohen, L. J. (1981). Can human irrationality be experimentally demonstrated? *Behavioral and Brain Sciences, 4*(3), 317–331.

Csikszentmihalyi, M. (2013). *Creativity: the psychology of discovery and invention.* New York: Harper Perennial Modern Classics.

Cummins, D. D. (1995). Naive theories and causal deduction. *Memory & Cognition, 23,* 646–658.

Darley, J. M. (2009). Morality in the law: The psychological foundations of citizens' desires to punish transgressions. *Annual Review of Law and Social Science*, *5*, 1–23.

De Neys, W., Schaeken, W., & d'Ydewalle, G. (2003a). Inference suppression and semantic memory retrieval: Every counterexample counts. *Memory & Cognition*, *31*, 581–595.

De Neys, W., Schaeken, W., & d'Ydewalle, G. (2003b). Causal conditional reasoning and strength of association: The disabling condition case. *European Journal of Cognitive Psychology*, *15*, 161–176.

Dieussaert, K., Schaeken, W., Neys, W. De, & d'Ydewalle, G. (2000). Initial belief state as a predictor of belief revision. *Current Psychology of Cognition*, *19*, 277–286.

Elio, R., & Pelletier, F. J. (1997). Belief change as propositional update. *Cognitive Science*, *21*(4), 419–460.

Elqayam, S. (2011). Grounded rationality: A relativist framework for normative rationality. In K. I. Manktelow, D. E. Over, & S. Elqayam (Eds.), *The Science of Reason: A Festschrift in Honour of Jonathan St.B.T. Evans*. Hove, UK: Psychology Press.

Elqayam, S., & Evans, J. S. B. (2011). Subtracting "ought" from "is": descriptivism versus normativism in the study of human thinking. *Behavioral and Brain Sciences*. *34*, 233–248.

Evans, J. S. B. T. (2012). Questions and challenges for the new psychology of reasoning. *Thinking & Reasoning,* 18, 5–31.

Evans, J. S. B. T., Newstead, S. E., & Byrne, R. (1993). *Human reasoning: The psychology of deduction*. Hove, UK: Erlbaum.

Evans, J. S. B. T, & Over, D. E. (2004). *If.* Oxford, UK: Oxford University Press.

Gable, P. A., & Harmon-Jones, E. (2013). Does arousal per se account for the influence of appetitive stimuli on attentional scope and the late positive potential? *Psychophysiology*, *50*(4), 344–350. doi: 10.1111/psyp.12023.

Gärdenfors, P. (1988). *Knowledge in flux*. Cambridge, MA: MIT Press.

Gärdenfors, P. (1992). Belief Revision: An introduction. In P. Gärdenfors (Ed.), *Belief revision* (pp. 1–28). Cambridge: Cambridge University Press.

Gazzo Castaneda, L. E., & Knauff, M. (2014). Intercultural differences in defeasible reasoning with legal conditionals. In A. C. Schütz, K. Drewing, & K. R. Gegenfurtner (Eds.), *Abstracts of the 56th Conference of Experimental Psychologists* (p. 81). Lengerich: Pabst.

Gazzo Castaneda, L. E., & Knauff, M. (2016a). When will is not the same as should: The role of modals in reasoning with legal conditionals. *The Quarterly Journal of Experimental Psychology,* 69, 1480–1497.

Gazzo Castaneda, L. E., & Knauff, M. (2016b). Defeasible reasoning with legal conditionals. *Memory & Cognition*, 44, 499–517.

Gazzo Castaneda, L. E., Richter, B., & Knauff, M. (2016). Negativity bias in defeasible reasoning. *Thinking & Reasoning*, *22*, 209–220.

Gazzo Castaneda, L. E., Stemmler, A., & Knauff, M. (2017). Reasoning with fundamental rights. In *Proceedings of the 39th Annual Conference of the Cognitive Science Society (pp. 2079 -2085) Austin, TX:* Cognitive Science Society.

Gilbert, N., Pyka, A., & Ahrweiler, P. (2001). Innovation Networks—A Simulation Approach. *Journal of Artificial Societies and Social Simulation*,*4*(3), 1–13.

Girotto, V., Johnson-Laird, P. N., Legrenzi, P., & Sonino, M. (2000). Reasoning to consistency: How people resolve logical inconsistencies. In J. Garcia-Madruga, M. Carriedo, & M. J. Gonzalez-Labra (Eds.), *Mental Models in Reasoning* (pp. 83–97). Madrid: UNED.

Harman, G. (1986). *Change in view*. Cambridge, MA: MIT Press.Hayward, W. G., & Tarr, M. J. (1995). Spatial language and spatial representation. *Cognition*, 55, 39 – 84.

Jahn, G., Knauff, M., & Johnson-Laird, P. N. (2007). Preferred mental models in reasoning about spatial relations. *Memory & Cognition, 35*, 2075–2087.

Johnson-Laird, P. N. (1983). *Mental models*. Cambridge: Cambridge University Press.

Johnson-Laird, P. N. (1999). Deductive reasoning. *Annual Review of Psychology, 50*, 109–135.

Johnson-Laird, P. N. (2006). *How we reason*. New York: Oxford University Press.

Johnson-Laird, P. N. (2010). Mental models and human reasoning. *Proceedings of the National Academy of Sciences. 107*, 18243–18250.

Johnson-Laird, P. N., & Byrne, R. M. J. (1991). *Deduction*. Hove, UK: Lawrence Erlbaum Associates.

Jung, N., Wranke, C., Hamburger, K., & Knauff, M. (2014). How emotions affect logical reasoning: Evidence from experiments with mood-manipulated participants, spider phobics, and people with exam anxiety. *Frontiers in Psychology, 5*, 1–12. doi: 10.3389/fpsyg.2014.00570.

Kahneman, D., & Tversky, A. (1974). Judgment under uncertainty: Heuristics and biases. *Science, 185*(4157), 1124–1131.

Kaplan, C. A., & Simon, H. A. (1990). In search of insight. *Cognitive Psychology, 22*, 374-419.

Khemlani, S., & Johnson-Laird, P. N. (2011). The need to explain. Quarterly Journal of Experimental Psychology, *64*, 2276–2288.

Kirman, A., Livet, P, & Teschl, M. (2010). *Rationality and emotion. Philos Trans R Soc Lond B Biol Sci. 365*(1538): 215–219.

Knauff, M. (1999). The cognitive adequacy of Allen's interval calculus for qualitative spatial representation and reasoning. *Spatial Cognition and Computation, 1*, 261–290.

Knauff, M. (2007). How our brains reason logically. *Topio, 26*, 19–36.

Knauff, M. (2009). A Neuro-Cognitive Theory of Deductive Relational Reasoning with Mental Models and Visual Images. *Spatial Cognition and Computation, 9*, 109–137.

Knauff, M. (2013). *Space to Reason: A Spatial Theory of Human Thought*. Cambridge, MA: MIT Press.

Knauff, M., Bucher, L., Krumnack, A., & Nejasmic, J. (2013). Spatial belief revision. *Journal of Cognitive Psychology, 25*, 147–156.

Knauff, M., Fangmeier, T., Ruff, C. C., & Johnson-Laird, P. N. (2003). Reasoning, models, and images: Behavioral measures and cortical activity. *Journal of Cognitive Neuroscience, 15*, 559–573.

Knauff, M., & Johnson-Laird, P. N. (2002). Visual imagery can impede reasoning. *Memory & Cognition, 30*, 363–371.

Knauff, M., & Knoblich, G. (2016). Logisches Denken. In: J. Müsseler & M. Rieger (Hrsg.). *Lehrbuch Allgemeine Psychologie* (3. Aufl.) (pp. 533–585). Berlin: Springer.

Knauff, M., & May, E. (2006). Mental imagery, reasoning, and blindness. *Quarterly Journal of Experimental Psychology, 59*, 161–177.

Knauff, M., Strube, G., Jola, C., Rauh, R., & Schlieder, C. (2004). The psychological validity of qualitative spatial reasoning in one dimension. *Spatial Cognition and Computation, 4*, 167–188.

Knauff, M., & Wolf, A. G. (2010). Complex Cognition: The Science of Human Reasoning, Problem-solving, and Decision-making (Editorial). *Cognitive Processing, 11*(2), 99–102.

Kosslyn, S. M. (1980). *Image and mind*. Cambridge, MA: Harvard University Press.

Kounios, J., & Jung-Beeman, M. (2009). Aha! The cognitive neuroscience of in-sight. *Current Directions in Psychological Science, 18*, 210–216.

Krumnack, A., Bucher, L., Nejasmic, J., Nebel, B., & Knauff, M. (2011). A model for relational reasoning as verbal reasoning. *Cognitive Systems Research*, 11, 377-392.

Manktelow, K. (2004). *Reasoning and Thinking*. Hove: Psychology Press.

Mayer, R. E. (2009). *Multimedia learning (2nd ed.)*. New York: Cambridge University Press.

Nebel, B. (1990). *Reasoning and Revision in Hybrid Representation Systems*, Lecture Notes in Computer Science, vol. 422, Berlin: Springer.

Oaksford, M., Morris, F., Grainger, B., & Williams, J. M. G. (1996). Mood, reasoning, and central executive processes. *J. Exp. Psychol. Learn. Mem. Cogn. 22*, 476–492.

Oaksford, M., & Chater, N. (2007). *Bayesian rationality the probabilistic approach to human reasoning*. New York, NY, US: Oxford University Press.

Politzer, G., & Carles, L. (2001). Belief revision and uncertain reasoning. *Thinking and reasoning, 7*, 217–234.

Prakken, H., & Sartor, G. (2004). The three faces of defeasibility in law. *Ratio Juris, 17*, 118–139.

Ragni, M., & Knauff, M. (2013). A theory and a computational model of spatial reasoning with preferred mental models, *Psychological Review*, 120, 561–588.

Ragni, M., Franzmeier, I., Maier, S., & Knauff, M. (2016). Uncertain relational reasoning in parietal cortex. *Brain & Cognition, 104*, 72–81.

Ragni, M., Fangmeier, T., Webber, L., & Knauff, M. (2006). Complexity in spatial reasoning. In R. Sun & N. Miyake (Eds.), *Proceedings of the 28th Annual Conference of the Cognitive Science Society (pp. 1986-1991)*. Mahwah, NJ: Erlbaum.

Ramsey, F. P. (1990). General propositions and causality. In D. H. Mellor (Ed.), *Philosophical Papers* (pp. 145–163). Cambridge, UK: Cambridge University Press. Original Publikation, 1929.

Rauh, R., Hagen, C., Knauff, M., Kuß, T., Schlieder, C., & Strube, G. (2005). From preferred to alternative mental models in spatial reasoning. *Spatial Cognition and Computation*, 5, 239–269.

Revlin, R., Cate, C. L., & Rouss, T. S. (2001). Reasoning counterfactually: Combining and rending. *Memory & Cognition, 29*, 1196–1208.

Revlis, R. (1975). Two models of syllogistic inference: Feature selection and conversion. *Journal of Verbal Learning and Verbal Behavior*, 14, 180–195.

Revlis, R., Lipkin, S. G., & Hayes, J. R. (1971). The importance of universal quantifiers in a hypothetical reasoning task. *Journal of Verbal Learning and Verbal Behavior, 10*, 86–91.

Rips, L. J. (1994). *The psychology of proof*. Cambridge, MA: M.I.T. Press.

Shepard, R. N., & Cooper, L. A. (1982). *Mental images and their transformations*. Cambridge, MA: MIT Press.

Skovgaard-Olsen, N. (2016). Ranking theory and conditional reasoning. *Cognitive Science, 40*(4), 848–880.

Spohn, W. (2012). *The Laws of Belief. Ranking Theory and Its Philosophical Applications*. Oxford: Oxford University Press.

Stenning, K. (2002). *Seeing reason*. Oxford: Oxford University Press.

Stupple, E.J.N. & Ball, L.J. (2014). The intersection between Descriptivism and Meliorism in reasoning research: further proposals in support of 'soft normativism'. *Frontiers in Psychology, 5*. doi.org/10.3389/fpsyg.2014.01269

Voss, A., Bartsch-Spörl, B., Börner, K., Coulon, C.-H., Durschke, H., Gräther, W., Knauff, M., Linowski, B., Schaaf, J. W., & Tammer, E. C. (1994). Retrieval of similar layouts - about a very hybrid approach in FABEL. In J. S. Gero, & F. Sudweeks (Eds.), *Artificial Intelligence in Design* (pp. 625–640). Dordrecht: Kluwer Academic Publishers.

Wolf, A. G., Rieger, S. & Knauff, M. (2012). The effects of source trustworthiness and inference type on human belief revision. *Thinking & Reasoning, 18*, 417–440.

.

A Concept for Quantitative Comparison of Mathematical and Natural Language and its possible Effect on Learning

Gabriel Wittum, Robert Jabs, Michael Hoffer, Arne Nägel, Walter Bisang, and Olga Zlatkin-Troitschanskaia

Abstract

Starting with the question whether there is a connection between the mathematical capabilities of a person and his or her mother tongue, we introduce a new modeling approach to quantitatively compare natural languages with mathematical language. The question arises from educational assessment studies that indicate such a relation. Texts written in natural languages can be deconstructed into a dependence graph, in simple cases a dependence tree. The same kind of deconstruction is also possible for mathematical texts. This gives an idea of how to quantitatively compare mathematical and natural language. To that end, we develop algorithms to define the distance between graphs. In this paper, we restrict the structure to trees. In order to measure the distance between trees, we use algorithms based on previous work measuring the distance of neurons using the constrained tree edit distance. Once a distance matrix has been computed, this matrix can be used to perform a cluster analysis.

Keywords

Mathematical Modeling; Mathematical Language; Natural Language; Comparing Trees; Constrained Tree Edit Distance; Learning; Cross-Linguistic Analysis; Hidden Complexity.

1   Introduction

Starting with the general question whether there is a connection between the mathematical abilities of a student and his or her native language, we aim at comparing natural languages with mathematical language quantitatively. The question arises from empirical studies that suggest such a connection and its relevance for learning (e.g., Brückner et al. 2015; Zlatkin-Troitschanskaia et al. 2016). Some basic issues concerning the relation between language and mathematics are addressed in Bisang's essay (this volume) on the expression of numerals in natural language from a cross-linguistic perspective.

Mathematics is the common language of quantitative theory in Science and Technology as well as in other disciplines like Economics, Psychology and many more. Mathematics is described by a specific language that has been worked out step by step by generations of mathematicians in the last centuries. Important rules date back to Leibniz (1684), Euler (1748), Lagrange (1797), Cauchy (1821), Weierstraß (1878) and many others. The core part is the mathematical formalism. This formalism is embedded into natural language which is usually simply structured and uses only a minimum, but very specific vocabulary. Wittum (1982) read mathematical publications in several languages unknown to him, but was able to understand the mathematical contents due to the mathematical formalism, which is used world-wide in the same way. This mathematical language is mainly based on the aim of expressing complex mathematical facts correctly, comprehensibly and at the same time simply, compactly and precisely. In this sense, the mathematical language maps the logical process and tries to avoid all deviations or embellishments.

Natural languages are also subject to structures. However, these structures are much more involved and less logical. They still form a set of rules which the language follows, called grammar. However, these rules often do not apply strictly, but may have some sidekicks and are applied fuzzily. These grammatical and syntactical rules form the abstract backbone of a text. In order to express something textually, a prior abstraction step is necessary, fitting the contents into such a rule-based construction.

These rules imply that a text can be deconstructed into a dependence graph, in simple cases a dependence tree. The same kind of deconstruction is also possible for mathematical texts. This gives an idea of how to quantitatively compare mathematical and natural language. To that end, we need an algorithm to define the distance between graphs. In this paper, we restrict the structure to trees, when comparing texts. This means that we do not consider texts with back referencing for now.

Heumann and Wittum (2009) dealt with a comparable question, but from a different area, investigating how to compare neurons. Neurons can be described as discrete trees. To compare these trees, one needs to measure the distance between them. To that end, the constrained tree edit distance by Zhang (1996) was used. The constrained tree edit distance can be computed in reasonable time, unlike the unconstrained version. The algorithms developed by Heumann and Wittum (2009) will also be applied in the present case, in order to measure the distance between trees (section 3 and 4). Once a distance matrix has been computed, this matrix can be used to perform a cluster analysis to visualise the relations between the items used in educational assessment (section 5). In the following section 2, we explain the details of the algorithm.

2   Deriving dependence trees from natural language texts

A graph $G = (V, E)$ is a set V of vertices and a set of edges E beginning and ending in a vertex. In the present paper, we consider rooted trees in the sense of graph theory with a root vertex (see https://en.wikipedia.org/wiki/Tree_(graph_theory)). As the child vertices do not have any special order imposed by the tree, these trees are called unordered. We can now assign one or more attributes or labels to each vertex and each edge.

There are tools to extract the dependency trees from texts available via Open Source license. They are all based on Probabilistic Context Free Grammars (PCFG), which have been trained on large data sets using machine learning. Pre-trained PCFGs are, for example, SpaCy, (SpaCy 2017), or CoreNLP, also known as Stanford parser (CoreNLP 2017). Both APIs come with their learning methods, in case the user seeks to train PCFGs for own data. An alternative is the Natural Language Toolkit (NLTK) which works without pretrained methods, is slower than the pretrained tools, but offers a larger set of methods (NLTK 2017). It is good for processing smaller samples. Both SpaCy and NLTK are written in Python, while CoreNLP is written in Java.

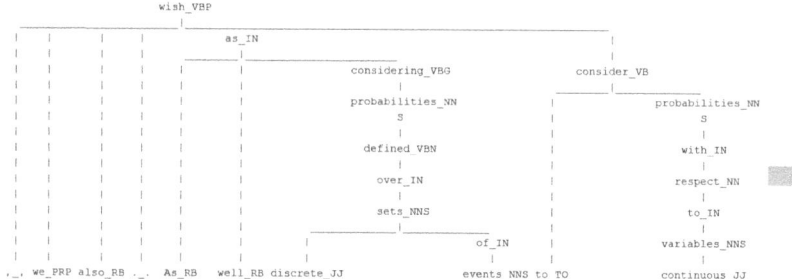

Fig. 1 A dependency tree derived by SpaCy; abbreviations:

IN	Preposition
JJ	Adjective
VBm	Verb, base form
VBG	Verb, gerund/present pple
VBN	Verb, past participle
VBP	Verb, non-3rd ps. sg. present
NN	Noun, singular or mass
NNS	Noun, plural
.	Sentence-final punctuation
,	Comma
PRP	Personal pronoun
RB	Adverb
TO	infinitival to

Figure 1 illustrates a dependency tree derived by SpaCy using the sentence: "As well as defined over discrete sets of events, we also wish to consider probabilities with respect to continuous variables." After constructing dependence trees from texts, we can compare two trees by computing their tree edit distance.

3   The tree edit distance

Following Heumann and Wittum (2009), we describe the constrained tree edit distance as a measure to quantify similarity of trees. Wagner and Fischer (1974) originally proposed a distance function between strings, which is the minimal cost of a sequence of edit-operations, which modify a string slightly by deleting, inserting or substituting characters. This is a generalization of the ideas of Levenshtein (1966) and Hamming (1950). The algorithm for computing such a distance is the basis for many problems which can be modelled as strings, such as DNA sequencing. Later on, the edit distance was generalised to trees (Tai 1979, Selkow 1977). There are algorithms for computing the edit-distance between ordered labeled trees, however, Kilpeläinen and Mannila (1991) and Zhang et al. (1992) showed that the computation of this tree edit distance is NP-complete for unordered trees. This makes it infeasible to be used for computational purposes. As a consequence, Zhang (1996) proposed an algorithm to compute a slightly modified distance, the constraint tree edit distance, which has quadratic complexity. We introduce these distances below.

Let a rooted tree $T = (V, E)$ with a set of labeled vertices and a set of edges connecting the vertices as, for example, shown in Figure 1 and Figure 2. We now introduce the three *basic edit operations* shown in Figure 3.

▷ **Definition 1 (*basic edit operation*).** The following basic operations on a labeled tree T are called *basic edit operations:*

(1) *Substitution: sub(b,g): Replace label b in vertex labeled b by label g*
(2) *Delete: del(g): Delete vertex labelled g. Connects the predecessor of vertex g with the successors of g.*
(3) *Insert: ins (f; a,d): Insert new vertex f between vertices a and d.*
    or: ins (f; d, λ) Adds new vertex f after vertex d. λ stands for an empty vertex.

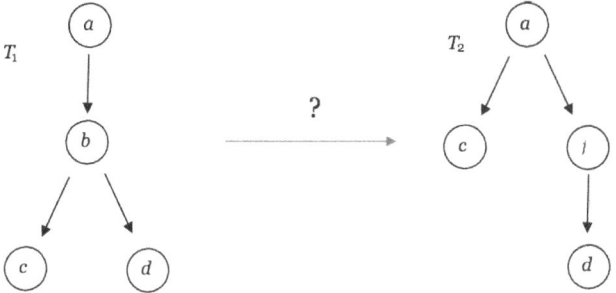

Fig. 2 How to define the distance of trees T_1 and T_2?

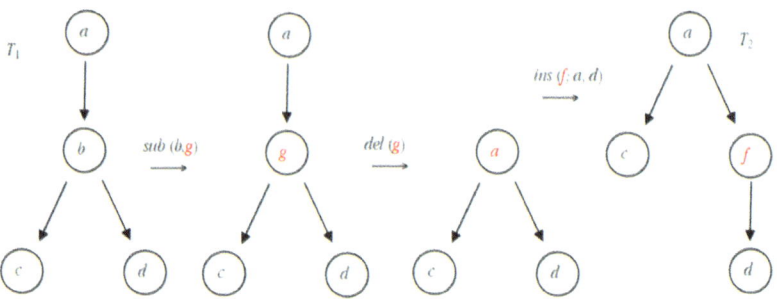

Fig. 3   Transforming T_1 into T_2

The three basic edit operations illustrated. Substitution of a label (left), deletion of a vertex (center) and insertion of a vertex between two other vertices (right). The substitution step (left) is not necessary and can be omitted when just determining the minimum sequence of elementary edit operations to transform T_1 into T_2.

Using these basic edit operations, we define the distance of two labeled trees, T_1 and T_2. Let a sequence $S = (Si)1{\le}i{\le}n$ of those atomic edit-operations transform tree T_1 into T_2. By assigning a weight $\gamma(Si) > 0$ to each basic edit operation Si, the weight $\gamma(S)$ of each of these sequences S is just defined as the sum of its elements $\gamma(S) = \sum_{i=1}^{n} \gamma(s_i)$. We can now define the *tree edit distance* of the two labeled trees T_1 and T_2.

▶ **Definition 2 (*tree edit distance*).**   The tree edit distance of two labeled trees T_1 and T_2 is given by

$$(4)\ d(T_1, T_2) := \min \{\ \gamma(S) = \sum_{i=1}^{n} \gamma(s_i)\ ;\ S = (si)_{1{\le}i{\le}n} \colon T_1\ T_2\ ,\ si\ \}.$$

It can be shown easily, that this distance is indeed a metric distance that means it satisfies non negativity, identity of indiscernibles, symmetry and the triangle inequality, if the weight γ of the edit-operations is a metric distance on the space of the labeled vertices joined with $\{\lambda\}$.

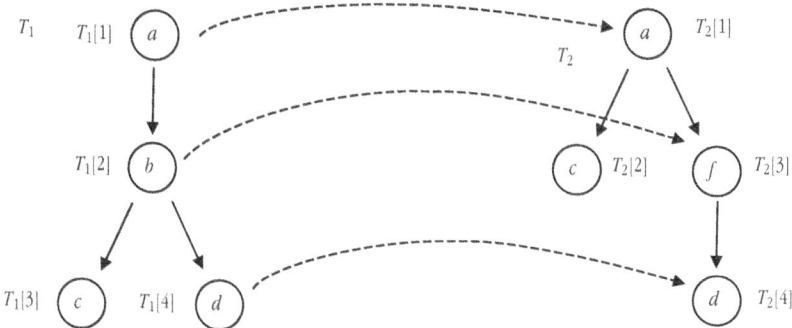

Fig. 4   Example of a matching M between trees T_1 and T_2
Formally, a matching M is a set of pairs of vertex indices: M = {(1, 1), (2, 3), (4, 4)}. *The set* M ∪ {(3, 2)} *is not a matching, because* $T_1[2]$ *is predecessor of* $T_1[3]$ *which is not true for the image vertices* $T_2[3]$ *and* $T_2[2]$. M *corresponds to the edit sequence* (del(c), sub(b, f), ins(c; a, λ)). *Using the discrete metric as local weight function* γ, *the weight of this matching is 3.*

Computing the tree edit distance between two arbitrary unordered trees is NP complete, meaning the tree edit distance is not realistically usable for practical computations. Due to the finiteness of trees, it is always possible to find a sequence $S = (si)_{1 \leq i \leq n}$ of basic edit operations si, which transfer a tree T_1 into another tree T_2. This means, that $0 \leq d(T_1, T_2) < \infty$. The NP completeness, however, makes it crucial to find a distance, which inherits the nice properties of the tree-edit-distance, but is of moderate complexity. Such a distance will be given in the next paragraph.

4   The constrained tree edit distance

To reduce the complexity and to get a computable distance, we introduce the concept of *matching* between unordered trees. We call a structure preserving bijective mapping between a part of the nodes of the trees a *matching*. A matching between trees, preserves the partial order imposed by the predecessor-successor-relationship of the vertices. This is important to keep complexity at bay. Given a matching M between trees T_1 and T_2, we only need to do structural changes on the rest of the tree, outside the matching. Within the matching part, we need at most to substitute vertices.

Every sequence $S = (si)_{1 \leq i \leq n}$ induces a matching. The weight of a matching γ(M) is defined by the weight γ(S) of its associated sequence S of edit operations: γ(M)

= $\gamma(S)$. Therefore, the distance between two trees can either be defined as the minimum weight of a feasible sequence or, equivalently, as the minimum weight of a matching between the vertices. Matching vertices are weighed as substitutions, all others are weighed as insertion or deletion operations. In the case of strings, the problem of finding the minimum weight of a feasible sequence is equivalent to a shortest path problem on a special graph, called edit graph, and can, therefore, be solved by dynamic programming.

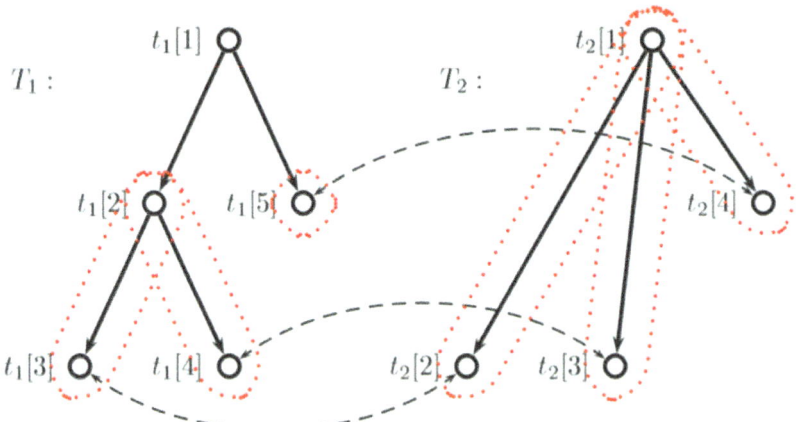

Fig. 5   Example for a matching M between trees T_1 and T_2
M *is not a constrained matching, since different subtrees of T_1 are mapped on the same subtree of T_2.*

To obtain a computable distance function for unordered trees, Zhang (1996) introduced so-called constrained matching. The idea behind this constraint is, that matching sub-trees should be mapped on each other. To that end, we introduce the *least common ancestor*, $lca(v_1, v_2)$, of two vertices v_1 and v_2. Considering the two paths from the vertices v_1 and v_2 to the root vertex of the tree the $lca(v_1, v_2)$ is the first vertex that is included in both paths. In Figure 3, for example, $lca(T_2[2], T_2[4])$ is the root vertex $T_2[1]$. Using the *least common ancestor* we can now introduce the constrained mapping. First, we define constrained matching formally.

▶ **Definition 3 (*Constrained matching*).**   Given two labeled unordered trees T_1 and T_2 with vertices $V_1 = \{T_1[1],...,T_1[n_1]\}$ and $V_2 = \{T_2[1],..., T_2[n_2]\}$, a constrained matching M is a set of ordered pairs of vertex indices:

(5) $M \subset \{1,...n_1\} \times \{1,...n_2\}$ such that, for (i_1, i_2), (j_1, j_2) and $(k_1, k_2) \in M$:

- $i_1 = j_1 \Leftrightarrow i_2 = j_2$;
- $T_1[i_1]$ is predecessor of $T_1[j_1] \Leftrightarrow T_2[i_2]$ is predecessor of $T_2[j_2]$;
- $lca(T_1[i_1], T_1[j_1])$ is predecessor of $T_1[k_1] \Leftrightarrow lca(T_2[i_2], T_2[j_2])$ is predecessor of $T_2[k_2]$.

These conditions just imply structure preservation. The weight $\gamma(M)$ of such a constrained matching M is given by

$$(6)\; \gamma(\mathfrak{M}) = \sum_{(i,j) \in \mathfrak{M}} \gamma(sub(T_1[i], T_2[j])) + \sum_{(i,.) \notin \mathfrak{M}} \gamma(del(T_1[i])) + \sum_{(.,j) \notin \mathfrak{M}} \gamma(ins(T_2[j]))$$

Now, we formulate the main statement on the constrained tree edit distance.

▶ Theorem 4 (*Constrained tree edit distance*).

Given two labeled unordered trees T_1 and T_2, the *constrained tree edit distance*
(7) $dc(T_1, T_2) = \min_{\{M:\, M \text{ constrained matching}\}} \gamma(M)$
        is a *metric* on the set of all labeled unordered trees.
The proof is given by Zhang (1996).

▶ Definition 5 (*Forest*).

Let T_1 be a tree with vertices $T_1[i]$. We call the set of all trees rooted in the children of $T_1[i]$ a *forest* $F_1[i]$.

According to Heumann and Wittum (2009), the distance between two forests F_1 and F_2 is then given by

$$(8)\;\; D(F_1[i], F_2[j]) = \min \begin{cases} D(\emptyset, F_2[j]) + \min_{1 \le t \le n_j}(D(F_1[i], F_2[j_t]) - D(\emptyset, F_2[j_t])), \\ D(F_1[i], \emptyset) + \min_{1 \le s \le n_i}(D(F_1[i_s], F_2[j]) - D(F_1[i_s], \emptyset)), \\ \min_{\mathfrak{M}_{lim}(i,j)} \Gamma(\mathfrak{M}_{lim}) MinCostMaxMatching. \end{cases}$$

To determine the minimal cost of a constrained matching between forests, we need to know the cost of matchings of substructures. The matching then either assigns subtrees of the first forest to subtrees of the second (*MinCostMaxMatching* in (8), line 3), or it assigns one forest, say $F_1[i]$, to a subforest $F_2[jt]$ of the second one. The cost is then the sum of the matching cost $D(F_1[i], F_2[jt])$ and the cost of deleting $F_2[j]$ except for its subforest $F_2[jt]$. These cases are covered by the first and second line in equation (8), where $\emptyset$ is placeholder for the empty forest. Knowing $D(F_1[i],$

$F_2[j]$) we can determine the distance between the trees T_1, i and T_2, j rooted at $T_1[i]$ and $T_2[j]$:

$$(9) \quad D(T_{1,i}, T_{2,j}) = min \begin{cases} D(\emptyset, T_{2,j}) + min_{1 \leq t \leq n_j}(T_{1,i}, T_{2,j_t}) - D(\emptyset, T_{2,j_t})), \\ D(T_{1,i}, \emptyset) + min_{1 \leq s \leq n_i}(D(T_{1,i_s}, T_{2,j}) - D(T_{1,i_s}, \emptyset)), \\ D(F_1[i], F_2[j]) + \gamma(i, j). \end{cases}$$

Here, a constrained matching is either a matching between the forests and the assignment of the roots (3rd line in equation (9)), or the assignment of one tree to a subtree of the second one (1st and 2nd lines in equation (9)). Hence, the distance between trees T_1, i and T_2, j is the minimal cost of all these cases. Still, complexity is a major issue. The following theorem states the complexity estimate for computing the constrained edit distance on unordered labeled trees.

▶ **Theorem 6 (Complexity).**

Let the number of direct children in the trees in question be bounded, then the complexity of the algorithm to compute the constrained tree edit distance is $O(|T_1||T_2|)$, where $|Tk|$ denotes the number of vertices in Tk.

That means, we end up with quadratic complexity. We refer to Zhang (1996) for further details on the complexity and the algorithm.

5   Application examples –
Comparing sentences in different natural languages

We constructed two groups of examples, comparing sentences in natural languages. First, we constructed a set of simple sentences to examine the capabilities of the natural language processing tools. Secondly, we selected sentences from a domain-specific knowledge test for students in economics. The following analyses are based on the English and German adapted and validated versions of the Test of Understanding in College Economics (TUCE IV, for US-original version see Walstad et al. 2007; for the German version see Zlatkin-Troitschanskaia et al. 2014), comprising 60 multiple choice items with and without numerical data. We complemented it with a simple exercise from Euler (1770), in order to include examples from different authors and different times. The following examples in German and English are used to show the feasibility of the intended approach.

5.1 Test set 1

To begin with, we choose a set of four simple sentences in German and translate them into English.

—*English*---
Sentence 0: Steven likes books.
Sentence 1: Steven likes long books.
Sentence 2: Steven likes long books and he also eats carrots.
Sentence 3: Steven likes long books and he also eats carrots, but he does not watch movies.

---*German*---
Sentence 4: Steven mag Bücher.
Sentence 5: Steven mag lange Bücher.
Sentence 6: Steven mag lange Bücher und er isst auch Karotten.
Sentence 7: Steven mag lange Bücher und er isst auch Karotten, aber er guckt keine Filme.

We used SpaCy to construct trees corresponding to these sentences. Two examples are shown in Figure 6. We then computed the constraint tree edit distance using the algorithm described in Section 4. The result is shown in Figure 7.

Comparing the simple sentences 0, 1 and 4, 5 the results are as expected. The word order is the same in both languages, so the distance is very low. The image changes strongly when comparing sentences 3 and 7. They are also translated verbally which leads to the expectation of a low distance. It is in fact one of the largest as can be seen in Figure 7. The reason can be found in Figure 6, where the trees of the two sentences are illustrated. Comparing the sentences shows that the German language processor deals with conjunctions in a different way to the English processor. This quite likely results from the data that has been used for training the language processors.

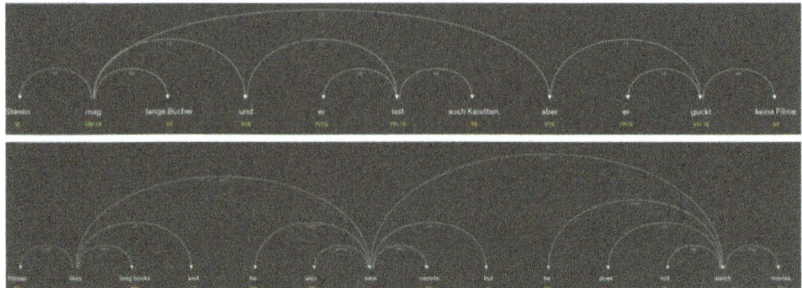

Fig. 6   The structural trees for sentences 3 and 7, both constructed by SpaCy

Fig. 7   The constrained tree edit distance for sentences 0 to 7
Interestingly, sentence 3 and 7 have a large distance, in spite of the fact that they are verbally translated.

5.2 Test set 2

To get a bit closer to mathematics, we selected questions from the English and German versions of the TUCE IV (Walstad et al. 2007; Zlatkin-Troitschanskaia et al. 2014) as a second test set and added an exercise by Euler (1770).

German

$S0$: In einem Land, in dem nur zwei Güter produziert und verbraucht werden, haben Produktion und Verbrauch von Gut X externe Nutzen zur Folge und Produktion und Verbrauch von Gut Y externe Kosten. Mit Blick auf die effiziente Produktionsmenge: Würde in einem unregulierten Markt zu viel oder zu wenig von Gut X bzw. Gut Y produziert werden?

$S1$: Die nachfolgende Tabelle gibt an, wie viele Tonnen Weizen und Roggen in einem Jahr in Land X und Land Y unter Verwendung derselben Menge an Produktionsfaktoren hergestellt werden können. Wie sollten die Unternehmen des Landes X gemäß der Theorie des komparativen Kostenvorteils vorgehen?

$S2$: Harter Frost hat die Hälfte der heimischen Apfelernte zerstört. Die Verbraucher reagieren auf den steigenden Apfelpreis mit dem vermehrten Kauf von Orangen, so dass für diese mit einem Anstieg der nachgefragten Menge und des Preises zu rechnen ist. Im Grundmodell von Angebot und Nachfrage bedeutet dies eine: …

$S3$: In einer Volkswirtschaft, in der hauptsächlich mit Heizöl geheizt wird, werden neue Vorkommen an Erdgas entdeckt, das Heizöl ersetzen und Wärme zu viel geringeren Kosten erzeugen kann. Wie wirkt sich dies wahrscheinlich auf den Marktpreis und die Produktionsmenge von Heizöl aus?

$S4$: In Neustadt-Sonnenbach agiert ein örtliches Eiscremeunternehmen in einem Arbeits- und Produktmarkt mit hohem Wettbewerb. Es kann Arbeitnehmer für 45 Euro am Tag einstellen und Eiswaffeln zu 1,00 Euro pro Stück verkaufen. Die nachfolgende Tabelle zeigt das Verhältnis zwischen der Arbeitnehmeranzahl und der Anzahl verkaufter Eiswaffeln. Wie viele Arbeitnehmer wird das Unternehmen während der gesamten Zeit, in der es tätig ist, anstellen, um den Gewinn zu maximieren bzw. den Verlust zu minimieren?

$S5$: Die beiden einzigen Cola-Hersteller eines Landes (A-Cola und B-Cola) entscheiden über Preiserhöhungen und -senkungen für ihre Colas. Die nachfolgende Tabelle zeigt die Preisstrategien der Unternehmen und den zu erwartenden Gewinn bzw. Verlust beider Unternehmen in Millionen Euro. Wenn beide Unternehmen davon ausgehen, dass die Mehrzahl der Verbraucher bald keine Cola mehr trinken, sondern auf andere Produkte umsteigen wird, was ist die logische Folge?

*S*6: Ein kleines Land, das in den vergangenen Jahrzehnten eine hohe Inflation zu verzeichnen hatte, beschließt, den Wert seiner Währung dem der Währung eines großen Landes anzugleichen, das in den vergangenen 50 Jahren nur eine äußerst geringe Inflationsrate zu verzeichnen hatte. Das kleine Land profitiert von diesem Schritt, weil …

*S*7: Ein Maultier und ein Esel beförderten Lasten von einigen hundert Pfund. Der Esel beklagte sich über die seine und sagte zu dem Maultier: Ich brauche nur hundert Pfund von deiner Last, um meine doppelt so schwer zu machen wie deine. Darauf antwortete das Maultier: Aber, wenn du mir hundert Pfund von deiner Last abgibst, trage ich dreimal so viel wie du. Wie schwer waren sie beladen?

English

*S*8: In a country where only two goods are produced and consumed, the production and consumption of Good X results in external benefits, while the production and consumption of Good Y results in external costs. Would unregulated markets produce too much or too little of Good X and Good Y, compared to the efficient output levels for these products?

*S*9: The table below shows the tons of rice and corn that can be produced in Country X and Country Y in one year, using the same amount of productive resources. According to the theory of comparative advantage, what should firms in Country X do?

*S*10: A recent hurricane destroyed half of the orange crop. Consumers are responding to an increase in the price of oranges by buying more apples. This change is expected to increase the price and quantity of apples sold. In terms of basic supply and demand analysis, there has been a: …

*S*11: In an economy where heating oil is the primary source of heat for most households, new supplies of natural gas, a substitute for heating oil, are discovered. Natural gas provides heat at a much lower cost. What is the most likely effect of these discoveries on the market price and quantity of heating oil produced?

*S*12: In Sunshine City, one local ice cream company operates in a competitive labor market and product market. It can hire workers for $45 a day and sell ice cream cones for $1.00 each. The table below shows the relationship between the number of workers hired and the number of ice cream cones produced and sold. As long as the company stays in business, how many workers will it hire to maximize profits or minimize losses?

*S*13: Suppose the only two cola companies (Acola and Bcola) in a nation are deciding whether to charge high or low prices for their colas. The companies' price strategies are shown in the table below. The four pairs of payoff values show what each company expects to earn or lose in millions of dollars, depending on what the other company does. If both companies believe that most consumers are soon going to quit drinking colas, and switch to other products, what is the equilibrium outcome?

*S*14: A small country that has experienced high inflation for the past decade decides to set the value of its currency equal to the value of a currency in a large nation that has had very low inflation for the past 50 years. The small country benefits because this action: ...

*S*15: A mule and an ass were carrying burdens amounting to several hundred weight. The ass complained of this, and said to the mule, I need only one hundred weight of your load, to make mine twice as heavy as yours; to which the mule answered, But if you give me a hundred weight of yours, I shall be loaded three times as much as you will be. How many hundred weight did each carry?

The resulting distance matrix is visualised in Figure. 8. This indicates that translated sentences may have a large distance from each other. This holds true for the pairs (*S*0, *S*8) and (*S*6, *S*14) in particular. These examples consist of larger sentences with a complex structure, which differs stronger in the two languages. On the other hand, for the pairs (*S*1, *S*9), (*S*2, *S*10) and Euler's exercise (*S*7, *S*15) the algorithm shows a relatively reasonable performance. These examples consist of shorter and simply structured sentences. With them, our current tools work better. In total, these examples demonstrate that using state of the art natural language processing tools for comparisons between natural languages is not yet sufficient for revealing the actual structure of more complicated texts in a comparable way. There, more algorithmic work has to be done and new tools have to be created to obtain a reliable basis for our planned comparison. One possible way to improve natural language processing could be using λ-calculus to analyse the derived trees.

Fig. 8   The constrained tree edit distance for S0 to S15
Translated sentences seem to have a large distance from each other. Short and simply structured sentences give the expected result, problems mainly occur with complicated sentences.

6   Further challenges and perspectives

Another level of difficulty in comparing languages is added by the so-called "hidden complexity". Hidden complexity means that words describing facts, which can also be taken from the context, are omitted (see Bisang 2015) without changing the meaning. To illustrate this, we quote an example from Bisang (2015).

Question: *Did you buy some apples?*
Answer (English): *I bought some.*
Chinese (English): *Bought.*

The Chinese answer is stripped of everything, which is not really necessary, but is still specific for the context. The meaning of both answers is identical. The Chinese answer reduces the tree

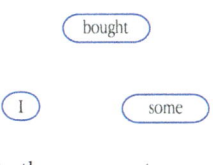

to the mere root

This level of complexity is still far from what natural language processors can handle.

As pointed out above, the conceptual approach presented here is feasible for comparing natural and mathematical language. State of the art natural language processing software, however, has several serious shortcomings when being applied in this context. Our analyses demonstrate that straightforward application of these tools to compare natural languages is not possible. To overcome this technical difficulty, we will develop improved tools.

The presented considerations and methods will form the foundation of an interdisciplinary cooperation between educational sciences, linguistics and mathematical modeling and simulation to achieve a quantitative understanding of the question concerning the relation between natural language and mathematics and its relevance to learning.

Bibliography

Bisang, W. (2015). Hidden Complexity - The Neglected Side of Complexity and its Implications. *Linguistics Vanguard, 1*(1), 177–187.

Brückner, S., Förster, M., Zlatkin-Troitschanskaia, O., & Walstad, W. B. (2015). Effects of prior economic education, native language, and gender on economic knowledge of first-year students in higher education. A comparative study between Germany and the USA. *Studies in Higher Education, 40*(3), 437–453. doi:10.1080/03075079.2015.1004235

Cauchy, A.-L. (1821). *Cours d'Analyse de l'Ecole royale polytechnique*. I.re Partie, L'Imprimerie Royale, Debure frères, Libraires du Roi et de la Bibliothèque du Roi.

CoreNLP (2017). Stanford CoreNLP oreNLP CoreNLP -07. du Ro. Retrieved from https://stanfordnlp.github.io/CoreNLP/. Accessed: June 10 2017.

Euler, L. (1748). Introductio in analysin infinitorum. *Opera Omnia*, Serie 1, Vol 8.

126 Gabriel Wittum et al.

Euler, L. (1770). *Vollständige Anleitung zur Algebra*, Bd. 1. Kaiserliche Akademie der Wissenschaften, St. Petersburg, 1770.

Hamming, R. W. (1950). Error detecting and error correcting codes. *Bell Systems Technical Journal, 26,* 147–160.

Heumann, H., & Wittum G. (2009). The tree-edit-distance, a measure for quantifying neuronal morphology. *Neuroinformatics 7*(3), 179–190.

Kilpeläinen, P., & Mannila, H. (1991). The tree inclusion problem. In Proc. Internat. Joint Conf. on the Theory and Practice of Software Development, Volume 1, (pp. 202–214).

Lagrange, J. L. (1797). *Théorie Des Fonctions Analytiques, Contenant Les Principes Du Calcul Différentiel, Dégagés De Toute Considération D'Infiniment Petits ou d'Évanouissans, De limites Ou de Fluxions, Et Réduits A L'Analyse Algébrique Des Quantités Finies*. Paris: Imprimerie de la République, Prairial an V.

Leibniz, G. W. (1684). Nova methodus pro maximis et minimis, itemque tangentibus, quae nec fractas nec irrationales quantitates moratur, et singulare pro illis calculi genus. *Acta Eruditorum Lipsiae, 1684.*

Levenshtein, V. I. (1966). Binary codes capable of correcting insertions and reversals. *Soviet Physics Doklady, 10*(8), 707–710.

NLTK (2017). Natural Language Toolkit. Retrieved from http://www.nltk.org/. Accessed: June 10 2017.

Selkow, S. (1977). The tree-to-tree editing problem. *Information Processing Letters, (6)*6, 184–186.

SpaCy (2017). https://spacy.io/. Accessed: June 10 2017.

Tai, K. (1979). The tree-to-tree correction problem. *Journal of the Association for Computing Machinery, 26*(3), 422–433.

Wagner, R., & Fischer, M. (1974). The string-to-string correction problem. *Journal of the Association for Computing Machinery, 12*(1), 168–173.

Walstad, W. B., Watts, M., & Rebeck, K. (2007). *Test of understanding in college economics: Examiner's manual* (4th ed.). New York, NY: National Council on Economic Education.

Weierstraß, K. (1878). Einleitung in die Theorien der Analytischen Funktionen. Vorlesung, gehalten in Berlin 1878. Mitschr. von Adolf Hurwitz.

Wittum, G. (1982). Diplomarbeit, Mathematik, Universität Karlsruhe.

Zhang, K., Statman, R., & Shasha, D. (1992). On the editing distance between unordered labeled trees. *Information Processing Letters, 42,* 133–139.

Zhang, K. (1996). A constrained edit distance between unordered labeled trees. *Algorithmica, 15,* 205–222.

Zlatkin-Troitschanskaia, O., Brückner, S., Schmidt, S., & Förster, M. (2016). Messung ökonomischen Fachwissens bei Studierenden in Deutschland und den USA – Eine mehrebenenanalytische Betrachtung der hochschulinstitutionellen und individuellen Einflussfaktoren. *Unterrichtswissenschaft, 44*(1), 73–88. doi: 10.3262/UW1601073

Zlatkin-Troitschanskaia, O., Förster, M., Brückner, S., & Happ, R. (2014). Insights from a German assessment of business and economics competence. In H. Coates (Ed.), *Higher Education Learning Outcomes Assessment: International Perspectives* (pp. 175–197). Frankfurt am Main: Lang. http://dx.doi.org/10.3726/978-3-653-04632-8

Knowledge Representation
and Cognitive Skills in Problem Solving

A View from Linguistic Typology

Walter Bisang

Abstract

This paper offers a programmatic view on the study of cross-linguistic variation and its effects on human cognitive skills. Based on Linguistic Typology and its methodology to account for cross-linguistic differences (section 2), it will show how the presence or absence of certain grammatical categories enhances or inhibits specific skills in the domain of quantification (section 3). In its main part (section 4), it will show how to describe structural differences between the source and the target language in translation and how to find out if these differences affect the performance of students in knowledge assessment tests. For that purpose, it will compare the English and the Japanese versions of the *US Test of Understanding in College Economics (TUCE)*. The paper will end in a short discussion on interdisciplinary cooperation for detecting the linguistic signal in data that are influenced by a multitude of different factors (section 5).

Keywords

Clause Combining; Cognition; Evidentials; Grammatical Categories; Language and Thought; Linguistic Typology; Number Words; Quantification; Thinking for Speaking; Translation; Knowledge; TUCE.

1   Introduction

It is a truism that languages are structurally different. What is much less trivial and is the field of extensive and partly controversial theoretical reasoning in linguistics is the question of how to model that difference. The present paper will look at cross-linguistic variation from the perspective of how it affects knowledge representation and human cognition with a particular focus on cognitive skills needed for problem solving. For that purpose, it will outline a method based on Linguistic Typology for detecting cross-linguistic differences that can be further tested as potential factors that may enhance or inhibit the application of certain cognitive skills to the solution of concrete (domain-specific) problems.

The paper starts with a short introduction to Linguistic Typology, its methods and its findings on regularities in cross-linguistic variation in section 2. Of particular relevance will be the question of grammatical categories and their presence or absence in a language. Section 3 illustrates how linguistic structures affect cognitive skills with examples from number words. How does the length of these words and the complexity of numeral systems affect the performance of our short-term memory? What is the cognitive advantage of actually having number words in a language? After these basic statements on how to find and describe structural differences and on how these differences work, section 4 will illustrate how the cross-linguistic analysis of structural differences can be applied to findings from higher-education knowledge tests. For that purpose, it will analyse the English and the Japanese versions of the *US Test of Understanding in College Economics (TUCE)* (for further information, see Walstad et al. 2007, Asano and Yamaoka 2015, Zlatkin-Troitschanskaia et al. 2016a). This test is of particular interest for the purpose of this paper because it shows language/culture-specific differences in performance (Brückner et al. 2015, Förster et al. 2015, Zlatkin-Troitschanskaia et al. 2016b). It will be shown how differences in clause combining between English and Japanese can be used for highlighting potential factors that may affect the test performance of the students.

Needless to say, it will only be possible to offer a programmatic view on the question of the specific relevance of fundamental cross-linguistic structural differences in knowledge representation. However, what will come out clearly is the fact that the translation of test items into different languages in assessment tests is not a trivial matter if typological differences between the grammars of the languages involved affect the way in which information is structured and in which certain parts of it may be highlighted or specified to different degrees (cf. Mehler et al. in this volume).

After having introduced the method of assessing structural differences across languages by the example of the English and the Japanese versions of TUCE, the conclusion in section 5 will briefly outline how the linguistic insights can be further tested in cooperation with other fields (as a part of the PLATO program, cf. Zlatkin-Troitschanskaia et al. in this volume). This cooperation is absolutely vital for filtering out the linguistic signal from other potential signals having to do with the general cultural background of the students, their life situation and the media that are used in the test situation.

2   Linguistic typology

Linguistic Typology starts out from cross-linguistic structural variation as it is found in the 7.000 languages[1] spoken worldwide and investigates the question of whether and to what extent it follows regular patterns. For that purpose, typologists have developed elaborate sampling methods for making sure that their findings and conclusions are based on statistically balanced sets of languages (Greenberg 1963, Dryer 1992, 1998, Rijkhoff et al. 1993, Rijkhoff and Bakker 1998, Miestamo et al. 2016). More recent studies are also based on Bayesian phylogenetic methods as they are used in evolutionary anthropology (Dunn et al. 2011 and the discussion in *Linguistic Typology* 15.2 (2011)). An important pattern of regularity that has been discovered by Greenberg (1963) are correlations between two (or more) structural properties of the type 'If a language has P, it also has Q' as illustrated by the following example on word order correlations (for a more detailed introduction, cf. Croft 2003):

(1) Universal 2 (Greenberg 1963):
    In languages with prepositions, the genitive almost always follows the governing noun, while in languages with postpositions it almost always precedes.

As one can see from the above statement, there are exceptions. After some initial optimism that there are many exceptionless universals, the domination of statistical universals has become increasingly important in typological research and culminated in the question of whether there are any exceptionless universals at all (Evans and Levinson 2009). As a consequence of this discussion, Linguistic Typology currently rather focuses on the factors that determine cross-linguistic variation (Dryer 1998). This more recent approach is based on an evolutionary

---

1   Cf. www.ethnologue.com, last access July 31, 2017.

model in which the environment consists of a pool of linguistic properties and a number of independent but interacting factors that determine their selection and successful diffusion within speech communities (Bisang 2006, 2016):

- Cognitive factors
- Communicative factors in the interaction between speaker and hearer
- Physiological factors related to the production and perception of linguistic sounds
- Sociohistorical and cultural factors that even may support the selection of cognitively unfavoured factors for sociocultural reasons

With these more recent questions, Linguistic Typology has developed into various directions (cf. Song 2011). One important aspect that is of particular relevance for the type of research suggested in this paper is the detailed analysis of grammatical categories, their properties and their presence or absence in a language. A good example is the category of evidentiality, which addresses the source of information. In a language with evidentials, the speaker has to express the type of source on which her/his expression is based. Depending on the grammar of individual languages, systems of evidentiality mark if the information is from direct evidence (seeing, hearing), from indirect evidenced based on inference or from hearsay (Aikhenvald 2004, p. 1). The use of a marker for this type of information in a language with evidentials is as compulsory as it is necessary to select a certain tense marker (present, past, etc.) in English main clauses. In Tariana, an Amazonian language spoken in Brazil, each clause has to occur with one marker out of a set of markers that express different values of evidentiality. Thus, the information 'José has played football' can be expressed by five different markers (printed in bold in the example below), depending on whether the statement is based on visual evidence (3a), on non-visual evidence (e.g., the speaker has heard it) (3b), on inference from context (e.g., the speaker sees the dirty socks of José) (3c), on an assumption mostly based on habitual activities (3d) or on information that was reported to the hearer (3e):[2]

---

2   The following abbreviations are used in the word-by-word glossing of the examples: 1, 2, 3 = 1st, 2nd, 3rd person, respectively, ACC = Accusative, ADJ = Adjective marker, ADV = Adverb marker, ASSUM = Evidential: Assumed, COND = Conditional converb, CVB = Converb, GEN = Genitive, INFER = Evidential: Inferred, NOM = Nominative, NONVIS = Evidential: Non-visual, PST = Past, REC = Recent, REP = Evidential: Reported, SG = Singular, TOP = Topic, VIS = Evidential: Visual.

(3)   Tariana (Aikhenvald 2004, pp. 2–3):
    a.   Visual evidence:
        Juse   *irida*   *di-manika-**ka***.
        José   football   3.SG-play-REC.PST.VIS
        'José has played football (we saw it).'

    b.   Non-visual: e.g., hearing:
        Juse   *irida*   *di-manika-**mahka***.
        José   football   3.SG-play-REC.PST.NONVIS
        'José has played football (we heard it).'

    c.   Inference from context:
        Juse   *irida*   *di-manika-**nihka***.
        José   football   3.SG-play-REC.PST.INFER
        'José has played football (we infer it from visual evidence).'

    d.   Asumed evidentiality:
        Juse   *irida*   *di-manika-**sika***.
        José   football   3.SG-play-REC.PST.ASSUM
        'José has played football (we assume this on the basis of what we already know).'

    e.   Reported evidentiality (hearsay):
        Juse   *irida*   *di-manika-**pidaka***.
        José   football   3.SG-play-REC.PST.REP
        'José has played football (we were told.)'

Since the grammar of Tariana constantly requires to address the source of information, this must have its effects on the perspective from which speakers look at their environment when they communicate (also cf. next section).

The data on evidentials in Tariana falls into the broader framework of this author's work on complexity from a cross-linguistic perspective. Starting out from the question of what grammatical categories are expressed in a language, one can then investigate the extent to which grammars force their speakers to explicitly mark that grammatical information or to leave it to the pragmatic inference of the reader/hearer. The combination of the grammatical categories present in a language and the extent to which they must be expressed generates two types of complexity, one that is visible in the surface realization of linguistic information (overt complexity) and one that is invisible and needs to be pragmatically inferred from context (hidden complexity) (Bisang 2009, 2014a, 2014b, 2015). Since evidentials are obligatory in Tariana, they contribute to the overt complexity of that language.

3   Language and the enhancement/inhibition of cognitive skills

The idea that language determines our worldview and our ways of thinking as it is commonly associated with the Sapir-Whorf hypothesis is rightly viewed with great scepticism in current linguistics[3]. Thus, statements like the following from Whorf (1956) have only very few adherents nowadays:

> "We are thus introduced to a new principle of relativity, which holds that all observers are not led by the same physical evidence to the same picture of the universe, unless their linguistic backgrounds are similar, or can in some way be calibrated". (Whorf 1956, p. 214).

The critical stance against a rigid determinism between language and thought does not exclude weaker hypotheses of linguistic relativity. One of them is Slobin's (1987, 1991, 2003) thinking for speaking hypothesis, which states that thinking takes a specific form when speakers are incorporating thoughts into the categories that are grammatically relevant in a given language. Slobin (1987) explains his hypothesis as follows:

> "A particular utterance is never a direct reflection of "objective" or perceived reality or of an inevitable and universal mental representation of a situation. This is evident within any given language, because the same situation can be described in different ways; and it is evident across languages, because each language provides a limited set of options for the grammatical encoding of characteristics of objects and events. "Thinking for speaking" involves picking those characteristics that (a) fit some conceptualization of the event, and (b) are readily encodable in the language". (Slobin 1987, p. 435).

The grammatical category of evidentiality as described in the previous section is a good example of how the presence of a category in a language is focusing the

---

3   For a particularly clear statement against the Sapir-Whorf hypothesis cf. Pinker (1994, pp. 57–65).

speaker's perspective on an event in the course of transforming it into linguistic structure (cf. Slobin and Aksu 1982, Slobin 2016).

The view presented in this paper takes up the idea that the categories that are relevant for the grammar of a language may have a certain impact on the cognition of its speakers but it looks at this impact rather from the more practical perspective of the solution of certain cognitive tasks than from the perspective of thought. Thus, it argues that certain properties of a language may enhance or inhibit certain cognitive skills. To start with, it will provide evidence for the enhancement of problem solving from two case studies on numerals (count words).

The first case is a test conducted by Dehaene (1997, pp. 102–103) in which the informants had to memorize sequences of digit numbers like 3 6 2 8 5 9 4. As it turned out, the performance of his participants depended on their mother tongue. While speakers of Chinese had no problems memorizing sequences of seven-digit numbers like the one above, only about 50% of the speakers of English performed equally well. The reason for this lies in the length of the numeral words and the limitations of the short-term memory. The shorter the number words are the more of them fit into the time slot determined by the short-term memory. As can be seen from the simple juxtaposition of the numerals in the above sequence in Chinese, English and Finnish, Finnish needs more space than English and English needs more space than Chinese:[4]

(4)   Chinese: *san, liu, er, ba, wu, jiu, si*
        English: *three, six, two, eight, five, six, four*
        Finnish: *kolme, kuusi, kaksi, kahdeksan, viisi, kuusi, neljä*

This example shows that the linguistic complexity with which numerals are expressed in a language has its impact on how many of them participants are able to memorize in their short-time memory (Dehaene 1997). What is even more remarkable is that the complexity of the numeral system also seems to have its impact on basic arithmetic skills. Thus, Welsh participants with their rather complex numeral system need somewhat more time for solving simple mathematical problems of the type 134 + 88 = 222 (Dehaene 1997) than English participants. If these findings are correct a simple linguistic property like the length of number words enhanc-

---

4   The representation of the numerals in (4) cannot be taken at face value because the orthographic systems used here represent individual phonemes differently. Nevertheless, the picture is basically the same if the numerals are represented by the sound symbols of the International Phonetic Association (IPA).

es or inhibits memory performance and the performance in simple mathematical calculations.

The second case is directly concerned with the cognitive foundations of our mathematical skills, in particular with our ability to count and to manipulate exact numbers. Even though most people may take the presence of number words for granted in any language, there are quite a few languages with a very limited inventory of only a few numerals (*one*, *two*, possibly *three* and *many*). Pirahã, a language spoken in the Amazonian area of Brazil, even lacks numerals as they are used for counting individual items completely, i.e., it does not even have an expression for the numeral *one* (Gordon 2004, Everett 2005)[5]. This fact gave rise to a number of questions. How do the Pirahãs quantify? Does this mean that they only represent approximate quantity but not exact quantity? As the experiments by Frank et al. (2008) show, the absence of number words does not necessarily imply the lack of the concept of exact number. To give an idea of how these experiments work, two tasks will be described briefly.

The fourteen participants (seven adult males and seven adult females) had to resolve matching tasks with spools of threads and uninflated rubber balloons, two materials which the informants knew well and which were easy to manipulate. In the first task of a series of five tasks, "the experimenter presented some quantity of spools and then asked the participant to put out the same quantity of balloons in a line" (Frank et al. 2008, p. 821). This task was no problem for the participants. They all performed nearly perfect. In the fifth task, the nuts-in-a-can task, "the experimenter dropped the spools one by one into an opaque cup into which the participant could not see" (Frank et al. 2008, p. 821). The task of the participants consisted in producing the same number of balloons. As it turned out, the participants performed less well in this task. The number of errors increased in magnitude with the cardinality of the set of spools used by the experimenter. The reason for that has to do with the fact that this experiment required the participants to memorize the exact number of items in the opaque cup—a task which became increasingly difficult with the increasing number of spools, since the Pirahãs had no numerals that enabled them to remember and to compare information about exact number through space and time.

---

5   Gordon (2004) and Everett (2005) describe three words that constitute the numerical vocabulary of Pirahã: *hói*, *hoí* and *baagiso*. Gordon (2004) states that these words do not express exact numbers. Thus, *hói* means 'roughly one' in his description. Everett (2005) argues that the language does not have any numerals at all. In his analysis, the three words mean 'small size or amount', 'somewhat larger size or amount' and 'cause to come together/many', respectively. Both authors basically agree that these terms do not simply denote exact numbers.

Based on these findings, Frank et al. (2008) conclude that the Pirahãs are clearly able to distinguish exact numbers but that they lack the tools for memorizing them. From such a perspective, numerals are "[a] cognitive technology for representing, storing, and manipulating the exact cardinality of sets" (Frank et al. 2008, p. 823). If this analysis is correct, the presence of number words in a language significantly enhances our cognitive ability to handle exact quantities but it does not determine our ability to think in terms of exact numbers. Moreover, this analysis also provides evidence against the Sapir-Whorf hypothesis, since the ability of manipulating exact numbers does not depend on the presence of numerals in a language. This fact is further supported by observations of how quickly speakers of languages with small inventories of numerals were able to acquire number words in contact with cultures which had them (cf. Dixon 1980, p. 108 on Warlpiri, an Australian aboriginal language, or Saxe 1981 on the Oksapmin of New Guinea).

4   English vs. Japanese—a first glance at data from the Test of Understanding in College Economics (TUCE)

This section looks at potential effects of language on the performance of students in the TUCE by comparing its English and Japanese versions. It is interested in what way linguistic representation may affect performance in knowledge assessment tests. In its first part, it will briefly point out the importance of the quality of the translation—a fact that seems to be underestimated in many international assessment tests. Its second more extensive part will show how differences in grammar may shape the tasks of the assessment tests in terms of information density and the perspective from which the information is presented.

The translation of a text is never quite the same as its original. This is a simple observation that is excellently illustrated by Eco (2003). In the case of the Japanese version of TUCE, the translator tries to provide the information that is necessary for the students to be able to solve the problem by sometimes adding additional information of cultural relevance that is not given in the English version. This is, for instance, the case in items 12 and 23. A comparative look at the students' test performance in these two items shows that the Japanese students performed much better than the US students and that, in contrast to the US students, the Japanese students' test performance constantly improved in the course of their economic studies (cf. Zlatkin-Troitschanskaia et al. 2016a, b). These are some first empirical hints that the quality of the translation and differences in the information provided in the source and in the target texts may have their effects on how students perform.

The more specific part of this section on the relevance of grammatical differences between the source and the target language needs some initial remarks
on the basic structure of Japanese. While English has the basic word order sub-
ject-verb-object (SVO), Japanese is subject-object-verb (SOV) and the nouns are
marked by case particles that immediately follow the noun:

(5)   Japanese:
        田中さんが新聞を読んでいます。
        Tanaka-san ga   *shinbun-o*   *yonde imasu.*
        Tanaka-Mr-NOM   newspaper-ACC   be reading
        'Mr Tanaka is reading a newspaper.'

As one can also see from (5), Japanese nouns have no articles and most of them do
not express number, i.e. they have no singular/plural distinction. Thus, *shinbun* in
(5) may actually mean 'the / a newspaper' as well as 'the newspapers / newspapers'.

Of particular interest for the purpose of this paper is clause combining and its
use for creating text coherence. There is a rich inventory of markers and constructions for combining two or more clauses into a complex multipredicate sentence in
Japanese. Some constructions are semantically very general, while others provide
very fine-grained information on the semantic relation between two clauses. The
construction with the marker *-te/-de*[6] directly added to the verb is characterized by
its semantic broadness. In (6), the semantic relation between the two states of affairs connected by *-de* could either be sequential (the second state of affairs starts
after the first one is finished (6a)) or simultaneous (the two states of affairs show
temporal overlapping (6b))[7]:

(6)   Japanese:
        茶を飲んで、新聞を読んだ。
        cha-o   *non-de*   *shinbun-o*   *yon-da.*
        tea-ACC   drink-CVB   newspaper-ACC   read-PST
        a. Sequential: 'He drank tea and then read the newspaper.'
        b. Simultaneous: 'He read the newspaper while drinking tea.'

---

6   This construction is called converb-construction (CVB) in linguistic typology. For an
      overview of the languages having that phenomenon, cf. Haspelmath (1995), Bisang
      (1995).

7   Depending on context, the marker *-te/-de* can express the following semantic relations:
      Additive, temporal sequence (sequential), cause, means, contrastive and concessive
      (Hasegawa 1996, pp. 6–7).

In contrast to the multifunctionality of the marker -*te*/-*de*, the marker -*tara* has a much more specific meaning. It marks conditionals in which the state of affairs must be completed (Hinds 1986, p. 67). In hypothetical contexts as in example (7) from TUCE (item 56), -*tara* denotes a hypothetical but entirely possible future event:

(7)   Japanese (TUCE, item 56):
       基準となる市場金利が７％であったら、...
       kijun-to naru   *shijōkinri-ga*   7%   *deat*-**tara**
       basic/key   market interest rate NOM   7%   be-COND
       'If [we assume that] the basic market interest rate will be 7% [and that is a
       possible scenario] …'

A first result of our comparative analysis of the Japanese and the English versions of TUCE shows that the Japanese translations make optimal use of the grammatical inventory that is available in that language for minimizing ambiguity. Since test scenarios normally have serious consequences for the participants, they require maximal precision. This objective is achieved by (i) addressing the test situation more explicitly than in the English version and (ii) by assessing the likelihood or the genericity of that situation more specifically and more explicitly. For both purposes, markers expressing fine-grained semantic relations between two or more states of affairs are preferred to markers with a broad functional range.

This will be illustrated by three Japanese examples from TUCE. The first one is based on the following English text, which starts with a series of three relatively simple independent sentences (the first sentence is put in square brackets because it will not be discussed):

[Suppose commercial banks have no excess reserves.] Then new deposits totaling $1 billion come into the banking system. The required reserve ratio is 20 percent. What is the maximum amount by which banks can increase deposits in the entire banking system? (TUCE, item 53)

The Japanese translation combines the three English sentences into a single sentence and establishes semantically fine-grained relations between each of the clauses that are simply juxtaposed in English:

(8)   Japanese (TUCE, item 53):

¹ その時に、銀行全体で総額１，０００億円の

sono toki-ni	ginkōzentai-de	sōgaku	1,000 oku	en-no
that time-at	banking system-in	whole amount	100 billion	Yen-GEN

² 新たな預金が追加され、支払い準備率が２０％

arata-na	yokin-ga	tsuika-**sare**	shiharaijunbiritsu-ga	20%
new-ADJ	deposit-NOM	being added	required reserve ration-NOM	20%

³ だとすると、銀行全体で増やせる預金の最大額は、

da to suru **to**	ginkōzentai-de	fuyaseru	yokin-no	saidaiga-ku-wa
if it is so	banking system-in	increase	deposit-GEN	maximum amount-TOP

'This time, [[new deposits totaling 100 billion Yen being added to the banking system] and [the required reserve ratio being 20%] [given that this is so]] the maximum amount by which deposits can be increased in the entire banking system is ...'

In line 2, the form *tsuika-sare* 'being added'[8] indicates that the two states of affairs, adding new deposits and the required reserve ratio being 20%, occur simultaneously, and/or are otherwise closely linked. This first state of affairs plus the next clause 'the required reserve ratio being 20%' are combined into a syntactic unit which together is marked by the conditional marker *to* in line 3, which indicates that both states of affairs represent a theoretically possible, generic scenario. Its use indicates that this is an example in a theoretical discussion. This information establishes very clear relations between the individual states of affairs which are left to the reader's inferential skills in the English version.

The second example (TUCE, item 56) is based on the following English task, which includes the structure already presented in (7):

If the price level is expected to increase by three percent next year and a key market interest rate is seven percent, the real rate of interest is: (TUCE, item 56)

The corresponding Japanese translation is as follows:

---

8   In a more detailed analysis, *tsuika* is a noun with the meaning 'addition', *sare* is a passive converb form of the verb *suru* 'make, do'.

(9)   Japanese (TUCE, item 56):

¹ 来年の物価水準が３％上昇すると予想され、

rainen-no	bukkasuijun-ga	3%	jōshō-suru-to	yosō-*sare*,
next year	price level-NOM	3%	whole amount	being predicted: CVB

² 基準となる市場金利が７％であったら、実質金利は、

kijun-to naru	shijōkinri-ga	7%	deat-**tara**,	jisshitsukinri-wa
basic/key	market interest		be-**COND**	real interest rate-TOP
	rate-NOM	7%		

'[[The price level being expected to increase by three percent next year] and [the key market interest rate if it is 7%]], the real interest rate is ...'

As in example (8), the verb form *yosō-**sare*** 'such a prediction being made' in line 1 indicates that this state of affairs and the one that is following it occur simultaneously and/or are otherwise closely linked (on *sare*, cf. fn. 8). In line 2, the predictive conditional verb form *deat-**tara*** 'if it were' in non-past use denotes a hypothetical but entirely possible future event. Its use instead of other conditional markers available in Japanese provides additional information to readers of the Japanese version, compared with the generic conditional conjunction 'if' in the English version.

The third example is based on the following English version of TUCE, item 23:

If both companies believe that most consumers are soon going to quit drinking colas, and switch to other products, what is the equilibrium outcome? (TUCE, item 23)

Its Japanese translation runs as follows:

(10)   Japanese (TUCE, item 23):

¹ 消費者の多くは、何かあれば、今飲んでいる

shōhisha-no	ōku-wa,	nani-ka	are-**ba**,	ima	nonde iru
consumer-GEN	many-TOP	something	be there-COND	now	drinking

² コーラを他の飲み物に簡単に代えるだろう。

kōra-o	hoka-no	nomimono-ni	kantan-ni	kaeru **darō**
Cola-ACC	other-GEN	beverage-to	easy-ADV	could switch

'As for most consumers, if something happens, they could easily switch from the Cola they are drinking now to another product.'

This example starts with the topic (short: TOP) of the whole passage, which is 'many consumers', and goes on with the most neutral form of the conditional marked by *-ba*, 'if something happens'. The rest of the example is the main clause, which is marked as a hypothetical irrealis by the form *darō* of the copula verb. What is remarkable about this translation is that it is constructed from the perspective of the consumers, while the English version takes the perspective of 'both companies'. Moreover, the English version uses the verb *believe*, which is absent from the Japanese text. The idea of uncertainty associated with this verb is taken over by the hypothetical irrealis form of the main verb. This information is enough for the readers of this task, the concept that there is an institution that 'believes' something is irrelevant. What matters for the text is its hypothetical status as it is typical of the situation in an examination.

To summarize, each of the three examples are focused on the test situation and they provide detailed information on the truth status of the events involved (their likelihood and their genericity). Moreover, they use specific verb forms for indicating the exact semantic relation between these states of affairs. Given the precision of these tasks, one may wonder to what extent this supports the test performance of the students. The following Tab. 1 presents a summary:

Tab. 1   Test performance of Japanese and US students in TUCE

Example (TUCE task)	Test performance
Example (8) (TUCE, 53)	Performance: Japanese and US students were similar.
Example (9) (TUCE, 56)	Performance: Japanese better.
Example (10) (TUCE, 23)	Performance: Japanese better.

Investigating the statistical significance of the assumed correlations would go beyond the scope und focus of this paper. However, what has become evident from the above discussion is that the English and the Japanese versions are clearly not the same. This was shown by the use of general typological methods of comparing languages. At a next stage, but this needs a lot more research, it will be necessary to apply this method to a larger text corpus for assessing effects of cross-linguistic typological differences (see also Mehler et al. in this volume).

5   Conclusion and short prospect about future work

This paper has tried to show how Linguistic Typology and its cross-linguistic perspective can identify grammatical domains by which languages differ (section 2) and how these domains may then be used for checking how the presence or absence of categories from that domain enhance or inhibit specific cognitive skills needed for knowledge acquisition and the solution of domain-specific problems (section 3). In applying this method to TUCE, it became clear that there are considerable differences between the English and Japanese versions (section 4). As it turned out, the Japanese version is focused consistently on the students in a test situation and their need of explicitness for being able to solve the test tasks. This shows that there are actually two aspects which are concerned with Linguistic Typology. The first one is directly concerned with the grammar of a language and its structural options, the second one has to do with conventions associated with certain text types (e.g., test tasks) and the grammatically available tools that are used in such a context. In the case of the Japanese version, the translation makes optimal use of the fine-grained distinctions available for expressing semantic relations between clauses and for marking the truth status of a clause.

In addition to these linguistic aspects, there is a large number of other, more indirect aspects that may potentially affect the students' test performance, among them interaction styles between learners and teachers, media use in learning, educational background, ethical and moral attitudes or the real life situation of students. Disentangling these factors needs interdisciplinary cooperation (cf. Zlatkin-Troitschanskaia et al. in this volume). At a first stage, the inventory of grammatical expression formats that are used in the specific languages included in knowledge assessment tests can be compared to the performance rate of the students. At a next stage, linguists can develop test material for grammatical phenomena that scored positively in the analysis of the knowledge assessment tests. Given the different degree of grammatical information density in the test tasks, one can create test material with different degrees of explicitly available grammatical information as far as it is allowed by the grammatical system of a language. This material can be used for experiments (e.g., eye tracking, EEG) to check for possible effects. In such a combination, it should be possible to detect potential language-based signals. For further corroboration, the test material could be presented in different media or in different learning situations.

Obviously, there will be a long way to go. The programmatic view outlined here is just the basis for further exchange with a multitude of disciplines on how to improve human knowledge from the perspective of Linguistic Typology (cf., e.g., Wittum et al. in this volume).

Bibliography

Aikhenvald, A. Y. (2004). *Evidentiality*. Oxford: Oxford University Press.

Asano, T., & Yamaoka, M. (2015). How to reason with economic concepts: Cognitive process of Japanese undergraduate students solving test items. *Studies in Higher Education, 40*(3), 412–436. doi: http://dx.doi.org/10.1080/03075079.2015.1004240.

Bisang, W. (1995). Verb serialization and converbs - differences and similarities. In M. Haspelmath & E. König (Eds.), *Converbs in Cross-linguistic Perspective* (pp. 37–188). Berlin: Mouton de Gruyter.

Bisang, W. (2006). Contact-induced convergence: Typology and reality. In K. Brown (Ed.), *Encyclopedia of Language and Linguistics, Vol. 3* (pp. 88–101). Oxford: Elsevier.

Bisang, W. (2009). On the evolution of complexity—sometimes less is more in East and mainland Southeast Asia. In G. Sampson, D. Gil & P. Trudgill (Eds.), *Language Complexity as an Evolving Variable* (pp. 34–49). Oxford: Oxford University Press.

Bisang, W. (2014a). Overt and hidden complexity—two types of complexity and their implications. *Poznan Studies in Contemporary Linguistics, 50*(2), 127–143.

Bisang, W. (2014b). On the strength of morphological paradigms—a historical account of radical pro-drop. In M. Robbeets & W. Bisang (Eds.), *Paradigm Change in Historical Reconstruction: The Transeurasian Languages and Beyond* (pp. 23–60). Amsterdam and Philadelphia: John Benjamins.

Bisang, W. (2015). Hidden complexity—the neglected side of complexity and its consequences. *Linguistics Vanguard, 1*(1), 177–187.

Bisang, W. (2016). Linguistic change in grammar. In K. Allan (Ed.), *The Routledge Handbook of Linguistics* (pp. 366–384). Oxford: Routledge.

Brückner, S., Förster, M., Zlatkin-Troitschanskaia, O., Happ, R., Walstad, W. B., Yamaoka, M., & Asano, T. (2015). Gender Effects in Assessment of Economic Knowledge and Understanding: Differences Among Undergraduate Business and Economics Students in Germany, Japan, and the United States. *Peabody Journal of Education, 90*(4), 503–518. doi: http://dx.doi.org/10.1080/0161956X.2015.1068079.

Croft, W. A. (2003). *Typology and Universals* (2nd edition). Cambridge: Cambridge University Press.

Dehaene, S. (1997). *The Number Sense. How the Mind Creates Mathematics*. Oxford & New York: Oxford University Press.

Dixon, R. M. W. (1980). *The Languages of Australia*. Cambridge: Cambridge University Press.

Dryer, M. S. (1992). The Greenbergian word order correlations. *Language, 13*, 257–292.

Dryer, M. S. (1998). Why statistical universals are better than absolute universals. *Chicago Linguistic Society: The Panels, 33*, 123–145.

Dunn, M., Greenhill, M., Levinson, S. C., & Gray, R. D. (2011). Evolved structure of language shows lineage-specific trends in word-order universals. *Nature, 473*, 79–82. doi:10.1038/nature09923.

Eco, U. (2003). *Dire quasi la stessa cosa. Esperienze di traduzione*. Milano: Bompiani.

Evans, N., & Levinson, S. C. (2009). The myth of language universals: Language diversity and its importance for cognitive science. *Behavioral and Brain Sciences, 32*, 429–448.

Everett, D. L. (2005). Cultural constraints on grammar and cognition in Pirahã. *Current Anthropology, 46*, 621–646.

Förster, M., Zlatkin-Troitschanskaia, O., Brückner, S., Happ, R., Hambelton, R. K., Walstad, W. B., Asano, T. & Yamaoka, M. (2015). Validating Test Score Interpretations by Cross-National Comparison Comparing the Results of Students from Japan and Germany on an American Test of Economic Knowledge in Higher Education. *Zeitschrift für Psychologie, 223*(1), 14–23. doi: 10.1027/2151-2604/a000195.

Frank, M. C., Everett, D. L., Fedorenko, E., & Gibson, E. (2008). Number as a cognitive technology: Evidence from Pirahã language and cognition. *Cognition,* 108, 819–824.

Gordon, P. (2004). Numerical cognition without words: Evidence from Amazonia. *Science,* 306, 496–499.

Greenberg, J. H. (1963). Some universals of grammar with particular reference to the order of meaningful elements. In J. H. Greenberg (Ed.), *Universals of Language* (pp. 73–113). Cambridge, MA.: The MIT Press.

Hasegawa, Y. (1996). *A Study of Japanese Clause Linkage. The Connective* TE *in Japanese.* Stanford: Center for the Study of Language and Information (CSLI) Publications.

Haspelmath, M. (1995). The converb as a cross-linguistically valid category. In M. Haspelmath & E. König (Eds.), *Converbs in Cross-linguistic Perspective* (pp. 1–55). Berlin: Mouton de Gruyter.

Hinds, J. (1986). *Japanese.* London & New York: Routledge.

Miestamo, M., Bakker, D., & Antti, A. (2016). Sampling for variety. *Linguistic Typology,* 20(2), 233–296.

Pinker, S. (1994). *The Language Instinct.* New York: Morrow.

Rijkhoff, J., Bakker, D., Hengeveld, K, & Kahrel, P. (1993). A method of language sampling. *Studies in Language,* 17, 169–203.

Rijkhoff, J., & Bakker, D. (1998). Language sampling. *Linguistic Typology,* 2, 263–314.

Saxe, G. B. (1981). The changing form of numerical reasoning among the Oksapmin. *Indigenous Mathematics Working Paper,* No. 14. UNESCO Education.

Slobin, D. I. (1987). Thinking for speaking. *Proceedings of the 13th Annual Meeting of the Berkeley Linguistics Society,* 435–444.

Slobin, D. I. (1991). Learning to think for speaking: Native language, cognition, and rhetorical style. *Pragmatics,* 1, 7–25.

Slobin, D. I. (2003). Language and thought online: Cognitive consequences of linguistic relativity. In D. Gentner & S. Goldin-Meadow (Eds.), *Language in Mind: Advances in the Study of Language and Thought* (pp. 157–192). Cambridge, MA: The MIT Press.

Slobin, D. I. (2016). Thinking for speaking and the construction of evidentiality in language contact. In M. Güven, D. Akar, B. Öztürk & M. Kelepir (Eds.), *Exploring the Turkish Linguistic Landscape: Essays in Honor of Eser Erguvanli-Taylan* (pp. 105–120). Amsterdam & Philadelphia: John Benjamins.

Slobin, D. I., & Aksu, A. A. (1982). Tense, aspect, and modality in the use of the Turkish evidential. In P. J. Hopper (Ed.), *Tense-Aspect between Semantics & Pragmatics* (pp. 185–200). Amsterdam & Philadelphia: John Benjamins.

Song, J. J. (Ed.) (2011). *The Oxford Handbook of Linguistic Typology.* Oxford: Oxford University Press.

Walstad, W. B., Watts, M., & Rebeck, K. (2007). *Test of Understanding in College Economics: Examiner's Manual* (4th Ed.). New York, NY: National Council on Economic Education.

Whorf, B. L. (1956). Science and linguistics. In J. B. Carroll (Ed.), *Language, Thought and Reality: Selected Writings of Benjamin Lee Whorf* (pp. 206–219). Cambridge, MA: The MIT Press.

Zlatkin-Troitschanskaia, O., Schmidt, S., Brückner, S., Förster, M., Yamaoka, M., & Asano, T. (2016a). Macroeconomic Knowledge of Higher Education Students in Germany and Japan – A Multilevel Analysis of Contextual and Personal Effects. *Assessment & Evaluation in Higher Education, 41*(5), 787–801. doi: http://dx.doi.org/10.1080/02602938.2016.1162279.

Zlatkin-Troitschanskaia, O., Brückner, S. Schmidt, S., & Förster, M. (2016b). Messung ökonomischen Fachwissens bei Studierenden in Deutschland und den USA – Eine mehrebenenanalytische Betrachtung der hochschulinstitutionellen und individuellen Einflussfaktoren. *Unterrichtswissenschaft, 44*(1), 73–88. doi: 10.3262/UW1601073.

Integrating Computational Linguistic Analysis of Multilingual Learning Data and Educational Measurement Approaches to Explore Learning in Higher Education

Alexander Mehler, Olga Zlatkin-Troitschanskaia, Wahed Hemati, Dimitri Molerov, Andy Lücking, and Susanne Schmidt

Abstract

This chapter develops a computational linguistic model for analyzing and comparing multilingual data as well as its application to a large body of standardized assessment data from higher education. The approach employs both an automatic and a manual annotation of the data on several linguistic layers (including parts of speech, text structure and content). Quantitative features of the textual data are explored that are related to both the students' (domain-specific knowledge) test results and their level of academic experience. The respective analysis involves statistics of distance correlation, text categorization with respect to text types (questions and response options) as well as languages (English and German), and network analysis to assess dependencies between features. The correlation between correct test results of students and linguistic features of the verbal presentations of tests indicate to what extent language influences higher education test performance. It has also been found that this influence relates to specialized language. Thus, this integrative modeling approach contributes a test basis for a large-scale analysis of learning data and points to a number of subsequent, more detailed research questions.

Keywords

Computational Modeling; Economic Knowledge Test; Educational Assessment Data; English; German; Linguistic Analysis; Multilingual Data; Network Analysis; Learning; Test Performance; TUCE.

1   Introduction

1.1   Motivation –
Findings from educational assessment research

The potential influence of language and phrasing of task description on students' performance in educational assessments and other psychometric instruments has long been discussed theoretically by test developers in national and international assessment research programs (e.g., Tremblay et al. 2013; Solano-Flores et al. 2006). This issue is particularly important when it comes to test instruments that assess the same construct in different countries with different languages; it must be ensured, for example, that the test does not differ in difficulty. Detailed guidelines for item formulation, translation and adaptation have been drafted and routine review procedures have been implemented, aiming to minimize language interference (e.g., Test Adaptation Guidelines (TAGs) by the International Test Commission (ITC) 2005, 2016). However, empirical examination of the effects of language features on educational assessment is still scarce. Language-focused studies are rare and are spread across various disciplines such as education, psychology, social and political sciences, with a lead in the social sciences in multilanguage, multinational, multicultural survey research (e.g., Mohler et al. 2016) and international reading research (e.g., on the Programme for International Student Assessment (PISA), see, e.g., Arffman 2010), as well as neighboring areas such as research on bilingual learning (e.g., Venkatram et al. 2006). Few recent studies examining item surface features and their effects on item performance have shown varied findings from no effect (e.g., Bühner and Pargent 2017) to significant influence of even small changes in meaning of single language features (e.g., on scale denotations, see Villar 2009). In few assessment fields relying on language, such as reading research, more detailed efforts have been made to define language features of stimuli as a core part of the construct assessed (e.g., Müller-Feldmeth et al. 2015, Snow 2002). This said, most assessments rely on language to tap test-takers abilities; yet while test developers rely on extensive validation procedures to minimize undesired language interference (AERA et al. 2014), fundamental language patterns still have a hitherto unexplored influence on mental operations such as information perception and task processing (e.g., Gentner and Goldin-Meadow 2003; Gleitman and Papafragou 2005).

International comparative studies demonstrate that students from different countries and linguistic and socio-cultural backgrounds perform differently on certain tasks (e.g., tasks containing numerical data), even when personal and institutional influence factors are controlled and the construct has been evidently measured invariantly between the different sub-groups (e.g., Förster et al. 2015; Zlatkin-Troitschanskaia et al. 2016a, c). Initial findings indicate that (native) proficiency in certain languages coincides with higher or lower test scores, for example, on items assessing numerical-mathematical understanding and quantitative reasoning (e.g., MacGregor and Price 1999; Vukovic and Lesaux 2013; Crossley and Kostyuk 2017) or cognitive abilities for knowledge acquisition in specific content domains, such as economics (Brückner et al. 2015b; Shavelson et al. in press). These effects differentiating native from non-native speakers persist over the course of studies in higher education, affecting students' acquisition and development of content knowledge in the domain (e.g., Zlatkin-Troitschanskaia et al. 2016a, c).

There are various explanatory approaches for these language-related differences in performance, which are still underresearched: one common explanation focuses on students' knowledge acquisition history and experiences with applying subject-specific concepts in pre-tertiary education, situated in a specific culture and language (e.g., in primary school and secondary school mathematics in Germany; e.g., Martin 2013; Rüede 2015). Nisbett's research (Nisbett and Masuda 2003; Nisbett et al. 2001) indicates, for example, that great cognitive differences between Westerners and East-Asians exist in terms of holistic and analytic thinking. Hatano (1982) also illustrates how linguistic factors facilitate the development of arithmetic competencies in Japanese children.[1] Accordingly, language-based differences can be assumed both across and within languages, as linguistic structures of different language systems and specific usages within individual languages can facilitate or complicate certain ways of thinking and conceptualization. Our prior research in economics education has indicated that student performance on content knowledge tests varies on the same tasks presented in various languages (e.g., German, English, Japanese) between the languages, but also within languages depending on participants' language proficiency, when many other relevant fac-

---

[1] Some research, however, indicates the differences are less evident; for instance, findings show Asians perform very well on international achievement tests created for the large part in the West (see, e.g., OECD 2013).

tors are controlled (e.g., Wang and Goldschmidt 1999; Brückner et al., 2015a, b; Zlatkin-Troitschanskaia et al. 2016a, c). This is the case both throughout the course of studies and at the end of studies. However, with the research so far and the modelled predictor variables, only small parts of the variance could be explained, which indicates that a more comprehensive, innovative approach is needed in order to explain greater parts of the differences in student performance.

A second popular explanatory approach foregrounds differences in cognitive load (e.g., Paas et al. 2003; Plass et al. 2010; Sweller et al. 2011) arising from higher or lower complexity of language structures in test items and students' familiarity with them. Correspondingly, assumptions that remain to be tested refer to knowledge acquisition in disciplines with an abundance of complex terminology that is new to learners and that differs significantly from previously taught concepts and languages. Current findings exemplify that reading behavior, and consequently learning and studying behavior, depends on factors such as text complexity and the readers' familiarity with certain (domain-specific) terminologies. Müller-Feldmeth et al. (2015), for instance, illustrate the relationship between a text's characteristics and a reader's knowledge level by using popular academic texts for studies on text comprehension. The findings indicate that readers who have prior knowledge of the topic are able to adapt their reading behavior to varying degrees of complexity in a text, while readers without prior knowledge have difficulty in doing so; Snow (2002) illustrates that understanding of subject-matter texts does not only depend on a reader's background schemata but also on their ability to parse the complex syntax and style of presentation of the text. However, the interaction between linguistic structures and empirically measured learning is still underresearched.

Language influences on test performance have been discussed for a long time, but rarely systematically analyzed. The reason might be that there are various challenges in analyzing language properties of domain-specific tasks and tests, such as notorious difficulty to statistically single out effects of individual linguistic factors and language effects. Furthermore, the question whether and to what extent language influences reflect a desirable part of the assessment, needs more differentiated and elaborated research: for instance, proficiency in the specialized language of a domain may be considered a relevant part of a domain-specific construct to be assessed (e.g., content knowledge; CEE 2010; cf. Avenia-Tapper and Llosa 2015). Language influences in assessments that do not claim to measure language skill as part of the construct facet may lead to rather construct-irrelevant noise in assessment data or even undesired differential functioning of items (DIFs) for sub-groups of students (e.g., non-native speaker) (AERA et al. 2014; Brückner et al. 2015a; Förster et al. 2015).

Different languages pose a particular challenge for comparative international assessment studies, for example, as illustrated in the comparison of the Test of Understanding in College Economics (TUCE, Walstad et al. 2007) between the US, Japan, and Germany (e.g., Zlatkin-Troitschanskaia et al. 2014; Förster et al. 2015). The standard approach in cross-national assessment relies on meticulous process quality assurance to produce equivalent translations to minimize language bias (cf. Solano-Flores et al. 2009; Mohler et al. 2016; Dept et al. 2017). Comparability is also determined statistically through measurement invariance analyses, and comprehensive validation analyses are carried out to ensure national suitability (e.g., Zlatkin-Troitschanskaia et al. 2014; Förster et al. 2015).

Despite state-of-the-art test design, adaptation, and validation processes, in particular, following the TAGs (ITC 2016; Hambleton 2005) and according to the Standards of Educational and Psychological Testing (AERA et al. 2004, 2014) which also include cognitive testing to ensure suitability also of the test language for the target population, only up to ca. 25% of variance in student responses could be explained by the controlled factors, such as attendance of economics courses in higher education, interest in economics topics, and attendance of specialized economics vocational schools or economics majors in pre-tertiary education (e.g., Zlatkin-Troitschanskaia et al. 2016c). Although such percentages of explained variance are not uncommon in empirical research in higher education (e.g., Zlatkin-Troitschanskaia et al. 2016b), follow-up studies comparing the performance of German and US students on the test showed undesired effects from different sources, such as gender differences and language differences. Gender effects in economic knowledge are a recurrent finding in empirical educational research and have in parts been explained, for example, by presence of numerical components or different response behavior on the multiple-choice format; for instance, male students have been found to be less averse to guessing on economics tests (Davies et al. 2005; Brückner et al. 2015b). Findings from previous research on the TUCE suggested that different language influences might also affect test scores.

Overall, student performance on the TUCE differed between students in Germany and the US, which still relied on two, albeit presumably parallel language versions (e.g., Zlatkin-Troitschanskaia et al. 2016c). As part of the validation, linguistic differences, particularly differential item functioning of single items, were also examined as potential influences on the equivalence of the test adaptations and the interpretation of results (e.g., Brückner et al. 2015a; Förster et al. 2015). The study juxtaposed the German adaptation with the English original and compared each item qualitatively across both versions.[2] The assessment results showed language effects depending on students' native language in Germany, i.e., test scores of native compared to non-native speakers of German, showed differences as well. On the German test, non-native speakers scored significantly lower, which was unexpected given that the construct is not modelled to rely on language skills (cf. Brückner et al. 2015a).

In addition to internationally established quality assurance guidelines prior to testing and having items reviewed (cf. TAGs, ITC 2016; AERA et al. 2014), rated by multiple (groups of) experts and pretested with a (small) sample of participants, test developers should also qualitatively analyze items that show differential functioning of items (DIFs) between countries (e.g., Förster et al. 2015). For instance, the degree to which an item relies on knowledge of certain terms may differ between languages and may augment the relevance of this specific linguistic feature for comparability. Few approaches exist that quantify qualitative evaluations of a test's language (cf. Solano-Flores et al. 2009). Overall, both international studies and studies within one language could benefit from a more detailed analysis of test language characteristics in order to gain a better understanding of how language in assessments functions as a fundamental vehicle for learning and to what extent it is part of the constructs assessed.

Initial language-related studies on the translation, adaptation, and validation of educational assessment tests (e.g., Zlatkin-Troitschanskaia et al. 2014; Förster et al. 2015) suggest that detailed linguistic analyses may provide important tools for detecting language influence on test performance. For instance, there may be certain grammatical structures that enhance or inhibit mental operations and are correlated to rates of correct solutions.

The problem at the base of the present study is an instantiation of a much more fundamental question raised in education, linguistics, psychology, philosophy, and other disciplines on the exact relation between language and learning. Its relevance for learning and assessment practice in higher education (and other educational sectors) is high in particular in view of migration and internationalization trends, better access and diversification of study paths, which lead to an increasingly heterogeneous student body in terms of students' prior knowledge and language proficiency (e.g., Zlatkin-Troitschanskaia et al. 2017). Current research indicates that linguistic effects might be more important for explaining and fos-

---

2   For a discussion of the translation and adaptation, see Zlatkin-Troitschanskaia et al. (2014). For an illustration of further linguistic and cultural differences that may shape performance as interpreted in the comparison of student performance on the German and Japanese TUCE, see, e.g., Brückner et al. (2015b); Förster et al. (2015).

tering knowledge acquisition than previously assumed (e.g., Brückner et al. 2015a; Zlatkin-Troitschanskaia et al. in press).

1.2 Research focus and framework

This study focuses on an assessment which has shown language effects that could not be explained from an educational research perspective alone (cf., e.g., Brückner et al. 2015a; Zlatkin-Troitschanskaia et al. 2016c), calling for a more in-depth analysis of the language in the test (e.g., Förster et al. 2015). The TUCE IV (Walstad et al. 2007) is one of several internationally established standardized test instruments for the study domain of economics. It was originally developed (by the Council for Economic Education) in English for college students in the United States and has been translated and adapted to diverse national contexts, such as Japan (e.g., Yamaoka et al. 2010) and Germany (Zlatkin-Troitschanskaia et al. 2014).

Diverse explanatory approaches have been offered. German and English differ in how challenging they are for learners, considering the many general differences between the languages, such as syntax, pragmatics, morphology, which might influence the understanding of test items (cf. also Bisang in this volume). For example, if response options are differentiated rather through lexical than grammatical aspects, this would respectively pose a different kind of challenge to learners. Depending on the language, specific terminology and jargon in economics might be more or less close to everyday language, which might again pose a different difficulty to learners. Furthermore, accessing economic information might be easier for non-native speakers if the information is in English rather than German, since more people learn English as a second language from early on in their education and are more likely to have reached the necessary proficiency level or acquired the necessary vocabulary to understand the test by the beginning of their studies. At least findings on the relation between native language and test language indicate such a difference between English and German (Walstad et al. 2007; Parker 2006; Brückner et al. 2015a). However, more detailed research that takes into account both the test-taker's language proficiency and the linguistic characteristics of a test instrument is still pending. As a necessary prerequisite for explaining any language effects in an empirically substantiated way, we carry out an in-depth analysis of linguistic features of the test instrument.

To explore the research question as to what extent students' test performance according to the TUCE scores as measured in our comparative study are related to the specific linguistic features and phrasing of test items, we formulate a number of fundamental assumptions (see Section 2) based on the abovementioned prior educational research and conduct both an exploratory and confirmatory analysis of the effects of different linguistic features in the test items. In Section 3, the test instrument, and sample are described, and also form the basis for the dependent variable of students' test performance. Section 4 describes the computational model that we built to quantify the data on linguistic features. This is done in order to perform four sorts of linguistic computation: *correlation analysis*, *Monte-Carlo simulation*, *automatic classification* and *feature analysis*. In Section 5, we present our experiments at large by utilizing the latter computational model.

The analyses include mostly automatically annotated features, such as part of speech (corpus-driven approach) and few manually annotated features, such as domain-specific terms and quantitative vocabulary (corpus-based approach) (see Section 4). Language patterns in test tasks were examined in detail using methods from computational linguistics, and relations between the specific language features and the measured students' response frequencies were analyzed by calculating distance correlations for each test item. The computational linguistics methods in the exploratory analysis part of this study include measuring distance correlations of language vectors, evolutionary searches, Monte Carlo simulations and automatic classifications to examine correlations between frequencies of dozens of the language features and the test-takers' response distributions on the multiple-choice test items. In sections 6, we discuss our findings and highlight some limitations, before drawing some conclusions for further research in section 7. The aim is to integrate our computational linguistic analysis into the landscape of educational measurement approaches. To this end, the analysis is guided by a couple of observational expectancies formulated in Section 2.

2   Research objectives and hypotheses

To integrate computational linguistic and educational measurement approaches we developed and tested a linguistic model of task descriptions for the German and English version of the TUCE for assessing students' economic knowledge in higher education. This newly developed linguistic model is used to generate quantitative representations of specific linguistic features (including content-related characteristics, see below) in both languages and phrasing of test items that can be related to rates of correct student responses on a task.

Based on the prior research, we formulate the following general assumptions of our approach:

(i)   We assume that certain linguistic features in the German and English TUCE versions correlate with test results on the TUCE, and

(ii)   in a way that allows for characterizing each language version by distinct patterns of linguistic features.

From this point of view, we may speak of a rather light version of Lucy's (1992) "reformulation of the linguistic relativity hypothesis" (cf. Lucy 1997) to which this paper adheres: describing the same task using different languages challenges students in different ways (see the task example in Figure 1 in Section 4.2) subject to measurable properties of these descriptions (cf. also Bisang in this volume).

(iii)   Accordingly, when students have problems in solving certain tasks, we assume that this effect also depends on the language in which the task description is given.

Generally speaking, language can be seen as an interference in cognition when the test taker has to understand the content being expressed by the corresponding task. It is important to note that we do not examine claims about the general possibilities of expression and task formulation in the languages involved. Rather, we take the specific language use in the TUCE as a given and assume the predictability of correct responses rates within the two language versions based on indices of quantitative text structure (which also include features used in readability metrics); in this line of thinking, we expect an effect of the use of words of certain classes in test task descriptions (known to affect readability) on the corresponding rates of correct responses (for more details see Section 4).

(iv)   Additionally, we assume that the longer students study a specific subject, i.e., economics, the more they become acquainted with and eventually proficient in the language of the domain, for example, with specialized terminology (cf. Section 1.2).

In order to explore these assumptions, the paper considers the following hypotheses:

Hypothesis 1

H1a: *Certain linguistic features of the tasks' verbal presentations are related to the rates of correct student responses on these tasks.*
Motivation: Based on the above considerations, we assume that one can predict the rates of correct student responses to a significant degree by analyzing quantitative features of the test tasks' verbal presentations. In so far, this hypothesis is not falsified by our results - or any further proof of the contrary. It provides general support for the suitability of our approach.

This motivation does not mean that we *identify* the reason of such a correlation with the readability of the linguistic input. Such a hypothesis would need further research that will be addressed by future work (see Section 7). However, schematic or redundant text organization might be a source of higher readability that might be directly related to our target variable: correct student responses to more readable questions. In order to reflect this conception, we will include a larger number of features into our analysis that consider the correlation of linguistic variables across observational units (such as sentences) of input texts: the higher this correlation, the more redundant the text organization in terms of these variables (for more details see Section 4.1).

H1b: The two *language versions of the TUCE differ regarding the degree of this correlation, but coincide in showing it.*

Motivation: In order to test this hypothesis, we analyze the task descriptions of the TUCE in two languages: *English* and *German*. We analyze the US original and German adaptation both developed for the same purpose of assessing economic knowledge among comparable samples of test takers. Note that by distinguishing the languages we do not qualify or compare them, nor do we presume perfect equivalence of items. Rather, we assume that the effect being predicted by Hypothesis 1a is manifested by *different linguistic features* of task descriptions.

Hypothesis 2

Linguistic features that are correlating with rates of correct responses allow for classifying the task descriptions in terms of the language in which they are written *(English and German)* and in terms of the *text type (i.e., question or response option) they manifest.*

Motivation: Together with Hypothesis 1b, this hypothesis relates to the notion of linguistic relativity (see above and Section 7). The validity of any linguistic features is supported beyond Hypothesis 1a and 1b to the extent that they additionally allow for classifying descriptions of tasks in different languages. Our results should show, *first*, that linguistic features of wording are correlated to rates of correct responses, and, *second*, that they allow for separating the texts of the two language versions. Thus, we aim at a quantitative model of task descriptions that allows for both interrelating verbal presentations of tasks and rates of correct responses while separating the languages in which these tasks are described. Insofar, one finds evidence in support of Hypothesis 1b, one knows that our feature model is able to reflect a language-related difference that is well-known to exist. However, any such observable difference is possibly not distinctive enough to allow for an automatic classification of the input items regarding the given target classes – moreover, it might be that these items unsystematically vary in this respect.

Therefore, it makes a difference to state Hypothesis 2 *in addition to* Hypothesis 1b – also because the latter is directly connected to Hypothesis 1a while Hypothesis 2

– as relating to a classification experiment – may also be tested irrespective of what is the outcome of testing Hypothesis 1a: even in cases where there is no correlation as predicted by Hypothesis 1a and 1b, a classification according to Hypothesis 2 may, nevertheless, be successful. The difference of Hypothesis 1b and 2 is also reflected by the different methods applied to test them: in the former case, it is correlation analysis, in the latter it relates to the apparatus of automatic classification. Additionally, *for H1 and H2*, we assume that single linguistic features are less likely to show correlations with rates of correct responses, and we, therefore, also include combinations of features, i.e., language patterns in the analyses.

Hypothesis 3

H3a: *The dependency postulated in H1 is affected by students' academic year: the more advanced they are, the weaker the dependency.*
Motivation: Studies in problem solving, expert-novice research and domain-specific learning have found that it takes novices longer to understand an item, and that they tend to give more consideration to surface features and the phrasing of tasks compared to students with more experience in the domain (cf. Alexander 2003; Ericsson 2008; Brückner et al. 2015a). We differentiated students according to their study progress in economics, including 1st, 2nd and 3rd-year undergraduate students in higher education in Germany and the US (see section 3.2), which is based on the assumption that the higher the academic year of a student, the longer and more intensive her or his training in the respective field of content knowledge will be. We expect freshmen to be most affected by linguistic characteristics of task descriptions; while students of higher years are expected to be more proficient in domain-specific language and have a broader base of domain knowledge that facilitates their responding; accordingly, students are less dependent on the linguistic description of a task the more formal training they have received. Thus, we shall observe that any effect in accordance with Hypothesis 1 is damped the more, the higher the academic year of the students under consideration.
H3b: *This effect should hold for both languages.*
Motivation: The domain-specific knowledge test (TUVE IV) was administered in the language that was used in the textbooks and classes in which students acquire the according knowledge. In German universities, undergraduate courses were taught in German, in the US colleges the contents of a study domain were taught in English. The institutional and curricular analysis of the economics education in the US and Germany indicate that in the majority of higher education institutions there are no systematic differences in the scope of economic contents taught in both countries (Brückner et al. 2015a). Hence, we expected students from both countries to have equal teaching conditions.

Hypothesis 4

H4a: *The dependency postulated in H1 is affected by the* specialized economic terms used in certain test tasks: *the more domain-specific terms are used, the stronger the dependency.*
Motivation: According to a model of domain learning (e.g., Alexander 2003), tasks might differ in how challenging they are for learners, if the *domain-specific terms are used,* which might influence the understanding of test items. Depending on the specific terminology and jargon in economics, the text presented in a task of the TUCE might be more or less close to everyday language, and therefore pose a different difficulty level to learners.
H4b: *Effects of specialized economic terms per item differ across languages.*
Motivation: The high-quality translation and adaptation of the TUCE aimed at generating an equivalent German-language test instrument. Validation and comparability analyses confirmed the functional and measurement equivalence of the German test version and, thus, suitability of both test versions (English and German) for comparisons between the United States and Germany (Zlatkin-Troitschanskaia et al. 2016a). This said, based on the linguistic relativity assumption, unnoticed linguistic differences in construct-relevant features such as terminology in test items can be expected to affect students' test scores across language versions.

Testing these hypotheses requires a quantitative model that includes a whole bunch of linguistic variables correlating with the rates of correct responses (our *target variable*) to varying degrees and for varying purposes (correlation analysis, difference analysis, automatic classification etc.). As a matter of fact, such a model does not exist out of the box. One reason is that TUCE data is structured in terms of questions and corresponding response options and, thus, is full of text snippets and short sentences making a straightforward application of well-established models of quantitative and computational linguistics rather difficult. Thus, we decided to build our own TUCE-related model which will be developed in Section 4. Before that, we inform about our data.

3   Assessment instrument and data

3.1   TUCE

The economic content assessed is based on content standards developed by the *Council for Economic Education* in the US (CEE 2010; Siegfried et al. 2010).

These standards differentiate various content areas within the fundamental areas micro and macroeconomics. There is an international consensus on the core curriculum in economics, which has been furthered as well by the international spread of economics textbooks developed in the US (e.g., OECD 2013). The understanding of the core economics curriculum is very similar in Germany, as illustrated by our curricular analysis of business and economics degree courses at 96 universities (see more details in Zlatkin-Troitschanskaia et al. 2014).

The economic content areas described in the tasks reference contexts that are touched upon not only in formal economic education, but rather realistic contexts that permeate the everyday life of all people, such as planning a household, taking on credit, insurances etc. as well as contexts referenced in public political debates, for instance in the current developments surrounding the British secession from the European Union, including such topic areas as public debt or international trade agreements. Hence, knowledge in these content areas can be acquired not only in formal higher education, but also through informal and unintentional learning, for example, while consuming mass media. While contexts are shared, the degree of abstraction and technicality of language may vary between these different communicative situations, registers and corresponding cognitive requirements. The TUCE is based on a cognitive model (Walstad et al. 2007; Yamaoka et al. 2010) following Bloom's cognitive taxonomy of teach-study objectives (Bloom et al. 1956) and the further developed version by Anderson and Krathwohl (2001), which were controlled in the adaptation and validation for Germany (Zlatkin-Troitschanskaia et al. 2014).[3]

The TUCE comprises 60 multiple-choice items with 1 correct response and 3 distractors, with respectively 30 items on microeconomics and 30 items on macroeconomics. In a thorough adaptation and comprehensive validation process the test was adapted and validated for use in higher education in Germany (Zlatkin-Troitschanskaia et al. 2014). Adaptation was carried out according to the TRAPD process (Harkness et al. 2003, 2011) and the TAGs by the ITC (2005) as well as recommendations by Solano-Flores, Contreras-Niño, and Backhoff (2006). The adaptation of the TUCE IV for Germany required hardly any modifications in content, and all 60 items were successfully adapted from the US version (Zlatkin-Troitschanskaia et al. 2014). An adaptation rate of hundred percent is far from the norm in international educational assessments and attests to the good quality of the original items and the similarity of curricula. Comparability analyses were carried out and measurement invariance between the German and US instrument was

---

3   For practical reasons, analyses of cognitive requirements are not included in this
    paper, but planned for future studies (see Section 7).

established (e.g., Brückner et al. 2015a, Förster et al. 2015; Zlatkin-Troitschanskaia et al. 2016c). These comprehensive analyses confirmed that the German and US instrument can be used for comparative studies. The two-dimensional structure of the construct was confirmed using confirmatory factor analysis (CFA). According-ly, in the following analyses, we differentiate between the item scores for both di-mensions, that is, micro and macro separately. Sufficient reliability was established for both the microeconomics and the macroeconomics parts (micro: alpha = 0.70; macro: alpha = 0.77).

3.2   Sample

The German TUCE data for this sub-study was collected in the winter term of 2012/2013 and the summer term of 2013 by administering a paper-pencil test to 1,629 students from business and economics degree courses from 33 universities in 14 German federal states, which included the largest business and economics faculties in Germany (for more details see Brückner et al. 2015a). The US data was provided by the CEE; the sub-sample for this study included 4,400 students from 51 colleges. In both countries, the test was administered to business and economics students in higher education at the beginning of their 1st, 2nd, and 3rd year of their undergraduate studies (the TUCE was also administered to German students in the 4th and 5th year of study, but those students were excluded from the present analy-sis). See Table 1 for the distribution of students across years of study. Overall, 51 observations from students beyond their 3rd year of studies were excluded.

Tab. 1   Distribution of students across years of studies

Year of Studies	Freq.	Percent	Cum.	Year of Studies	Freq.	Percent	Cum.
1st	571	36.19	36.19	1st	1,040	23.64	23.64
2nd	639	40.49	76.68	2nd	2,000	45.45	69.09
3rd	368	23.32	100.00	3rd	1,360	30.91	100.00
total	1,578	100.00		total	4,400	100.00	

Left: Germany; right: United States

The microeconomics part was completed by 1,392 students from Germany, and 2,243 students from the US; the macroeconomics part was completed by 1,398 students from Germany, and 2157 students from the US. Most of the students were native speakers of German and English in Germany and the US respectively (for more details see Brückner et al. 2015a).

4 Quantifying test task descriptions

In this section, we describe our computational model for testing the hypotheses of Section 2. Our conceptual background is *quantitative linguistics* according to which natural language texts exhibit certain numerical distributions in a law-like manner so that their *genre-, register-, topic- and function-related characteristics* are more or less systematically reflected by these distributions (cf. Mehler 2005). In this sense, our approach is in line with efforts to *automatic text classification* according to which texts of different *topics, styles, genres* or *registers* (Pieper 1975; Biber 1995; Mehler et al. 2010) can be classified by means of machine learning (Sebastiani 2002).

Since Hypothesis 4 is domain- and terminology-related, the register-oriented differentiation of texts is of special interest here. To this end, we differentiate among four classes of words of general language and terminology, respectively (see below). In this way, we go beyond classical approaches to feature analysis in quantitative linguistics in the sense that a great deal of our model is semantically grounded in the domain under consideration, that is, economics.

4.1 Identifying and collecting specific language features

While seeking a model for interrelating test tasks with rates of correct responses in a language-*independent* manner (see Hypothesis 1a), we also seek a model that is expressive enough to perform the desired language-related classification (see Hypothesis 1b and especially Hypothesis 2). In spite of the methodical orthogonality of these two subtasks, we nevertheless derive both models from the same text-linguistic basis. More specifically, we start from a range of related research on *text classification* (Liiv and Tuldava 1993), *quantitative stylistics* (Pieper 1975), *plagiarism detection* (Stein et al. 2011) and *authorship attribution* (Stamatatos 2011), *readability assessment* (Islam and Mehler 2013) and *text similarity measurement* (Bär et al. 2012) to derive candidate features for quantifying the textual data of the corpus of Section 3. In order to arrive at a first guess, we concentrate on rather easy-to-compute indices as summarized in Table 2. To this end, we collected features from five different areas:

1. **Basic features:** First and foremost, we distinguish so called basic features (as, for example, *hapax legomena* and *dis legomena*) irrespective of their part of speech (POS). This also includes character-based features. The idea behind this approach is to study the expressiveness of these rather simple features in line with Occam's razor: *the simpler the model generating the same results, the better this model.*

2. **Quantitative text structure:** Secondly, we experiment with features (frequencies and ratios) that have been used to characterize texts quantitatively in order to make them an input to automatic classification. In this way, we adhere to the tradition of quantitative text linguistics and especially to classificatory approaches based on numerical features addressing text structure (Joachims 2002; cf. also the literature in Mehler 2005) based thereon. This group of features directly relates to Hypothesis 2.

3. **Part-of-speech-related features:** Thirdly, we compute features (once more frequencies and ratios) that are sensitive to the parts of speech of lexical text constituents. The idea is to distinguish the impact of adjectives, nouns, verbs and adverbs. Evidently, using adjectives, verbs and adverbs rather than abstract nouns makes a text less abstract and more active (Altmann 1988). This group of features relates – at least indirectly – to Hypotheses 1a, 3 and 4.

4. **Semantic features** are computed and explore the membership of words to certain semantically demarcated word classes (as distinguished below). By using such semantic features, we draw on restrictions induced by the domain of the tasks under consideration, that is, *economics* (cf. Section 3.1). In the case of semantic features, we utilize *manually annotated data*. This relates to the classification of words as belonging to one of the following semantic classes:

   1. *General-Language Words* (GLW) are words which are used rather often in economic texts.
   2. *Economic Terms* (ET1) are words including a general-language sense, i.e., terms in a broader sense.
   3. *Economic Terms* (ET2) are words that do not include a general-language sense, i.e., terms in a stronger domain-specific sense.
   4. *Mathematical and Statistical Expressions* (MSE) concern a group of units including symbols and formulae (see an example in Figure 1).

MSE were examined in particular since the task requirement to handle quantitative data was shown to influence item difficulty and test scores (Brückner et al. 2015b; Shavelson et al. in press). However, in the present study, we did not yet differentiate the type and structure of MSE (cf. Wittum et al. in this volume) to warrant a dedicated hypothesis. Still, a frequency of MSE members, a number of MSE members in relation to text length, an average number of MSE pre-sentence and an average length of MSE were included in the analyses (see Table 2). Generally, the presence of technical terms is hypothesized to increase item difficulty, due to higher information density, to an increase of the average number of syllables per word and to adding construct-relevant features, that is, domain terminology to be understood. Thus, using these semantic features relates to Hypotheses 4.

5. **Correlation-based features interrelating frequencies of different parts of speech:** As an additional set of features, we compute the distance correlation[4] (Kosorok 2009) between random variables computed from input texts seen as stochastic processes. More specifically, for any given observational unit (e.g., sentence) of any textual input, we compute several random variables (e.g., *sentence length*, *number of adverbs* etc.) and ask for the mutual statistical dependence of these variables. The higher this dependence for the more pairs of variables, the more schematic the textual organization.

This approach is motivated by the conception that the more schematic the organization of a text (in our case this relates to its lexical organization), the higher its redundancy, the more readable the text and, finally, the easier to give the correct answer to the question manifested by that text in the context of TUCE. This group of features directly relates to Hypothesis 1a.

Semantic features as considered here are mainly given by ratios that are relating frequencies of class membership to the number of sentences per question or response option. We also interpret class membership observed per sentence as a random variable to compute its distance correlation to the corresponding frequencies of parts of speech. In this way, we do not only measure the degree of schematic lexical organization of texts, but also receive insights into the degree by which these texts manifest technical domain-specific language.

4.2   The manual annotation of semantic features

The manual annotation of terms (see Feature Set 4 in the section 4.1) was carried out by two economics experts and one linguist, who decided on the selection and classification of terms by consensus (on the importance of mixed teams in content validation, see ITC, 2016). The first round of annotation showed disagreements particularly on categories 1 and 2., i.e., domain terminology with a general-language sense and general-language words used in economics. Annotators disagreed

---

4   This method is known for outperforming by far other correlation measures.

in particular on the limits of compound and separable terms and degree of term usage and domain-specificity.[5] For practical reasons, all categories were included in the analysis. Most economic terms in the stronger sense were selected unanimously in the first round and were all accepted in the second round after their appearance in domain textbooks in higher education economics was confirmed (cf. Mankiw and Taylor 2010; Samuelson and Nordhaus 2010).

Mathematical and statistical terms included mathematical symbols and formulae (with coherent strings counted as one term), measurement unit lexemes, abbreviations, and symbols (e.g., currency symbols), as well as general language terms indicating a specific or abstract quantitative relationship between two units, which requires students to make a comparison, mathematical or statistical operation (e.g., "increase"/"decrease", "higher"/"lower", "as high as", "one additional", "share", "percent", "probability"). Mathematical-statistical terms appeared in clusters within items with low and high shares; i.e., mostly a quantitative relation in the item stem would be followed by further quantitative terms in the response options. A decision was made to not include general monetary terms in this category (e.g., "price" or "cost"), but only to mark specific quantities and relations (e.g., "$1" or "more expensive"). All words belonging to either of the two classes were marked and tagged for part-of-speech. In this way, the difficult decision about multi-word expressions to either manifest a (usually more technical) compound term or a sequence of (usually less technical) single-word terms was not relevant for the subsequent analyses. Figure 1 shows one example item from macroeconomics with corresponding annotations of economic and quantitative terms.

---

5   A detailed classification and internal differentiation of these categories would have required a more elaborate annotation scheme as well as additional expert rating, reference consultation or corpus analyses, which would have been beyond the scope of this initial study (see Sections 6 and 7). On the challenges of classifying terminology see also Janich (1998).

50. Der Verbraucherpreisindex einer Volkswirtschaft beträgt in einem Jahr 180 und im nächsten Jahr 189. Die Inflationsrate in der Volkswirtschaft für diesen Zeitraum beträgt	The consumer price index in an economy is 180 one year and 189 the next year. The rate of inflation in the economy over that year period is:
☐ 1 Prozent. ☐ 5 Prozent. ☐ 8 Prozent. ☐ 18 Prozent.	☐ 1 percent. ☐ 5 percent. ☐ 8 percent. ☐ 18 percent.

Fig. 1 Example annotations on one TUCE item in macroeconomics in German and English ET1=*yellow*, ET2=*red*; MSE=*blue*. ET2 (red) include a domain-specific, not a general-language sense, i.e., these are the technical terms in a stronger domain-specific sense

4.3   Computational modeling and analyzing of different language features

We computed all features of Section 4.1 for both questions and response options of TUCE separately as well as jointly. Further, we took the same feature list for quantifying texts in both languages considered here. In this way, we considered *264 different features* (i.e., three times the number of features listed as rows in Table 2).[6] In order to compute these features we first preprocessed our input corpus. This was done by means of *TextImager* (Hemati et al. 2016), a distributed web-based system for automatically analyzing and visualizing natural language texts. More specifically, we used the LanguageTool segmenter, lemmatizer and Stanford tagger (Toutanova et al. 2003) to process both German and English texts. Since we lack an adequate tagger of grammatical categories for English, we did not distinguish syntactic words. Therefore, we only considered the difference between word forms and lemmas to analyze German and English texts using the same quantitative model.

---

6   This approach ranges among those using rather larger vector spaces for quantifying
     natural language texts based on the sort of quantitative features considered here.

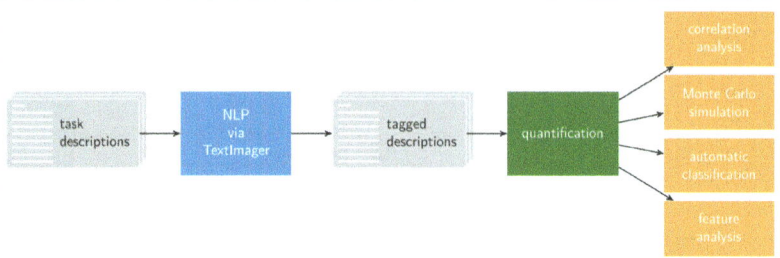

Fig. 2 NLP architecture for quantifying task descriptions as input to correlation analysis, automatic classification and feature visualization

The overall architecture of our approach to quantifying task descriptions is depicted in Figure 2. It distinguishes four computational subtasks to be performed all of which start from the same quantification of task descriptions based on the feature model of Section 4.1:

1. **Correlation analysis:** we compute distance correlations (Kosorok 2009) to explore the dependence between linguistic features of test task descriptions and rates of correct responses. Further, we compute Spearman's rank correlation to also qualify the latter correlations. As will be shown in Section 5, the features listed in Table 2 correlate rather differently with rates of correct responses. Since we additionally expect that single features correlate worse than combinations thereof, we perform an evolutionary search for the subset of features that best correlates with rates of correct responses.

2. We perform a **Monte Carlo simulation** to assess the significance of the latter correlation analysis. For each linguistic feature, we randomly reassign its values according to an urn model (drawing without replacement) and re-compute the corresponding distance correlations. Values are finally averaged for 10,000 runs of this simulation. The randomization focuses on the subset of best performing features in order to estimate the probability by which randomization yields a distance correlation at least as high as the one being returned by our evolutionary search.

3. **Automatic classification** serves for assessing the expressiveness of our model with respect to language classification and speech act detection. To this end, we perform three experiments: (i) in a *language-related* classification we consider *German* against *English texts* (in both cases irrespective of the underlying text type, that is, *question* and *response option*), (ii) in a *text genre-related classifi-*

cation we consider *questions* in opposition to *response option* (irrespective of the underlying language), while (iii) in a combined *genre- and language-related* classification we contrast *German questions*, *German response options*, *English questions* and *English response options* among each other. Rather than using a neural network (Joulin et al. 2016), we rely on *Support Vector Machines* (SVM) and linear kernels (Joachims 2002) for performing these classifications. The reason is that we want to secure easier interpretability of our classification results, while gaining plausibility by not relying on classification techniques that are too elaborate.

4. **Feature Analysis:** Finally, we utilize network theory (Newman 2003) to detect redundancy in our model. To this end, we compute a series of networks whose nodes denote features as selected by our correlation analysis while their edges are weighted by the distance correlations between these features. In this way, we get access to the degree by which most "expressive" features depend on each other: *the higher this expected dependence, the higher the redundancy in our model.*

Tab. 2 The set of 264 features which were calculated to quantify task descriptions (first part)

Feature	ID (Q)	ID (D)	ID (Q+D)	Description	Reference
	F1	F89	F177	Number of characters	(Zheng et al. 2006)
	F2	F90	F178	Number of sentences	(Zheng et al. 2006)
	F3	F91	F179	Number of tokens	
	F4	F92	F180	Number of lemmas	
	F5	F93	F181	Average number of tokens per sentence	(Zheng et al. 2006)
	F6	F94	F182	Number of sentences in relation to text length (aka number of tokens)	
	F7	F95	F183	Average number of characters per sentence	(Zheng et al. 2006)
	F8	F96	F184	Average number of characters per token	(Zheng et al. 2006)
	F9	F97	F185	Number of hapax legomena (task context)	(Zheng et al. 2006)
	F10	F98	F186	Number of dis legomena (task context)	(Zheng et al. 2006)
	F11	F99	F187	Number of hapax legomena (corpus context)	
	F12	F100	F188	Number of dis legomena (corpus context)	
Basic features	F13	F101	F189	Number of hapax legomena in relation to text length (task context)	
	F14	F102	F190	Number of dis legomena in relation to text length (task context)	
	F15	F103	F191	Number of hapax legomena in relation to text length (corpus context)	
	F16	F104	F192	Number of dis legomena in relation to text length (corpus context)	
	F17	F105	F193	Yule's Index	(Köhler, Altmann, and Piotrowski 2005; Greg and Udny Yule 1944)
	F18	F106	F194	Flesch Kincaid grade level	(Peter Kincaid 1975; Flesch 1948)
Quantitative text characteristics	F19	F107	F195	Typen-token ratio	(Zheng et al. 2006; Greg and Udny Yule 1944; Holmes 1998)
	F20	F108	F196	Entropy of word form frequencies	(Islam, Rahman, and Mehler 2014)
	F21	F109	F197	Entropy of lemma frequencies	(Islam, Rahman, and Mehler 2014)
	F22	F110	F198	Entropy of sentence lengths	(Islam, Rahman, and Mehler 2014)
	F23	F111	F199	Number of verbs	
	F24	F112	F200	Number of nouns	
	F25	F113	F201	Number of adjectives	
	F26	F114	F202	Number of adverbs	
	F27	F115	F203	Average number of verbs per sentence	(Stamatatos 2009)
PoS-related features	F28	F116	F204	Average number of nouns per sentence	(Stamatatos 2009)
	F29	F117	F205	Average number of adjectives per sentence	(Stamatatos 2009)
	F30	F118	F206	Average number of adverbs per sentence	(Stamatatos 2009)
	F31	F119	F207	Number of verbs in relation to text length	
	F32	F120	F208	Number of nouns in relation to text length	
	F33	F121	F209	Number of adjectives in relation to text length	
	F34	F122	F210	Number of adverbs in relation to text length	
	F35	F123	F211	Number of sentences in relation to number of adjectives	
	F36	F124	F212	Number of sentences in relation to number of adverbs	
	F37	F125	F213	Number of sentences in relation to number of nouns	
	F38	F126	F214	Number of sentences in relation to number of verbs	
	F39	F127	F215	Text length in relation to number of adjectives	
	F40	F128	F216	Text length in relation to number of adverb	
	F41	F129	F217	Text length in relation to number of noun	
	F42	F130	F218	Text length in relation to number of verb	

Tab. 2 (continued) The set of 264 features which were calculated to quantify task descriptions

Feature	ID (Q)	ID (D)	ID (Q+D)	Description	Reference
Distance correlation-based features	F43	F131	F219	dCorr(#Adjectives,#Adverbs)	
	F44	F132	F220	dCorr(#Adjectives,#Nouns)	
	F45	F133	F221	dCorr(#Adjectives,#Verbs)	
	F46	F134	F222	dCorr(#Adverbs,#Nouns)	
	F47	F135	F223	dCorr(#Adverbs,#Verbs)	
	F48	F136	F224	dCorr(#Nouns,#Verbs)	
	F49	F137	F225	dCorr(#Nouns,#GLW)	
	F50	F138	F226	dCorr(#Nouns,#MSE)	
	F51	F139	F227	dCorr(#Nouns,#ET1)	
	F52	F140	F228	dCorr(#Nouns,#ET2)	
	F53	F141	F229	dCorr(#Verbs,#GLW)	
	F54	F142	F230	dCorr(#Verbs,#MSE)	
	F55	F143	F231	dCorr(#Verbs,#ET1)	
	F56	F144	F232	dCorr(#Verbs,#ET2)	
	F57	F145	F233	dCorr(#Adjectives,#GLW)	
	F58	F146	F234	dCorr(#Adjectives,#MSE)	
	F59	F147	F235	dCorr(#Adjectives,#ET1)	
	F60	F148	F236	dCorr(#Adjectives,#ET2)	
	F61	F149	F237	dCorr(#Adverbs,#GLW)	
	F62	F150	F238	dCorr(#Adverbs,#MSE)	
	F63	F151	F239	dCorr(#Adverbs,#ET1)	
	F64	F152	F240	dCorr(#Adverbs,#ET2)	
	F65	F153	F241	dCorr(#GLW,#MSE)	
	F66	F154	F242	dCorr(#GLW,#ET1)	
	F67	F155	F243	dCorr(#GLW,#ET2)	
	F68	F156	F244	dCorr(#MSE,#ET1)	
	F69	F157	F245	dCorr(#MSE,#ET2)	
	F70	F158	F246	dCorr(#ET1,#ET2)	
Semantic features	F71	F159	F247	Frequency of GLW members	
	F72	F160	F248	Frequency of MSE members	
	F73	F161	F249	Frequency of ET1 members	
	F74	F162	F250	Frequency of ET2 members	
	F75	F163	F251	Number of GLW members in relation to text length	
	F76	F164	F252	Number of MSE members in relation to text length	
	F77	F165	F253	Number of ET1 members in relation to text length	
	F78	F166	F254	Number of ET2 members in relation to text length	
	F79	F167	F255	Average number of GLW per sentence	
	F80	F168	F256	Average number of MSE per sentence	
	F81	F169	F257	Average number of ET1 per sentence	
	F82	F170	F258	Average number of ET2 per sentence	
	F83	F171	F259	Average length of GLW	
	F84	F172	F260	Average length of MSE	
	F85	F173	F261	Average length of ET1	
	F86	F174	F262	Average length of ET2	
	F87	F175	F263	#V/(#V+#ADV)	
	F88	F176	F264	#V/(#V+#ADJ)	

5   Experimentation

According to Section 4, we subsequently present a series of experimental results with respect to correlation analysis (Section 5.1), Monte Carlo simulation (Section 5.2), automatic classification (Section 5.3) and feature analysis based on complex network theory (Section 5.4).

Tab. 3   Distance correlations regarding German and English task descriptions separately

	De	En
All features	0.22	0.27
Top 20 features	0.24	0.33
Top 10 features	0.24	0.33
Top 5 features	0.31	0.40

The row called *All features* denotes the scenario in which all 264 features of Table 2 are taken to perform the correlation analysis, rows denoted as *Top n features* denote the scenario in which the set of *n* features of highest distance correlation is used to calculate its correlation with the rate of correct responses.

5.1   Correlation analysis

For each of the features listed in Table 2 and for each of the text analytic scenarios distinguished in Section 4 (that is, by distinguishing the quantitative analysis of questions (Q) from that of response options (D) as well as from Q+D – see Table 2, columns 2-4), we compute the corresponding value distributions using the TUCE data of Section 3. This enables an evolutionary search on the space of feature vectors to search for the subset of features that best correlates with the number of correct student responses on a task: *the smaller the number of these features and the higher the correlation, the less linguistic information is needed to predict the rate of correct responses, the higher the expected dependency according to Hypothesis 1* (see Section 2). One reason to perform this evolutionary search is exploratory data analysis. That is, we do not start with a hypothesis about the exact nature of linguistic features that are supposed to correlate with the rate of correct responses; rather, we are looking for such features by starting from the classes of features distinguished in Section 4.

Tab. 4   Distance correlations

	De	En
1st Year	0.46	0.45
2nd Year	0.50	0.44
3rd Year	0.50	0.47
All	0.50	0.45

Distance correlations were calculated by using the best performing feature subset S (last row in Tab. 4) by means of an evolutionary search. The search space for calculating S considers all features and all students for each language separately and then uses S to calculate the corresponding distance correlation by distinguishing between 1st, 2nd, and 3rd year students.

In the present case, an evolutionary search can be seen to generate a population of vectors indicating which of the features of Table 2 are effective (1) or not (0). Any such vector codes a candidate subset of features whose distance correlation with the rate of correct responses is measured to assess the fitness of this selection. For each round of this search, best performing individual features are taken and crossed-over to form candidate feature sub-sets of the next generation. The search stops after having performed a given number of iterations (while it may converge before reaching the maximum number of iterations). For performing these evolutionary searches, we used *genalg* (Willighagen et al. 2015). The number of iterations and the size of the populations are both equal to 2,000.

Tab. 5   Distance correlations of optimized feature subset

	De	En
1st Year	0.46	0.44
2nd Year	0.42	0.43
3rd Year	0.42	0.46
All	0.44	0.44

In this experiment, the feature subset S was optimized starting from the set of 1ˢᵗ year students and then used to calculate the distance correlations regarding the remaining set of scenarios (including the scenario denoted by *All*).

We performed 8 different optimizations using *genalg* (see the Tables 4-7). More specifically, we separated German from English task descriptions by regarding all students, 1st year students, 2nd year students and 3rd year students in separate evolutionary searches. For each of these scenarios, we calculate the best fitting feature subset to predict the respective target variable. Table 5 shows distance correlations being computed for German and for English task descriptions separately. It demonstrates a monotone increase in correlation starting from taking all features into account and ending with the subset of n highest ranked features where features are ranked according to their distance correlation with the target variable when being considered in isolation.

Table 3 also shows that English texts are always better correlated with the rates of correct responses than their German counterparts. According to Section 2, we do not take any of these assessments as a starting point for qualifying the languages under consideration but just state a difference between the two languages (see Hypothesis 1b).[7]

Notably, a weak correlation of at least 30% is first reached by means of the set of top 10 features (English) and the set of top 5 features (German), respectively. A stronger correlation of 40% is realized only in the case of English task descriptions when using the set of top 5 features. In any event, Table 3 demonstrates that by concentrating on fewer features distance correlation increases. Thus, it makes sense to

---

7   Our observation may hint at a difference between original and translation (cf., e.g., Baker 1996), a general language difference, a difference between learners in the US being more dependent on specific language patterns than German students, etc.; further analyses are needed to explain this finding (see Sections 6 and 7).

search for best performing feature subsets as described above. The corresponding results are shown in Tables 4, 5, 6 and 7. Table 4 starts with searching for this optimal subset S by using all features and by considering all students (irrespective of the year) (see last row) and then uses S to compute the respective correlations per year.

The results are striking: correlation increases up to 50% – in this sense we can speak of stronger correlation (Hypothesis 1a) as well as of differences between English and German (Hypothesis 1b): the task descriptions of both languages exhibit the targeted correlation but to different degrees. Obviously, correlation analysis now performs better for German than for English texts thereby reversing the order induced by Table 3.

Moreover, regarding Hypothesis 3, we state that the higher the academic year the higher the correlation – at least it is equal to the year before (3rd year, German texts). In a single case, it is smaller (2nd year, English texts, compared with 1st year students). This finding is *not* in support of Hypothesis 3. Thus, in order to shed more light on this hypothesis, we differentiate our analysis by optimizing the years separately and then taking the optimal subset to compute correlations for the remaining years. In Table 5, we optimize the 1st year, in Table 6 the 2nd year and in Table 7 the third year. Once more, the results cannot be fully interpreted in support of Hypothesis 3. However, in Table 5 we see the best match with the prediction made by this hypothesis showing only one exception in the broader sense (En, year 3 in relation to year 2) and one stationarity not being predicted (De, year 3 in relation to year 2). One reason for these failures might be that the differences between the 3rd and the 2nd academic year are not as pronounced as assumed by Hypothesis 3. Nevertheless, correlations reported in Tables 5, 6 and 7 are remarkably high – in several cases they equal 50% while in a single case correlation is even above 50% (Table 6, 2nd year, German texts).

Tab. 6   Distance correlation of optimized features subset (2 year)

	De	En
1st Year	0.46	0.43
2nd Year	0.51	0.43
3rd Year	0.50	0.45
All	0.50	0.44

In this experiment, the feature subset S was optimized starting from the set of 2nd year students and then used to calculate the distance correlations regarding the remaining set of scenarios (including the scenario denoted by *All*).

Tab. 7   Distance correlation of optimized features subset (3 year)

	De	En
1st Year	0.46	0.45
2nd Year	0.50	0.44
3rd Year	0.50	0.46
All	0.50	0.45

In this experiment, the feature subset S was optimized starting from the set of 3rd year students and then used to calculate the distance correlations regarding the remaining set of scenarios (including the scenario denoted by *All*).

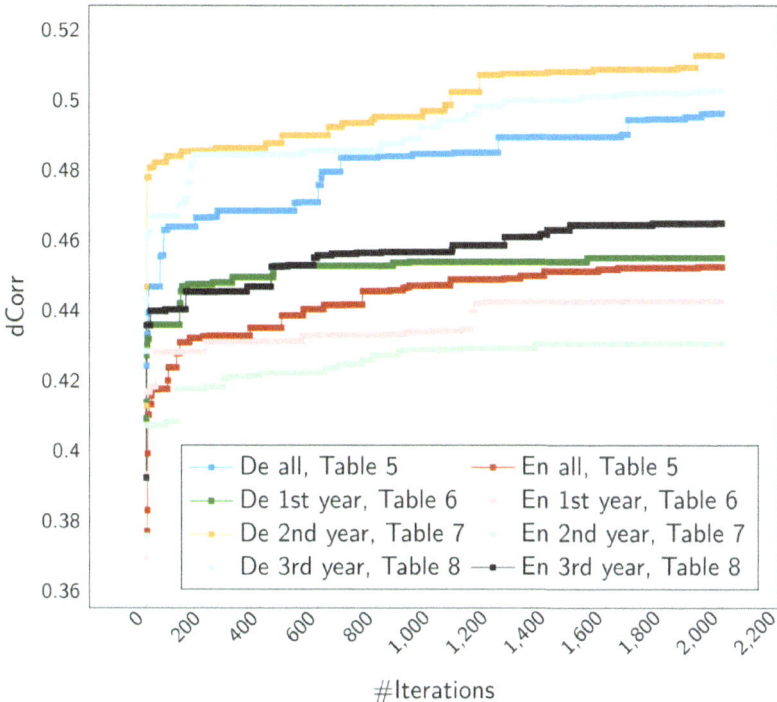

Fig. 3 Distance correlation as a function of the number of iterations in evolutionary searches. The analyses are based on genalg; highest correlation of 51% is reached for the scenario documented in Table 7

Figure 3 presents the increase in distance correlation as a function of the number of iterations of *genalg* by distinguishing between the different scenarios as reported in Table 4, 5, 6 and 7. It shows that the final outcome is rapidly approximated already for lower numbers of iterations. Thus, our findings are rather stable making further searches by means of more iterations rather obsolete.

Summing up our findings in terms of correlation analysis, we observe a stronger correlation between linguistic features on the one hand and the rate of correct answers of students on the other (Hypothesis 1a). We also see that the languages differ in this respect even if this variation is less systematic than expected (Hypothesis 1b). Finally, regarding Hypothesis 3, we do not detect the expected damping effect as a function of the academic year in the full range but only in a reduced version.

In Figure 4, we additionally display the distribution of distance correlation and Spearman's rank correlation induced by the list of features of Table 2. This is done to detect whether distance correlation measures dependencies not being measured by the latter. Obviously, we can identify many features for which distance correlation is higher than Spearman's correlation indicating that, indeed, the former index detects correlations which are hidden for the latter. This result is confirmed for German as well as for English as shown by the boxplots in Figure 4.

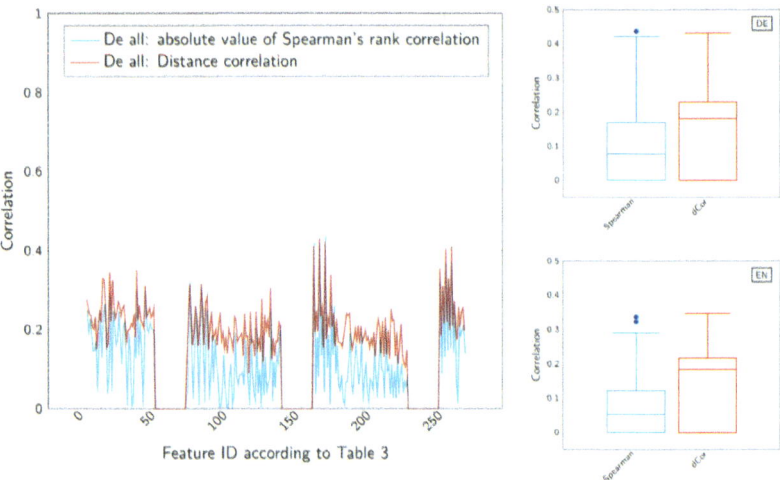

Fig. 4   Comparing distance and Spearman's rank correlation by means of a distribution (left) and two boxplots (right).
Left: Distance correlation and absolute values of Spearman's rank correlation per feature of Table 2 with respect to the target variable when using the German data.
Right above: the corresponding boxplot.
Right below: the corresponding boxplot for the English data.

Finally, Table 8 (below) shows the frequency distribution of (a subset of) the features of Table 2. These frequencies denote the numbers by which the features have been selected as members of best performing subsets as documented in Table 4, 5, 6 or 7, respectively. While there is no feature that is always selected (i.e., eight times: four optimizations, two languages), several features reach a maximum of five selections. This concerns the *text length in relation to adverbs per question (Q) (F40)*, the *average number of general-language words (GLW) per sentence per Q* (F79), the *frequency of GLW per response option* (D) (F159) and the *number of sentences in relation to the number of adjectives per Q&D* (F211). A feature being selected four times is, for example, the *average number of economic terms not including a general-language sense (ET2) per sentence in response options* (F170).

Obviously, semantic features tend to be informative in terms of the dependencies measured here (cf. Hypothesis 4a). Table 8 displays 125 features of Table 2 which were selected at least once. In this subset, 23 features have been selected for German and English texts, 49 only for English texts and 53 only for German texts.

Tab. 8 Frequency distribution of features

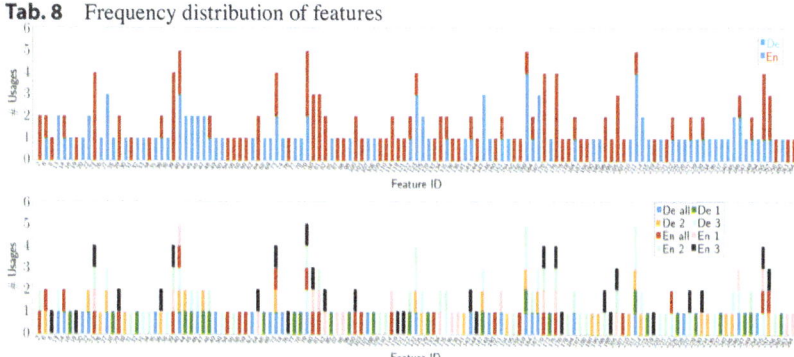

Above: Starting from the correlation analyses reported in Tables 4, 5, 6, and 7, this table displays the frequencies per feature by which they were selected by the respective evolutionary search. Features are colored depending on whether they have been selected for German (*blue*) or English (*red*) task descriptions. The x-axis shows the corresponding feature ID according to Table 2. Features that have not been selected in any of these searches are not displayed.
Below: The same frequency distribution now being differentiated regarding the experiments documented in Tables 4, 5, 6 and 7.

5.2   Monte-Carlo simulation

In order to assess the significance of our correlation analysis (Section 5.1), we performed a Monte-Carlo test. We tested the null hypothesis according to which the correlation of random permutations of feature values across data items (defined by the corresponding pair of question and response option) is higher than in the case of the experiments reported in Section 5.1 when regarding the same target variable, that is, rate of correct responses. In order to average findings over random permutations, we generated 10,000 such permutations. Basically, these permutations are computed by shuffling values of question/response option pairs per feature. Table 9 (left) shows the corresponding probability to find such a random permutation that performs at least as well as the distributions observed in Section 5.1 (see Tables 4, 5, 6 and 7). Obviously, this probability is in all cases below 1%. Thus, we may conclude that correlations as being measured by our approach are significantly high.

This assessment neither depends on the academic year, nor on the language (cf. Hypotheses 3 and 4). Table 9 (*right*) additionally shows the corresponding average distance correlations based on the set of 10,000 shuffled variants. Obviously, shuffling results in remarkably reduced correlations with a loss of up to 31% (this is seen by comparing row 4 (3rd year) of Table 9 (*right*) with the corresponding row of Table 6). In any of these scenarios (all, 1st year etc.), shuffling only concerns the corresponding subset of features that were output by the corresponding optimization routine of Section 6.1 for the respective scenario. By means of this Monte-Carlo simulation we can conclude that the distance correlations documented in Section 5.1 are non-random.

Tab. 9 Results of a Monte-Carlo simulation in terms of probabilities (*left*) and expected distance correlations (*right*)

	De	En		De	En
1st Year	0.003	0.004	1st Year	0.221	0.227
2nd Year	0.004	0.007	2nd Year	0.203	0.255
3rd Year	0.005	0.001	3rd Year	0.190	0.246
All	0.001	0.006	All	0.203	0.244

Left: The probability $P(dCorr_{rand} \geq dCorr_{observed})$ to find a random permutation of values shuffled per feature resulting in a correlation at least as high as the ones reported in Section 5.1.
Right: Distance correlations of random counterparts of observed correlations averaged over 10,000 random samples.

5.3   Automatic classification

As a third experiment, we computed three classifications by drawing on the difference between the languages considered in our study as well as the different text types (or speech acts), that is, questions and response options as collected in our corpus. This experiment relates to Hypothesis 2. We perform this experiment in order to learn about the possibility of using the model of Section 4 not only for detecting dependencies between text characteristics but also response rates. Rather, we also want to know how well it serves as a way of finding differences between objects that are well-known separable, that is, languages and text types. By reconstructing such differences, we learn how to detect statistical dependencies as well as classifying target languages and text types by means of the same model of Section 4. Once more, this would be a strong argument in support of our computational approach. In order to do this, we performed the following classifications:

1. **Language-related classification:** The goal of this experiment is to predict the language of task descriptions (including the corresponding question and its response option). This is done by representing each description by a vector whose dimensions are defined by the feature list of Table 2. Each of these vectors is then labeled by the corresponding target class (i.e., *de* and *en*) and made input to training a *Support Vector Machines*(SVM)-based classifier. In all these experiments, we used linear kernels provided by LibSVM (Chang and Lin 2001) as part of Weka (Hall et al. 2009) to compute a 10-fold cross-validation and to finally compute the corresponding F-score[8] of the predicted classification.[9] In the present case this score is 0.90 using all features indicating a rather good separability of the languages.
2. **Text type-related classification:** This second experiment aims at predicting the text type or speech act (*question* or *response option*) of text segments irrespective of the language in which they are written. To this end, we construct for each question and each response option in our corpus a separate feature vector by now considering only the features of Column 2 and 3 of Table 2. We use the same setting of SVM-based classification as before and finally reach an average F-score of 0.93. Once more, this indicates a very good separability now concerning the two speech acts considered here.
3. **Joint classification:** In this third experiment, we jointly classify text segments in terms of speech acts and their underlying language. That is, we consider four target classes: *English questions*, *English response option*, *German questions* and *German response option*. Feature vectors are constructed and SVMs are trained as before. Using the features of Column 2 and 3 of Table 2 to generate vector representations, this experiment results in an F-score of 0.80 – obviously, this joint classification is more demanding leading into a reduced score.

---

8   The F-score is the harmonic mean of precision and recall. In this paper we compute micro-averaged F-scores.

9   The kernels' parameters are as follows: *cost* = 1, *degree* = 3, *eps* = 0.001, *gamma* = 0 and *loss* = 0.1.

In order to further substantiate these experiments, we additionally performed an evolutionary search on the feature space of Table 2 to approximate the best performing subsets of features optimizing the corresponding F-score.[10] The results are shown in Table 10: now, the language-related classification is nearly perfect while the text type-related one is also improved remarkably (for the third scenario of a joint classification, the evolutionary search failed). We also repeated all three experiments by taking only those features into account that have been selected in Table 8 (see Table 10, 2nd column) – this experiment directly addresses Hypothesis 2: while the joint classification for language and text type drops down dramatically – showing that this classification does not work at all – the two other categorizations are still highly competitive. Thus, we can conclude that the languages under consideration are very well separable as are the two text types. In conjunction with our findings of Section 5.1 we also state that our linguistic model is both informative in terms of the latter classifications *and* expressive enough to predict our target variable, that is, rates of correct student responses.

Tab. 10 *F*-scores of three categorization experiments

	E1	E2	E3
E/G	0.90	0.85	0.99
Q/D	0.93	0.88	0.96
E/G × Q/D	0.80	0.22	∅

Note: *E:* English, *G:* German; *Q:* Question, *D:* Response option according to three different scenarios: *E1* considers all features of Table 2, *E2* only those features that were selected according to Table 8, and *E3* performs an evolutionary search for the best performing subset of all features of Table 2. Cells show the respective *F*-score. A zero in the last cell indicates a failed evolutionary search.

5.4   Feature analysis

In this section, we analyze the features of Table 2 for their redundancy. To this end, we span networks whose vertices denote features while their edges are spanned among pairs of features whose distance correlation is at least as high as a the lower

---

10   We did not use neural network-based classifiers since we expected to get competitive results already by using much simpler classifiers. This is also the reason why we used linear kernels instead of more powerful ones.

bound selected to generate that network: Figure 5 shows the distribution of cohesion[11] values of the resulting networks as a function of this bound. Analogously, Figure 6 exhibits the distribution of the fraction of vertices belonging to the largest connected component of these networks as a function of the same bound. While cohesion is rapidly reduced even for smaller bounds, the latter fraction is higher for the same bounds. For a distance correlation of approximately 50% (lower bound) cohesion is only about 4%, while in this case the fraction is still above 25%. The lower the cohesion and the smaller the fraction for the lower bounds, the lower the correlation among features in Table 2, the lower the redundancy in the feature model. Due to the fact that cohesion drops to 4% for a bound of 50%, for which we observe correlations between feature subsets and the target variable (see Tables 4, 5, 6 and 7), we find that on the level of this bound, redundancy is remarkably low in our model.

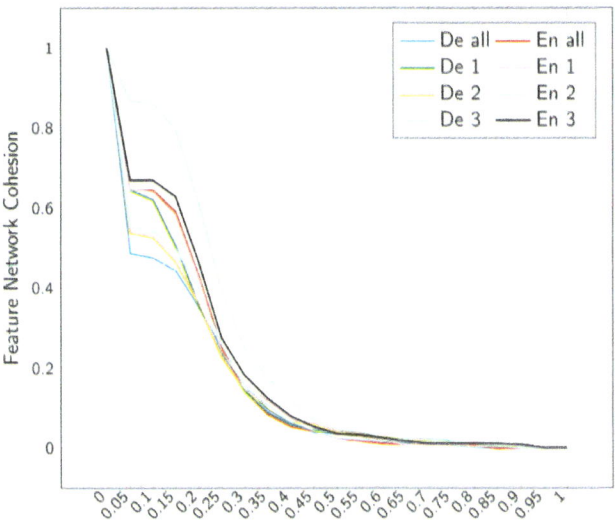

Fig. 5 Network cohesion as a function of permissible minimum distance correlation per feature-to-feature edge: For each value of dCor (x-axis) a separate feature network is computed, whose cohesion value is shown on the y-axis.

---

11 The cohesion of a graph is the ratio of the number of its edges and the number of edges in a completely connected graph of the same order.

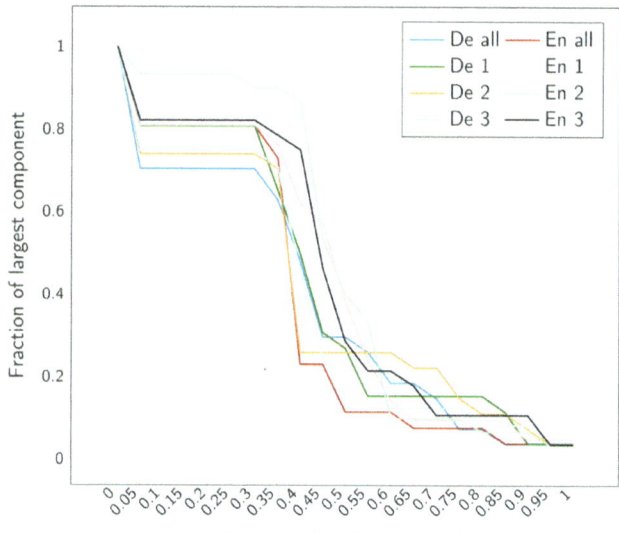

Distance Correlation Bound

Fig. 6   Fraction of vertices belonging to the largest connected component of the networks of Figure 5 (y-axis) as a function of permissible minimum distance correlation per feature-to-feature edge (x-axis)

6   Discussion

6.1   Interpretation

In this section, we interpret our findings of Section 5 with respect to our hypotheses of Section 2:

1. **Hypothesis 1a and 1b:** H1a: "*Certain linguistic features of the tasks' verbal presentations are related to the rates of correct student responses on these tasks*". Our findings (see Section 5.1) indicate a strong correlation between linguistic features of task descriptions and expected rates of correct student responses on these test tasks. This correlation gets remarkably higher (by up to 10 percent – compare Figure 4 with Tables 4, 5, 6 and 7) if feature subsets are considered in contrast to single features. This assessment is also supported by the Monte-Carlo test of Section 5.2 according to which we can speak of significant correlations. These findings indicate a certain statistical interdependence among the analyzed linguistic features making the target variable that is

rate of correct responses, more predictable than in cases where single features are considered. By means of the feature analysis of Section 5.4, we assessed a rather low redundancy in our model. Thus, we may conclude that there is a statistical dependence between groups of linguistic features of task descriptions and response rates: *to a significant degree one knows the expected outcome of a test when knowing how it is verbally presented and vice versa and H1a cannot be falsified completely.* Because of the limited range of our study this interpretation is seemingly too bold. It is probably more valid to say that the way a task is verbally presented has a high impact on the expected outcome of student responses. According to Hypothesis 1b, *"The two language versions of the TUCE differ regarding the degree of this correlation, but coincide in show-ing it"*, this effect is observed for both English and German task descriptions. However, while both languages coincide with regard to this effect, they do so according to different scales (see Section 5.1). Hence, H1b was partly falsified. By Table 8 we know that only 23 out of 264 features were selected for charac-terizing texts of both languages. Most notably, feature F170[12] is a semantic one that predominates in selections starting from English texts. This observation possibly hints at a semantic difference between both languages *in the context of TUCE* (cf. Bisang in this volume). Further, F23 and F175 are features regarding the verb-related structure of texts that also dominated in selections related to English texts. This observation additionally hints on a systematic difference between both languages. In a nutshell: the statistical dependence is observed for task descriptions irrespective of the underlying language while the varia-tion according to which this effect is observed for these languages might be explainable by the affinity of certain features (*domain-specific economic terms* and *verb-related vocabulary structures*) for certain languages – this finding already relates to Hypothesis 4 (see below). Testing this assessment requires further research (see Section 7).

2. **Hypothesis 2:** *"Linguistic features that are correlating with rates of correct responses allow for classifying the task descriptions* in terms of the language in which they are written *(English and German)* and in terms of the *text type (i.e., question or response option) they manifest"*. In Section 5.3 we performed an experiment in text categorization by distinguishing texts written in different languages, texts of different text types and texts varying these two variables jointly. Our findings indicate that the analyzed linguistic features correlating with rate of correct responses (see Table 8) are informative in that they allow for

---

12   The average number of economic terms not including a general-language sense (ET2) per sentence in response options (see Table 2).

the first two of these classifications. In other words: *our feature model enables both assessing the targeted correlations while recognizing differences between languages on the one hand and text types on the other*. Further research is needed to consolidate this evaluation in terms of every single feature of Table 8. In any event, however, German and English texts are remarkably well separable when using the subset of features documented in Table 8, thus, H2 cannot be falsified.

3. **Hypothesis 3:** Our study did not provide much evidence in support of Hypothesis 3 (H3a: "*The dependency postulated in H1 is affected by students' academic year: the more advanced they are, the weaker the dependency*" and H3b: "*This effect should hold for both languages*"). Though we expected a correlation dampening effect the higher the academic year of test takers, we could not substantiate this effect in any respect. However, starting from an optimal feature model characterizing students of the 1st academic year, we found that to some degree the expected effect really occurs: at least regarding the 2nd academic year. Though this finding concerns a downgraded version of Hypothesis 3a, it nevertheless hints at a potential of further research into this direction. Further, since this assessment holds for both languages, we also address Hypothesis 3b to this minor degree. The reason for not having fully falsified the alternative of Hypothesis 3 is at least twofold: either Hypothesis 3 is not reflected by our data or our model is not expressive enough to provide enough evidence. Following the latter reading we aim at extending our linguistic model in future work in order to further study this putative dampening effect.

4. **Hypothesis 4:** H4a: "*The dependency postulated in H1 is affected by the* specialized economic terms used in certain test tasks: *the more domain-specific terms are used, the stronger the dependency*" and H4b: "*Effects of specialized economic terms per item differ across languages*". Though not having been studied in detail we nevertheless detected a difference across target languages regarding the effect of specialized economic terms. This relates in particular to Feature F170 calculating the *average number of economic terms (lacking a general-language meaning) per sentences in response options*. This feature is highly informative in the case of English texts when studying respective correlations (see above). 28 *semantic* features are documented in Table 8 that are selected by one of the optimization experiments of Section 5.1. Beyond feature F170, this also includes the features F81 and F82. Both of them consider average numbers of economic terms per sentence – but now in questions. Once more, these features are highly informative only with respect to English texts when trying to optimize distance correlations (see Table 8). Thus, we may conclude that the effect of using economic terms differs across languages in the

context of TUCE (Hypothesis 4b): the English data is more affected by these semantic, terminology-related features than the German data. In any event, distance correlation does not consider the direction of the statistical dependence. Further effort is needed to clarify this effect (see Section 7).

6.2   Limitations

The findings of this study should be interpreted with some limitations in mind. In regard to the manually annotated features, further differentiations might yield more meaningful results. In this study, for example, we did not differentiate the type and structure of quantitative data given in the test items. Further, more detailed analyses of numeracy and difficulty components can draw on a model of mathematical language (cf. also Wittum et al. in this volume). With regard to the economic terminology, the classification of single vs. multi-word terms and terminology with varying degrees of technicality and usage in general language prove difficult to differentiate - especially terminology that can be inferred from everyday experience vs. terminology known only through economics studies - and should be addressed in future studies based on a more detailed annotation scheme and corpus analyses.

The language versions differed in that one was the original test designed for assessing students in the US, the other was a translation and adaptation for assessing students in Germany, which was additionally meant to ensure cross-national comparability (e.g., Brückner et al. 2015a; Förster et al. 2015). The German adaptation of the TUCE was carried out by a team of translation experts, domain experts in economics education, and US and German test developers; and it was cognitively pretested (Zlatkin-Troitschanskaia et al. 2014). This reduces the likelihood of one particular personal style shaping the language of the tasks of the German version[13]; still, there are a number of possible factors that may influence the language characteristics of the test. Translation research suggests that translated texts can differ in their linguistic characteristics from non-translated texts (e.g., Baker 1996; Sireci et al. 2006). By virtue of a continuous reference of a translated text

---

13   Examination of the effects of editors on translations has started only recently in corpus-based translation research (Bisiada 2017). There are recommendations on how to select and train translators for the specific demands of translating psychometric instruments (see e.g., ITC 2016; Survey Research Center 2016). However, more comprehensive research on the effects of all parties influencing the phrasing of a test item, including expert team compositions and team decision-making, on the final product is still needed.

to a source text, a translator's training as language, a translator's strife to achieve acceptability of the text among the target audience, the communication maxims of the testing situation, as well as the specifics of the translation assignment, translated texts are hypothesized – and often empirically found (e.g., Hansen-Schirra et al. in this volume) – to display features differentiating them from non-translated texts. Such trends are discussed as translation universals (e.g., Baker 1996), including for instance normalization (preference for standard phrasings), shining through (of source-language structures in the target text), or explications. General translation tendencies are counter-balanced by area-specific translation guidelines and practices, such as the typical instruction to not alter syntactic complexity of questions and items, i.e., to not make them more readable than the original in order to preserve comparability (Mohler et al. 2016). Even though the validation findings provide support for functional and measurement equivalence between both language versions (Zlatkin-Troitschanskaia et al. 2014; Förster et al. 2015), it would be difficult to draw direct conclusions about effects of such fine-grained linguistic features as used in this study across the two language versions. Hence, our interpretation refers to within-country effects for two countries and comparison of quality of original and translation using this approach remains a further research.

Our quantitative model provides many starting points for extensions and replacements: This relates to more fine-grained features including syntactic words as well as to semantic features drawing on the specifics of the focal domain. To this end, in future work, we plan to build classifiers for fine-grained classifications of general language as well as for different layers of terminology in order to better predict the expected outcomes of students in the framework of TUCE as a function of the content of questions and their response options. This may foster the integration of educational measurement approaches on the one hand and computational linguistics on the other – the present work is a first effort into this direction.

7 Overall conclusions

To summarize the information we gained from the analyzed linguistic features: Among the 264 linguistic features analyzed, we repeatedly selected the best fitting ones for each year of studies, examining the distance correlations between their distribution and the distribution of correct and incorrect response options, and applying the feature set also to the other two years of studies. We also examined whether patterns of occurrence of linguistic features allowed us to predict the text type or language version where they occurred. This would indicate that the item texts are to a certain extent schematic in their language version – which, if generalizable, would set the basis for automatic recognition of text type and language versions. For each year of studies, the analyses showed correlations more than twice as high as values for other influence factors obtained with common correlation methods (i.e., up to 50%). Thus, item phrasing seems to be more related to student responses than anticipated.

Interpreting the practical meaning of correlations with very basic features in line with theory remains a challenge. For instance, what does it mean when correct student responses are correlated with adverbs? At this point, we would not be able to make straightforward recommendations to test developers to use more, less, or a certain amount or share of specific linguistic features (and gauging item versions to have a percentage of a given part-of-speech would make no sense in practice). Instead, linguistic theory offers tentative explanations of what larger patterns such features may indicate, which need to be integrated in relation to student responses. For instance, adverb use can be considered indicative of an ornate style of writing, to which various groups of students may respond in a given way (e.g., neutrally, biased, focused, etc.)[14]. Thus, follow-up studies which further substantiate effects should likely enable recommendations rather at the level of styles and tendencies which writers can consciously operationalize.

A second avenue explored in this paper is to start with linguistic features that are already assumed to have a certain theoretical relevance, i.e., semantic features, which however are also more complex and error-prone to identify and classify than more grammar-based categories. Hence, for semantic features, while measurement error increases due to judgment in manual annotation, interpretations of effects become easier. For instance, domain-specific terminology can easily be considered a linguistic feature that contributes to item difficulty and is meaningful to the assessed construct, i.e., understanding economic terminology can be considered part of economic knowledge. Calibrating for an optimum between theoretical interpretability and measurement error may be an important goal for future research.

The mathematical-quantitative terms analyzed point to a third perspective. These terms were easy to identify, and prior research offers a good basis for interpretation in terms of cognitive difficulty (Brückner 2017). Evaluation of cognitive properties by experts, for example, ratings of difficulty, is a routine part of test development (cf. AERA et al. 2014). In this study, we did not yet consider cognitive

---

14 A useful metaphor could be a given teaching style to different groups of students' respond differently; similarly, an assessment style can be conceived that shapes the communicative situation between respondent and item and specific parts therein interacting with students.

levels (cf. Zlatkin-Troitschanskaia et al. 2014) and their links with linguistic item features, but they will very likely be examined in follow-up studies.

Educational research offers various further topics to be examined. Prior knowledge is only one example. We know that prior knowledge at the beginning of studies plays an important role in knowledge acquisition over the further course of studies (e.g., Dochy et al. 2002). For instance, prior knowledge was found to be the strongest predictor of microeconomic knowledge in Germany and the United States (for a detailed analysis of the effects of prior knowledge on students' test results, see Brückner et al. 2015a).

Given that students interact with the items, studies on linguistic effects might also include a more differentiated or more objective assessment of students' language abilities in order to examine to what extent language proficiency or deficits affect students' responses to the test. For instance, Brückner et al. (2015a) indicate that students' native language had no substantial effect on the microeconomic knowledge score, but on the macroeconomic knowledge score in Germany and the US. Therefore, in follow-up studies, reading and listening comprehension should be assessed using a separate language test to objectively measure and analyze the language abilities of non-native speakers in both countries.

Information on differential item functioning depending on language features as well as detailed information on students' language proficiency should enable further differentiation of construct-relevant vs. irrelevant influences of language, and contribute to a better understanding of the interplay between domain-specific and generic knowledge and skills in assessment and learning.

Finally, we emphasize the importance of studies such as this integrating multiple disciplines and examining the linguistic underpinnings of test performance by closing with a broader argument on how this study contributes to understanding the fundamental connections between language and learning (as one of the focuses of the PLATO program, cf. Zlatkin-Troitschanskaia et al. in this volume) and what further connections we see with research in other disciplines.

As a concluding point, we offer some brief considerations on the wider implications of our study and its positioning with a special focus on linguistic relativity. In Section 1, we reviewed some findings and assumptions concerning the role of language in accounting for differences in (economic) tests results. These considerations do not aim at linguistic features (like word order, readability, number of parts of speech or morphological typology), but at individual languages (like English or German). As such, they are related to what has become known as the "Linguistic Relativity Hypothesis" (cf. Lucy 1997). The relativity argument runs as follows: Languages differ with respect to their morphological, syntactic and semantic features (cf. also Bisang in this volume). The meanings of words influence how we conceptualize what we talk about. Therefore, speakers using different language(s) *think* differently.

Reasoning along this line is known as *linguistic relativism* (roughly, thinking is influenced by language) or, even stronger, *linguistic determinism* (language unavoidably predefines how we think).[15] Based on theoretical and empirical reasons, it is generally assumed that a deterministic position cannot be maintained (cf. Davidson 1973/1974; Levinson 1997; Malt et al. 1999 and the review given by Wolff and Holmes 2011; also languages' "hidden complexity" (Bisang 2015) may be considered as counter evidence). However, there is evidence from the cognitive sciences that linguistic relativism may be operative at the interface of embodied mental representations between linguistic and non-linguistic processing (e.g., Papafragou et al. 2008; Frank et al. 2008; Lupyan et al. 2007). Roughly, languages provide containers (linguistic processing) that may interfere with organizing sensations and habits (non-linguistic processing). Interference, notably, may happen both ways, facilitating as well as competing (Wolff and Holmes 2011) and becomes apparent mainly in processing speed.

Understanding and solving assessment tasks surely are cognitive achievements. Therefore, it cannot be ruled out in advance that certain test tasks may be processed faster in a certain language (by a native speaker of that language). Evidence for an effect of individual languages in our study can only be assessed indirectly, assuming that faster processing also leads to "better" processing in the sense that the task in question can be solved more correctly (for findings from cognitive validation of the TUCE see Brückner 2017). In order to address these issues, further studies could examine non-linguistic processing in learning more directly, for example, using eye-tracking or neurophysiological methods. This involves identifying language differences that can be described and operationalized for measurement with these methods (cf. Bisang in this volume).

Following the view that language is primarily for communication rather than for thinking (Clark 1996), acquaintance with technical vocabulary and with domain-specific knowledge (i.e., common ground-based language of a sub-community) will very likely result in a better mastery of using language in domain-specific learning. Remarkably, in our study, more advanced students performed better on the economics knowledge test than beginning students, but the correlation between students' test results and item language features did not become weaker with years of studies. That is, even though, domain-specific knowledge and terminology

---

15   These hypotheses are bound up with linguistic field work of Edward Sapir and Benjamin Lee Whorf (see, e.g., Kay and Kempton 1984).

are assumed to be acquired over the course of studies, they had a similar effect towards the end of studies as in the beginning (e.g., Happ et al. 2016).

To our knowledge, an integrative multidisciplinary approach such as the one presented in this study has not been taken before. It addresses a number of specific difficulties that have prevented quantitative analyses of test language and learning outcomes in the past. Thus, our study paves the way for future more innovative research with more explanatory power along the avenues outlined above to approximate such complex and yet fundamental influences on learning.

Bibliography

AERA (American Educational Research Association), APA (American Psychological Association), & NCME (National Council on Measurement in Education (2014). *Standards for educational and psychological testing.* Washington, DC: American Educational Research Association.

Alexander, P. A. (2003). The Development of Expertise: The Journey from Acclimation to Proficiency. *Educational Researcher, 32*(8), 10–14.

Altmann, G. (1988). *Wiederholungen in Texten.* Bochum: Brockmeyer.

Anderson, L. W., & Krathwohl, D. R. (Eds.) (2001). *A Taxonomy for Learning, Teaching, and Assessing: A revision of Bloom's taxonomy of educational objectives.* New York: Longman.

Arffman, I. (2010). Equivalence of Translations in International Reading Literacy Studies. *Scandinavian Journal of Educational Research, 54*(1), 37–59.

Avenia-Tapper, B., & Llosa, L. (2015). Construct Relevant or Irrelevant? The Role of Linguistic Complexity in the Assessment of English Language Learners' Science Knowledge. *Journal for Educational Assessment, 20*(2), 95–111.

Baker, M. (1996). Corpus-based translation studies: The challenges that lie ahead. In H. Somers (Ed.), *Terminology, LSP and Translation. Studies in Language Engineering in Honour of Juan C. Sager* (pp. 175–186). Amsterdam & Philadelphia: John Benjamins.

Bär, D., Biemann, C., Gurevych, I., & Zesch. T. (2012). UKP: computing semantic textual similarity by combining multiple content similarity measures. In *Proceedings of the 1st Joint Conference on Lexical and Computational Semantics* (pp. 435-440). Association for Computational Linguistics.

Biber, D. (1995). *Dimensions of Register Variation: A Cross-Linguistic Comparison.* Cambridge: Cambridge University Press.

Bisang, W. (2015). Hidden complexity–the neglected side of complexity and its implications. *Linguistics Vanguard, 1*(1), 179. doi: https://doi.org/10.1515/lingvan-2014-1014

Bisiada, M. (2017). Translation and editing: a study of editorial treatment of nominalisations in draft translations. *Perspectives,* 1–15. doi:10.1080/0907676X.2017.1290121

Bloom, B. S., Englehart, M. B., Furst, E. J., Hill, W. H. & Krathwohl, D. R. (Eds.) (1956). *Taxonomy of educational objectives, the classification of educational goals–Handbook I: Cognitive Domain.* New York: McKay.

Brückner, S. (2017). *Prozessbezogene Validierung anhand von mentalen Operationen bei der Bearbeitung wirtschaftswissenschaftlicher Testaufgaben.* Landau: Empirische Pädagogik.

Brückner, S., Förster, M., Zlatkin-Troitschanskaia, O., & Walstad, W. B. (2015a). Effects of prior economic education, native language, and gender on economic knowledge of first-year students in higher education. a comparative study between Germany and the USA. *Studies in Higher Education, 40*(3), 437–453.

Brückner, S., Förster, M., Zlatkin-Troitschanskaia, O., Happ, R., Walstad, W. B., Yamaoka, M., & Asano, T. (2015b). Gender Effects in Assessment of Economic Knowledge and Understanding: Differences among Undergraduate Business and Economics Students in Germany, Japan, and the United States. *Peabody Journal of Education, 90*(4), 503–518.

Bühner, M., & Pargent, F. (2017). *Gute Items, schlechte Items bei der Messung von Persönlichkeit. Auch schlechte Items funktionieren prima. [Good items, bad items. bad items work fine, as well.].* Presented at the Conference of the German Society for Empirical Educational Research (GEBF).

Chang, C.-C., & Lin, C.-J. (2001). LIBSVM: a library for support vector machines. *ACM Transactions on Intelligent Systems and Technology (TIST), 2*(3), 1–27.

Clark, H. H. (1996). Communities, commonalities, and communication. In J. Gumperz & S. Levinson (Eds.), *Rethinking linguistic relativity* (pp. 324–355). Cambridge: Cambridge University Press.

Council for Economic Education (CEE) (2010). *Voluntary National Content Standards in Economics.* (2nd ed.) Retrieved from http://councilforeconed.org/wp/wp-content/uploads/2012/03/voluntary-national-content-standards-2010.pdf

Crossley, S., & Kostyuk, V. (2017, June). Letting the Genie Out of the Lamp: Using Natural Language Processing Tools to Predict Math Performance. *In International Conference on Language, Data and Knowledge* (pp. 330–342). Springer, Cham.

Davidson, D. (1973/1974). On the very idea of a conceptual scheme. *Proceedings and Addresses of the American Philosophical Association, 47,* 5–20.

Davies, P., Mangan, J., & Telhaj, S. (2005). Bold, reckless and adaptable? Explaining gender differences in economic thinking and attitudes. *British Educational Research Journal, 31*(1), 29–48.

Dept, S., Ferrari, A., & Halleux, B. (2017). Translation and Cultural Appropriateness of Survey Material in Large-Scale Assessments. In P. Lietz, J. C. Cresswell, K. F. Rust & R. J. Adams (Eds.), *Implementation of Large-Scale Education Assessments* (pp. 168–192). Wiley.

Dochy, F., De Rijdt, C., & Dyck, W. (2002). Cognitive prerequisites and learning: How far have we progressed since Bloom? Implications for educational practice and teaching. *Active learning in higher education, 3*(3), 265-284.

Ericsson, K. A. (2008). Deliberate practice and acquisition of expert performance: a general overview. *Academic Emergency Medicine, 15*(11), 988–994. doi:10.1111/j.1553-2712.2008.00227.x. PMID: 18778378.

Förster, M., Zlatkin-Troitschanskaia, O., Brückner, S., Happ, R., Hambleton, R. K., Walstad, W. B., Asano, T., & Yamaoka, M. (2015). Validating test score interpretations by comparing the results of students from the United States, Japan and Germany on a test of economic knowledge in higher education. *Zeitschrift für Psychologie, 223*(1), 14–23.

Frank, M. C., Everett, D. L., Fedorenko, E., & Gibson, E. (2008). Number as a cognitive technology: Evidence from Pirahã language and cognition. *Cognition, 108*(3), 819–824.

Gentner, D., & Goldin-Meadow, S. (Eds.) (2003). *Language in mind: Advances in the study of language and thought*. Cambridge, London: MIT Press.

Gleitman, L., & Papafragou, A. (2005). Language and thought. In K. J. Holyoak & R. G. Morrison (Eds.), *Cambridge handbook of thinking and reasoning* (pp. 633–661). Cambridge: Cambridge University Press.

Hall, M., Frank, E., Holmes, G., Pfahringer, B., Reutemann, P., & Witten, I. H. (2009). The WEKA data mining software: an update. *SIGKDD Explorations Newsletter, 11*(1), 10–18.

Hambleton, R. K. (2005). Issues, designs, and technical guidelines for adapting tests into multiple languages and cultures. In R. K. Hambleton, P. Merenda & C. Spielberger (Eds.), *Adapting educational and psychological tests for cross-cultural assessment* (pp. 3–38). Mahwah, NJ: Lawrence Erlbaum.

Happ, R., Zlatkin-Troitschanskaia, O., & Schmidt, S. (2016). An Analysis of Economic Learning Among Undergraduates in Introductory Economics Courses in Germany. *Journal of Economic Education, 47*(4), 300–310. doi:10.1080/00220485.2016.1213686

Harkness, J., Vijver, van de F. J. R., & Mohler, P. Ph. (Eds.) (2003). *Cross-Cultural Survey Methods*. New York: Wiley.

Harkness, J. (2011). *Guidelines for best practice in cross-cultural surveys*. Survey Research Center, Institute for Social Research, University of Michigan.

Hatano, G. (1982). Learning to add and subtract: A Japanese perspective. In: T.P Carpenter, J. M. Moser & T. A. Romberg (Eds.), *Addition and subtraction: A cognitive perspective* (pp. 211–223). Hillsdale, NJ: Erlbaum Associates.

Hemati, W., Uslu, T., & Mehler, A. (2016). TextImager: a distributed UIMA-based system for NLP. *Proceedings of the COLING 2016, the 26th International Conference on Computational Linguistics: System Demonstrations, Osaka, Japan, 59–63*.

Holz-Mänttäri, J. (Hrsg.). (1988). *Translationstheorie - Grundlagen und Standorte*. (1st ed.). Finnland: University of Tampere.

International Test Commission (ITC). (2005). *International Guidelines on Test Adaptation*. [www.InTestCom.org]

International Test Commission (ITC). (2016). *The ITC Guidelines for Translating and Adapting Tests* (2nd ed.). [www.InTestCom.org]

Islam, Z., & Mehler, A. (2013). Automatic readability classification of crowd-sourced data based on linguistic and information-theoretic features. *Proceedings of the 14th International Conference on Intelligent Text Processing and Computational Linguistics* (CICLing 2013).

Janich, N. (1998). *Fachliche Information und inszenierte Wissenschaft: Fachlichkeitskonzepte in der Wirtschaftswerbung. [Technical information and staged science. Concepts of specialism in business advertisement.]* (Forum für Fachsprachen-Forschung, vol. 48). Tübingen: Gunter Narr Verlag.

Joachims, T. (2002). *Learning to classify text using support vector machines*. Boston: Kluwer.

Joulin, A., Grave, E., Bojanowski, P., & Mikolov, T. (2016). Bag of tricks for efficient text classification. *Proceedings of the 15th Conference of the European Chapter of the Association for Computational Linguistics: Vol. 2, Short Papers*, (pp. 427–431). Valencia: Association for Computational Linguistics.

Kay, P., & Kempton, W. (1984). What is the Sapir-Whorf Hypothesis? *American Anthropologist, 86*(1), 65–79.

Kosorok, M. R. (2009). On Brownian distance covariance and high dimensional data. *The annals of applied statistics, 3*(4), 1266–1269.

Levinson, S. C. (1997). From outer to inner space: linguistic categories and non-linguistic thinking. In J. Nuyts & E. Pederson (Eds.), *Language and conceptualization* (pp. 13–45).

Liiv, H., & Tuldava, J. (1993). On classifying texts. In L. Hrebíček & G. Altmann (Eds.), *Quantitative text analysis: Quantitative linguistics* (Vol. 52, pp. 253–262). Trier: Wissenschaftlicher Verlag Trier.

Lucy, J. A. (1992). *Language diversity and thought: A reformulation of the linguistic relativity hypothesis.* Cambridge: Cambridge University Press.

Lucy, J. A. (1997). The linguistics of "color". In C. Hardin & L. Maffi (Eds.), *Color Categories in Thought and Language* (pp. 320–346). Cambridge: Cambridge University Press.

Lupyan, G., Rakison, D. H., & McClelland, J. L. (2007). Language is not just for talking: Redundant labels facilitate learning of novel categories. *Psychological science, 18*(12), 1077–1083.

MacGregor, M., & Price, E. (1999). An exploration of aspects of language proficiency and algebra learning. *Journal for Research in Mathematics Education, 30*(4) 449-467.

Malt, B. C., Sloman, S. A., Gennari, S., Shi, M., & Wang, Y. (1999). Knowing versus naming: Similarity and the linguistic categorization of artifacts. *Journal of Memory and Language, 40*(2), 230–262.

Mankiw, N. G., & Taylor, M. P. (2010). Economics (Special ed. with coverage of the world financial crisis). London: Thomson.

Martin, J. (2013). Differences between experts' and students' conceptual images of the mathematical structure of Taylor series convergence. *Educational Studies in Mathematics, 82*(2), 267–283. doi:10.1007/s10649-012-9425-7

Mehler, A. (2005). Eigenschaften der textuellen Einheiten und Systeme [Properties of Textual Units and Systems]. In R. Köhler, G. Altmann & R. G. Piotrowski (Eds.), *Quantitative Linguistik. Ein internationales Handbuch [Quantitative Linguistics. An International Handbook]* (pp. 325–348). Berlin/New York: De Gruyter.

Mehler, A., Sharp, S., & Santini, M. (Eds.). (2010). *Genres on the Web: Computational Models and Empirical Studies.* Dordrecht: Springer.

Mohler, P., Dorer, B., de Jong, J., & Hu, M. (2016). *Translation: Overview. Guidelines for Best Practice in Cross-Cultural Surveys.* MI: Survey Research Center, Institute for Social Research, University of Michigan.

Müller-Feldmeth, D., Held, U., Auer, P., Hansen, S., Hansen-Schirra, S., Maksymski, K., Wolfer, S., & Koniecny (2015). Investigating comprehensibility of German popular science writing. In K. Maksymski, S. Gutermuth, S. Hansen-Schirra (Eds.), *Translation and comprehensibility* (p. 227-261). Berlin: Frank & Timme.

Newman, M. E. J. (2003). The structure and function of complex networks. *SIAM Review, 45*, 167–256.

Nisbett, R. E., & Masuda, T. (2003). Culture and point of view. *Proceedings of the National Academy of Sciences of the United States of America, 100*(19), 11163–11170. doi:10.1073/pnas.1934527100

Nisbett, R., Peng, K., Choi, I., & Norenzayan, A. (2001). Culture and Systems of Tought: Holistic Versus Analytic Cognition. *Psychological Review, 108*(2), 291–310.

Paas, F., Renkl, A., & Sweller, J. (2003). Cognitive load theory and instructional design: Recent developments. *Educational psychologist, 38*(1), 1–4.

Papafragou, A., Hulbert, J., & Trueswell, J. (2008). Does language guide event perception? Evidence from eye movements. *Cognition, 108*(1), 155–184.

Parker, K. (2006). The effect of students characteristics on achievement in introductory microeconomics in South Africa. *South African Journal of Economics, 74*(1), 137–149.

Pieper, U. (1975). Differenzierung von Texten nach numerischen Kriterien. *Folia Linguistica, VII,* 61–113.

Plass, J. L., Moreno, R., & Brünken, R. (2010). *Cognitive load theory.* Cambridge University Press.

Rüede, C. (2015). *Strukturierungen von Termen und Gleichungen: Theorie und Empirie des Gebrauchs algebraischer Zeichen durch Experten und Novizen.* Wiesbaden: Springer Fachmedien.

Samuelson, P. A., & Nordhaus, W. D. (2010). *Economics* (19th ed.). Boston: McGraw-Hill.

Sebastiani, F. (2002). Machine learning in automated text categorization. *ACM Computing Surveys, 34*(1), 1–47.

Shavelson, R. J., Marino, J., Zlatkin-Troitschanskaia, O., & Schmidt, S. (in press). Reflections on the Assessment of Quantitative Reasoning. In B. L. Madison & L. A. Steen (Eds.), *Calculation vs. context: Quantitative literacy and its implications for teacher education* (2nd ed.). Washington, DC: Mathematical Association of America.

Siegfried, J., Krueger, A., Collins, S., Frank, R., McGoldrick, K., MacDonald, R., Taylor, J., & Vredeveld, G. (2010). *Voluntary national content standards in economics* (2nd ed.) New York: Council for Economic Education.

Sireci, S. G., Yang, Y., Harter, J., & Ehrlich, E. J. (2006). Evaluating guidelines for test adaptations: A methodological analysis of translation quality. *Journal of Cross-Cultural Psychology, 37*(5), 557–567.

Snow, C. (2002). *Reading for Understanding: Toward an R&D Program in Reading Comprehension.* Santa Monica: RAND Corporation. Retrieved from http://ebookcentral.proquest.com/lib/umainz/detail.action?docID=227837

Solano-Flores, G., Backhoff, E., & Contreras-Niño, L. A. (2009). Theory of test translation error. *International Journal of Testing, 9*(2), 78–91.

Solano-Flores, G., Contreras-Niño, L., & Backhoff-Escudero, E. (2006). Translation and adaptation of tests: lessons learned and recommendations for countries participating in TIMSS, PISA and other international comparisons. *Revista electrónica de investigación educativa, 8*(2).

Stamatatos, E. (2011). Plagiarism Detection Using Stopword n-grams. *Journal of the American Society for Information Science and Technology, 62*(12), 2512–2527.

Stein, B., Lipka, N., & Prettenhofer, P. (2011). Intrinsic plagiarism analysis. *Language Resources and Evaluation, 45,* 63–82.

Sweller, J., Ayres, P., & Kalyuga, S. (2011). *Cognitive Load Theory. Explorations in the Learning Sciences, Instructional Systems and Performance Technologies* (Vol. 1.). New York, NY: Springer Science+Business Media LLC. doi:10.1007/978-1-4419-8126-4

Toutanova, K., Klein, D., Manning, C. D., & Singer, Y. (2003). Feature-rich part-of-speech tagging with a cyclic dependency network. *Proceedings of the 2003 Conference of the North American Chapter of the Association for Computational Linguistics on Human Language Technology: Vol. 1,* (pp. 173–180). Edmonton, Canada.

Tremblay, K., Lalancette, D., & Roseveare, D. (2013). *Assessment of Higher Education Learning Outcomes. AHELO Feasibility Study Report – Volume 2. Data analysis and national experiences.* Paris: OECD Publishing.

Villar, A. (2009). *Agreement answer scale design for multilingual surveys: Effects of translation-related changes in verbal labels on response styles and response distributions.* (Doctoral dissertation). The University of Nebraska-Lincoln.

Venkatraman, V., Siong, S. C., Chee, M. W., & Ansari D. (2006). Effect of Language Switching on Arithmetic: A Bilingual fMRI Study. *Journal of Cognitive Neuroscience, 18*(1), 64–74.

Vukovic, R. K., & Lesaux, N. K. (2013). The relationship between linguistic skills and arithmetic knowledge. *Learning and Individual Differences, 23,* 87–91.

Walstad, W. B., Watts, M. W., & Rebeck, K. (2007). *Test of understanding in college economics* (4ᵗʰ ed., Examiner's manual). New York: Council for Economic Education.

Wang, J., & Goldschmidt, P. (1999). Opportunity to learn, language proficiency, and immigrant status effects on mathematics achievement. *The Journal of Educational Research, 93*(2), 101–111.

Willighagen, E., Ehrhart, F., Rieswijk, L., Jeliazkova, N., Evelo, C. T. A., Farcal, L., Hardy, B., & Sarimveis, H. (2015). eNanoMapper updates and its collaborations with the community. *NanoSafety Cluster Newsletter, 6,* 14-17.

Wol, P., & Holmes, K. J. (2011). Linguistic relativity. *Wiley Interdisciplinary Reviews: Cognitive Science, 2*(3), 253–265.

Yamaoka, M., Walstad, W. B., Watts, M. W., Asano, T., & Abe, S. (2010). *Comparative studies on economic education in Asia-Pacific region.* Tokyo, Japan: Shumpusha Publishing.

Zlatkin-Troitschanskaia, O., Förster, M., Brückner, S., & Happ, R. (2014). Insights from a German assessment of business and economics competence. In H. Coates (Ed.), *Higher Education Learning Outcomes Assessment –International Perspectives* (pp. 175–197). Frankfurt am Main: Peter Lang.

Zlatkin-Troitschanskaia, O., Brückner, S., Schmidt, S., & Förster, M. (2016a). Messung ökonomischen Fachwissens bei Studierenden in Deutschland und den USA - Eine mehrebenenanalytische Betrachtung der hochschulinstitutionellen und individuellen Einflussfaktoren. *Unterrichtswissenschaft, 44*(1), 73–88.

Zlatkin-Troitschanskaia, O., Pant, H. A., Kuhn, C., Toepper, M., & Lautenbach, C. (2016b). *Messung akademisch vermittelter Kompetenzen von Studierenden und Hochschulabsolventen. Ein Überblick zum nationalen und internationalen Forschungsstand.* Wiesbaden: Springer VS.

Zlatkin-Troitschanskaia, O., Schmidt, S., Brückner, S., Förster, M., Yamaoka, M., & Asano, T. (2016c). Macroeconomic knowledge of higher education students in Germany and Japan – a multilevel analysis of contextual and personal effects. *Assessment & Evaluation in Higher Education, 41*(5), 787–801.

Zlatkin-Troitschanskaia, O., Pant, H. A., Lautenbach, C., Molerov, D., Toepper, M., & Brückner, S. (2017). *Modeling and Measuring Competencies in Higher Education: Approaches to Challenges in Higher Education Policy and Practice.* Wiesbaden: Springer VS.

Zlatkin-Troitschanskaia, O., Happ, R., Toepper, M., Nell-Müller, S., Brandt, S., Suter, R., & Rampelt, F. (in press). Opportunities for Refugees to Obtain and Succeed in Higher Education – Initial Empirical Insights. *Journal Refugee Review.*

PART III
Learning as Interaction and Communication Processes in Formal and Informal Learning Environments

Media Effects on Positive and Negative Learning

Marcus Maurer, Oliver Quiring, and Christian Schemer

Abstract

While educational science in the past mainly focused on students' formal or intentional learning from courses, textbooks, or online tutorials in university contexts, communication science usually deals with ordinary citizens' informal or unintentional learning from the mass media in everyday life. One of the general aims of the PLATO project is to bring these research traditions together. Therefore, this paper sums up research on media effects on positive and negative learning recently conducted; our studies show that media coverage is often biased and news media, therefore, contribute to negative as well as positive learning. Which kind of learning occurs, heavily depends on the way information is presented.

Keywords

News Media; Social Media; Media Effects; Political Communication; Knowledge; Media Content; Media Bias; Media Exposure; Content Analysis; Survey; Experiment; Misinformation.

1   Introduction

Learning is in the focus of a variety of scientific disciplines. While education-al science in the past mainly focused on student's formal or intentional learning from courses, textbooks, or online tutorials in university contexts, communication science usually deals with ordinary citizens' informal or unintentional learning from the mass media in everyday life. One of the general aims of the PLATO project is to bring these research traditions together (see Zlatkin-Troitschanskaia et al. 2017). This seems to be fruitful for at least two reasons: First, during formal learning students expose themselves to various non-academic sources including social media, online encyclopedias, and many more. Second, during their everyday media reception students are exposed to various online and offline news media that contain information on socially relevant issues like politics, manmade and technological risks, or the economy. As many academic disciplines are concerned with these issues, media effects on student's learning are quite likely (cf. also Koretz in this volume).

In democracies, mass media function as an important institution to provide information about societal sub-systems, such as the political system, the economy and many other domains (McQuail 2005). Mass media provide information that gives citizens orientation and helps them making up their mind in various societal domains. For instance, political news may give people orientation during election times by presenting and commenting on policy programs of different political parties and candidates (Reinemann et al. 2013). News about health is likely to improve health literacy in the public and can result in better health care (Schäfer et al. 2015). Additionally, news media publish information on stock markets or the economy as a whole that can enhance economic literacy in the public and can facility financial and economic decision making (Mitchell and Mulherin 1994; Quiring et al. 2013). Finally, even in academia students are likely to benefit from the availability of free information in traditional media and media platforms on the web. In this sense, mass media provide information that can enable positive learning, i.e., desirable outcomes, for example, informed votes, health care choices, or financial decision.

However, two problems arise nowadays that can impede positive learning out-comes. First, the abundance of information can result in information and commu-nication overload for consumers. This raises the question for information seekers where to find information that is relevant and suitable for their personal situation and how they can escape from distracting information. Second, information is often not unbiased (D'Alessio and Allen 2000). Among the sources of bias are public relation efforts of organized interests of economic or political actors, the general tendency of an outlet, or journalists who pursue their own interest. Information retrieved from search engines or social media can be biased by algorithmic selection (Epstein and Robertson 2015). The increasing proliferation of fake news, rumors, and conspiracy theories online is another issue that can seriously distort the news that consumers encounter (Schultz et al. 2017). Moreover, incivil online user comments more and more challenge the neutral presentation of facts (e.g., Ziegele et al. 2017). Such influences that undermine knowledge gain, distract from learning, or result in learning misinformation is considered negative learning (cf. Zlatkin-Troitschanskaia et al. 2017).

The present paper focuses on three aspects related to media effects on positive and negative learning: First, we demonstrate which features on the supply side of information affect positive and negative learning from the media. Second, we focus on what news sources people use to get information about politics, science, and the economy. Third, we present evidence for media effects on positive and negative learning.

2   Theoretical background

The theories used to explain and predict learning from media information differ with respect to the locus of explanation. Economic theories (e.g., news diffusion) and news selection theories (e.g., news value theory) help explain the *supply* of media information. For example, news value theory (Galtung and Ruge 1965) assumes that certain criteria like negativity, personalization, and conflict (so-called news factors) increase the newsworthiness of an event. Therefore, journalists tend to over-report negative and personalized events such as economic crises, natural catastrophes, and statements by politicians criticizing their opponents, which frequently causes biases in media content. Although journalists are expected to follow the norm of objective reporting, news media differ in their editorial lines (more or less conservative versus more or less liberal). Therefore, news stories are also assumed to show a more or less obvious ideological bias (news bias theory). Consequently, the presentation of the same events in different news media often heavily differs with respect to its slant.

Studies on information based *media use* are theoretically grounded in theories of media selection, for example, uses and gratifications approach (Rubin 2002), selective exposure (Frey 1986), or most recently fragmentation theory (Sunstein 2001). These theories assume that citizens more or less actively search for media content that either helps them to satisfy their needs (e.g., information, entertainment, or escapism) or helps them to confirm their already existing attitudes. Especially the tendency to confirm already existing attitudes may result in a largely fragmented society: instead of being open for new arguments many citizens are captured in so-called echo chambers in which they only expose themselves to information from likeminded others. Given the well-known editorial lines of established news media (see above) and the various even more biased new online sources discussing socially relevant issues (e.g., websites of interest groups, social media, and blogs) it seems to get more and more easy to avoid any information challenging already existing worldviews.

In order to explain *learning from the mass media*, two different research traditions can be distinguished (Maurer and Oschatz 2016): First, theories such as knowledge gap (Tichenor et al. 1970) and digital divide (Norris 2001) are based on traditional learning theory. They try to explain citizens' factual knowledge of political or scientific issues by their media exposure and a variety of social variables like education, gender, or age. Second, information processing models (Lang 2000) and persuasion models (Chaiken and Trope 1999) are rather focused on the role of motivational processes that guide individual information processing. They try to explain why different people often process, understand, and remember the same given media content quite differently.

3   Methods and data

In order to study media effects on positive and negative learning communication scholars can apply different methods. The study of *supply side*, for example, diversity or quality of news information, is commonly done based on (qualitative or quantitative) content analysis using human coders or automated coding of a corpus of news sampled from a given population of news (Krippendorff 2004). Exposure to information, for example, news is assessed in public opinion surveys in which news consumers explicitly report on their media use habits such as importance of media outlets or frequency of use (Slater 2004). News exposure is also gauged with tracking data, for example, log file and eye-tracking analyses of reading behavior on websites. Media effects research relies on observational data obtained in cross-sectional or panel surveys on the one hand and experimental studies on the other (Potter 2012). In survey studies, representative poll data is combined with data from content analyses to measure the effects of media content on the individual or aggregate level. In experimental studies, researchers vary the amount of information, the features of presentation, or the context in which information is conveyed in order to test for different effects.

The aim of this paper is to give an overview about the recent research on positive and negative learning. The paper presents data from various studies recently conducted by the three authors using all of the above-mentioned methods. It includes (I) content analyses on the presentation of party's issue stances in elections, the economic situation, and climate change in German news media, (II) a content analysis of user comments on news websites and Facebook, (III) experimental research on the effects of Facebook use on knowledge acquisition, (IV) survey data on the effects of media exposure on the belief in conspiracy theories, (V) eye-tracking and panel survey data on the effects of media content on knowledge gain about climate change, and (VI) panel survey data on the effects of misinformation in televised debates.

4 Findings

4.1 Supply of information

Various content analyses show that traditional news media do not provide exhaustive and unbiased information. Instead, they lay emphasis on negative events, exaggerate problems and rather seldom explain causes and effects of these problems. First, this holds true for media information on politics: comparing media presentation of political party programs in the 2005 German national election to the original programs, Maurer (2009) found that in leading German news media only about 25 percent of all issue stances have been mentioned at least once in a period of twelve weeks before the election. Instead of providing full information about party's issue stances, the news media focused on a few election pledges that were especially controversial. Second, it holds true for media information about science. When comparing media information about the recent IPCC reports on climate change with the original reports, various studies (Haßler et al. 2014; Maurer 2011) found that German news media tend to portray scientific findings as certain catastrophes that the original report presented as uncertain at least to some extent. Third, it holds true for media information about the economy (Geiß et al. 2016; Quiring 2003). When comparing German media reports on unemployment with official statistics on the unemployment rate during the 1990s, it becomes obvious that an increase in the number of people being unemployed sometimes boosts media reports on unemployment, while media sometimes completely fail to accurately present the unemployment rate (Figure 1).

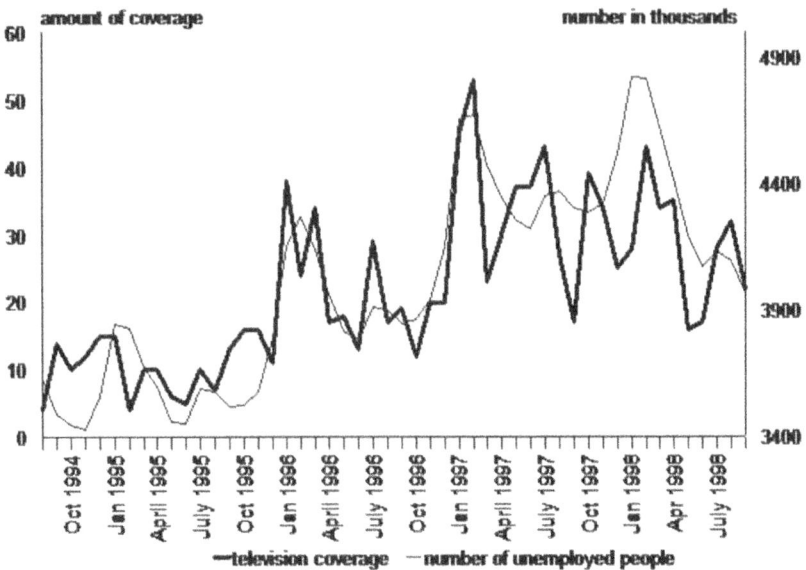

Fig. 1 Media reports on unemployment and unemployment rate in Germany, 1994-1998
Source: Quiring (2003, p. 11)

Nevertheless, the coverage of these issues in social media is even less accurate, as it generally follows the same criteria of newsworthiness and citizens are not expected to follow the journalistic norm of objective reporting (Ziegele and Quiring 2013). The same holds true for political talk-shows and televised debates, where the audience is frequently misinformed by political actors on political and economic facts (Maurer and Reinemann 2006).

4.2 Use of information

Especially in Germany, traditional offline news media are still citizens' most relevant sources of information on politics (Reinemann et al. 2013) and science (Oschatz et al. 2015). Moreover, they are considered as more credible than alternative sources of information on the web (Schultz et al. 2017). As especially younger citizens frequently rely on online news media and social media, this may change in future probably leading to a further fragmentation of media use, as citizens tend to expose themselves to online news media that confirm their prior attitudes (cf. Koretz in this volume).

4.3 Media effects on learning

In general, traditional news media show moderate but nevertheless relevant effects on citizens' knowledge. This, for instance, holds true for political knowledge (Maurer 2008) and knowledge on climate change (Oschatz et al. 2017). For example, a two-wave panel survey before and after the release of the recent IPCC report on climate change found that the more information on the consequences of climate change citizens read in daily newspapers between the two panel waves, the more knowledge on the consequences of climate change they acquired. This held true even after controlling for various other factors influencing knowledge gain. No similar effects were found for television news and online media (Figure 2).

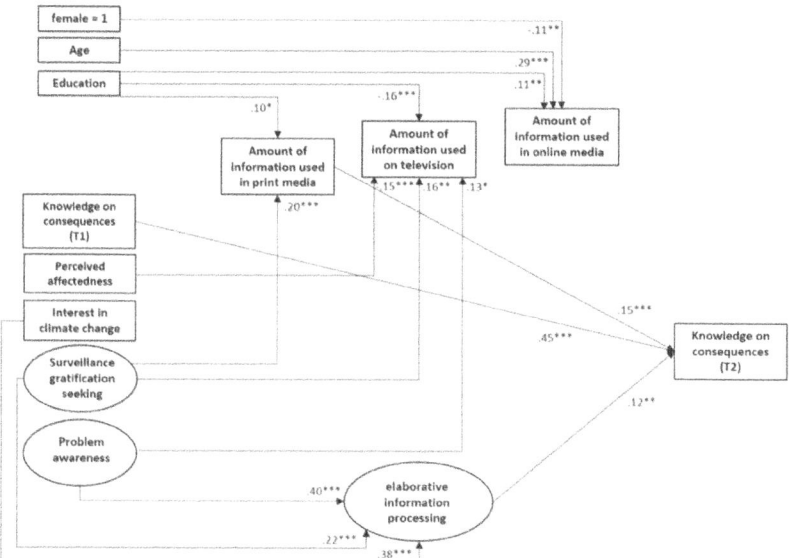

Fig. 2 Media effects on knowledge gain about the consequences of climate change
Source: Oschatz et al. (2017)

In an experimental study combining log-file, eye-tracking, and survey data, Haßler et al. (2017) found that also learning from online media can directly be traced back to the individual patterns of reading behavior. When being exposed to a news website on climate change including various website elements like a news article, user comments, videos, audio files, popularity cues, and hyperlinks, subjects spend by far the most time reading the central text article. Consequently, the time spend reading this article was by far the best predictor of knowledge gain, while receiving the same information from an online video did not contribute to knowledge acquisition.

Concerning the effects of alternative and social media, there is evidence that taming the information tide on social media just by scanning headlines and teasers of news results in the subjective experience of being informed. As a consequence of this feeling of knowing, news consumers are less likely to use in-depth news or background information as compared to news users that have a realistic perception of their own knowledge. For example, in an experimental study (Schäfer et al. 2017) subjects were introduced to read Facebook posts on various political issues. The more posts they read, the more the gap between their subjective and objective knowledge about these issues increased. Obviously, reading the posts increased their feeling of being informed, although they did not gain factual knowledge (Figure 3).

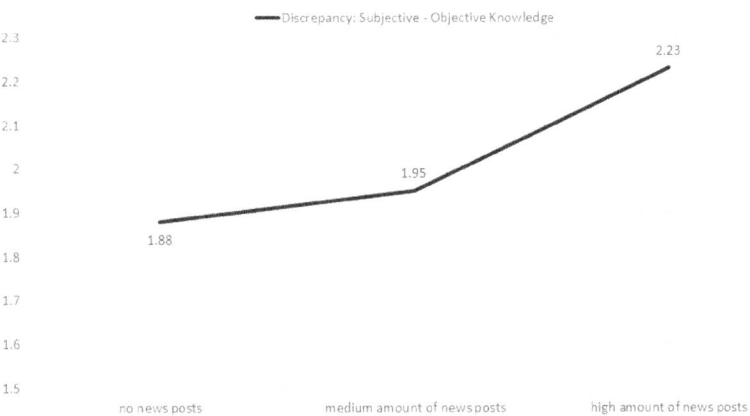

Fig. 3   Subjective and objective knowledge gain by reading Facebook posts
Source: Schäfer et al. (2017)

While social media do not seem to contribute much to factual knowledge gain, there is evidence that media exposure in some cases even leads to negative learning (cf. Oeberst et al. in this volume). First, a recent survey study shows that exposure to non-mainstream websites and blogs seems to increase the belief in conspiracy theories (Schultz et al. 2017). Second, a panel survey on the effects of a televised debate in the 2002 German national election shows that voters that are frequently misinformed by candidate statements on political issues – in this case the economic situation in Germany – tend to change their beliefs in the direction of the incorrect statements. Before the debate, a majority of the viewers was aware of the fact that the number of Germans being unemployed increased from 1998 to 2002. After the debate, a majority falsely believed that unemployment decreased (Maurer and Reinemann 2006). Finally, users of online media further bias the already existing biases in the coverage of traditional news media in their online comments of news stories because they tend to forget the source of the information and its credibility (Heinbach et al. 2017). Taken together, recent research from communication science shows that media coverage contributes to positive as well as negative learning. Which kind of learning occurs, heavily depends on the way information is presented.

5   Discussion and avenues for future research in PLATO

Mass media are by far the most important source of information on socially relevant issues like politics, science, and the economy. This holds true for traditional news media, but increasingly also for non-journalistic online sources like blogs, social media, and websites of interest groups. They can be a valuable source of knowledge gain but also mislead the public in case they provide biased or even wrong information. So far, most studies in media effects research focused on what the audience can learn from media information be it factual or fictional. These studies shed light on what features of information (e.g., overall supply, content, form, context) can facilitate positive learning. At the same time, research has been devoted to the features that impede positive learning or foster negative learning (e.g., abundance, distractors, bias). Much less scholarly work focused on the interference of knowledge gain in one domain, for example, news about politics or the economy, on knowledge in another domain such as academic knowledge about politics or economic knowledge. On the one hand, increases in the knowledge in one domain can certainly foster learning in another given that the former learning experience was a positive one. On the other hand, negative learning in one domain will unvoluntarily undermine knowledge acquisition in another one since information in the latter domain may contradict what learners learned in the first place. Therefore, especially integrating research on media effects on positive and negative learning in established models explaining students' knowledge gain (or loss) as a part of the PLATO program might be fruitful.

Bibliography

Chaiken, S., & Trope, Y. (Eds.). (1999). *Dual-process theories in social psychology*. New York: Guildford.

D'Alessio, D., & Allen, M. (2000). Media bias in presidential elections: A meta-analysis. *Journal of Communication*, *50*(4), 133–156.

Epstein, R., & Robertson, R. E. (2015). The search engine manipulation effect (SEME) and its possible impact on the outcomes of elections. *Proceedings of the National Academy of Sciences of the United States of America*, *112*(33), E4512–E4521.

Frey, D. (1986). Recent research on selective exposure to information. *Advances in Experimental Social Psychology*, *19*, 41–76.

Galtung, J., & Ruge, H. M. (1965). The Structure of Foreign News. The Presentation of the Congo, Cuba and Cyprus Crises in Four Norwegian Newspapers. *Journal of Peace Research*, *2*, 64–91.

Geiß, S., Weber, M., & Quiring, O. (2016). Frame competition after key events: A longitudinal study of media framing of economic policy after the Lehman Brothers bankruptcy 2008–2009. *International Journal of Public Opinion Research*, published online first 16 May 2016.

Haßler, J., Maurer, M., & Oschatz, C. (2014). Media logic and political logic online and offline: The case of climate change communication. *Journalism Practice*, *8*, 326–341.

Haßler, J., Maurer, M., & Oschatz, C. (2017). *Der Einfluss des Involvements und des Blickverhaltens auf den Wissenserwerb von Onlinenutzern*. Paper presented at the Jahrestagung der Fachgruppe Rezeptions- und Wirkungsforschung der DGPuK, Erfurt.

Heinbach, D., Ziegele, M., & Quiring, O. (2017). *Sleeper Effect from Below. Long-Term Effects of Source Credibility and User Comments on the Persuasiveness of News Articles*. Paper presented at the Annual Conference of the International Communication Association, San Diego, CA

Krippendorff, K. (2004). *Content analysis: An introduction to its methodology* (2 ed.). Thousand Oaks, CA: Sage.

Lang, A. (2000). The limited capacity model of mediated message processing. *Journal of Communication*, *50*(1), 46–70.

Maurer, M. (2008). Wissensvermittlung im Wahlkampf. Ursachen und Folgen politischen Wissenserwerbs im Bundestagswahlkampf 2005. In C. Wünsch, W. Früh & V. Gehrau (Eds.), *Integrative Modelle in der Rezeptions- und Wirkungsforschung: Dynamische und transaktionale Perspektiven* (pp. 65–80). München: Verlag Reinhard Fischer.

Maurer, M. (2009). Wissensvermittlung in der Mediendemokratie. Wie Medien und politische Akteure die Inhalte von Wahlprogrammen kommunizieren. *Politische Vierteljahresschrift*, Sonderheft 42, 151–173.

Maurer, M. (2011). Wie Journalisten mit Ungewissheit umgehen. Eine Untersuchung am Beispiel der Berichterstattung über die Folgen des Klimawandels. *Medien & Kommunikationswissenschaft, 59*, 60–74.

Maurer, M., & Oschatz, C. (2016). The influence of online media on political knowledge. In G. Vowe & P. Henn (Eds.), *Political communication in the online world* (pp. 73-87). New York: Routledge.

Maurer, M., & Reinemann, C. (2006). Learning versus knowing: Effects of misinformation in televised debates. *Communication Research, 33*, 489–506.

McQuail, D. (2005). *Mass Communication Theory* (5. ed.). London: Sage.

Mitchell, M. L., & Mulherin, H. J. (1994). The impact of public information on the stock market. *Journal of Finance, 49*(3), 923–950.

Norris, P. (2001). *Digital divide. Citizen engagement, information poverty, and the internet worldwide*. Cambridge: Cambridge University Press.

Oschatz, C., Maurer, M., & Haßler, J. (2015). Klimawandel im Netz. Die Digitalisierung von Informationskanälen und ihre Folgen für die Öffentlichkeit. In O. Hahn, R. Hohlfeld & T. Knieper (Eds.), *Digitale Öffentlichkeit* (pp. 149-163). Konstanz: UVK.

Oschatz, C., Maurer, M., & Haßler, J. (2017). *Media effects on the acquisition of knowledge on the consequences of climate change: A panel study*. Unpublished research paper.

Potter, W. J. (2012). *Media effects*. Thousand Oaks, CA: SAGE.

Quiring, O. (2003). Die Fernsehberichterstattung über die Arbeitslosigkeit und ihr Einfluss auf wahlrelevante Vorstellungen der Bevölkerung – eine Zeitreihenanalyse 1994-1998. *Publizistik, 48*, 1–24.

Quiring, O., Kepplinger, H. M., & Weber, M. (2013). *Lehman Brothers und die Folgen: Berichterstattung zu wirtschaftlichen Interventionen des Staates*. Wiesbaden: Springer VS.

Reinemann, C., Maurer, M., Zerback, T., & Jandura, O. (2013). *Die Spätentscheider. Medieneinflüsse auf kurzfristige Wahlentscheidungen*. Wiesbaden: Springer VS.

Rubin, A. M. (2002). The uses-and-gratification perspective of media effects. In J. Bryant & D. Zillmann (Eds.), *Media effects: Advances in theory and research* (pp. 525-548). Mahwah, NJ: Lawrence Erlbaum Associates.

Schäfer, M., Quiring, O., Rossmann, C., Hastall, M. R., & Baumann, E. (Eds.). (2015). *Gesundheitskommunikation im gesellschaftlichen Wandel*. Baden-Baden: Nomos.

Schäfer, S., Schmitt, J. B., & Schemer, C. (2017). *The more the better?! An experiment on the influence of political Facebook news posts on subjective knowledge*. Paper presented at the Annual Conference of the International Communication Association, San Diego, CA.

Schultz, T., Jackob, N., Ziegele, M., Quiring, O., & Schemer, C. (2017). Erosion des Vertrauens zwischen Medien und Publikum? *Media Perspektiven, 5*, 246-259.

Slater, M. D. (2004). Operationalizing and analyzing exposure: The foundation of media effects research. *Journalism & Mass Communication Quarterly, 81*(1), 168–183.

Sunstein, C. R. (2001). *Republic.com*. Princeton: Princeton University Press.

Tichenor, P., J., Donohue, G. A., & Olien, C. N. (1970). Mass media flow and differential growth in knowledge. *Public Opinion Quarterly, 34*(2), 159–170.

Ziegele, M., & Quiring, O. (2013). Conceptualizing Online Discussion Value. A Multidimensional Framework for Analyzing User Comments on Mass-Media Websites. *Annals of the International Communication Association, 37*, 125–153.

Ziegele, M., Weber, M., Quiring, O., & Breiner, T. (2017). The dynamics of online news discussions: Effects of news articles and reader comments on users' involvement, willingness to participate, and the civility of their contributions. *Information, Communication & Society*, published online first 12 May 2017.

Zlatkin-Troitschanskaia et al. (2017). *Positive Learning in the Age of Information*. Unpublished Manuscript, Draft Proposal Cluster of Excellence, Johannes Gutenberg University Mainz.

The Norm of Neutrality in Collaborative Knowledge Construction

A Comparison between Wikipedia and the Extreme Right-wing Metapedia

Aileen Oeberst, Jort de Vreeze, and Ulrike Cress

Abstract

Social media enabled collaboration at unprecedented levels. And while research points to the benefits of mass collaboration, it has also revealed challenges and problems. Here we explore biases in collaboratively constructed knowledge. To this end, we compared two online encyclopedias: Wikipedia and the extreme right-wing Metapedia. Both urge users to present topics from a neutral point of view. Using different measures we found that Metapedia articles (vs. Wikipedia articles) are significantly shorter, contain fewer references, contain relatively more anger- and anxiety-related words, rarely present more than one point of view in controversies, and often convey opinions – for inctance, by using pejorative language. Thus, norms might not be very effective in preventing biases – particularly if they largely remain a projection screen.

Keywords

Collaborative Knowledge Construction; Norms; Neutral Point of View; Wikipedia; Metapedia; Hostile Media Effect.

1   Research questions

Social media has revolutionized the production of web contents. With the development of the Web 2.0 Internet users have risen from passive perceivers to active producers of web contents. Moreover, it has enabled collaboration at unprecedented
levels. While research points to the benefits and potentials of mass collaboration
in order to collect and construct knowledge (e.g., Cress et al. 2016; Giles 2005;
Gowers and Nielsen 2009), it has also revealed challenges and problems (e.g., Holt
and Rinaldo 2014; Koretz in this volume, Lutz and Hofmann 2017; Pfeiffer 2015;
Maurer et al. in this volume, Zlatkin-Troitschanskaia et al. 2017). In this paper, we
explore biases in collaboratively created knowledge. We will focus on two online
encyclopedias that both aim at presenting *knowledge* (vs. opinions, as in discussion forums): Wikipedia and the extreme right-wing Metapedia. Both urge users
to present topics from a neutral point of view. We make use of different objective
measures to explore their success.

2   Theoretical background

Much research from psychology demonstrates that information processing is often
biased (e.g., Pohl 2017; Kunda 1990; Knauff in this volume). However, since collaborative knowledge construction differs substantially from the typical psychological lab studies, the generalizability of prior findings is limited (Nestler et al.
2017). Collaborative knowledge construction, for instance, takes place in a social
context (Cress and Kimmerle 2008), which operates on a number of implicit or
explicit norms in order to facilitate collaboration and to achieve the self-set goals
regarding contents. One of the frequently found norms is the demand for neutrality: Wikipedia, the flagship of mass collaboration, employs the Neutral Point of
View policy[1], but so do others, such as Citizendium[2] or the extreme right-wing
encyclopedia Metapedia[3]. Particularly the latter example raises the question as to
the effectiveness of such a neutrality norm (cf. Maurer et al. in this volume). In fact,
research has shown that perceptions of neutrality differ as a function of one's attitude. In their seminal study on the hostile media phenomenon, Vallone, Ross and
Lepper (1985) demonstrated that both, pro-Israeli and pro-Arab partisans rated
identical media contents as being biased against their side. Interestingly, this effect

---

1   https://en.wikipedia.org/wiki/Wikipedia:Neutral_point_of_view [May 15, 2017]

2   http://en.citizendium.org/wiki/CZ:Approval_Standards [May 15, 2017]

3   http://en.metapedia.org/wiki/Metapedia:Style_guide [May 15, 2017]

resulted not only from a biased perception of the contents, but was also based on a biased endorsement of fairness and objectivity. A meta-analysis suggested that the effect is robust and pronounced in people, who are more involved with the topic (Hansen and Kim 2011). It is plausible to assume that people, who contribute to an online encyclopedia *are* involved in the topic they write about. Thus, one may question the effectiveness of neutrality norms. In the present study, we explored this issue by comparing articles from Wikipedia and Metapedia.

3   Methods, materials and analyses

Altogether we selected 60 articles from the German Wikipedia and Metapedia, respectively (120 in total). In order to test for neutrality in more and less controversial topics, we chose articles from politics (foreign politics, migration politics, Europe, history, see Table 1) and natural sciences (biology, chemistry, information technology, mathematics; see Table 2). Thus, the study comprises a 2 (encyclopedia: Wikipedia, Metapedia) x 2 (discipline: politics, natural sciences) quasi-experimental design.

Tab. 1   Articles about political topics compared between Wikipedia and Metapedia

Topic	Article title in Wikipedia	Article title in Metapedia
Absolutism	Absolutismus	Absolutismus
Agenda 2010	Agenda 2010	Agenda 2010
Aristocracy	Aristokratie	Aristokratie
European migrant crisis since 2015	Flüchtlingskrise in Europa ab 2015	Asylantenflut in Europa 2015
Asylum law	Asylrecht (Deutschland)	Asylrecht
Residence law	Aufenthaltsgesetz	Aufenthaltsgesetz
Brexit	EU-Austritt des Vereinigten Königreichs	Brexit
German Democratic Republic	Deutsche Demokratische Republik	DDR
Democracy	Demokratie	Demokratie
Demonstration (protest)	Demonstration	Demonstration
Energy transition	Energiewende	Energiewende
World War I	Erster Weltkrieg	Erster Weltkrieg
Feminism	Feminismus	Feminismus
Gender	Gender	Geschlechtergleichschaltung

Tab. 1 (continued)

Topic	Article title in Wikipedia	Article title in Metapedia
Social Pension Programme	Gesetzliche Rentenversicherung (Deutschland)	Gesetzliche Rentenversicherung
Basic Law for the Federal Republic of Germany	Grundgesetz für die Bundesrepublik Deutschland	Grundgesetz Bundesrepublik Deutschland (Gründung der BRD)
Unemployment compensation	Arbeitslosengeld II	Hartz4
Treaty of Lisbon	Vertrag von Lissabon	Vertrag von Lissabon
German reunification	Deutsche Wiedervereinigung	Mauerfall
Multi-party system	Mehrparteiensystem	Mehrparteiensystem
Monarchy	Monarchie	Monarchie
NATO	NATO	NATO
Parliament	Parlament	Parlament
Republic	Republik	Republik
State (polity)	Staat	Staat
Referendum	Volksentscheid	Volksabstimmung
Ukraine-European Union Association Agreement	Assoziierungsakommen zwischen der Europäischen Union und der Ukraine	Assoziierungsabkommen zwischen der EU und Ukraine und den Niederlanden 2016
Weimar Republic	Weimarer Republik	Weimarer Republik
World War II	Zweiter Weltkrieg	Zweiter Weltkrieg

Tab. 2 Articles about topics from the natural sciences compared between Wikipedia and Metapedia

Topic	Article title in Wikipedia	Article title in Metapedia
Addition	Addition	Addition
Approximation	Approximation	Approximation
Atom	Atom	Atom
Binary number system	Dualsystem	Binärsystem
Biology	Biologie	Biologie
Bear	Bären	Bären
Chemistry	Chemie	Chemie
Differential equation	Differentialgleichung	Differentialgleichung
eCall	eCall	E-Call (Automobilnotrufsystem)

Tab. 2   (continued)

Topic	Article title in Wikipedia	Article title in Metapedia
Theory of relativity	Relativitätstheorie	Einsteinismus
Evolution	Evolutionstheorie	Evolutionstheorie
g-force	g-Kraft	G-Kraft
Light bulb	Glühlampe	Glühlampe
Invasive species	Biologische Invasion	Introduktion (Biologie)
Compact disc	CompactDisc	Kompaktscheibe
Magnet	Magnet	Magnet
Mathematics	Mathematik	Mathematik
Mobile phone	Mobiltelefon	Mobiltelefon
Motorcycle	Motorrad	Motorrad
Periodic table	Periodensystem	Periodensystem der Elemente
Photosynthesis	Photosynthese	Photosynthese
Physics	Physik	Physik
Speed of sound	Schallgeschwindigkeit	Schallgeschwindigkeit
Melting point	Schmelzpunkt	Schmelzpunkt
Boiling point	Siedepunkt	Siedepunkt
Vector	Vektor	Vektor
Mendelian inheritance	Mendelsche Regeln	Vererbungslehre
Viscosity	Viskosität	Viskosität
Internet	Internet	Weltnetz
Time	Zeit	Zeit

All articles were retrieved in July 2016 (Sargizi 2016) and analyzed in three different ways: First, we made use of automatic text analyses in order to obtain objective, quantitative measures of the emotionality of contents (with *LIWC*, Tauszcik and Pennebaker 2010). Based on expert-defined dictionaries, LIWC determines the percentage of word categories. In the present study, we made use of three global indices of LIWC: we assessed (a) the overall number of words per article as an indicator of elaboration, (b) the relative frequency of different emotion words (see below) as an inverse measure of factuality and neutrality, and (c) the percentage of science-related words as an indicator of the scientific basis of the articles. Secondly, we analyzed the number of sources of the articles as another indicator of the scientific basis of the articles. Finally, we provide some insights from a content exploration (not a thorough content analysis!) of the articles. Materials, data, as well as scripts for analyses are available here: osf.io/fe2r7.

4   Results

4.1   Automatic text analyses

4.1.1   Elaboration

The overall number of words per article was used as an indicator of elaboration. A mixed measures ANOVA with encyclopedia (Wikipedia, Metapedia) as within-topic factor and discipline (science, politics) as between-topic factor revealed a significant main effect of encyclopedia, $F(1,58) = 38.96$, $p < .001$, $\eta_p^2 = .40$, a significant main effect of discipline, $F(1,58) = 13.06$, $p = .001$, $\eta_p^2 = .18$, as well as a significant interaction, $F(1,58) = 5.41$, $p = .024$, $\eta_p^2 = .09$. Overall, Wikipedia articles contained significantly more words than Metapedia articles, and in general, political articles were longer than articles about scientific topics. This difference was pronounced for Metapedia articles (see Table 3).

Tab. 3   Results of the automatic text analysis as well as the source analysis as a function of encyclopedia (Wikipedia, Metapedia) and discipline (science, politics)

	Wikipedia		Metapedia	
	Science (N = 30)	Politics (N = 30)	Science (N = 30)	Politics (N = 30)
Word count	4085.30 (3061.47)	10292.90 (9945.17)	638.40 (762.78)	2751.20 (4143.91)
Anxiety	0.04 (0.07)	0.07 (0.05)	0.02 (0.08)	0.11 (0.11)
Anger	0.07 (0.12)	0.13 (0.09)	0.07 (0.17)	0.26 (0.22)
Sadness	0.10 (0.08)	0.19 (0.11)	0.08 (0.16)	0.16 (0.13)
Positive Feelings	0.01 (0.02)	0.03 (0.04)	0.04 (0.05)	0.05 (0.08)
Optimism	0.36 (0.18)	0.52 (0.27)	0.33 (0.33)	0.54 (0.36)
STEM	3.67 (2.80)	0.21 (0.44)	3.59 (3.69)	0.16 (0.28)
Sources	31.33 (37.61)	114.73 (129.77)	3.07 (4.43)	14.07 (22.21)

4.1.2   Emotionality

We conducted separate mixed measures ANOVAs for each type of emotion words (anxiety, anger, sadness, positive feelings, optimism). For three types of emotion words – sadness, positive feelings, and optimism – we did not find any effects (main effects or interactions) for encyclopedia, all $Fs < 2.73$, $ps > .10$. For anger and anxiety, however, we obtained the following differences: for anger there was a significant main effect of encyclopedia, $F(1,58) = 5.76$, $p = .02$, $\eta_p^2 = .09$, a significant main effect of discipline, $F(1,58) = 14.50$, $p < .001$, $\eta_p^2 = .20$, and a significant interaction, $F(1,58) = 6.31$, $p = .015$, $\eta_p^2 = .10$. Follow-up t-tests revealed that Wikipedia and Metapedia did not differ in the relative frequency of anger-related words, when analyzing scientific articles, $t(29) = .08$, $p = .94$. For political articles, however, Metapedia contained a significantly higher percentage of anger-related words, $t(29) = 3.42$, $p = .002$, $d = .37$ (see Table 3). With regard to anxiety, the ANOVA revealed a significant main effect of discipline, $F(1,58) = 12.57$, $p = .001$, $\eta_p^2 = .18$, no significant main effect of encyclopedia, $F(1,58) = 0.56$, $p = .46$, $\eta_p^2 = .01$, but a significant interaction, $F(1,58) = 4.48$, $p = .039$, $\eta_p^2 = .07$. Follow-up t-tests revealed that Wikipedia and Metapedia articles about scientific topics did not differ, $t(29) = 1.11$, $p = .278$, whereas Metapedia articles about political topics contained by trend more anxiety-related words than did the same Wikipedia articles, $t(29) = 1.82$, $p = .079$, $d = .13$.

4.1.3   Science-related words

We made use of the STEM dictionary (science, technology, engineering, mathematics; Heilemann 2016). Specifically, we submitted the supra-category 1-MINT to a mixed measures ANOVA with encyclopedia (Wikipedia, Metapedia) as within-topic factor and discipline (science, politics) as between-topic factor. We only obtained a significant main effect of discipline, $F(1,58) = 56.86$, $p < .001$, $\eta_p^2 = .50$, all other $Fs < 0.2$, $ps > .72$. In both encyclopedias did articles about scientific (vs. political) topics contain a significantly larger percentage of STEM words.

4.2   Sources

The number of sources[4] was submitted to a mixed measures ANOVA with encyclopedia (Wikipedia, Metapedia) as within-topic factor and discipline (science, politics) as between-topic factor. It yielded a significant main effect of encyclopedia, $F(1,58) = 31.64$, $p < .001$, $\eta_p^2 = .35$, a significant main effect of discipline, $F(1,58) = 12.28$, $p = .001$, $\eta_p^2 = .18$, and a significant interaction, $F(1,58) = 9.98$, $p < .01$, $\eta_p^2 = .15$. Wikipedia articles contained generally significantly more sources ($M = 73.03$, $SD = 103.64$) than did Metapedia articles ($M = 8.57$, $SD = 16.81$).

In consideration of the fact that Wikipedia articles were also much longer than Metapedia articles, we also compared the number of sources relative to article length. To this end we divided the number of sources by the number of words for each article. A mixed measures ANOVA with encyclopedia (Wikipedia, Metapedia) as within-topic factor and discipline (science, politics) as between-topic factor yielded neither a main effect of encyclopedia, $F(1,58) = 2.34$, $p < .001$, $\eta_p^2 = .04$, nor a significant main effect of discipline, $F(1,58) = 1.36$, $p = .252$, $\eta_p^2 = .02$, nor a significant interaction, $F(1,58) = 1.34$, $p = .248$, $\eta_p^2 = .02$.

Thus, Wikipedia articles did not cite more sources per (fixed amount of) content but rather contained generally longer elaborations and – accordingly – more sources.

4.3   Content exploration

During article analyses some aspects attracted our attention and seem worth mentioning here. It must be stressed, however, that this is no elaborate content analysis, which would be an effortful but desirable endeavor for future research.

Language. Metapedia values original language (here: German) and therefore despises and avoids anglicisms. For instance, the Metapedia article about the Internet is titled "Weltnetz" ("world net", see also compact disc in Table 1). Beyond that, Metapedia uses more words that already imply an opinion or world-view. The title of the article about the European migration crisis, for instance, makes use of the word "Asylantenflut", which refers to a flood of asylum seekers that is termed in clearly negative ways (Link 1982) as there is a more neutral German word for asylum seekers (Asylsuchende). Similarly, the article about "Gender" is

---

4   From Wikipedia we summed up the entries cited under the "references" as well as the "literature" section. From Metapedia the sum was made of "literature", "references" and "sources".

termed "Geschlechtergleichschaltung" and "Gleichschaltung" is a Nazi term for standardization/ unification, which, however, does not fully tap the connotation of the German word. The articles themselves likewise often convey a clear attitude towards the topic, which is indicated by the use of highly negative words for critical topics (e.g., "global misandry", "mental-psychological poisoning of the relationship between the sexes" in the article about feminism; "flooded with Africans and Orientals", "transforming our occidental homeland into a battle field" in the article about the migration crisis[5]).

Content. Metapedia articles repeatedly take certain positions. Sometimes this is a certain focus when it comes to content. The Metapedia article about the motor cycle, for instance, focuses almost entirely on its use as a military vehicle. Other times, articles convey up-front and point-blank criticisms of well-established scientific theories (e.g., "the illogical and non-scientific character of this 'theory'" in the article about the relativity theory) and social-political movements (e.g., "Within the ideological orbit of feminism there are pseudo sciences that come along under militant names such as 'Women Studies', 'Gender Studies' and 'Critical Men Studies'" in the article about feminism) before even describing the topic from a neutral point of view. Interestingly, Metapedia articles even contain criticisms that are unrelated to the topic of the article. The article about energy transition, for instance, criticizes politicians, who "otherwise do not get tired to complain about 'marked distortion', 'bureaucracy', 'regulatory overkill' and national politico-economic 'statism' (using the same to justify the erosion of border protection to enforce mass immigration)" (exclamation marks in the original). All those observations seriously question the neutrality of Metapedia articles.

5   Discussion and implications

Our quantitative analyses show that Metapedia articles differ from Wikipedia articles in that they are significantly shorter, contain significantly fewer references, but a significantly greater percentage of anger-related and anxiety-related words. It must be acknowledged, however, that the use of emotion words was generally rather low – even in Metapedia. An exploration of the very article contents, however, hints towards the limitations of dictionary-based automatic text analyses, as we found many examples of pejorative language and presentation, which might not be captured by LIWC (e.g., as in the case of "Asylanten", see Grabczyk 2015, for similar findings). On the other hand, the examples of our content exploration need

---

5   All translations by the first author.

to be interpreted with great care, too. After all, we did not conduct a proper content analysis with blind raters. Such would be an effortful but highly desirable endeavor for future research (see also Koretz in this volume).

Still, our findings speak to the argument that a norm of neutrality might not be very effective, since perceptions of neutrality differ according to own attitudes (Vallone et al. 1985; see also Holt and Rinaldo 2014; Dormann et al. in this volume). Obviously, neutrality was not the only norm – neither in Wikipedia, nor in Metapedia. On the other hand, neutrality might not be the only norm that is flexibly interpreted: The concept of knowledge itself, for instance, may vary substantially (Oeberst et al. 2016; Kimmerle et al. 2013). Similarly, the requirement to provide references for the contributed contents may miss the mark if solely references are used and cited, that are in line with one's own perspective. Therefore, norms might be less effective than assumed – as long as they remain largely a projection screen. It might still heighten the threshold for bias, however. In a recent series of studies we found that Wikipedia articles are not immune to hindsight bias, but they show less bias than individuals do (Oeberst et al. 2017).

Bibliography

Cress, U., & Kimmerle, J. (2008). A systemic and cognitive view on collaborative knowledge building with wikis. *International Journal of Computer-Supported Collaborative Learning, 3*, 105–122.

Cress, U., Jeong, H., & Moskaliuk, J. (2016). *Mass collaboration and education*. Cham, Switzerland: Springer International Publishing.

Giles, J. (2005). Internet encyclopaedias go head to head. *Nature, 438*, 900–901.

Gowers, T., & Nielsen, M. (2009). Massively collaborative mathematics. *Nature, 461*, 879–881.

Grabczyk, M. (2015). The terminology of contemporary national socialist online communities. *Folio, 1*(14), 79–88. Retrieved from http://www.ia.uw.edu.pl/images/Folio_142015.pdf#page=81. Accessed: 24 May 2017.

Hansen, G. J., & Kim, H. (2011). Is the media biased against me? A meta-analysis of the hostile media effect research. *Communication Research Reports, 28*, 169–179.

Heilemann, M. (2016). *Gütekriterien diktionärsbasierter Textanalysen zur Erfassung domänenspezifischer Kommunikationsinhalte*. Berlin: Logos.

Holt, K., & Rinaldo, M. (2014, May). *Exploring the dark side of participatory online media: Online participation, identitarian discourse and media criticism at Metapedia.org*. Paper presented at Journalism in Transition: Crisis or opportunity? JSS-ECREA conference Thessaloniki, Greece.

Kimmerle, J., Thiel, A., Gerbing, K.-K., Bientzle, M., Halatchliyski, I., & Cress, U. (2013). Knowledge construction in an outsider community: Extending the communities of practice concept. Computers in Human Behavior, 29, 1078–1090.

Kunda, Z. (1990). The case for motivated reasoning. *Psychological Bulletin, 108*, 480–498.

Link, J. (1982). Kollektivsymbolik und Mediendiskurse, *kultuRRevolution. Zeitschrift für Angewandte Diskurstheorie, 1*, 6–21.

Lutz, C., & Hofmann, C. P. (2017). The dark side of online participation: exploring non-, passive and negative participation. *Information, Communication & Society, 20*(6), 876–897. http://dx.doi.org/10.1080/1369118X.2017.1293129

Nestler, S., Leckelt, M., Back, M. D., von der Beck, I., Cress, U., & Oeberst, A. (2017). Produktion von naturwissenschaftlichen Informationen im Internet am Beispiel von Wikipedia. *Psychologische Rundschau, 68*, 172–176.

Oeberst, A., Kimmerle, J., & Cress, U. (2016). What is knowledge? How is it constructed and who possesses it? The need for a new answer to old questions. In U. Cress, H. Jeong & J. Moskaliuk (Eds). *Mass collaboration and education*. Cham, Switzerland: Springer International Publishing.

Oeberst A., von der Beck, I., Cress, U., Back, M. D., & Nestler, S. (2017). Biases in the production and reception of collective knowledge: The case of hindsight bias in Wikipedia. *Psychological Research*, https://doi.org/10.1007/s00426-017-0865-7

Pfeiffer, T. (2015). Gegenöffentlichkeit und Aufbruch im Netz. Welche strategischen Funktionen erfüllen Websites und Angebote im Web 2.0 für den deutschen Rechtsextremismus? In S. Braun, A. Geisler & M. Gerster (Eds). *Strategien der extremen Rechten. Hintergründe – Analysen – Antworten* (pp 257–286). Springer.

Pohl, R. F. (2017). *Cognitive illusions: Intriguing phenomena in thinking, judgment, and memory* (2nd ed., pp. 424–445). London: Routledge.

Sargizi, S. (2016). *Schaffen es Online-Enzyklopädien durch die Festlegung von Richtlinien für neutrale Standpunkte in ihren Artikeln zu sorgen? Eine empirische Untersuchung von Neutralitätsmerkmalen in Wikipedia und Metapedia.* (Unpublished Bachelor Thesis) University of Tuebingen.

Tausczik, Y. R., & Pennebaker, J. W. (2010). The psychological meaning of words: LIWC and computerized text analysis methods. *Journal of Language and Social Psychology, 29*, 24–54.

Vallone, R. P., Ross, L., & Lepper, M. R. (1985). The hostile media phenomenon: biased perceptions and perceptions of media bias in coverage of the Beirut massacre. *Journal of Personality and Social Psychology, 49*, 577–585.

Zlatkin-Troitschanskaia et al. (2017). *Positive Learning in the Age of Information*. Unpublished Manuscript, Draft Proposal Cluster of Excellence, Johannes Gutenberg University Mainz.

Why Google Can't Save Us

The Challenges of our Post-Gutenberg Moment

Sam Wineburg, Joel Breakstone, Sarah McGrew,
and Teresa Ortega

Abstract

The Stanford History Education Group has prototyped, field tested, and validated a bank of assessments that tap *civic online reasoning*—the ability to judge the credibility of the information that floods young people's smartphones, tablets, and computers. We developed 56 tasks and administered them to students across 12 states. In total, we collected and analyzed 7,804 student responses. From pre-teens to seniors in college, students struggled mightily to evaluate online information. To investigate how people determine the credibility of digital information, we sampled 45 individuals: 10 PhD historians, 10 professional fact checkers, and 25 Stanford University undergraduates. We observed them as they evaluated websites and engaged in open web searches on social and political issues. Historians and students often fell victim to easily manipulated features of websites, such as official-looking logos and domain names.

Keywords

Civic Online Reasoning; Critical Thinking; Digital Literacy; Internet; Media Literacy; Information; Credibility.

Coverage of "fake news" has been everywhere since the 2016 U.S. presidential elections. It's impossible to turn on the TV or radio without hearing the term. Tens of thousands of words have been devoted to columns about how to address this menace. Google and Facebook have announced initiatives to address the problem. Governments have introduced legislation to mandate instruction on the topic in schools.

Fake news is a big problem, but unfortunately it's not our biggest. The Internet is filled with content that defies simple "fake" or "real" binaries. For every issue of social and political importance, there are websites that blast half-true headlines, blog posts that manipulate data, and websites that advance specific agendas. Some of these outlets are transparent about who they are and who they represent. Others carefully conceal their backing, in some cases portraying themselves as grassroots efforts when, in fact, they are sponsored by corporate or political interests. Such funding doesn't necessarily render the information false. But citizens trying to make decisions about, say, energy policy have a right to know that ExxonMobil sponsored the article they're reading. Determining where information comes from and who's behind it are crucial parts of deciding whether it is credibile. In a digital age, such skills are essential for gathering credible information—the lifeblood of informed citizenship.

We are particularly concerned about young people, our future citizens, because the Internet dominates their lives (American Press Institute 2015). With optimism, trepidation, and, at times, annoyance, we've witnessed young people's digital dexterity and astonishing screen stamina. Students today are now more likely to learn about the world through social media than through traditional sources like print newspapers (Gasser et al. 2012). Given this reality, it is critical that students are able to evaluate the content they find online.

Unfortunately, our research demonstrates that, right now, they can't. Between January 2015 and June 2016, we administered 56 tasks to students across 12 states. In total, we collected and analyzed 7,804 student responses. Our college assessments were administered online at six different universities that ranged from Stanford, a school that rejects 95% of its applicants, to large state universities in the United States that admit the majority of students who apply.

When thousands of students respond to dozens of tasks there are bound to be endless variations. However, these variations paled in comparison to a stunning and dismaying consistency. Overall, young people's ability to reason about information on the Internet can be summed up in one word: Bleak.

These "digital natives" may be able to flit between Facebook and Twitter while simultaneously uploading a selfie to Instagram and texting a friend. But when it comes to evaluating information that flows through social media channels, they are easily duped. We did not design our exercises to make hairsplitting distinctions between a "good" and a "better" answer. Rather, we sought to establish a reasonable bar, a level of performance we believed was within reach of most teenagers and college students.

Our tasks measured three core competencies of civic online reasoning: identifying who is behind the source of information, evaluating the evidence presented, and investigating what other sources have to say (McGrew et al. 2017). Some of our assessments were paper-and-pencil tasks; others were administered online. For the paper-and-pencil assessments, we used screen shots of tweets, Facebook posts, websites, and other content that students would likely encounter online. We are mindful of the criticism of using paper-and-pencil measures to assess students' ability to judge online sources. However, we wanted to ensure that our assessments could be used in all schools, no matter their technological resources.

One of our paper-and-pencil tasks presented students with screenshots of two articles, both from a prominent American news website, on approaches to solving global climate change. One was a traditional news story from the website's "Science" section; the other was a post sponsored by an oil company. Students had to explain which of the two sources was a more reliable source of information about climate change.

Native advertisements—that is, advertisements designed to look like editorial content—are a relatively new source of revenue for news outlets. Native ads are made to look like news stories, complete with eye-catching visuals and data displays. But, as with all advertisements, their purpose is to promote, not to inform. Our task assessed whether students could identify who was behind an article and to consider how that *who* might influence its content. Successful students recognized that one of the articles was actually an advertisement for an oil company and reasoned that, due to the company's vested interest in fossil fuels, it was less likely to be an objective source than a news article on the same topic.

We administered the final version of this task to over 200 high school students. Nearly 70% selected the oil company ad as the more reliable source. Responses showed that rather than considering the source and purpose of each article, many students were taken in by a pie chart in the native ad. Although there was no evidence that the chart presented reliable data, students concluded that the oil company's post was fact-based. One student wrote, "I believe [the oil company's article] is more reliable, because it's easier to understand with the graph and seems more reliable because the chart shows facts right in front of you." In contrast, only about 15% of students concluded that the news article was more reliable than the advertisement. A task we designed for middle school students yielded similar results: 82% of students failed to identify as an advertisement a story that was clearly marked "sponsored content." Together these findings suggests that many students have no idea what "sponsored content" means. Until they do, these students risk being deceived by groups seeking to influence them.

For every challenge facing digital citizens, there are scores of websites pretending to be something they are not. Ordinary people once relied on publishers, editors, and subject matter experts to vet the information they consumed. But on the unregulated Internet, all bets are off. Michael Lynch, a philosopher who studies technological change, observed that the Internet is "both the world's best fact-checker and the world's best bias confirmer— often at the same time" (2016). Never have we had so much information at our fingertips. Whether this bounty will make us smarter and better informed or more ignorant and narrow-minded will depend on our awareness of this problem and our educational response to it. At present, democratic reasoning is threatened by the ease at which disinformation is allowed to spread and flourish.

The results of our study, combined with findings from other researchers (e.g., Hargittai et al. 2010; see Kirschner and van Merriënboer 2013, for review), provide evidence that the myth of the digital native is precisely that—a myth. As Christopher Scanlon (2009), a scholar of digital journalism, put it:

> "Those writing about digital natives confuse the ability to navigate around ready-made online environments [...] for a general ease with technology." He continued, "Once students stray outside of the safe confines of pre-built, pre-configured online environments [...] they often turn out to be just as confused as the rest of us."

If Scanlon is right that digital natives are no better at navigating online content than the rest of us, to whom can we turn to show us the way? We wanted to explore how experts judge the credibility of digital information. Before we could start, though, we needed to figure out who qualifies as an "expert."

We turned first to a group of professionals who evaluate sources for a living: historians. Ample research has established how historians *source* documents, interrogating a document's author and the circumstances of its creation as keys to determining its trustworthiness (Wineburg 1998, 2001, in press). The majority of historians, however, still conduct their research in archives of print documents. We thus recruited a second group: fact checkers, whose job it is to ascertain truth in digital form. Finally, we drafted a group of undergraduates at Stanford University. These university students are drawn from the tail of the ability distribution and earmarked—at least according to Stanford University brochures—to lead the digital future.

We observed the groups as they evaluated live websites and searched for information on social and political issues. What we found was not what we expected. Both historians and students often fell victim to easily manipulated features of websites, such as official-looking logos and domain names, and took at face value claims that were anchored to dubious scholarly references.

We asked participants to evaluate the website of the American College of Pediatricians, a small splinter group of doctors that broke with the mainstream, 64,000-member American Academy of Pediatrics after the latter endorsed adoptions by same-sex couples. The American College makes no secret of its hostility to the LGBT community, posting statements such as one that advocates adding the letter P, for "pedophilia," to the acronym LGBT, because pedophilia is "intrinsically woven into their agenda" (American College of Pediatricians 2015). After evaluating an article on this site and comparing it to one on the site of the American Academy of Pediatrics, participants judged the trustworthiness of the two sites.

The differences among groups were dramatic. Every fact checker viewed the American Academy's site as the more reliable; historians often equivocated; and university students overwhelmingly judged the American College's site the more reliable (see Figure 1). What, then, did fact checkers do that distinguished their approach from historians and students?

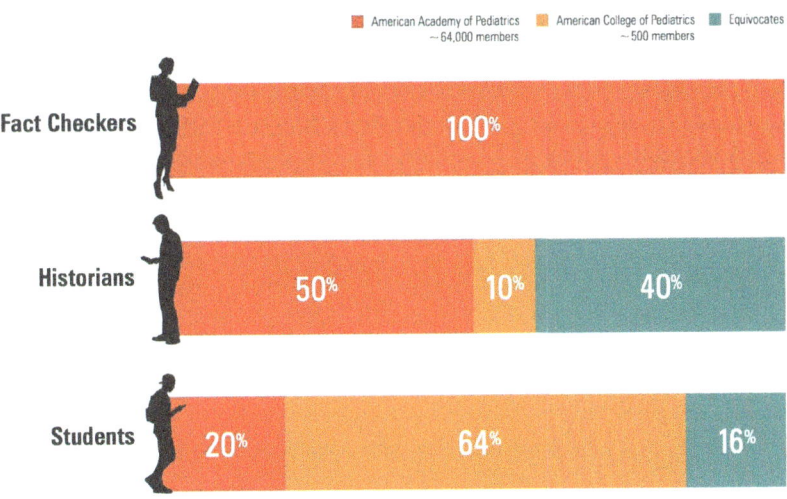

Fig. 1   Percentage of participants in each group selecting the College or the Academy as more reliable

Historians and students approached web content by reading *vertically*, their eyes moving up and down the screen as though it were a page of print. They engaged in close reading (Shanahan 2012) of web content, asking: Does a site look professional? Is it free of typos and banner ads? Does it quote well-known sources? Are bias or faulty logic detectable? In contrast, fact checkers read *laterally*, leaping off an unfamiliar site almost immediately and opening up multiple search windows. They ignored the internal features of sites that swayed historians and students, and instead prioritized finding out what other sources had to say about the original site. The horizontal scan of other sites gave fact checkers a near-instantaneous fix on where they had originally landed. Fact checkers demonstrated that the close reading of a digital source, when one doesn't even know if the source can be trusted (or is what it says it is)—proves to be a *colossal* waste of time (McGrew and Wineburg 2016; Wineburg and McGrew 2016, 2017).

Paradoxically, a key feature of lateral reading is *not reading*. Fact checkers intelligently ignored massive amounts of irrelevant (or less crucial) text when making an informed judgment. In their evaluations, historians and students relied on common but deeply flawed *weak heuristics*, like viewing a domain designation as a proxy for trustworthiness. Fact checkers instead relied on *strong heuristics*, which not only saved them time but led to more accurate judgments. Over the past two decades, Gerd Gigerenzer and colleagues (see Gigerenzer and Gaissmaier 2011, for review) have redeemed heuristics from the dungeon of cognitive biases (Tversky and Kahneman 1974) and demonstrated how some of these cognitive shortcuts can help problem solvers make judgments "more quickly, frugally, and/or accurately than more complex methods" (2011, p. 454). Lateral reading fits Gigerenzer and Gaissmaier's definition of a "fast and frugal" heuristic. Fact checkers read less and learned more—with a speediness that often left other participants in the dust.

The Stanford students in our study—along with the thousands of high school students who completed our tasks—rarely showed evidence of reading laterally. After reviewing some of the most widely available resources for teaching students to evaluate web content, this isn't surprising. A common curriculuar approach in the United States is to give students checklists and have them answer a series of questions about a website, such as whether a site is registered as an NGO or what an organization says about itself on an "About" page. In no case did we observe fact checkers begin their evaluations by answering long lists of questions.

The checklist approach cuts searchers off from the most efficient route to learning more about a website: finding out what the rest of the web has to say. Fact checkers evaluated unfamiliar websites by leaving them. For them, the direct route to credibility was indirect. As the blogger and Internet critic Mike Caulfield put it (2017), "the World Wide Web is a *web*, and the way to establish authority and truth on the web is to use its web-like properties." This is what professional fact checkers do. It is what we should be teaching students to do as well.

Bibliography

American College of Pediatricians (2015). *"P" for pedophile.* Retrieved from http://www.acpeds.org/p-for-pedophile

American Press Institute (2015). *How millennials get news: Inside the habits of America's first digital generation.* Retrieved from https://www.americanpressinstitute.org/publications/reports/survey-research/millennials-news/

Caulfield, M. (2017). *How "news literacy" gets the web wrong.* Retrieved from https://hapgood.us/2017/03/04/how-news-literacy-gets-the-web-wrong/

Gasser, U., Cortesi, S., Malik, M., & Lee, A. (2012). *Youth and digital media: From credibility to information quality.* Cambridge, MA: The Berkman Center for Internet and Society.

Gigerenzer, G., & Gaissmaier, W. (2011). Heuristic decision making. *Annual Review of Psychology, 62,* 451–482. doi:10.1146/annurev-psych-120709-145346

Hargittai, E., Fullerton, L., Menchen-Trevino, E., & Thomas, K. Y. (2010). Trust online: Young adults' evaluation of web content. *International Journal of Communication, 4,* 468–494. doi:1932–8036/20100468

Kirschner, P. A., & van Merriënboer, J. J. G. (2013). Do learners really know best? Urban legends in education. *Educational Psychologist, 48*(3), 169–183. doi:10.1080/00461520.2013.804395

Lynch, M. P. (2016). Googling is believing: Trumping the informed citizen. *New York Times.* Retrieved from http://opinionator.blogs.nytimes.com/2016/03/09/googling-is-believingtrumping-the-informed-citizen/

McGrew, S., & Wineburg, S. (2016). *Reading Less and Learning More: Expertise in Evaluating the Credibility of Online Information.* Paper presented at the annual meeting of the American Educational Research Association, San Antonio, TX.

McGrew, S., Ortega, T., Breakstone, J., & Wineburg, S. (2017). The challenge that's bigger than fake news: Teaching students in engage in online civic reasoning. *American Educator.*

Scanlon, C. (2009, January 21). The natives aren't quite so Restless. *The Australian.* Retrieved from http://www.theaustralian.com.au/higher-education/opinion/the-natives-arent-quite-so-restless/story-e6frgcko-1111118616452

Shanahan, T. (2012). *What is close reading?* Retrieved from http://shanahanonliteracy.com/blog/what-is-close-reading#sthash.mxxi0paG.rtIrn0KW.dpbs

Tversky, A., & Kahneman, D. (1974). Judgment under uncertainty: Heuristics and biases. *Science, 185*(4157), 1124–1131. doi:10.1126/science.185.4157.1124

Wineburg, S. (1998). Reading Abraham Lincoln: An expert/expert study in the interpretation of historical texts. *Cognitive Science, 22*(3), 319–346. doi:10.1016/S0364-0213(99)80043-3

Wineburg, S. (2001). *Historical thinking & other unnatural Acts: Charting the future of teaching the past.* Philadelphia, PA: Temple University Press.

Wineburg, S. (in press). *Stuck in the past: Why learn history when it is already on your iPhone?* Chicago: University of Chicago Press.

Wineburg, S., & McGrew, S. (2016). Why students can't Google their way to truth. *Education Week*. Retrieved from http://www.edweek.org/ew/articles/2016/11/02/why-students-cant-google-their-way-to.html

Wineburg, S., & McGrew, S. (2017). *Lateral reading and the nature of Expertise: Learning more and reading less when evaluating digital information*. Technical Report No. 1701. Stanford, CA: Stanford History Education Group.

Approaches to the Study of Negative Learning

Daniel Koretz

Abstract

This paper presents several suggestions about the study of negative learning. First, while much negative learning is both factually incorrect and social undesirable, we should separate these two attributes, as they are distinct and can reflect different causal mechanisms. Second, it is essential that we investigate negative learning in the context of larger societal and political trends, and doing so will often require complex models with moderation and reciprocal causation. Third, we should apply three criteria in selecting sources to examine: archetypal content, readership, and impact. Devising appropriate measures of impact will be challenging for both technical and ethical reasons. Finally, while basic research is important in this domain, it is essential that we also focus on applied research with practical implications.

Keywords

Negative Learning; Social Context; Causal Models; Moderation; Reciprocal Causation; Outcome Measurement.

I will make three suggestions about investigating negative learning, focusing on how we define the phenomenon, how we approach analysis, and which aspects of new media should be a primary focus. I will reference aspects of the papers by Maurer, Quiring, and Schemer (in this volume) and Oeberst, de Vreeze and Cress (in this volume), but the larger framing for my comments is the societal and political trends of recent years in Europe and especially the United States. I will then suggest a sequential approach for investigating the impact of online sources of negative learning. In conclusion, I will put these specifics aside and offer some more general suggestions about research on negative learning.

First, I suggest that for purposes of scientific investigation, it is essential to separate two aspects of what is now labeled as negative learning. Zlatkin-Troitschanskaia et al. (2017) develop this definition:

> "Negative learning [is] ... the acquisition of false ... concepts, counterfactual misconceptions and/or socially opportunistic knowledge (e.g., to justify racism), attitudes, and prejudices that contradict widespread societal values and norms ..." (Zlatkin-Troitschanskaia et al. 2017, p. 6).

This definition includes both factual inaccuracy and social undesirability. In contrast, Maurer et al. (in this volume) use a narrower definition that encompasses only factual inaccuracy:

> "Influences that undermine knowledge ..., distract from learning, or result in learning misinformation [are] considered negative learning" (p. 199).

In practice, we will often be concerned with learning that is both false and socially undesirable—for example, the spread of racist and anti-Semitic lies on the Internet in the US—and I focus my comments on examples that have both of these characteristics. However, from a scientific perspective, the two are distinct. For example, a mechanism may foster the spread of false information regardless of its social desirability. Maurer et al. (in this volume) provide a clear example of this. They noted:

> "Taming the information tide on social media just by scanning headlines ... results in the subjective experience of being informed" (p. 204).

This important conclusion has no necessary connection to social desirability.

My second point is that we will need complex causal models to study important aspects of negative learning. The causal model in the Maurer et al. quotation above is recursive: changes in technology and the media encourage overconfidence in the accuracy of information, which presumably facilitates the spread of false information. This simple model was entirely appropriate for that question, and it will be for many other important questions about positive and negative learning. However, for many important questions, we will need more complex models.

Recent trends in negative learning in the US and the associated societal and political trends illustrate the importance of more complex causal models. Note that I deliberately used the ambiguous phrase "associated with." It is apparent that there are causal links between the societal trends, the political trends, and trends in negative learning involving new technologies, but the precise nature of those causal relationships is unclear.

The spread of false information via information technology during the US election has been amply documented. Much of this was spread via social media, but one can also see clear trends in the number of visitors to right-wing, racist, and conspiracy-theory websites. Use of many of these sites increased rapidly during the Trump campaign and shortly after his election in November 2016. This is apparent in the rankings of websites by number of visitors published by Alexa (an Amazon company). For example, the Alexa ranking of the Daily Stormer, which some observers consider the most influential of the American neo-Nazi websites, increased from about 35,000 in the summer of 2016 to about 14,000 by March of 2017 (Alexa 2017a). Another example is the Infowars site, which is the most influential right-wing conspiracy-theory website in the US. Trump uses this site as a source of "information," and before his election, he appeared on the radio show hosted by Alex Jones, who runs Infowars. Its ranking increased from over 3,000 in the summer of 2016 to 865 at the beginning of 2017. The Daily Stormer has maintained its higher readership, while the rank of Infowars has since dropped back to near 3,000 (Alexa 2017b). Obviously, social media such as Reddit amplified the impact of these sites, as users used these media to disseminate postings that they found particularly appealing.

Information on both hate incidents and hate crimes in the US is extremely incomplete, but the limited available data show similar patterns, that is, an increase during the campaign and immediately after the election. For example, national data from the Anti-Defamation League showed an increase of 34% in anti-Semitic incidents in 2016 compared with the year before and an 84% increase in the first three months of 2017 compared with the first three months of 2016. New York City reported an 81% increase in hate crimes during the first six weeks of 2017, compared with the first weeks of 2016.

Anecdotal data strongly suggest that these social and political trends are related. For example, the Trump campaign received open support from white supremacist organizations, which it disavowed weakly or not at all. The press, social media, and anti-hate organizations have publicized many instances in which both children and adults cited Trump while abusing or bullying ethnic minorities, Jews, and others.

Identifying the contribution of new technologies to these trends, however, will be difficult, in part because these trends were accompanied by—and presumably supported by—a worsening of old problems that predate information technology. For example, the right in the US has managed to make "culture" and identity, rather than positions about policy and legislation, a primary motivation for their supporters. The dissemination of false information is routine in political campaigns, but the Trump campaign greatly increased this, openly and frequently proclaiming "facts" that were demonstrably false. They coupled this steady stream of lies with greatly increased attacks on the legitimate press, which tried to rebut the lies (while often carefully avoiding the word "lie" and substituting milder terms). Trump still rarely refers to the media without labeling them "fake media" or "fake news," even when they are reporting facts that he or his associates have admitted. Some of the American racist organizations have been using the German term Lügenpresse (not always with the umlaut), and signs with this term appeared at Trump rallies. (The Daily Stormer goes further and sometimes uses the term Judenpresse.) Obviously, these are all techniques used successfully in the past by authoritarian politicians and regimes.

The analytical challenge is to identify the causal effects of new technologies and media on negative learning in the context of these other societal and political trends. To accomplish this, we first need to consider reciprocal causation. While it seems clear that both right-wing websites and social media contributed to these societal and political trends, trends in the rankings of sites like the Daily Stormer suggest that the reverse is also true: societal and political trends influenced the use of new media. Second, and perhaps more important, we will need to consider moderation effects. For example, it seems likely that new media amplified the effects of more traditional mechanisms, such as the use of the big lie. Conversely, societal and political trends are likely to have moderated the effects of new media. Although evaluating both moderation and reciprocal causation will likely prove very difficult in practice, these are the models that should guide our thinking about many of the important questions about negative learning and new technologies.

Third, I would offer suggestions about the sites and sources that offer the most payoff for investigation. Oeberst et al. (in this volume) contrasted two sites, one associated with negative learning and another not: Metapedia and Wikipedia. While contrasting sites is a useful approach in general, I don't believe this was an optimal choice of sources. Metapedia has a small number of visitors, and I suspect that it is not particularly influential.

I suggest selecting negative-learning sites for analysis based on three criteria: archetypal content, consumption (e.g., number of unique visitors, frequency of links and posts on social media), and potential impact or influence. As an example, in the US at present, infowars.com meets all three criteria. I suspect that Metapedia meets only the first.

Investigations of the characteristics and impact of negative-learning sources could follow a four-step sequence. The first stage is selecting contrasting groups of sites based on the three criteria above. The second stage is examining patterns that differentiate the two groups. Oeberst et al. (in this volume) illustrated two techniques for doing this: content analysis and automated text analysis. While Oeberst's exploratory content analysis was fruitful, the automated text analysis, which relied on *a priori* linguistic categories, proved only modestly informative. An alternative that might prove more productive is an exploratory approach, using machine learning to identify differentiating patterns in the two groups. The third stage, which I believe is still relatively unexplored, is constructing and evaluating measures of impact. Examples of potentially useful measures are uploads to specific social media sites and repetition of new memes in other sites and on social media. The final stage is exploring the impact of sites and, over the course of numerous studies, accumulating information on the attributes that characterize the sources with the greatest impact.

There are two types of barriers to investigating the impact of these sites. The first is common to many studies in the social sciences: lack of ready access to adequate data. In many cases, the available data will be systematically incomplete and weak in other respects, and the people who control access to the data may not provide access to researchers. The second, more unusual barrier is a moral one. Identifying and publishing the attributes that make some negative-learning sites particularly effective would be doing their market research for them, giving them tools to become yet more effective.

In conclusion, I would offer several more general suggestions about research on negative learning. First, most of the papers in this volume focus on either attributes of technology or intrapersonal factors. It seems clear we need to complement these approaches with consideration of societal trends.

Second, while the importance of basic research is apparent, recent societal and political trends underscore the importance of applied research in this domain. Shavelson (in this volume) put this a different way: he noted that we need research that fall into Pasteur's Quadrant. I entirely agree.

Finally, we are only at the early stages of work on negative learning, still striving to find the best approaches for understanding the role of information technology and new media on its propagation. Ultimately, however, the societal value of our work will hinge on whether we find ways to lessen negative learning and increase positive learning. For example, Ciampaglia (in this volume) showed how the use of social media contribute to a 'bubble effect,' in which people rapidly lose exposure to contrary views. Once we understand the mechanisms that help create and strengthen these bubbles, we must explore mechanisms for weakening them.

Bibliography

Alexa (2017a). How popular is dailystormer.com? http://www.alexa.com/siteinfo/daily-stormer.com. Accessed: 25 June 2017.

Alexa (2017b). How popular is infowars.com? http://www.alexa.com/siteinfo/infowars.com. Accessed: 25 June 2017.

Zlatkin-Troitschanskaia et al. (2017). *Positive Learning in the Age of Information*. Unpublished Manuscript, Draft Proposal Cluster of Excellence, Johannes Gutenberg University Mainz.

Positive Learning and Pluriliteracies

Growth in Higher Education and Implications
for Course Design, Assessment and Research

Oliver Meyer, Margarete Imhof, Do Coyle, and Mita Banerjee

Abstract

Deeper learning and the development of transferable knowledge and skills are highly desirable goals in Higher Education programs. However, current studies indicate that these goals are rarely achieved. In this article, we will present a model of deeper learning that promotes the development of disciplinary literacies and transferable knowledge. Based on our joint work we will outline a revised course design that aims at putting the principles of deeper learning into practice through a focus on affect, student engagement, knowledge construction, meaning making and active demonstration of understanding as well as reflective practice. Further, we will outline a research agenda for evaluating and assessing deeper learning processes and outcomes in Higher Education and discuss how deeper learning might pertain to the notion of positive learning envisioned by PLATO.

Keywords

Constructive Competence Development; Deeper Learning; Designing Teaching and Assessment for Learning Quality; Evidence-Based Teaching; Higher Education; Instructional Science; Learner Engagement; Pluriliteracies; Systems Model of Learning and Teaching; Teaching and Learning; Teaching and Learning Ecologies.

1   Deeper learning and 21st century universities: Aspirations and reality

"Colleges and universities, for all the benefits they bring, accomplish far less for their students than they should." (Derek Bok, former president of Harvard University, quoted in Arum and Roksa 2010, p. 1).

What do graduates from institutions of Higher Education take away from their years of study? In the most recent effort to reform colleges and universities the German Rectors' Conference (HRK) identified four categories of competences which would need to be secured through higher education: academic subject knowledge, employability, ability for civil engagement, and positive personal growth. This comprehensive set of competences is considered to be pre-requisite for the problems entailed in the intertwined complexities of political, social, environmental, and economic challenges of the 21st century. In a global economy which demands for highly skilled "knowledge workers" who can apply "theoretical and analytical knowledge acquired through formal education to develop new products and services" (Chiriac and Ghitiu-Bratescu 2011, p. 15), economic success rests in large parts on the skills of these highly literate knowledge workers. The key competence is to transfer knowledge through acquiring, processing, and communicating information in contextually relevant, meaningful and appropriate ways (Eppler and Burkhard 2004; Kale et al. 2011; cf. Shavelson in this volume).

By attaching occupational skill measurements to population surveys, Liu und Grusky (2013) have been able to evidence increases in both skill requirements of occupations and economic returns. They conclude that "the defining feature [...] of the last 30 years has been a precipitous increase in the wage payoff to jobs requiring synthesis, critical thinking, and deductive and inductive reasoning" (Liu and Grusky 2013, p. 1332).

According to national surveys (Hart Research Associates 2015), 91% of US employers agree that for career success, "a candidate's demonstrated capacity to think critically, communicate clearly, and solve complex problems is more important than his or her undergraduate major." That implies that such general collegiate or baseline skills are considered to be as or even more important than subject specific or hard skills. According to a recent article in the Washington Post (Selingo 2017), writing skills are reported to be "the biggest differentiator in business" and the third highest ranking baseline skills across a wide range of career areas.

A series of studies (Arum and Roska 2010, 2014; Astin 1993; Blaich 2007) demonstrated only marginal student learning despite the rhetoric. Arum and Roksa's (2010) study raises serious concerns since no significant gains in critical thinking, complex reasoning, and writing skills for at least 45 percent of participants (N = 2300) could be found. As Arum and Roksa (2014) report, US universities fail to adequately develop these generic collegiate skills in their graduates. Citing a number of relevant studies, they report that only a quarter of college graduates entering the US labor market have excellent skills in critical thinking and problem solving and that only 16 % have excellent communication skills. Recent findings of the KoKoHS research program even indicate that students' competencies may even decline over the course of their university studies (e.g., Happ et al. 2016; Schmidt et al. 2016; Zlatkin-Troitschanskaia et al. 2017a).

According to the OECD's Programme for the International Assessment of Adult Competencies (OECD 2016b) which measures adults' proficiency in key information-processing skills – literacy, numeracy, and problem solving in technology-rich environments, German universities seem equally unfit to prepare their students for the challenges of working in the 21st century: Only 20,2 % of all people with university education in Germany perform at the highest level of literacy, which is 0,7% below OECD average, 4% lower than the US and 16% less than in Finland or Japan.

Arum and Roksa (2014) list a number of cultural, sociological and historical reasons to explain the character of 21st century higher education and its shortcomings: they argue that 'academic capitalism', a deepening marketisation of university life threatens to marginalize the role of student learning (cf. also Gardner in this volume). Astin (1993) shows that a faculty's research orientation correlates strongly negatively with their orientation on student development.

Further, a shift from students' academic and moral development towards personal growth and well-being has resulted in authority being ceded to students. Ironically, rather than increasing the quality of learning, the introduction of course evaluations seems to have further exacerbated the problem and led to what Kuh (2003) has coined a 'disengagement compact' between students and faculty members.

This complex, dynamic interrelationship is compounded by the fact that the students themselves have undergone significant change in terms of their psychological development: sociologists and psychologists have proposed to look at individuals in the age group from 18-29 as emerging adults (Arnett 2000). This life stage is characterized by transitions, identity explorations, and experimentation (Skulborstad and Hermann 2016). In high-income countries, emerging adults typically attend institutions of tertiary education and face developmental challenges as they explore the new educational and social environment (Arnett et al. 2014; Trautwein and Bosse 2017).

As a consequence, higher education institutions need to acknowledge their responsibility for their student body because "what is accomplished and what fails to be accomplished at college is [...] central to the transitions of many emerging adults" (Arum and Roksa 2014, p. 416–417). The quality of the learning experience including the personal relationships with the teachers have a lasting impact both on personality development, in particular self-esteem and self-efficacy, and on the development of professional skills (Gonzales et al. 2017; Roberts and Davis 2016). Values and attitudes, which a person forms during these years, are likely to persist, and decisions and career-choices made in this stage often have implications for a lifetime. It needs to be acknowledged that 21st century university education will have to provide environments where students can both build knowledge and increase their skill-sets and also safely grow into responsible adults (cf. also Kosslyn in this volume).

In this article, we would like to propose the Pluriliteracies Approach to Teaching for Learning (PTL) as a model for 21st century university teaching and learning. It focuses on the development of subject specific literacies and transferable knowledge and skills as well as on personal growth. We presume that generic collegiate skills and domain specific skills are closely inter-dependent and inter-related sets of skills. We argue that critical thinking, effective communication, and transferable knowledge and skills are the product of deeper learning processes which will only occur if learning is embedded in disciplinary contexts and cultures and if there is an explicit focus on the development of specific literacies. Our model shows how such ecologies for deeper learning can be designed. In this article, we will describe a course structure to illustrate how PTL can be implemented in higher education teaching and learning. Based on that course design, we will outline a research agenda for deeper learning which we would like to pursue in the course of the PLATO program (cf. Zlatkin-Troitschanskaia et al. 2017b).

2   Pluriliteracies teaching for deeper learning

Pluriliteracies Teaching for Learning (PTL) is an approach to learning which has been developed in the course of a project for the European Center of Modern Languages (ECML) in order to address conceptual and methodological shortcomings and problems identified by Content and Language Integrated Learning (CLIL) researchers and practitioners (Meyer et al. 2015; Meyer & Coyle 2017). Taken together, the reported deficits in academic language use, especially in student writing (Vollmer 2008) and the notable absence of cognitive discourse functions such as 'defining', 'explaining', or 'hypothesizing' in CLIL classrooms (Dalton-Puffer

2007, 2015) indicate that the teaching of academic language tends to be neglected, not only in CLIL or immersion settings but also across content-classrooms in general.

In systemic functional linguistics, language is considered to be the "primary evidence for learning" (Mohan et al. 2010, p. 221). If that is indeed the case, these findings point to a bigger problem of education in general: if learners are not able to articulate their knowledge and understanding adequately, then it stands to reason that they have not fully understood the contents in the first place. We believe that neglecting to actively teach the language of schooling to promote the development of academic literacies may result in surface learning, "where new knowledge is arbitrarily and non-substantively incorporated into cognitive structure" (Novak 2002, p. 549). Deeper learning, "the process through which an individual becomes capable of taking what was learned in one situation and applying it to new situation (i.e. transfer)" (Pellegrino and Hilton 2012, p. 5) is dependent on "the way in which the individual and the community structures and organizes the intertwined knowledge and skills" (Pellegrino and Hilton 2012, p. 6).

Deeper learning takes place when "the learner chooses conscientiously to integrate new knowledge to knowledge that the learner already possesses" and involves "substantive, non-arbitrary incorporations of concepts into cognitive structure" (Novak 2002, p. 549) and may eventually lead to the development of transferable knowledge and skills.

PTL centres on the development of subject specific literacies in more than one language, and models and provides pathways for deeper learning into and across languages, disciplines, and cultures (see Figure 1). Becoming pluriliterate (= acquiring subject literacy in more than one language) will empower learners to purposefully and successfully construct and communicate knowledge across languages and cultures, and will prepare them for living and working in the Knowledge Age.

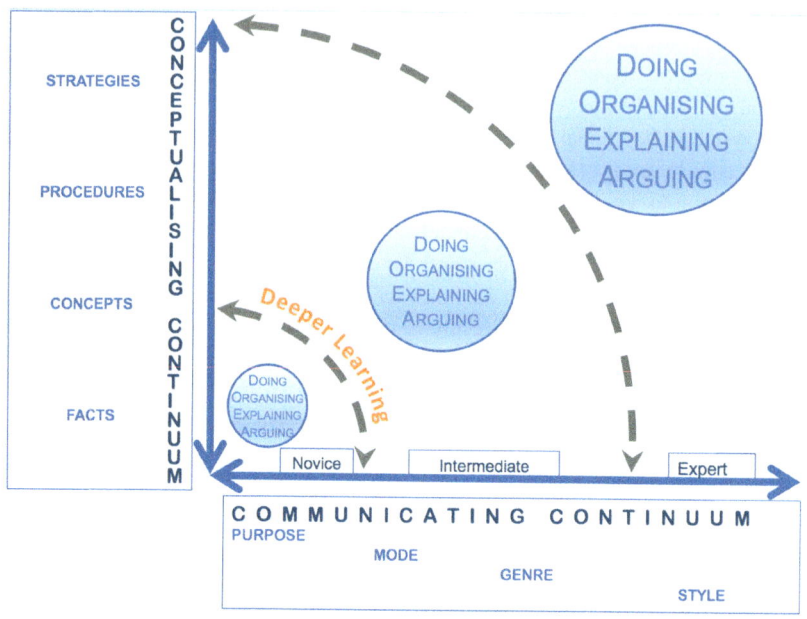

Fig. 1 The Graz Group Pluriliteracies Model (Meyer et al. 2015, p. 49)

Our model serves multiple purposes: Firstly, it centers on the co-dependent processes of knowledge construction and knowledge sharing as the main drivers of subject literacies. Building new knowledge requires learners to use strategies and skills to transform facts and observations into conceptual knowledge. Besides, learners need to integrate new information into pre-existing knowledge structures or schemata, beliefs and attitudes.

Since most of the new knowledge resides in media texts, learners need to be empowered to "critically interpret biases and distortions" (Kim 2016, p. 68) in those texts as well as "critically negotiate meanings, engage with the problems of misrepresentations and under-representations, and produce their own alternative media" (Kim 2016, p. 69).

Secondly, the model emphasizes the need for learners to establish connections between the two continua as they engage in the prototypical activities of constructing and communicating knowledge within a subject (i.e., doing science, organizing science, explaining science and arguing science). As we have argued before (Meyer et al. 2015, 2017), deeper learning processes are triggered when learners language their understanding by actively linking the conceptual and the communicative continuum. In our model, progress becomes manifest in the growth of learners' meaning-making potential which we have visualized as moving outwards along the continuum from novice to expert.

3 Ecologies for deeper learning

So far, this article has focused primarily on the cognitive and linguistic dimensions of deeper learning. Such a narrow view, however, runs the risk of overemphasizing the process of learning while neglecting the participants and their roles in that process. Learning and education are deeply social in nature (Walqui 2006) and recent research underlines the importance of the learning environment on learner achievement via behavioral, emotional and cognitive engagement (Ning and Downing 2012). Pietarinen et al. (2014) report that student well-being and emotional engagement, which becomes evident in the quality of the relationships with teachers and peers, contributes to cognitive engagement which in turn further increases behavioral engagement and may therefore lead to improved task performance and more successful learning. Student engagement thus seems to be socially embedded and highly dependent on the quality of interaction with and the pedagogical practices adopted by their teachers. Logically, Pietarinen et al. (2014) consider student well-being to be the key mediator that enhances emotional and cognitive engagement in school.

The fundamental importance of student well-being, emotional engagement and its relationship to deeper learning has led us to thoroughly revise our model. We have added a new dimension which focuses on variables that are vital to generating and sustaining learner commitment and achievement.

By adding a mentoring dimension which is supposed to counterbalance the added personal growth dimension, we believe to have arrived at a truly integrated model of teaching and learning that allows for the design of deeper learning ecologies where mentors and mentees are engaged in the processes of constructing and communicating of knowledge (see Figure 2).

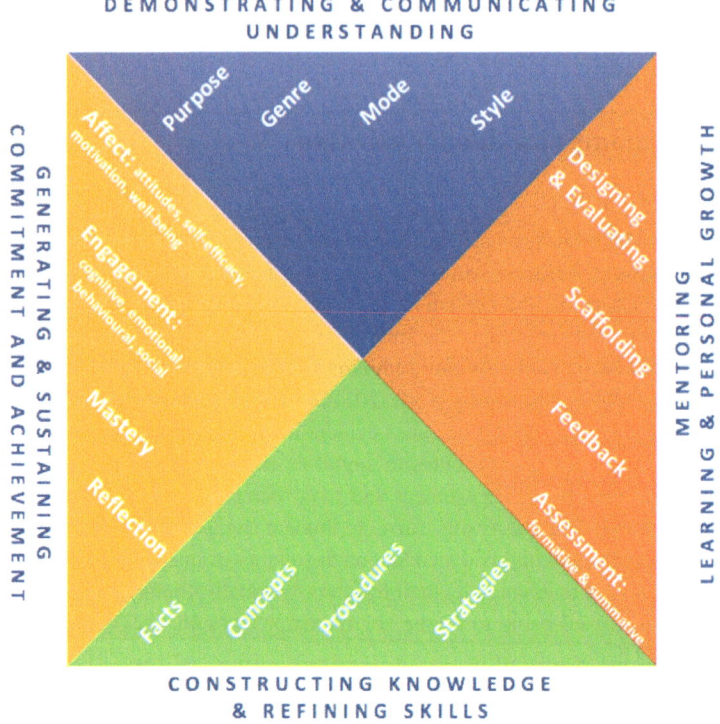

Fig. 2 Revised Model of Pluriliteracies Teaching for Learning

We define learning as long-term change in behavior, both in terms of achievement and engagement, and in mental representations, including attitudes resulting from experience (Ormrod 2011). The flip-side of change by learning is teaching, at least as far as formal settings are concerned. Teaching has been defined as "[…] an intentional intervention designed to result in a cognitive, affective, or behavioral change in another person" (Forsyth 2016, p. 3). It is vital for teachers as experts for stimulating personal growth of their students to understand the goals and principles of creating appropriate learning environments. In the remainder of this section, the scope of intended learning outcomes (ILO, Biggs and Tang 2011) will be captured in terms of four equally relevant aspects: Affect, Engagement, Mastery, and Reflection.

3.1 Affect

Affective objectives of teaching and learning comprise attitudes, self-efficacy, motivation and well-being. Pellegrino and Hilton (2012, p. 4) have listed affective learning outcomes, i.e. "intellectual openness, work ethic and conscientiousness, and positive core self-evaluation" as high priority objectives for Education in the 21st century. Research shows that individual differences in attitudes and thinking styles are systematically related to learning experiences (Kuhn 1991), and that the development of the ability and willingness to use rational arguments to make a case, to balance reasons, and to handle conflicting information, is a function of specific characteristics of the learning environment (Hefter et al. 2014, 2015).

Learning experiences are facilitated by and shape individual motivation to invest effort in learning. Learner behavior depends on the degree to which the basic motivational needs are satisfied (Deci and Ryan 2000), for example, how much students feel that they have a choice in what and how they study, how much they sense that they can use and increase their competences, and how safe they feel in the social environment.

Self-efficacy, defined as a strong belief in one's ability to solve a problem and the expectation to succeed in a task is "a key personal resource in self-development, successful adaptation, and change" (Bandura 2006, p. 4). Self-efficacy has an impact on the long-term and short-term choices individuals make, on the persistence in the face of task difficulty, on the willingness to invest effort, and on the self-evaluation after completing a task. Research has shown that not only have teachers an influence on the development of adolescents' self-efficacy, but that also teachers' own self-efficacy substantially predicts learners' achievement (Blazar and Kraft 2017; Woolfolk and Davis 2006).

Emotional well-being has been recognized as an important source for personal growth and as a relevant outcome aspect. Well-being is defined as a multi-faceted construct referring to the psychological, cognitive, social and physical functioning as determined by a multitude of factors (OECD 2017, p. 62). For the first time in 2015, the PISA study collected data on students' well-being in school contexts. Well-being has been shown to have considerable impact on student life and growth. Studies suggests that well-being is closely related to good health (Konu and Lintonen 2006; Suhrcke and de Paz Nieves 2011) and impacts on student motivation, learning, and achievement. Research also shows that successful students do not necessarily report high levels of satisfaction with their life and studies. There is evidence for system-specific associations between willingness and ability to invest effort into studying, on the one hand, and tension and anxiety, on the other hand.

3.2   Engagement

Student engagement captures the degree to which a student is actively involved in activities designed for learning (cf. Dormann et al. in this volume). It is conceptualized as a multidimensional construct composed of behavioral, cognitive, emotional, and social patterns of behavior, which, in combination, contribute to learning and to developing successful learning habits and attitudes. Cognitive engagement is visible as investment of cognitive effort in instructional situations, persistence, and positive emotions towards learning and the school setting, including peers and teachers (Ulmanen et al. 2016). Student engagement reflects both classroom behavior (Shernoff et al. 2016), and the pursuit of educational and academic activities beyond school, for example, as in developing personal goals and making career choices (Wang and Degol 2014a, 2014b; Wang et al. 2016).

3.3   Mastery

Mastery of knowledge and skills is a core goal of teaching and learning (cf. Kosslyn in this volume). Following Anderson and Krathwohl's (2013) revision of Bloom et al.'s (1971) taxonomy and in line with Dalton-Puffer's interpretation (2013), the categorization of knowledge and skills is arranged in terms of complexity of (mental) operations which a person is required and able to perform to solve a problem. Teachers design tasks which help students understand their progress, how they achieved it, and where they are headed. Constructive feedback from teachers to students on the degree of mastery supports individual experience of competence and is the backdrop against which new goals will be set to drive further learning.

3.4   Reflection

Self-reflection is both a way of learning and a goal for learning. Current theories of self-regulated learning contain self-reflection as a core construct (Boekaerts 1999; Zimmerman 2000). Successful self-regulated learning needs students to understand how to set adequate goals for themselves, how to plan a learning episode including, selecting learning strategies, to monitor reiterating goals when they meet difficulties and errors (Heemsoth and Heinze 2016), and to adapt their learning and study behavior accordingly.

Self-regulation as a goal for learning and teaching addresses the development of a positive attitude and pertaining skills towards lifelong learning (LLL). This has become a major guideline for educational policy and curriculum development in many places (e.g., European Commission 2001). Encouragement for self-reflection could be identified as a predictor for interest, for the motivation to continually learn and improve on one's skills and competences, for a growing confidence in one's ability to master new challenges, and the use of metacognitive strategies and skills to monitor learning (Lüftenegger et al. 2017).

3.5   Interdependence of growth areas

To complete the picture of the teaching and learning relationship, two more aspects need to be taken into account: Firstly, personal growth in all aspects occurs both in the student and in the teacher. Second, the aspects of personal growth are mutually interdependent and interact in a complex pattern. In search of sources and effects of teacher self-efficacy, Zee and Koomen (2016, p. 7) were able show that teacher self-efficacy impacts on the quality of classroom processes which are critical for student achievement, which in turn supports teacher self-efficacy. The complex interrelationship of well-being, motivation, achievement, and (teacher) self-efficacy requires that all relevant aspects need to be considered carefully. If one aspect is neglected, it is likely to negatively affect the entire system, for example, a lack of emotional support in the classroom may well lead to diminished teacher and student well-being and lower academic achievement, resulting in low self-efficacy in both the teacher and the student. Conversely, more positive predictions emerge through fostering positive behaviours, for example, teacher self-efficacy, and improvements may emerge in more distal areas, such as student motivation and academic achievement.

4   Mentoring learning and personal growth

"Every student deserves a great teacher, not by chance but by design" (Fisher et al. 2016, p. 2).

The consideration of the role of the student in terms of affect, engagement and commitment to learning needs to be complemented by a discussion of the role of the teacher's pedagogic understanding in higher education. These procedures and strategies which stimulate growth processes, require students to construct knowledge and refine their skills and demonstrate and communicate their understanding. This will not function effectively unless the learner connects with learning objectives and engages in content development through a sense of commitment to successfully achieve those goals. Developing a growth mindset brings together all three dimensions in the PTL model discussed thus far i.e. (1) *generating and sustaining achievement and commitment,* (2) *constructing knowledge and refining skills,* and (3) *demonstrating and communicating understanding.* The fourth dimension comprises the teacher's role in fostering growth mindsets and mentoring learner progression. In this section, therefore, we examine key aspects of the role of teachers – regardless of the ages and stages of students - which focus on designing and evaluating learning, scaffolding and supporting learners, and providing feedback for assessing learning by individuals, peers and teachers.

4.1   Designing and evaluating learning

For students to leverage deeper learning, the dynamic processes involved in designing and evaluating a conducive learning environment suggests a reorientation of UNESCO's 'four pillars' (Delors 1996) in terms of teacher knowing, doing, being and enabling in the classroom. Drawing on the work of van Lier (1996), if teachers articulate their own 'Theory of Practice' based on an understanding and interpretation of the principles underpinning PTL, this will bring into question the purposes and enactment of day to day classroom practices. Whilst there is extensive research on teacher knowledge and pedagogic understanding in schools (e.g., Banks et al. 1999; Bernstein 2000; Shulman and Shulman 2009; Verloop et al. 2001) transforming the rhetoric into teacher-owned distinctive practices or 'signature pedagogies' (Shulman 2005) in higher education demands significant shifts in designing different 'patterns of actions, activities and interactions' (Schatzki et al. 2001) for different classes and different learners. This assertion is based on the premise that learning progression not only involves cognitive and metacognitive development but also self-efficacy, affect and teacher guidance. This is summarised by Fullan and Langworthy (2014, p. 8) as leading to "sophisticated pedagogic capacities, which require expertise across a repertoire of different teaching strategies and continuous evaluation of where students are in their learning progressions." In the literature, it is often suggested that moving away from teacher-led classrooms implies adopting student-led approaches where teachers become 'facilitators' or 'guides on the side'. We propose, however, that enabling deeper learning requires the teacher to take a highly proactive role in 'driving the learning process forward' using whichever strategy works best according to individual learners and tasks. This involves interacting with learners to make thinking more visible and to encourage dialogue about learning – an interesting point given the traditional foundations of the role of Socratic dialogue in tertiary education. Hattie (2014) suggests that the teacher's role is both that of facilitator and activator of learning, where teacher as activator is significantly more powerful than facilitator in terms of enabling learning. Yet, teaching for learning does not lie in determining the extent to which a teacher is more 'facilitator' or 'activator' or any other descriptor, but rather in emphasizing how growth processes are stimulated when teachers and students work together to achieve shared goals. All learning contexts, therefore, require a wide range of teaching approaches and a repertoire of strategies from teacher-based input to project-based learning though direct instruction to an inquiry-based model.

> "Teachers who play dynamic, interactive roles with students – pushing students to clearly define their own learning goals, helping them gain the learning muscle to effectively pursue those goals, and supporting them in monitoring how they are doing in achieving those goals – have extremely strong impacts on their students' learning. Such teachers do not 'let the students learn on their own' but instead help them master the difficult and demanding process of learning." (Fullan and Langworthy 2014, p. 20).

The need for teachers to 'partner' learners to co-create personal and transparent learning pathways mutually negotiated and achieved through challenging learning tasks, prioritises what we call teacher 'mentoring'. Stoll and Louis (2007) underline the importance of teacher-learner connectedness where mentoring involves enabling learners "to learn about themselves as learners and continuously assess and reflect upon their own progress" (Fullan and Langworthy 2014, p. ii). It also emphasises the need for teachers to be reflexive in their practices echoing the principle 'everyone a teacher everyone a learner' (NFER 2014). 'Mentoring for learning' a term coined by Tillema et al. (2015) is characterized by exploring joint goals, actions and evaluations through conversations that construct and reconstruct meaningful conceptualisations and communication that go "beyond the information given and shape unique episodes of knowledge productive interaction" (Tillema et al. 2015, p. 16). Yet there seems to be a disconnect between what is perceived as typical approaches to learning in higher education and current practices. Rather than describing the teacher as mentor, PTL requires teachers to design and evaluate the dynamic processes involved in mentoring for learning. The centrality of meaning-making in mentoring for learning emphasizes progressive conversations to support informed participation and scaffold learning through appropriate feedback, assessment and personal growth.

4.2　Pathways for scaffolding and supporting learning

A constant challenge for teachers concerns planning, activating and negotiating the 'right approach, at the right time for the right type of learning'. There are, of course, no straightforward formulas and solutions but a range of emergent flexible learning pathways which lie at the intersection between student growth and mentoring learning, drawing together the dimension for demonstrating and communicating understanding with that of constructing knowledge and refining skills (see Figure 4). Navigating these pathways requires scaffolding and support by teachers not only to develop conceptual and linguistic tools but also to build student confidence and a sense of achievement through feedback and assessments. Involving students in defining and redefining learning tasks and the sequencing of activities goes some way to ensuring that goals and intentions are clear. Similarly, designing opportunities with and for individuals enables learning to become visible to themselves and others. Students are encouraged to engage in problem-solving and opportunities for 'transferring' learning thereby connecting to their own sense of achievement and aspirations. The transfer from surface learning to deeper learning – both of which are essential (Marton and Säljö 1976) involve students and teachers together in collaborative enterprise (Stoll and Louis 2007) across spaces where physical and virtual tools are co-developed and used.

Marzano (2017) details a range of fundamental teacher strategies which focus on engaging students, building positive learning relationships and crucially communicating high teacher expectations for all learners including 'reluctant' individuals. Whilst it could be argued that these strategies are not new for teachers, we argue that what is distinctive in PTL is the way in which the repertoire of teacher strategies has to transparently cohere with all four PTL dimensions when mapping out learning pathways and designing tasks and activities to support deeper learning progression. In other words, deploying engagement strategies which foster student commitment alongside those which enable student choice in navigating cognitive and linguistic pathways, build confidence and a sense of agency – thereby seeking to provide learners with the range of tools needed to encourage personal growth and autonomous lifelong learning.

4.3　Feedback for assessing learning

Feedback between and among teachers and students stands at the critical nexus between learning goals, deeper learning tasks and deeper learning outcomes (Fullan and Langworthy, 2014, p. 16). Feedback essentially develops a mutual understanding of what learning progression in pluriliteracies growth looks like. It actively engages students in evaluating progress by adjusting and refining their work. Where appropriate learning goals and success criteria are defined, co-created or designed by students and guided by the 'experts' in advance of task implementation, using rubrics that make levels of success transparent, then capacities for students to build new knowledge and lead their own learning effectively is practised, refined and advanced. Formative assessment embodies feedback from different sources, especially peers, and becomes integral to developing iterative self-assessment and collaborative assessment which is critical for understanding and meaning-making. Carefully designed and agreed principles for different kinds of assessment are fundamental to raising student awareness and confidence in the 'how to do it better' mindset and drives progression within the PTL continua. This is mentored learning.

According to Dweck (2007), Tough (2012) and Duckworth (2013), appropriate feedback in its different forms also contributes to the development of student capacities essential for overcoming challenges – such as grit, tenacity and perseverance – defined as commitment to successful learning and growth mindsets (Claxton et al. 2011). In other words, adaptive feedback and integrated assessment are essential for learning progression; it contributes to the development of essential skills that enable learners to cope with and learn through making mistakes and experiencing dissatisfaction with progress. Through PTL we are proposing a more holistic conceptualisation of learning and teaching which repositions the student and the teacher in a 'safe', yet challenging and dialogic environment which unifies all four dimensions to grow interconnected learning ecologies. This resonates with Fullan's notion of learning partnerships built on principles of 'equity, transparency, reciprocal accountability and mutual benefit' (cf. Fullan and Langworthy 2014).

There has been a significant shift on a global scale in terms of how the quality of higher education is measured (LEAP 2007). In contexts where neo-liberal attitudes and policies are dominant, some students may have to pay for their higher education and the marketisation of 'excellence' is based on 'customer' satisfaction. The criteria for assessing the quality of teaching in universities is commonly based on rhetoric around employability, transferability of skills, impact in terms of addressing specific skill shortages, and student feedback – all of which are used as a benchmark for funding for universities. Claims about student attributes and learning outcomes based on generic skills influence teaching agendas in tertiary education which have more recently paid particular attention to competitive marketing by promoting the importance of learning and teaching experiences as well as research excellence.

In some contexts, such as the UK, there are awards for achieving teaching excellence standards using institution-wide data, which have led to a national teaching excellence framework for higher education (TEF) designed to attract the 'best' international students. Increasing demands are being made on university teachers to undergo some form of training to teach in higher education contexts, yet a focus on how to enable and facilitate deeper learning for students receives little attention. Individual institutions promote goals based on 'distinctiveness' and 'improved student experiences' (Douglas and McClelland 2008) yet the gap between teaching and high-quality student learning, we would argue, is widening. In this paper, we suggest that the criteria for understanding how approaches to teaching in higher education can provide students with opportunities to engage in critical thinking, problem-solving and using a range of literacies, need to be critically re-conceptualized. In other words, exploring the conditions necessary for the kind of learning which is talked about but not achieved across a range of rapidly changing contexts is essential for educating a future global workforce.

5   Putting a pluriliteracies approach into practice: Designing interconnected university classes

Based on our personal experiences as well as regular feedback from pre- and in-service teacher educators, student teachers following literature courses, experience considerable difficulty in making optimal use of their theoretical knowledge about literary genres and literary periods in terms of conceptual-depth and linguistic competence. In tasks which require the reading, analysis and writing of literary texts, the nature of student difficulties suggests that key concepts have not been internalized and that relevant skills are not fully automatized thereby indicating that deeper learning processes have not been activated and the task is not completed successfully.

To address these challenges, we decided to redesign our courses based on a more integrated approach to providing opportunities for deeper learning. According to Lantolf and Poehner (2014), the successful internalization of conceptual knowledge follows three phases: from understanding to abstraction to transfer. They posit that in order to fully understand a concept so that it can be applied in subject specific activities and tasks, learners require an initial material or 'hands-on' phase: "The advantage of materializing a concept over providing a purely verbal definition is that the latter lends itself to memorization without understanding, while the former is difficult to memorize without understanding" (Lantolf and Poehner 2014, p. 65).

In order to deepen understanding, learners need to engage in articulating their understanding as it evolves through social communication (e.g., another learner or to themselves as in private speech in order to "gain mastery over the concept through dialogic speech" (Lantolf and Poehner 2014, p. 67). Languaging their understanding will help students move towards an abstraction of the concept which is fundamental for using and applying it in different contexts.

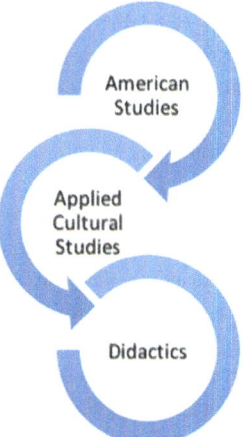

Fig. 3   Revised course structure

Instead of planning and designing our courses separately, our revised three-part course structure is the result of an intense collaboration between three distinct disciplines which form a mandatory part of our teacher training programme: American Literature, Cultural Studies and Didactics (see Figure 3). The revised structure and interconnected nature of these courses is based on the above-mentioned principles to initiate and sustain deeper learning processes in our students:

1. In the American Literature class, we intend to facilitate understanding and practice empathic positioning as well as maximize student engagement and interaction through group role plays. Research has shown that role-play activities can increase self-reflection, awareness, retention of knowledge (Westrup and Planander 2013) and create deeper cognitive links to the learning content (McEwen et al. 2014). In each session, students are required to role-play a specific novel or drama in groups. The role play is followed by a teacher-led phase

where the instructor clarifies how the novel or drama which the students had to capture in their role-play reflects the philosophical and cultural ideas of that specific literary period.

2. Building on those experiences, students attend a Cultural Studies course where they move to a more abstract understanding of their newly gained conceptual knowledge by being taught how to write a literary essay based on the work of literature that they chose for their role-play. This is new in several ways: Traditionally, Cultural Studies courses tend to have no connections to literary classes and the essay assignments are typically not based on prior reading or learning experiences. In addition, instructors will receive specific training in functional linguistics to ensure that student feedback on essays will not be based on a traditional, grammar-based view of language but serve to help students maximize their meaning making potential.

3. To promote transfer of conceptual knowledge and to demonstrate a deeper understanding of the novels/dramas as well as the literary periods and genres that they have studied in the previous two courses, students will be asked to design and produce digital teaching materials for upper-secondary students in the form of highly interactive ibooks for iPad classrooms in a subsequent Didactics Class. According to the Revised Bloom Taxonomy, creating those materials requires the reorganization of knowledge elements into new patterns or structures through the processes of generating, planning and producing and is considered to be a highly complex and demanding cognitive operation (Anderson and Krathwohl 2013).

6   Towards a research agenda for deeper learning

Building on Bigg's 3P Model (Presage-Process-Product; Biggs 1999) which frames a complexity of factors which come into play during any teaching and learning process, we present a research agenda for deeper learning which acknowledges that what teachers and learners bring with them in terms of previous experiences, attitudes, perceptions and predispositions (Presage), will impact on teacher instructional decisions and materials design for learning as well as learner readiness and willingness to actively engage in the set tasks (Processes), thereby shaping the quality of learning and feedback (Product; see Figure 4). Learning outcomes are conceptualized as subject specific achievement and performance, including attitudinal and motivational competences as personal assets. Whilst there is nothing new about these factors, we argue that the quality of learning is dependent on the *interaction* of contributory factors and characteristics defined by the learners and teachers, the physical and social spaces which situate the learning and constant feedback which account for dynamic influences and determine the quality of learning. We posit that when the ecological potential of learning is shared and understood by those involved – as set out in the PTL approach – then the quality of learning is transparent and driven by participants. In other words, emergent ecological systems shape each learning and teaching episode which we refer to as shared learning spaces.

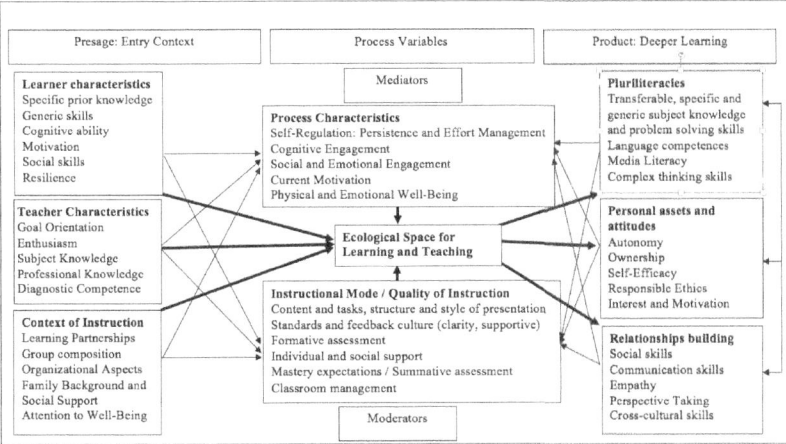

Fig. 4   Systems model of arena for learning and teaching

According to van Ewijk (2011) teacher performance and expectations are likely to vary depending on learner characteristics. In a similar vein, learner motivation and achievement might be a function of the group composition in the context of instruction (van Ewijk and Sleegers 2010). Moreover, drawing on the assumption that teacher characteristics in combination and interaction with student characteristics and the instructional context impact on the scope and depth of learning spaces (Keller et al. 2017; Schiefele and Schaffner 2015) we propose our first set of research questions:

(RQ 1) What are the factors that initially contribute to creating shared learning spaces?
(RQ 2) How do learner characteristics, teacher characteristics, and the context of instruction interact with each other to create shared learning spaces?
(RQ 3) What is the impact of learner characteristics, teacher characteristics, and the context of instruction on the subsequent mediators in the learning process?

Learning outcomes operate at distinct levels of immediacy and complexity (Anderson and Krathwohl 2013; Biggs and Tang 2011). Therefore, we propose that measuring outcomes to encourage increasing relevance of comprehensive and transferable skills and competences (Pellegrino and Hilton 2012) requires specific attention with a focus on three elements:

- pluriliteracies, which involve transferable knowledge and competences and skills;
- personal assets and attitudes, based on self-efficacy, interest, and motivation to invest effort and to contribute to society in a responsible and ethical manner;
- relationship building through communication competences.

How these contributory elements are transformed into an inclusive, yet accessible and practical framework for assessing and evaluating learning, leads to the following:

(RQ 4) How do we define the complex yet relevant descriptors of deeper learning outcomes in the areas of pluriliteracies, personal assets, and relationship building?
(RQ 5) How can we align teaching, learning and assessing developing competences in terms of immediate and sustainable learning?

Outcomes of a learning process are rarely a final or static 'product'. Experiences in one learning episode serve as a bridge or a barrier to the next depending on how mediating variables, especially the sense of self-efficacy, impact on the learner and teacher (Bandura 2006). The processes and outcomes involved in linking learning episodes, therefore, shape perceptions of self, of others, and of the relationships between all the people involved in the learning episode. Based on these considerations, we propose the next research question:

(RQ 6) How does previous learning stimulate and reinforce deeper learning?

In an ecological model, we view learning outcomes as integrated and mutually dependent across and within the levels described. In particular, subject specific skills, language skills, and complex thinking skills are interdependent. In addition, we assume that investing effort in developing and using these skills is driven by a set of interconnected self-competences, such as motivation and self-efficacy. Applying knowledge and skills to different learning episodes involves additional cognitive and motivational competences which help learners to reflect on and adjust their skills for successful transfer (Larsen-Freeman 2013; Trench and Minervino 2017). Taken together, we arrive at the following research questions:

(RQ 7) How is domain-specific and generic content of deeper learning reflected in language and self-competences?
(RQ 8) What are the conditions under which learners transform, transfer and apply their competences to solve complex problems?

Learning is non-linear and teaching is not a transmissive process from expert to novice –teaching and learning interconnects through dynamic cyclical processes and conditions. Individuals develop learning trajectories through which skills and competences are developed. Our adaptation of Bigg's (1999) model especially emphasizes the influence and relevance of prior knowledge, experiences, attitudes and values of both learners and teachers in shaping learning episodes. When teachers and learners invest effort into cognitive, social, and emotional engagement, their self-regulation skills become increasingly refined. Empirical research in the field of instructional science identifies factors which mediate and impact on learning and learning outcomes. In addition to that, we suggest investigating the mediating processes as they are enacted in classrooms. Investigating these processes may provide further evidence which in turn may help us define optimal conditions for learning, for example, the structure and presentation style of content and tasks; the type and frequency of assessments; clarity and motivational potential of feedback; support for student learning; and the social control of group dynamics in the classroom (e.g., Hattie 2014; OECD 2016a, 2017). In essence, we believe that we need a more detailed understanding of how the principles of learning work for the challenges of deeper learning:

(RQ 9) What are moderating factors which determine the instructional mode and quality of teaching?
(RQ 10) What are the dynamic interactions between the characteristics of the instruction and the moderating variables?

(RQ 11) How do characteristics of instruction affect the mediating variables, and, eventually, the outcomes of learning?
(RQ 12) How can we map a range of learning trajectories and/or learning cycles typical of deeper learning?
(RQ 13) What are appropriate instruments, tasks, challenges, and materials that support deeper learning?
(RQ 14) How can or must teaching and learning be tailored to the content and the target competences to navigate a learner through mediating processes into deeper learning?

Throughout this article, the importance of learner-teacher 'partnerships' for learning including peer relationships has been emphasized (Langworthy and Fullan 2014; King 2015; OECD 2017; Oga-Baldwin et al. 2017; Schroeder et al. 2011). Whilst affective factors impacting learning and teaching in schools are well researched, much less attention has been paid to such contributory variables in the tertiary sector.

(RQ 15) What are the contributory factors which foster learning partnerships for deeper learning?
(RQ 16) How does the quality of learning partnerships impact on the sustainability of deeper learning over time?

The research questions outlined above are suggestions for ways in which a shared understanding of the dynamics of the learning and teaching processes may be discussed, debated and critiqued. In order to develop appropriate measurement strategies that represent the complexity of the model and learner development or change over time, the need to focus on a multi-level content- and competence-oriented assessment of cognition (knowledge), metacognition, and self-competences emerges. Constructing a research agenda such as this requires time. It will involve measurements of both immediate learning and transferable skills using subject-specific and generic problem-solving tasks as well as affective elements such as self-efficacy, motivational strength, persistence, willingness to learn, cognitive and emotional engagement, all of which are fundamental contributors to the quality of learning partnerships.

In sum, we propose a framework for (quasi-)experimental research to investigate the scope of deeper learning, which will identify more specific teaching and learning challenges involved in such dynamic processes. In particular, we wish to further our understanding of complex learning and the acquisition of transferable competences in higher education contexts, where student experiences leading to and determining quality learning outcomes have not been given adequate attention. The rhetoric driving the student experience agenda in universities and higher education institutions has not – as far as we know – focused on articulating more finely granulated interpretations of the fundamental processes of learning which in essence reveal much more than measurable degree examination results (cf. Zlatkin-Troitschanskaia et al. 2017a).

7   Conclusion: From deeper learning to positive learning

"If we choose to ignore the Sustainable Development Goals (SDGs), higher education will become the dinosaurs of tomorrow." (Ogbuigwe 2017).

To conclude this article, we will address the question as to how pluriliteracies development and deeper learning pertain to the more ambitious goals and envisioned outcomes of the PLATO program: The goals of positive learning can be summarized as empowering students to not only become critical, highly informed and reflective citizens with the ability to evaluate situations and take informed decisions but, more importantly, to act responsibly and ethically for the good of our planet and its population (cf. Zlatkin-Troitschanskaia et al. 2017b). The UNESCO four pillars of education, state that 21st century students must learn how to know, how to do, how to be and how to live together. The UNESCO (2017) suggests a number of steps universities should take to reach these goals (see Figure 5):

• Providing the cognitive tools required to better comprehend the world and its complexities, and to provide an appropriate and adequate foundation for future learning.
• Providing the skills that would enable individuals to effectively participate in the global economy and society.
• Providing self-analytical and social skills to enable individuals to develop to their fullest potential psycho-socially, affectively as well as physically, for an all-round complete person.
• Exposing individuals to the values implicit within human rights, democratic principles, intercultural understanding and respect and peace at all levels of society and human relationships to enable individuals and societies to live in peace and harmony.

The arguments developed throughout this article purport that a focus on pluriliteracies and deeper learning forms the nexus of positive learning, since the ability to critically evaluate situations and take informed decisions requires deep understanding as well as transferable knowledge and skills.

However, positive learning also encompasses acting and behaving responsibly and ethically which involves more than knowledge and understanding: it calls for attributes and behaviours such as strength, long-term engagement and persistence, resourcefulness, resilience, agency, community involvement (cf. Zlatkin-Troitschanskaia et al. 2017b). In order to instill these qualities and values in young emerging adults, universities need to provide environments that support the positive and healthy development of their students (see Mercier 2016, Taylor et al. 2017).

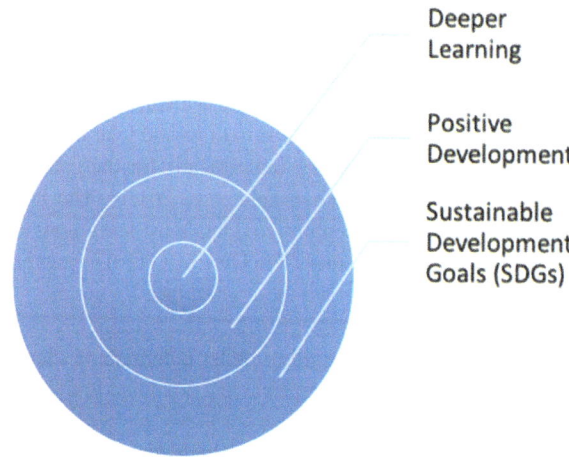

Deeper
Learning

Positive
Development

Sustainable
Development
Goals (SDGs)

Fig. 5   Model of Positive Learning

Finally, an ethical dimension is a fundamental component of positive learning since it informs potential trajectories for responsible and moral behavior of young people. The 17 Sustainable Development Goals (SDGS) and their associated 169 targets which were agreed upon by all countries at the United Nations in September 2015 could serve this purpose and provide an "ethos for higher education to reinvent itself and to rethink teaching, research, and community engagement" (Ogbuigwe 2017) with the goal of preparing students to face global, social, economic and environmental challenges by: raising awareness of sustainable development through interdisciplinary, pluricultural and plurilingual activities; encouraging participatory research on sustainable development, for example, through green campuses and local sustainability initiatives, and engaging with and sharing information with international networks (UN 2017).

As is so often the case, the successful application of the SDGS does not rest on empty rhetoric or easily and sometimes hastily marketed commitments by anonymous universities, but on the individual teachers and lecturers and the learning spaces they co-create in individual classrooms and lecture halls. Our pluriliteracies model for deeper learning addresses this 'disconnect' by offering a way to fuse the concentric circles of positive learning, by showcasing how to design ecologies for deeper learning and positive growth and by providing evidence of how this can be enacted in higher education.

Bibliography

Anderson, L. W., & Krathwohl, D. (Eds.). (2013). *A Taxonomy for learning, teaching, and assessing: A revision of Bloom's taxonomy of educational objectives*. Boston: Pearson.

Arnett, J. (2000). Emerging adulthood. A theory of development from the late teens through the twenties. *American Psychologist, 55*(5), 469–480.

Arnett, J., Zukauskiene, R., & Sagimura, K. (2014). The new life stage of emerging adulthood 18-29 years: Implications for mental health. *Lancet Psychiatry, 1*(7), 569–576.

Arum, R., & Roksa, J. (2010). *Academically adrift: Limited learning on college campuses*. Chicago: University of Chicago Press.

Arum, R., & Roksa, J. (2014). *Aspiring adults adrift: Tentative transitions of college graduates*. Chicago: University of Chicago Press.

Astin, A. (1993). *What matters in college? Four critical years revisited*. San Francisco: Joessey-Bass.

Bandura, A. (2006). Adolescents' development from an agentic perspective. In F. Pajares & T. Urdan (Eds.), *Self-Efficacy Beliefs of Adolescents* (pp. 1–45). Greenwich, CT: Information Age Publishing.

Banks, F., Leach, J., & Moon, B. (1999). New understandings of teachers' pedagogic knowledge. In J. Leach & B. Moon (Eds.), *Learners and Pedagogy* (pp. 89–110). London: Paul Chapman Publishing.

Bernstein, B. (2000). *Pedagogy, symbolic control and identity: Theory, research and critique*. London: Taylor and Francis.

Biggs, J. (1999). *Teaching for quality learning at university*. Buckingham, UK: Society for Research on Higher Education.

Biggs, J., & Tang, C. (2011). *Teaching for quality learning at university*. New York: McGraw Hill.

Blaich, C. (2007). *Overview of findings from the first year of the Wabash National Study of Liberal Arts Education*. Retrieved from http://www.liberalarts.wabash.edu/research

Blazar, D., & Kraft, M. A. (2017). Teacher and teaching effects on students' attitudes and behaviors. *Educational Evaluation and Policy Analysis, 39*(1), 146–170.

Bloom, B. S., Hastings, J. T., & Madaus, G. F. (1971). *Handbook on formative and summative evaluation of student learning.* New York: McGraw Hill.

Boekaerts, M. (1999). Self-regulated learning: Where we are today. *International Journal of Educational Research, 31*(6), 445–457. doi:10.1016/S0883-0355(99)00014-2

Chiriac, S. E., & Ghitu-Bratescu, A. (2011). Linking globalisation, sustainable development and knowledge transfer - A network based approach. *Journal of Doctoral Research in Economics, 3*(1), 13–22.

Claxton, G., Chambers, M., Powell, G., & Lucas, B. (2011). *The learning powered school: Pioneering 21st century education.* Bristol: TLO Publishers.

Dalton-Puffer, C. (2007). *Discourse in content and language integrated learning (CLIL) classrooms.* Philadelphia: John Benjamins.

Dalton-Puffer, C. (2013). A construct of cognitive discourse functions for conceptualising content-language integration in CLIL and multilingual education. *European Journal of Applied Linguistics, 1*(2), 216–253.

Dalton-Puffer, C. (2015). *Cognitive discourse functions: Combining content and language perspectives for CLIL teacher development.* Conference presentation. CLIL Colloquium: Integrating content and language for teacher development in bilingual / multilingual settings: From research to practice. Madrid, June 2015.

Deci, E. L., & Ryan, R. M. (2000). The „what" and „why" of goal pursuits: Human needs and the self-determination of behavior. *Psychological Inquiry, 11*(4), 227–268. doi:10.1207/S15327965PLI1104_01

Delors, J. (1996). *The treasure within.* A Report for the European Commission.

Douglas, J., & McClelland, Davies, J. (2008). The development of a conceptual model of student satisfaction with their experience in higher education. *Quality Assurance in Education, 16*(1), 19–35. doi:10.1108/09684880810848396

Duckworth, A. (2013). *Grit: The power of passion and perseverance.* TED: Ideas Worth Spreading. Retrieved from https://www.ted.com/talks/angela_lee_duckworth_grit_the_power_of_passion_and_perseverance

Dweck, C. (2007). *Mindset: The new psychology of success.* New York: Ballantine Books.

Eppler, M.J. & Burkhard, R.A. (2004). *Knowledge Visualization: Towards a New Discipline and its Fields of Application. Institute for Corporate Communication.* Retrieved from http://doc.rero.ch/record/5196/files/1_wpca0402.pdf

European Commission (2001). *Making a European area of lifelong learning a reality.* Brussels: Commission of the European Communities.

Fisher, D., Frey, N., & Hattie, J. (2016). *Visible learning for literacy.* Thousand Oaks, CA: Corwin Press.

Forsyth, D. R. (2016). *College teaching.* Washington, DC: American Psychological Association.

Fullan, M., & Langworthy, M. (2014). *A rich seam: How new pedagogies find deep learning.* Toronto, ON: Pearson.

González, A., Conde, Á., Díaz, P., García, M., & Ricoy, C. (2017). Instructors' teaching styles: Relation with competences, self-efficacy, and commitment in pre-service teachers. *Higher Education.* doi:10.1007/s10734-017-0160-y

Hart Research Associates (2015). *Falling Short? College learning and career success. Selected findings from online surveys of employers and college students conducted on behalf of the Association of American Colleges & Universities.* Retrieved from https://www.aacu.org/leap/public-opinion-research

Happ, R., Zlatkin-Troitschanskaia, O., & Schmidt, S. (2016). An Analysis of Economic Learning among Undergraduates in Introductory Economics Courses in Germany. *Journal of Economic Education, 47*(4), 300–310. doi:10.1080/00220485.2016.1213686

Hattie, J. (2014). *Visible learning for teachers: Maximizing impact on learning.* London: Routledge.

Heemsoth, T., & Heinze, A. (2016). Secondary school students learning from reflections on the rationale behind self-made errors: A field experiment. *Journal of Experimental Education, 84*(1), 98–118.

Hefter, M. H., Berthold, K., Renkl, A., Riess, W., Schmid, S., & Fries, S. (2014). Effects of a training intervention to foster argumentative skills while processing conflicting scientific positions. *Instructional Science, 42*(6), 929–947.

Hefter, M. H., Renkl, A., Riess, W., Schmid, S., Fries, S., & Berthold, K. (2015). Effects of a training intervention to foster precursors of evaluativist epistemological understanding and intellectual values. *Learning and Instruction, 39,* 11–22. doi:10.1016/j.learninstruc.2015.05.002

Kale, D., Little, S. and Hinton, M. (2011). Reconfiguration of Knowledge Management Practices in New Product Development: The Case of the Indian Pharmaceutical Industry. In K.A. Grant (Ed.), *Case Studies in Knowledge Management Research* (pp. 102–119). Reading, UK: Academic Publishing International Ltd.

Keller, M. M., Neumann, K., & Fischer, H. E. (2017). The impact of physics teachers' pedagogical content knowledge and motivation on students' achievement and interest. *Journal of Research in Science Teaching, 54*(5), 586–614.

Kim, J. H. (2016). Pedagogical approaches to media literacy education in the United States. In M. N. Yildiz & J. Keengwe (Eds.), *Handbook of research on media literacy in the digital age* (pp. 52–74). Hershey, PA: IGI Global.

King, R. B. (2015). Sense of relatedness boosts engagement, achievement, and well-being: A latent growth model study. *Contemporary Educational Psychology, 42,* 26–38.

Konu, A. I., & Lintonen, T. P. (2006). School well-being in grades 4–12. *Health Education Research, 21*(5), 633–642. doi:10.1093/her/cyl032

Kuh, G. D. (2003). What we're learning about student engagement from NSSE: Benchmarks for Effective Educational Practices. *Change, 35*(2), 24–32.

Kuhn, D. (1991). *The skills of argument.* Cambridge, MA: Cambridge University Press.

Lantolf, J. P., & Poehner, M. E. (2014). *Sociocultural theory and the pedagogical imperative in L2 education: Vygotskian praxis and the research/practice divide.* New York: Routledge.

Larsen-Freeman, D. (2013). Transfer of learning transformed. *Language Learning, 63*(s1), 107–129. doi: 10.1111/j.1467-9922.2012.00740.x

Liu, Y. & Grusky, D. B. (2013). The payoff to skill in the third industrial revolution. *American Journal of Sociology, 118*(5), 1330–1374.

Lüftenegger, M., Schober, B., van de Schoot, R., Wagner, P., Finsterwald, M., & Spiel, C. (2017). Lifelong learning as a goal – Do autonomy and self-regulation in school result in well-prepared pupils? *Learning and Instruction, 22*(1), 27–36.

Marton, F., & Säljö, R. (1976). On qualitative differences in learning. 1 – Outcome and process. *British Journal of Educational Psychology, 46*(1), 4–11.

Marzano, R. J. (2017). *The new art and science of teaching.* Alexandria, VA: ASCD and Solution Tree.

McEwen, L., Stokes, A., Crowley, K. & Roberts, C. (2014). Using role-play for expert science communication with professional stakeholders in flood risk management. *Journal of Geography in Higher Education, 38*(2), 277–300. doi:10.1080/03098265.2014.911827

Mercier, J. (2016). Embedding positive youth development into tertiary learning and teaching. In H. Hamerton & C. Fraser (Eds.), *Te Tipuranga - Growing Capability: Proceedings of the 2015 National Tertiary Learning and Teaching Conference* (pp. 27–34). Tauranga, NZ: Bay of Plenty Polytechnic.

Meyer, O., & Coyle, D. (2017). Pluriliteracies teaching for learning: conceptualizing progression for deeper learning in literacies development. *European Journal of Applied Linguistics, 5.* doi:10.1515/eujal-2017-0006

Meyer, O., Coyle, D., Halbach, A., Schuck, K., & Ting, T. (2015). A pluriliteracies approach to content and language integrated learning – Mapping learner progressions in knowledge construction and meaning-making. *Language, Culture, and Curriculum, 28*(1), 41–57.

Mohan, B., Leung, C., & Slater, T. (2010). Assessing language and content: A functional perspective. In A. Paran & L. Sercu (Eds.), *Testing the untestable in language education* (pp. 217–240). Clevedon: Multilingual Matters.

National Foundation for Educational Research (NFER). (2014). *Everyone a teacher, everyone a learner at New NFER Enquiring School.* Retrieved from https://www.nfer.ac.uk/about-nfer/media-and-events/everyone-a-teacher-everyone-a-learner-at-new-nfer-enquiring-school/

National Leadership Council for Liberal Education & America's Promise (LEAP) (2007). *College Learning for the New Global Century.* Washington: Association of American Colleges and Universities.

Ning, K., & Downing, K. (2010). The reciprocal relationship between motivation and self-regulation: A longitudinal study on academic performance. *Learning and Individual Differences, 20*(6), 682–686.

Novak, J. D. (2002). Meaningful learning: The essential factor for conceptual change in limited or inappropriate propositional hierarchies leading to empowerment of learners. *Science Education, 86*(4), 548–571.

OECD (2016a). *PISA 2015 Results (Volume II): Policies and practices for successful schools.* Paris: OECD Publishing.

OECD (2016b). *The survey of adult skills: Reader's companion.* Paris: OECD Publishing.

OECD (2017). *PISA 2015 Results (Volume III): Students' well-being.* Paris: OECD Publishing.

Oga-Baldwin, W. Q., Nakata, Y., Parker, P., & Ryan, R. M. (2017). Motivating young language learners: A longitudinal model of self-determined motivation in elementary school foreign language classes. *Contemporary Educational Psychology, 49,* 140–150. doi:10.1016/j.cedpsych.2017.01.010

Ogbuigwe, A. (2017). *Advancing sustainability in higher education through the UN's sustainable development goals.* Retrieved from https://sustainability.mit.edu/article/advancing-sustainability-higher-education-through-uns-sustainable-development-goals

Ormrod, J. E. (2011). *Educational Psychology: Developing Learners.* Boston: Pearson.

Pellegrino, J. W., & Hilton, M. L. (Eds.). (2012). *Education for Life and Work. Developing Transferable Knowledge and Skills in the 21st Century.* Washington, DC: The National Academies Press.

Pietarinen, Soini, T., & Pyhältö, K. (2014). Students' emotional and cognitive engagement as the determinants of well-being and achievement in school. *International Journal of Educational Research, 67,* 40–51. doi:10.1016/j.ijer.2014.05.001

Roberts, B. W., & Davis, J. P. (2016). Young Adulthood Is the Crucible of Personality Development. *Emerging Adulthood, 4*(5), 318–326.

Schatzki, T. R., Cetina, K., & von Savigny, E. (Eds.). (2001). *The Practice Turn in Contemporary Theory.* London: Routledge.

Schiefele, U., & Schaffner, E. (2015). Teacher interests, mastery goals, and self-efficacy as predictors of instructional practices and student motivation. *Contemporary Educational Psychology, 42,* 159–171. doi:10.1016/j.cedpsych.2015.06.005

Schmidt, S., Zlatkin-Troitschanskaia, O., & Fox, J.-P. (2016). Pretest-Posttest-Posttest Multilevel IRT Modeling of Competence Growth of Students in Higher Education in Germany. *Journal of Educational Measurement, 53*(3), 332–351. DOI: 10.1111/jedm.12115

Schroeder, S., Richter, T., McElvany, N., Hachfeld, A., Baumert, J., Schnotz, W., Horz, H., & Ullrich, M. (2011). Teachers' beliefs, instructional behaviors, and students' engagement in learning from texts with instructional pictures. *Learning and Instruction, 21*(3), 403–415. doi:10.1016/j.learninstruc.2010.06.001

Selingo, J. J. (2017). *Why can't college graduates write coherent prose? Washington Post, August 11.* Retrieved from https://www.washingtonpost.com/news/grade-point/wp/2017/08/11/why-cant-college-graduates-write/

Shernoff, D. J., Kelly, S., Tonks, S. M., Anderson, B., Cavanagh, R. F., Sinha, S., & Abdi, B. (2016). Student engagement as a function of environmental complexity in high school classrooms. *Learning and Instruction, 43,* 52–60. doi:10.1016/j.learninstruc.2015.12.003

Shulman, L. S. (2005). Signature pedagogies in the professions. *Daedalus 134* (3), 52–59.

Shulman, L. S., & Shulman, J. H. (2004). How and what teachers learn: A shifting perspective. *Journal of Curriculum Studies, 36*(2), 257–271.

Skulborstad, H. M., & Hermann, A. D. (2015). Individual Difference Predictors of the Experience of Emerging Adulthood. *Emerging Adulthood, 4*(3), 168–175.

Stoll, L., & Louis, K. S. (2007). *Professional Learning Communities: Divergence, Depth and Dilemmas.* Maidenhead: Open University Press/McGraw Hill.

Suhrcke, M., & de Paz Nieves, C. (2011). *The impact of health and health behaviours on educational outcomes in high-income countries: A review of the evidence.* Kopenhagen: WHO.

Taylor, R. D., Oberle, E., Durlak, J. A., & Weissberg, R. P. (2017). Promoting positive youth development through school-based social and emotional learning interventions: A meta-analysis of follow-up effects. *Child Development, 88*(4), 1156–1171. doi:10.1111/cdev.12864

Tillema, H. H., van der Westhuizen, G. J., & van der Merwe, M. P. (2015). Knowledge building through conversation. In H. Tillema, G. J. Westyhuizen & K. Smith (Eds.), *Mentoring for learning "Climbing the Mountain"* (pp. 1–19). Rotterdam: Sense Publishers.

Tough, P. (2012). *How children succeed: Grit, curiosity and the hidden power of character.* New York: Houghton Mifflin Harcourt.

Trautwein, C., & Bosse, E. (2017). The first year in higher education—critical requirements from the student perspective. *Higher Education, 73*(3), 371–387.

Trench, M., & Minervino, R. A. (2017). Cracking the problem of inert knowledge. In B. H. Ross (Ed.), *Psychology of Learning and Motivation* (Vol. 66, pp. 1–41). Oxford: Elsevier.

Ulmanen, S., Soini, T., Pietarinen, J., & Pyhältö, K. (2016). The anatomy of adolescents' emotional engagement in schoolwork. *Social Psychology of Education, 19*(3), 587–606.

United Nations (UN) (2017). *Substainable Development. Knowledge Platform*. Retrieved from https://sustainabledevelopment.un.org/sdinaction/hesi

United Nations Educational, Scientific and Cultural Organization (UNESCO) (2017). *Education. The four pillars of learning*. Retrieved from http://www.unesco.org/new/en/education/networks/global-networks/aspnet/about-us/strategy/the-four-pillars-of-learning/

van Ewijk, R. (2011). Same work, lower grade? Student ethnicity and teachers' subjective assessments. *Economics of Education Review, 30*(5), 1045–1058. doi:10.1016/j.econedurev.2011.05.008

van Ewijk, R., & Sleegers, P. (2010). Peer ethnicity and achievement: A meta-analysis into the compositional effect. *School Effectiveness and School Improvement, 21*(3), 237–265.

van Lier, L. (1996). *Interaction in the Language Curriculum: Awareness, Autonomy, and Authenticity*. London: Longman.

Verloop, N., van Driel, J., & Meijer, P. (2001). Teacher knowledge and the knowledge base of teaching. *International Journal of Educational Research, 35*(5), 441–461. doi:10.1016/S0883-0355(02)00003-4

Vollmer, H. J. (2008). Constructing Tasks for Content and Language Integrated Learning and Assessment. In O. Eckerth & S. Siekmann (Eds.), *Task-Based Language Learning and Teaching – Theoretical, Methodological, and Pedagogical Perspectives* (pp. 227–290). Frankfurt am Main: Peter Lang.

Walqui, A. (2006). Scaffolding instruction for English language learners: A conceptual framework. *The International Journal of Bilingual Education and Bilingualism, 9*(2), 159–180. doi:10.1080/13670050608668639

Wang, M. T., & Degol, J. (2014a). Motivational pathways to STEM career choices: Using expectancy-value perspective to understand individual and gender differences in STEM fields. *Developmental Review, 33*(4), 304–340. doi:10.1016/j.dr.2013.08.001

Wang, M. T., & Degol, J. (2014b). Staying engaged: Knowledge and research needs in student engagement. *Child Development Perspectives, 8*(3), 137–143. doi:10.1111/cdep.12073

Wang, M.-T., Fredricks, J. A., Ye, F., Hofkens, T. L., & Linn, J. S. (2016). The math and science engagement scales: Scale development, validation, and psychometric properties. *Learning and Instruction, 43*, 16–26. doi:10.1016/j.learninstruc.2016.01.008

Westrup, U., & Planander, A. (2013). Role-play as a pedagogical method to prepare students for practice: the students' voice. *Högre utbildning, 3*(3), 199–220.

Woolfolk, A., & Davis, H. A. (2006). Teacher self-efficacy and its influence on the achievement of adolescents. In F. Pajares & T. Urdan (Eds.), *Self-Efficacy Beliefs of Adolescents* (pp. 117–138). Greenwich, CT: Information Age Publishing.

Zee, M., & Koomen, H. M. Y. (2016). Teacher self-efficacy and its effects on classroom processes, student academic adjustment, and teacher well-being: A synthesis of 40 years of research. *Review of Educational Research, 86*(4), 981–1015. doi:10.3102/0034654315626801

Zimmerman, B. J. (2000). Attaining self-regulation: A social cognitive perspective. In M. Boekaerts, P. R. Pintrich & M. Zeidner (Eds.), *Handbook of Self-Regulation* (pp. 13–39). San Diego, CA: Academic Press.

Zlatkin-Troitschanskaia, O., Pant, H. A., Lautenbach, C., Molerov, D., Toepper, M., & Brückner, S. (2017a). *Modeling and Measuring Competencies in Higher Education: Approaches to Challenges in Higher Education Policy and Practice*. Wiesbaden: Springer VS.

Zlatkin-Troitschanskaia et al. (2017b). *Positive Learning in the Age of Information*. Unpublished Manuscript, Draft Proposal Cluster of Excellence, Johannes Gutenberg University Mainz.

Acquisition of Generic Competencies Through Project Simulation in Translation Studies

Silvia Hansen-Schirra, Sascha Hofmann, and Jean Nitzke

Abstract

Motivated by the research in several international and interdisciplinary initiatives, for example, P21 Partnership for 21st Century Learning or the Collegiate Learning Assessment instruments, we seek for a scalable and measureable set of generic competencies for translation studies. Up to now, the acquisition of competencies in translation studies has primarily been operationalized by implementing authentic projects in higher education classes using socio-constructivist approaches. This results in a hybridization of subject-specific competencies and generic competencies in translator education. Because of the necessity to focus on the acquisition of generic competencies as a primary learning outcome, an additional teaching approach, the simulated project, will be discussed and tested as a new method for a solid generic competence development within higher education.

Keywords

Authentic Projects; Generic Competencies; Reflective Practitioner; Self-Reporting Method; Simulated Projects; Translation Studies.

1   Motivation

In our field translation studies, the research on domain-specific competencies has made serious progress (cf. PACTE 2003; Göpferich 2008; EMT 2009) and led to a range of competence models, nowadays in strong relation to employability and the market readiness of the educated translator. Whereas the modeling of domain-specific cognitive competencies as well as some soft skills in translation studies has been well researched in the last years, especially through translation process studies (cf. Carl et al. 2016), many aspects of the generic cognitive competencies have either not been properly defined yet, not to mention their empirical investigation. Generic cognitive competencies that address abilities like problem solving strategies, argumentation, research strategies and reading as well as non-cognitive generic competencies that concern self-regulating aspects, such as a positive self-concept, socio-emotional traits and others are here commonly only defined as parts of strategies to solve translation problems within the core process of translation (cf. Göpferich 2008; PACTE 2003). They are strongly linked to the subjects involved in the field, for instance, linguistics, cultural studies or translation technology but are not singularly investigated.

Motivated by the research in several international and interdisciplinary initiatives (cf. Zlatkin-Troitschanskaia et al. 2015, 2017), for example, P21 Partnership for 21st Century Learning[1] or the Collegiate Learning Assessment instruments on generic competencies (Zlatkin-Troitschanskaia et al. 2018; see also Klein et al. 2007; Pellegrino and Hilton 2012) and the common competence definition by Weinert (2001a, 2001b)[2] we seek for a scalable and measureable set of generic competencies for translation studies. Using the frameworks that differentiate between cognitive generic competencies[3], we demand a proper set of generic competencies in respect to the needs of the translation profession. Together with the exploration of a competence set we also see a necessity to adopt existing teaching approaches in translation studies to foster their development during translator education. Up to now, this acquisition of especially generic competencies in translation studies has primarily been operationalized by implementing authentic projects in higher education classes using socio-constructivist approaches. This results in a hybridization of subject-specific competencies and generic competencies in translator

---

[1]   http://www.p21.org/our-work/p21-framework (Accessed: May 31st, 2017)

[2]   https://www.oecd.org/skills/piaac/Skills%20volume%201%20(eng)--full%20v12--eBook%20(04%2011%202013).pdf (Accessed: May 31st, 2017)

[3]   https://www.oecd.org/skills/piaac/Skills%20volume%201%20(eng)--full%20v12--eBook%20(04%2011%202013).pdf (Accessed: May 31st, 2017)

education. Because of the necessity to develop the skills of a translator as a final product on a macro-level, the acquisition of generic competencies is often a secondary learning outcome. Due to this strong focus on authentic translator training (e.g., Massey and Ehrensberger-Dow 2011), an additional teaching approach, the simulated project, as a new method for a solid generic competence development within higher education processes will be described within this paper.

2 From authentic to simulated project work in translator education

If we take a look at initiatives focussing on competence oriented learning in the translation studies community that were mentioned in the introduction, we can acknowledge that authentic projects are one of the most prominent methods used in the curricula of translator education programmes (Kelly 2005; Hansen-Schirra and Kiraly 2013; Kiraly et al. 2013; Kiraly 2013; Massey 2017). Many of these initiatives base their projects on the work of the translation studies scholar Donald Kiraly (1995, 2000, 2012), itself derived from social constructivism and the concept of project based learning, that can be traced back to the first half of the 20th century manifested in the works of John Dewey (1938).[4]

In Kiraly's works, progression through the programme of studies is portrayed not in conventional fashion, but instead in terms of movement from less to more complex. Moving beyond basic skills and knowledge, students will be exposed to scaffolded problem-solving activities where they can practice the application of the basic skills they have acquired to realistic situations. The final stage of the curriculum involves facilitated project work, where the students tackle authentic projects supported by facilitators rather than teachers. Course design progresses from more to less contrived; learning proceeds from more conscious to more intuitive; activities proceed from the less contextualized to more contextualized; and didactic style proceeds from more instructive to more constructive and facilitative. Learning is a holistic, emergent, self-perpetuating and embodied lifelong process that proceeds both within the individual and within communities of practice at different levels and in different contexts. The learner is taken from a simple to a more complex level of competence acquisition, leaving the nutshell of instruction towards an authentic, less contextualized and more intuitive setting in the classroom.

---

4   For Project Based Learning (PBL) see also Knoll (1997), Markham (2011), Blumenfeld et al. (1991).

Most of the approaches focus on the basic idea of scaffolded project based learning in which procedures applied in the real workplace are performed between the commission and the delivery of a real product in our case of a translation. During these procedures or operations, students or teams of students can be compared to freelance translators or small translation agencies that deliver translations directly to an existing customer, a recently published example is the collaborative translation project by Massey and Brändli (2016). These classroom-based translation bureaus simulate real translation-agency environments in which real assignments for real customers are undertaken. The International Network of Simulated Translation Bureaus (INSTB) chaired by the Zuyd Hogeschool in Maastricht defines such a project bureau as follows: "a translation bureau that is staffed and run by students as a real translation bureau. It is part of the curriculum and earns credit points".[5]

In our opinion though most of these authentic projects, however, face one major problem if we consider the acquisition of generic competencies: The learners are directly exposed to real market requirements with all the risks, danger and threats that such a real assignment has to offer. This most certainly puts a lot of pressure on any participant in an authentic project. Furthermore, it requires a certain level of proficiency in translation to cope with these problems and to be able to produce a high-quality translation that meets industry standards. Adding the necessary high level of self-assessment proficiency to evaluate one's own actions and mistakes, the authentic project sets a high standard in terms of acquired competencies for the degree and quality of student participation.

It is precisely this high level of fidelity, proficiency and competence that seems to be one of the problems in the process of translator education. If we assume that beginner students receive instruction in basic knowledge and competence about translation, it would appear to be a huge step from this rather simple learning phase to the very complex learning environment involving authentic projects were generic competencies have to be developed in addition to the domain specific ones.

A solution proposed in this paper is the simulation of a real working environment in the classroom without the stress and time pressure of the real workplace by offering mixed forms of instructive and constructive teaching within a classroom setting with a high degree of authenticity. If we define the translation process as a problem-solving activity, as Massey (2017) describes it, and if we want to link this

---

5   See http://www.instb.eu/. Consisting of nine higher education institutions mainly in the Benelux countries and France, the INSTB is at the moment probably one of the largest academic networks that is running authentic project work in a real-life environment and a good example of the operationalization of the concept of authentic project work in translator education.

to established learning concepts as the concept of deeper learning, as proposed, for example, by the U. S. National Research Council (2012), which suggests that the learning individual should develop transferable knowledge through a high level of authenticity in their academic work, we have to use a more flexible approach to existing teaching techniques. Bringing the focussed, adrenaline-driving and here-and-now urgency of real-life projects into the classroom by designing simulated projects is the next step in a subsequent evolution of competence acquisition. The exposure to scaffolded problem-solving activities within the context of such a simulated project is the second phase of learning after the early more instructive phase at the very beginning of the educational process. In the context of in-class work, the major advantage of the simulator concept is the possibility for the facilitator to manipulate the often almost mechanically regular learning process or even research work at any time and take an influence on the competencies that are involved. We no longer have to wait for authentic problems to occur and a generic competence being applied; we can generate and manipulate them within the process and in accordance with the level of competence of the group or even a single student. By adding the spirit of real-life authenticity but remaining within a protected environment, we can bring the complexity of an authentic project into the classroom and still be independent of market issues like time pressure, cost effectiveness and entrepreneurial success. Following Hertel and Mills (2002), who define educational simulation as sequential decision-making events in which realistic tasks are fulfilled within an environment that models reality (2002, p. 15), the simulated projects in class can be run much like an airplane simulator, where tasks and problems can be initiated by the facilitator while using the device. By adopting the level of fidelity of the simulation[6] we then will be able to reproduce reality according to the level of competence acquisition that is required as the specific learning outcome of the specific course. While we increase the level of fidelity from low to high we will on the one hand raise complexity of the simulation, and on the other hand it will lead to a concrete level of abstraction in the learning situation. This enables us to pinpoint problems that can either be linked to missing knowledge that should have been picked up by student by that point of the educational process, or to procedural knowledge that has not yet been learned (cf. Alves 2005). This form of reflective translation-process problem solving is possible due to the ability to pause the simulator at any point in the translation process chain. When we do pause it, we will be able to identify the specific problem at hand and

---

6   High fidelity simulations are a common training concept used in clinical training, see Gilley (1990), Lasater (2007) or Maran and Glavin (2003), see also Shavelon in this volume.

to reflect on it in an appropriate manner, unlike the situation for existing projects, whether they be authentic or not, which usually do not intentionally take a step back from the process to recover missed learning goals during the performance of the translation task. As a final consequence, this approach could even lead to a return to more basic instruction if a set problem is solved in an inadequate way by a large number of participants.

From an interdisciplinary perspective, a positive effect in using simulated projects is the possibility of applying simulation expertise to translator education as a sub-field of translation studies. Bakken, Gould and Kim (1992), who investigated the use of a flight simulator for management training, determined that by giving direct feedback in a protected environment, a simulator makes use of a shortened period of time between the arising of a problem and its resolution, which enhances the learning effect. According to Hertel and Mills (2002), they can even bridge gaps between disciplines and immediately foster deeper learning because the active role of the learner within any simulation significantly promotes better understanding, longer remembrance and leads to a more successful (self-)evaluation (Lasater 2007). All the simulation proposals are strongly linked to the work of Kolb (1984) and his concept of experiential learning, which suggests that simulating activity can actually intensify the cycle of learning because the challenging situations that are evoked through it can lead to cognitive conflicts, resulting in more rapid changes in the decision-making process (Kolb et al. 2001).

Another cornerstone of our theoretical framework is furthermore relying on problem solving, which is undoubtedly one of the very important aspects of Donald Schön's (1987) concept of the reflective practitioner. We hope to integrate the often forgotten problem-setting process and lead the students towards a consolidation of their personal problem-solving strategies. They will be empowered to use new strategies they have not used before.[7] This "process by which we define the decision to be made, the ends to be achieved, the means which may be chosen" (Schön 1987, p. 40) will be at the focus of attention of these tools for translational problem setting, with which we can situate the problem-setting and problem-solving process in the safe environment of an educational institution. Simulated projects will be just as powerful as authentic projects but will offer a laboratory environment for immediate problem solving which, unlike a truly authentic, real-time project, can be paused at any time. This view on simulation is supported by Gilley (1990), who sees one of the advantages of simulations in allowing the learner to make mistakes

---

7   The concept of problem solving is also a key concept in translation-process research, especially using the methodology of think-aloud protocols; see Tirkkonen-Condit and Jääskelainen (2000) or Shreve and Angelone (2010).

in a controlled, high fidelity environment. With reference once again to Schön's concept of problem setting (1987, p. 40), in which the things that we will attend to will be named and the context will be framed, the advantage is that we can influence the things that are framed, or at least be sure that these things are framed at all. In Schön's (1987, p. 40) terms: "in real world practice, problems do not present themselves to the practitioner as givens. They must be constructed from the materials of problem situations which are puzzling, troubling, and uncertain". In this way, we are able to get a handle on the 'chaos' that an authentic project has to offer. As a result, we can get our students to reflect in action and on their action, which represent cornerstones of the reflective practitioner perspective.

3   Generic competence data in simulated projects

By defining the simulated project approach as the most promising underlying concept of generic competence acquisition during a higher education program, our first aim is to test the validity of this hypothesis and proof the advantages in comparison to classic or standard teaching approaches. We assume that a student in a simulated authentic project who is exposed to all sorts of problems from the professional world while performing the requested task, will enhance his generic competencies better than a regular enrolled student in another seminar.

To test our hypothesis we designed a small pilot study, which is based on a simulated research project aimed at introducing empirical research methods in translation classes. In winter term 2009/2010, we developed a simulated project, in which 40 translation students worked together on the empirical investigation of cognitive processes during the translation process. The students were grouped into six project teams. They all shared one common research question, i.e. whether it is cognitively more demanding to process nominal structures compared to verbal structures during translation. And although the topic of noun-verb shifts and their processing effort has been addressed by various researchers (e.g., Hansen-Schirra et al. 2012; Čulo et al. 2008; Alves et al. 2010), data triangulation is still an open issue with respect to empirically modeling the cognitive processes involved.

Therefore, the students were asked to address these research gaps by using a multi-method approach (cf. Alves 2003) using one method per team and triangulating the data afterwards. The following methods were used in collaborative group work: translation corpora, thinking-aloud, keylogging, eyetracking, comprehensibility ratings and retrospective interviews. This mixture involves offline and online methods (cf. Krings 2005; Göpferich 2008) tapping on conscious as well as unconscious cognitive processing. The teams collected data under realistic research environments (e.g., using an eyetracker or keylogging software), however the amount of data (in terms of corpus size or subject group size) was still on an example-based level. As a consequence, only rough tendencies could be observed, which did not allow for an empirical interpretation or a statistical data triangulation. We met the teams separately in the laboratory for consultations, without offering classes on a regular basis. The teams presented and discussed their results at a mock conference. Additionally, they had to write a research report on their findings.

From a didactic perspective, the simulated project was designed to strengthen the following competencies by performing the project-inherent tasks:

Tab. 1 Didactic aims of the simulated project

project tasks	didactic aims
development of hypotheses and operationalization in the experiment	transfer capability, analytical thinking, creativity
organization of team work	communication skills, ability to work autonomously, self-discipline, decision making, stress resistance, flexibility, ability to take on responsibility
data collection and interpretation	project management, time management, problem-solving strategies
conference presentation, research report	information and knowledge management, presentation skills, writing skills

For the pilot study we are presenting here, we used a self-report method and asked the students to fill out standardized rating questionnaires developed by our university's Center for Quality Assurance and Development in order to evaluate classes (cf. Hiltmann 2002). Self-reporting is an established method in social sciences (Döring and Bortz 2016) as well as in translation studies (Göpferich 2008). However, we are totally aware of the disadvantages of this method: Self-ratings are biased by subjective opinions, impressions and memory capacities, which may influence the validity of the method. In order to improve inter-subjectivity and validity, we avoided leading and open questions. The ratings included a Likert scale from 1 (= strongest learning effect) to 7 (= weakest learning effect). We carried out the rating in the last seminar session. Participation was anonymous and on a voluntary basis. 17 students took part in the rating; the results are presented in table 2, comparing the simulated project seminar to the cumulated values of all seminars at our faculty[8]:

Tab. 2 Mean ratings of the project group vs. mean ratings of all seminars

Competence	Simulated project group (average)	All seminars at FTSK (average)	Difference
Transfer capability	2.0	3.0	1.0
Communication skills	1.8	2.8	1.0
Teamwork competence	1.3	3.6	2.3
Oral communication	2.1	2.6	0.5
Writing skills	2.6	3.3	0.7
Ability to take on responsibilities	1.6	3.4	1.8
Self-assessment ability	1.8	3.4	1.5
Ability to work autonomously	1.4	2.4	1.0
Flexibility	1.5	3.1	1.6
Stress resistance	2.1	3.1	1.0
Ability to learn	2.4	2.7	0.3
Self-discipline	1.5	2.7	1.2
Creativity	2.2	3.4	1.2
Decision making	1.8	3.2	1.4
Ability to identify one's knowledge gaps and fill them	2.3	2.8	0.5
Time management	2.0	3.5	1.5
Information and knowledge management	1.6	3.1	1.5
Project management	1.4	3.5	2.1
Presentation skills	1.4	3.5	2.1
Scientific writing	2.6	4.1	1.5
Problem solving	1.8	3.5	2.7
Analytical thinking	1.7	3.2	1.5

The ratings for the project seminar were better for all competencies compared to the mean ratings of all seminars at the faculty. On the basis of a normal distribution, a t-test showed that the differences were statistically significant ($t(42)=11.04$,

---

8   Faculty of Translation Studies, Linguistics and Cultural Studies in Germersheim (FTSK) at Johannes Gutenberg University Mainz

p<0.0001). Further, with a Pearson correlation test, it was tested whether the ratings of the competencies correlate with each other, which would show that some competencies are always rated better/worse than others, but the correlation did not become significant (r(20)=0.08, p=0.7194).

In summary, this means that the competencies we especially addressed with the simulated project (see table 1), yielded better judgements than the average at our faculty. This may be interpreted in such a way that the simulated project resulted in stronger learning effects for these generic competencies compared to traditional didactic concepts.

4   Discussion and outlook

A result from the previous discourse would lead us to a new hypothesis that simulated projects are not only the more promising teaching approach, we shall also be able to elaborate a set of translation-related generic competencies for our field by observing such simulated project scenarios. Here, the research done in our field, for example, by Massey and Ehrensberger-Dow (2011, 2012) and by Massey and Jud (2015) have yielded initial results. But qualitative research work in the community of practice through industry contacts, for example, SAP or Daimler will also enlarge the data base. Furthermore, we are able to analyse a considerable volume of Moodle-course data and discussions on Slack from already run authentic projects at the Faculty of Translation Studies, Linguistics and Cultural Studies in Germersheim (FTSK).[9]

It is quite obvious that such a complex toolset will also require a high level of competence on the part of the teacher, who will need an overt understanding not only of the learning process but also of the process of teaching in a simulated environment. The simulated project will require experts in the community of theory and practice to run the tool in an adequate manner. This highly skilled teaching personnel will have to know the entire translation process from top to bottom, have deep insight into the potential problems that can actually arise during the translation process and possess a high level of proficiency in initiating these problems at the right time and with the right emphasis. Furthermore, the question of complexity and fidelity has to be addressed within this realm.

To achieve this, the exchange of teachers, researchers and practitioners in the respective field as well as across neighbouring fields (e.g., cross-fertilising with

---

9   Slack is a team communication device that is based on the instant messaging principle. See www.slack.com.

roleplay approaches from American studies courses, see Meyer et al. in this volume) is one of the key requirements for a successful simulator. Only if we can expose our teaching staff to the realities of the professional world of translation will any kind of simulated authentic or authentic project be a feasible teaching technique for translator education. Yet we may also assume that the role of the facilitator will surely be transformed. Until now, the teacher has usually taken on the role of a project manager (Kiraly and Hofmann 2016) or perhaps the customer. With project simulation, this will change as the teacher adopts the role of an operator. The teacher will run the simulator and set problems in certain frames in order for the students to achieve an appropriate level of problem-solving capability.

Bibliography

Alves, F., Pagano, A., Neumann, S., Steiner, E., & Hansen-Schirra, S. (2010). Translation Units and Grammatical Shifts: Towards an Integration of Product- and Process-based Translation Research. In G.M. Shreve & E. Anglone (Eds.), *Translation and Cognition* (pp. 109–142). Amsterdam: John Benjamins.

Alves, F. (2003). *Triangulating Translation. Perspectives in process oriented research.* Amsterdam: John Benjamins.

Alves, F. (2005). Bridging the Gap between Declarative and Procedural Knowledge in the Training of Translators: Meta-reflection under Scrutiny. *Meta, 50*(4). Retrieved from https://www.erudit.org/revue/meta/2005/v50/n4/019861ar.pdf

Bakken, B. E., Gould, D., & Kim, D. (1992). Experimentation in Learning Organizations: A Management Flight Simulator Approach. *European Journal of Operational Research, 59*(1), 167–182.

Blumenfeld, P. C., Soloway, E., Marx, R. W., Krajcik, J. S., Guzdial, M., & Palincsar, A. (1991). Motivating project-based learning: sustaining the doing, supporting the learning. *Educational Psychologist, 26,* 369–398.

Carl, M., Schaeffer, M., & Bangalore, M. (2016). The CRITT Translation Process Research Database. In M. Carl, S. Bangalore & M. Schaeffer (Eds.), *New Directions in Empirical Translation Process Research* (pp. 13–54). Berlin: Springer.

Čulo, O., Hansen-Schirra, S., Neumann, S., & Vela, M. (2008). Empirical studies on language contrast using the English-German comparable and parallel CroCo corpus. *Proceedings of the LREC Workshop on Comparable Corpora, Marrakesch,* 47–51.

Dewey, J. (1938). *Experience and education.* New York: Macmillan.

Döring, N., & Bortz, J. (2016). *Forschungsmethoden und Evaluation in den Sozial- und Humanwissenschaften.* Berlin, Heidelberg: Springer.

EMT Expert Group (2009). *Competences for Professional Translators, Experts in Multilingual and Multimedia Communication.* Brussels: European Commission. Retrieved from http://ec.europa.eu/dgs/translation/programmes/emt/key_documents/emt_competences_translators_en.pdf

Gilley, J. W. (1990). Demonstration and simulation. In M. W. Galbraith (Ed.), *Adult learning methods: A guide for effective instruction* (pp. 261–281). Malabar, FL: Krieger.

Göpferich, S. (2008): *Translationsprozessforschung: Stand –Methoden – Perspektiven*. Tübingen: Narr.

Hansen-Schirra, S., Neumann, S., & Steiner, E. (2012). *Cross-linguistic Corpora for the Study of Translations. Insights from the Language Pair English-German*. Berlin, Boston: De Gryter.

Hansen-Schirra, S., & Kiraly, D. (2013). *Projekte und Projektionen in der translatorischen Kompetenzentwicklung*. Frankfurt: Peter Lang.

Hertel, J. P., & Millis, B. J. (2002). *Using simulations to promote learning in higher education: An introduction*. Sterling, VA: Stylus.

Hiltmann, M. (2002). Die Erfassung des Konstrukts „gute Lehre" im Fragebogen-Verfahren. In Zentrum für Qualitätssicherung und -entwicklung (Series Ed.), *Mainzer Beiträge zur Hochschulentwicklung, Vol. 6*., Mainz.

Kelly, D. (2005). *A Handbook for Translator Trainers. A Guide to Reflective Practice*. Manchester: St Jerome.

Kiraly, D. (1995). *Pathways to Translation*. Kent OH: Kent State University Press.

Kiraly, D. (2000). *A Social Constructivist Approach to Translator Education: Empowerment from Theory to Practice*. Manchester: St. Jerome.

Kiraly, D. (2012). Growing a Project-based Translation Pedagogy: A Fractal Perspective. *Meta, 57*(1), 82–95.

Kiraly, D. (2013). Towards a View of Translator Competence as an Emergent Phenomenon: Thinking Outside the Box(es) in Translator Education. In D. Kiraly, S. Hansen-Schirra & K. Maksymski (Eds.), *New Prospects and Perspectives for Educating Language Mediators* (pp. 197–224). Tübingen: Narr Francke Attempto.

Kiraly, D., & Hofmann, S. (2016). Towards a Postpositivist Curriculum Development Model for Translator Education. In D. Kiraly et al. (Ed.): *Towards Authentic Experiential Learning in Translator Education* (pp. 67–87). Göttingen: Mainz University Press at V&R unipress.

Klein, S., Benjamin, R., Shavelson, R. J., & Bolus, R. (2007). The Collegiate Learning Assessment: Facts and Fantasies. *Evaluation Review, 31*(5), 415–439.

Knoll, M. (1997). The project method: its origin and international development. *Journal of Industrial Teacher Education, 34*(3), 59–80.

Kolb, D. A. (1984). *Experiential Learning: Experience as the Source of Learning and Development*. Englewood Cliffs, NJ: Prentice Hall.

Kolb, D. A., Boyatzis, R. E., & Mainemelis, C. (2001). Experiential Learning Theory: Previous Research and New Directions. In R. J. Sternberg & L. Zhang (Eds.), *Perspectives on Thinking, Learning, and Cognitive Styles* (pp. 227–47). Mahwah, NJ: Lawrence Erlbaum.

Krings, H. P. (2005). Wege ins Labyrinth – Fragestellungen und Methoden der Übersetzungsprozessforschung im Überblick. *Meta, 50*(2), 342–358.

Lasater, K. (2007). High-fidelity simulation and the development of clinical judgment: students' experiences. *Journal of Nursing Education, 46*(6), 269–277.

Maran, N., & Glavin, R. (2003). Low- to High fidelity simulation – a continuum of medical education. *Medical Education, 37*(S1), 22–28.

Markham, T. (2011). Project Based Learning. *Teacher Librarian, 39*(2), 38–42.

Massey, G. (2017/forthcoming). Translation Competence Development and Process-oriented Pedagogy. In J. W. Schwieter & A. Ferreira (Eds.), *The Handbook of Translation and Cognition* (pp. 520–544). Chichester: Wiley-Blackwell.

Massey, G., & Brändli, B. (2016). Collaborative Feedback Flows and How We Can Learn from Them: Investigating a Synergetic Experience in Translator Education. In D. Kiraly et al. (Eds.), *Towards Authentic Experiential Learning in Translator Education* (pp. 177-199). Göttingen: Mainz University Press at V&R unipress.

Massey, G., & Ehrensberger-Dow, M. (2011). Commenting on Translation: Implications for Translator Training. *Journal of Specialised Translation, 16*, 26–41.

Massey, G., & Ehrensberger-Dow, M. (2012). Evaluating the Process: Implications for Curriculum Development. In L. Zybatow, A. Petrova & M. Ustaszewski (Eds.), *Translationswissenschaft interdisziplinär: Fragen der Theorie und der Didaktik* (pp. 95–100). Frankfurt/Main: Lang.

Massey, G., & Jud, P. (2015). Teaching Audiovisual Translation with Products and Processes: Subtitling as a Case in Point. In L. Bogucki & M. Deckert (Eds.), *Accessing Audiovisual Translation* (pp. 99–116). Frankfurt/Main: Peter Lang.

National Research Council (2012). *Education for Life and Work: Developing Transferable Knowledge and Skills in the 21st Century.* Washington, DC: The National Academies Press.

PACTE (2003). Building a Translation Competence Model. In F. Alves (Ed.): *Triangulating Translation: Perspectives in Process Oriented Research* (pp. 43–66). Amsterdam/Philadelphia: Benjamins.

Pellegrino, J. W., & Hilton, M. L. (2012). *Education for Life and Work: Developing Transferable Knowledge and Skills in the 21st Century.* Committee on Defining Deeper Learning and 21st Century Skills, Board on Testing and Assessment and Board on Science Education, Division of Behavioral and Social Sciences and Education. Washington, DC: The National Academies Press.

Schön, D. A. (1987). *Educating the Reflective Practitioner.* San Francisco CA: Jossey-Bass.

Shreve, G. M., & Angelone, E. (Eds.) (2010). *Translation and Cognition.* Amsterdam/Philadelphia: John Benjamins.

Tirkkonen-Condit, S., & Jääskeläinen, R. (Eds.) (2000). *Tapping and Mapping the Processes of Translation and Interpreting. Outlooks on Empirical Research.* Benjamins Translation Library 37. Amsterdam/Philadelphia: John Benjamins.

Weinert, F. E. (2001a). Competencies and Key Competencies: Educational Perspective. In N. J. Smelser & P. B. Baltes (Eds.), *International Encyclopedia of the Social and Behavioral Sciences* (pp. 2433–2436). Amsterdam u. a.: Elsevier.

Weinert, F. E. (2001b). Concept of Competence: A Conceptual Clarification. In D. S. Rychen & L. H. Salganik (Eds.), *Defining and Selecting Key Competencies* (pp. 45–65). Seattle u. a.: Hogrefe & Huber.

Zlatkin-Troitschanskaia, O., Blömeke, S., & Pant, H. A. (Eds.) (2015). Competency Research in Higher Education. *Peabody Journal of Education, 90*(4), 459–464.

Zlatkin-Troitschanskaia, O., Pant, H. A., Lautenbach, C., Molerov, D., Toepper, M., & Brückner, S. (2017). *Modeling and Measuring Competencies in Higher Education: Approaches to Challenges in Higher Education Policy and Practice.* Wiesbaden: Springer VS.

Zlatkin-Troitschanskaia, O., Toepper, M., Molerov, D., Buske, R., Brückner, S., Pant, H. A., Hofmann, S., & Hansen-Schirra, S. (2018). Adapting and Validating the Collegiate Learning Assessment to Measure Generic Academic Skills of Students in Germany – Implications for International Assessment Studies in Higher Education. In O. Zlatkin-Troitschanskaia, M. Toepper, C. Kuhn, H. A. Pant & C. Lautenbach (Eds.), *Assessment of Learning Outcomes in Higher Education – Cross-national Comparisons and Perspectives*. Wiesbaden: Springer.

Positive Learning in the Age of Information (PLATO) – Critical Remarks[1]

Richard J. Shavelson

Abstract

Access to information in mass and social media was once thought of as a universal "leveler" for all. Unfortunately learning opportunities have been corrupted by biased, false, deliberately inaccurate, and unverified information. Negative learning (NL) occurs when Internet users are unable to recognize this. Positive learning (PL), the acquisition of new, warranted and morally justified knowledge, is PLATO's focus. PLATO should capitalize on high fidelity simulations to: (a) study NL and PL, (b) teach PL skills, and (c) assess PL skills. A model of teaching and learning developed for "Pluraliteracies" provides a framework for PLATO to develop, teach and assess PL competencies. Two warnings as PLATO progresses: (1) education alone cannot overcome NL opportunities; technologies (e.g., artificial intelligence) are needed to assist citizens in identifying NL environments; and (2) research must go beyond "person" to "person-in-context" recognizing that environments can foster either NL or PL.

Keywords

Negative Learning; Positive Learning; Simulation; Teaching; Learning; Assessing; PLATO; Artificial Intelligence Technology.

---

1   This paper is based on my discussant remarks at the June 2017 PLATO conference at the University of Mainz, Germany; for more information about the PLATO program see Zlatkin-Troitschanskaia et al. (2017).

1   Introduction

Information in mass and social media reaches people around the globe. While some believed the Internet would be a universal "leveler" providing users with access to information and learning opportunities, much of what is found is biased, false, deliberately inaccurate, conflicting, unverified, and purposely preselected. Negative learning (NL) occurs, often unintentionally or unconsciously, when Internet users are unable to recognize biased or false information, are misguided by it, and use it as a basis for generating knowledge. In contrast, positive learning (PL), defined as the acquisition of new warranted knowledge that is in line with ethical and moral values, is at the heart of the research program, Positive Learning in the Age of Information (PLATO) (Zlatkin-Troitschanskaia et al. 2017, p. 3ff.).

This paper briefly reviews and uses as a springboard two papers in this volume to reflect on PLATO's research agenda. The first, "Acquisition of Generic Competencies through Project Simulation in Translation Studies" by Hansen-Schirra, Hoffmann and Nitzke deals with the use of simulation in teaching and learning. Building on "Acquisition," this paper shows how simulation might impact PLATO's research, teaching and assessment agenda. The second paper, "Positive Learning and Pluriliteracies: Growth in Higher Education and Implications for course design, assessment and research" by Meyer, Imhof, Coyle and Banerjee presents a Teaching for Learning Model that provides an opportunity to turn the model toward PLATO's research that aims to build new knowledge about NL and PL. The paper concludes with two recommendations for PLATO research that might otherwise be missed.

2   Acquisition of generic competencies

"Acquisition" makes a strong argument for using simulation in the field of higher education generally and translation studies specifically to educate professionals. Simulations seem especially useful in this field due to their:

- High fidelity with actual practice (translating actual documents into English),
- Usefulness as an instructional tool where complexity of documents and context can be controlled by moving from substantial simplification to full simulation of actual practice, and
- Usefulness not only for instruction but also for assessment of competence.

Building on "Acquisition" it seems as if PLATO might capitalize on high-fidelity simulations of actual or "criterion" social media/Internet situations to:

- Research,
- Teach, and
- Assess.

More specifically, the paper attempts to show that high-fidelity simulations of actual or "criterion" situations to research, teach, and assess are at the core of research and development in PLATO.

Years ago while work was being carried out on the United States' mission to put man on the moon, zero and lunar gravity was simulated as a way of studying the impact of gravity and space suits on astronaut performance (see Shavelson and Seminara 1968). In carrying out the research two dimensions of simulation were particularly informative when deciding what type of simulation was to be used in which context (Shavelson 1968):

- *Level of Abstraction*:   Low (Concrete) — High (Symbolic or Mathematical)
- *Level of Fidelity*:   Low (Unlike Real World) — High (Accurate Portrayal of Real World)

In conducting research into uncharted territory, then, typically simulations low in abstraction and high in fidelity are used. This means that simulations used in these uncharted situations should concretely replicate the real world or criterion situation as closely as possible to the research claims to be made about performance (see Shavelson 1968). In the case of an extraterrestrial simulation of gravity, three alternatives were used in research and training. Moving from the lowest level of abstraction and highest level of fidelity, these are: (a) parabolic flight, (b) water flotation, and (c) counterbalance. Parabolic flight only lasted a matter of seconds or minutes. So while strong in verisimilitude, parabolic flight was impractical. Counterbalance was rejected, ultimately, by the astronauts because their movement was limited in by the cumbersome simulation method. In the end, astronauts were trained with water flotation at 0 or space gravity and 1/6 or lunar gravity (e.g., Shavelson 1968).

In particular, what "Acquisition" argues for is simulation that is concrete and which varies in its level of fidelity. As they point out, initially in teaching, students would work on lower fidelity tasks. They would focus, for example, on translating documents under "ideal" conditions. As students develop, the bar would be raised. Simulation fidelity would move to high fidelity conditions consistent with the realistic situation: high pressure to perform, limited time, demands for accuracy and so on. That is, a document that has been professionally translated by experts could serve as the simulation task given to students. Students' translations could then be compared to the experts'. The conditions under which the translations were carried out would vary from ideal to realistic as students' competence developed.

Simulation could make a significant contribution to PLATO's goal of studying negative and positive learning. Simulations could serve as experimental tasks, as performance assessments for measuring the outcomes of experiments, and as educational "treatments" for preparing students and citizens more generally for the post-factual age. Just as with Translation Studies and the translation of documents, high fidelity simulations of Internet encounters are part of PLATO's agenda. By building a simulated Internet—a high fidelity, low abstraction "Intranet"—researchers and educators could manipulate the variables of interest from basic research all the way to very applied research.

To make this claim concrete, consider Sam Wineburg' work (cf. in this volume). He and his research team started out by measuring news literacy and quickly expanded to on-line civic reasoning using multiple news sources, especially those readily available on the Internet and social media. In reviewing the scant literature on the topic, he noted that most research used multiple-choice tests or Likert-type rating scales of civic or media literacy (see Stanford History Education Group (SHEG hereafter) 2016):

"Writing a press release is typically the job of:
a) A reporter for CNN.com;
b) A spokesperson for Coca-Cola;
c) A lawyer for Yahoo!;
d) A producer for NBC Nightly News;
e) Don't know" (p. 5).

He concluded: "No doubt it is important to know that corporate spokespeople write press releases. But we're not certain that knowing this tells us what students can do when confronted by a statement issued by, say, Volkswagen in response to its emissions scandal. Instead of proxies, our approach directly measured student capabilities" (p. 7).

Wineburg and his team developed performance tasks that were high fidelity, concrete simulations of Internet/social network encounters for middle- and high-school students and college students. He sampled diverse students and colleges. The following five tasks were used with college students (SHEG 2016, p. 6):

1. *Article Evaluation*: In an open web search, students decide if a website can be trusted.
2. *Research a Claim*: Students search online to verify a claim about a controversial topic.
3. *Website Reliability*: Students determine whether a partisan site is trustworthy.
4. *Social Media Video*: Students watch an online video and identify its strengths and weaknesses.
5. *Claims on Social Media*: Students read a tweet and explain why it might or might not be a useful source of information.

One task exemplified "cloaked" websites. These are websites that abound on the Internet. They are professional-looking with neutral descriptions. However, they advocate, on behalf of their parent organizations while actively concealing their true identities and funding source. Wineburg used an open web search to see if college students confronted with an article from a cloaked sight could determine its source.

Students were told to go to an article, "Denmark's Dollar Forty-One Menu," on the website *MinimumWage.com*. The article argues that if the US followed the example of countries like Denmark and raised the minimum wage, food prices in the US would increase and jobs would decrease. The article makes reference to the *New York Times* and the *Columbia Journalism Review* regarding minimum wage policy and employment. *MinimumWage.com* looks profession and contains "Research" and "Media" pages ; the website's "About" page says that it is a "non-profit research organization dedicated to studying public policy issues surrounding employment growth."

In the assessment students are asked to determine whether "Denmark's Dollar Forty-One Menu" is a reliable information source. Successful students will discover that, despite its appearance, *MinimumWage.com* is managed by lobbyists for the food and beverage industry. Its parent organization, the Employment Policies Institute, is a front for Berman and Company, a lobbying firm. According to the *New York Times*, Richard Berman creates "official-sounding nonprofit groups" to disseminate information on behalf of corporate clients.

College students struggled mostly unsuccessfully when faced with a site that deviously conceals its sponsors. Far too many accepted the website at face value. Of 58 undergraduates only 4 found the Berman source. Over 80 percent gave naive responses; easy dupes of the Internet. Some of these students pointed to the "About" page that vouched for the site's trustworthyness; others noted links to the *New York Times* as credible sources, and others noted the article was biased against the minimum wage.

Wineburg (SHEG 2016) summarized his findings on college students' Internet savvy in one word: *bleak*.

He went on to say that our "digital natives" may be able to flit between Facebook and Twitter while simultaneously uploading a selfie to Instagram and texting a friend. But when it comes to evaluating information that flows through social media channels, they are easily duped. Wineburg and his team did not design their exercises to make fine distinctions among answers. Rather they sought to establish a reasonable performance level of they hoped was within most middle school, high school and college students' reach. And they hoped college students, who spend hours each day online, would ask who is behind a site that presents one side of a contentious issue. In every case and at every level, they said that they were taken aback by students' lack of preparation. Ordinary citizens once relied on publishers, editors, and subject matter experts to vet the information they consumed. But on the unregulated Internet, this isn't the case.

3   Positive learning in higher education – Promoting pluraliteracies development

"Deeper Learning" provides an important framework not only for teaching and learning languages, disciplines and cultures in German higher education but also for most professions. In the professions, the knowledge base is often multidisciplinary and this knowledge must be put into action where it has interpersonal, social, moral impact or some combination of them. Indeed, Derek Bok, former Harvard University president, and Stanford undergrad, was concerned that Harvard's medical training was too narrow. He believed that the everyday problems patients presented physicians with went beyond what Harvard medical students learned in school. He went so far as to recommend the use of the Collegiate Learning Assessment—a high-fidelity simulation in the form of performance tasks—to index students' capacity to think critically, solve problems, and communicate about everyday events (personal communication; see Shavelson 2010).

The four facets of the Teaching for Learning model (see Figure 1) contribute importantly to our thinking about what teaching and learning in higher education might look like in the 21st century and what can be done about it.

Fig. 1   Revised Model of Pluriliteracies Teaching for Learning (from Meyer et al., p. 242, in this volume)

The authors of "Deeper Learning" might consider two possible additions to the model. This suggestion is made somewhat reluctantly because the model is already complex. However, the additions might be important enough to warrant the added complexity.

First of all, every time we act individually, socially, environmentally, etc., that act involves knowledge, motivation, communication and learning, as the model shows (Figure 1). But action also carries with it a moral component: "Should I do this?", "In what way does it affect other people?", "How does it affect the environment?", "How does it affect me?" Indeed, this moral component of action is the focus of one of the four areas of research envisioned for PLATO. Hence, the Teaching for Learning model might consider a moral facet in addition.

People's beliefs, attitudes and prior knowledge impact how and what is learned and consequently impacts people's actions. Prior beliefs act as a filter for new learning. What appears to be a clear statement is interpreted through belief, attitude and prior knowledge filters leading to different interpretations of that statement. We know that very young children begin to develop beliefs about the world and people around them through their parents' behavior and teaching (Bloom and Weisberg 2007). For example, parents' religious beliefs are transmitted to children such that they impact on how students interpret what they are learning. Several studies in the US have shown that while college students succeed in passing a course on evolution, including at Stanford, many who believed in divine creation or intelligent design held onto those beliefs, handed down by their parents and churches, after completing the course (e.g., Barnes and Brownell 2016; Hokayem and Boujaoude 2008). It seems that given the strength and impact of beliefs and prior learning on subsequent learning, the model might incorporate a facet along these lines.

Deep Learning leads to the question: "What does the Deep Learning model of teaching for learning tell us about one of PLATO's concerns?":

> "When Internet users are unable to recognize biased or false information, are misguided by it, and use it as a basis to generate knowledge, *negative learning (NL)* occurs. In the digital age, individual beliefs or prejudices become more important than objective knowledge, as most Internet users struggle to filter and process vast amounts of information and rely on the first few hits in an online search. NL is difficult to avoid because it often is unintentional and unconscious." (Zlatkin-Troitschanskaia et al. 2017, p. 3).

The model suggests hypotheses for intervention by educating citizens—students and adults alike—about *constructing knowledge* from the Internet and *refining skills* in judging the truth value of assertions they encounter. The facts, concepts, procedures and strategies aren't those of a particular discipline or profession but need to be developed by PLATO to provide the basis for enhancing the capacity of citizens to learn from the various media sources in an era of (mis)information.

Perhaps in *demonstrating and communicating understanding*, the model suggests that we become informed of the purpose, genre, mode and style of Internet and social media communications.

Moreover it suggests that a concerted effort needs to be made in *mentoring learning and personal growth* by what Anders Ericsson calls deliberative practice—a practice with clear goals, feedback on how to improve and a constant raising of the bar for performance leading to expertise (e.g., Ericsson et al. 1993). Does this sound like the Teaching for Learning's facet of assessment, feedback, scaffolding, and designing and evaluating?

And the Teaching for Learning model suggests that *generating and sustaining commitment and achievement* be turned toward understanding how messages are intentionally designed to persuade, play to prior beliefs and biases and attempt to engage viewers emotionally and rapidly so as to reduce time and mental effort for reflection. Moreover, the model's focus on cognition, affect and especially *action* is consistent with views of the use of simulation as a critical instructional device to move from negative to positive learning simulations, and then, could contribute to PLATO's research.

Sam Wineburg and his colleague, Sarah McGrew, studied experts' approach when evaluating online information (McGrew and Wineburg 2017). The experts were (1) university history professors; (2) online fact checkers who are charged by American news and political fact-checking organizations with evaluating claims, sources, and evidence; and (3) Stanford undergraduates who grew up as "digital natives". One task used in this research is familiar to us now—minimumwage.com. Here are the results consistently reached with this task: All online fact checkers found the underlying source in a matter of minutes; historians and students took much longer and only very few found the source.

McGrew et al. (2017, pp. 6–7) were interested in what skills or strategies distinguished fact checkers from historians and students; they reported:

- *Reading Laterally*: Fact checkers opened up new tabs on a horizontal axis to research minimumwage.com before reading the article or settling on a judgment of the site. Faced with a website that masks its mission or funding source, going outside the site helped fact checkers arrive at a better understanding—and ultimately a more informed evaluation. 80% of students devoted no time to investigating the source behind minimumwage.com until explicitly prompted to do so. History professors acted more like college students than fact checkers.
- *Taking Bearing*: Rather than clicking randomly, readers actively try to figure out where they have landed, who is behind the information being provided, and what the creators of the information want the user to take from the site. Bearing-less reading refers to almost exclusively focusing on surface aesthetics and the ease of accessing information. Again fact checkers took bearings; most students and history professors did not.
- *Site Selection and Verification*: Fact checkers systematically choose sites preferring "news sources" or "press reports" and verified sites by cross-checking from other sites. Less so students and historians.
- *Footing*: Footing is not about possessing technological skill or savvy strategies for evaluating information. Instead, it is about one's sense of self vis-à-vis digital content. It asks: "Do I see myself as someone who can outsmart the Internet?" or "Am I acutely aware that the Internet can outsmart me?".

This research just scratches the surface and suggests a major research agenda. This agenda includes coming to understand the knowledge, skills, and affective characteristics that go into using media to foster positive learning and avoid negative learning. PLATO is positioned to carry forward this and myriad other important studies.

4   Closing reflections

In pursuing its agenda, PLATO researchers need to be mindful of two points. The first point is that education and educating college students and citizens in a democracy is insufficient. For over 100 years, the US included environmental education in the curriculum; today it can be seen what good that has done. We need education to develop in students and citizens the new 21st Century skill of Internet/ Social Media savvy. In addition to education, we need to provide technologies to combat negative learning. For example, an Artificial Intelligence sitting on Google delving into the source of Internet sites and red flagging questionable sites and providing evidence for the flag. Without such technology, the amount and rapidity of information is overwhelming and thinking fast rather than reflectively thinking slow is a reasonable response to survive information overload.

A second point is that researchers need to avoid is a narrow focus on "the person"—the student or the citizen—in studying the impact of media on negative and positive learning. It behooves researchers to look beyond the person and beyond educating the person. People live in environments that support and foster either PL or NL. We need to understand the nature of these environments and their impact on thought, feeling and action. This is not about the way news is manipulated but about micro-cultures that exist in neighborhoods, religious groups or in societies that afford fake news that support strongly held if untested or unethical beliefs. Research needs to focus on person in place, and understand how place influences behavior. Simply put, *context matters* and understanding knowledge, affect and action in context is essential to combating negative learning. It also suggests policy instruments that might lead from NL to PL.

Bibliography

Barnes, M. E., & Brownell, S. E. (2016). Practices and perspectives of college instructors on addressing religious beliefs when teaching evolution. *CBE Life Science Education, 15*, Retrieved from https://www.ncbi.nlm.nih.gov/pmc/articles/PMC4909340/. Accessed: 8 July 2017.

Bloom, P., & Weisberg, D. S. (2007). Childhood origins of adult resistance to science. *Science, 316*, 996–997.

Ericsson, K. A., Krampe, R. T., & Tesch-Romer, C. (1993). The role of deliberate practice in the acquisition of expert performance. *Psychological review, 100*(3), 363–406.

Hokayem, H., & Boujaoude, S. B. (2008). College students' perceptions of the theory of evolution. *Journal of Research in Science Teaching, 45*(4), 395–419.

McGrew, S., Ortega, T., Breakstone, J., & Wineburg, S. (2017). The challenge that's bigger than fake news: Teaching students to engage in civic online reasoning. *American Educator*.

McGrew, S., & Wineburg, S. (2017, April). *Taking Bearing: Reading less and learning more when assessing digital information*. Paper presented at the annual meeting of the American Educational Research Association, San Antonio, Texas.

Shavelson, R. J. (1968). Lunar gravity stimulation and its effect on man's performance. *Human Factors, 10*(4), 393–402.

Shavelson, R. J. (2010). *Measuring college learning responsibly: Accountability in a new era*. Stanford, CA: Stanford University Press.

Shavelson, R. J., & Seminara, J. L. (1968). Effect of lunar gravity on man's performance of basic maintenance tasks. *Journal of Applied Psychology, 52*, 177–183.

Stanford History Education Group (2016). *From history assessments to assessments of news literacy*. Retrieved from https://ed.stanford.edu/news/stanford-researchers-find-students-have-trouble-judging-credibility-information-online. Accessed: 15 June 2017.

Zlatkin-Troitschanskaia et al. (2017). *Positive Learning in the Age of Information*. Unpublished Manuscript, Draft Proposal Cluster of Excellence, Johannes Gutenberg University Mainz.

PART IV
Learning with Ethics and Morality

Ethics of Beliefs

On Some Conceptual and Empirical Obstacles to Teaching the Ability for Positive Learning

Wanja Wiese

Abstract

This paper deals with the concept of positive learning (PL). The main goal is to provide a working definition of PL on which further refinements and extensions can be based. First, I formulate a list of desiderata for a definition of PL: I argue that a working definition of PL should *(i)* make the involved epistemic norms explicit, *(ii)* be flexible, and *(iii)* be empirically tractable. After that, I argue that a working definition of PL should focus on three basic epistemic norms (which I call *Evidentialism*, *Degrees of Plausibility*, and *Non-Arbitrary Updates*). Drawing on work on the ethics of belief and Bayesian inference, I highlight theoretical and empirical challenges that already follow from such basic assumptions. Finally, I formulate a working definition of PL based on the three epistemic norms and show that it fulfills the desiderata given above. Furthermore, I also provide a tentative agenda for future research that seeks to develop the notion of PL in various ways that are relevant to PLATO in general, and to a "practical philosophy of mind" in particular.

Keywords

Bayesian Inference; Beneficial Misrepresentation; Cognitive Bias; Epistemic Norms; Ethics of Belief; Moral Value; Positive Illusion; Positive Learning; Prudential Value.

1   What does "Positive Learning" mean?

One of the aims of PLATO is finding out how people can be guarded against biased information, and how they can be assisted in detecting fake news (cf. Zlatkin-Troitschanskaia et al. 2017). There are at least three (complementary) ways in which this can be done. A first option is to find a way to reduce the amount of biased or false information in media like the Internet (cf., e.g., Ciampaglia in this volume). This could decrease the likelihood that people encounter biased information and are negatively affected by it. However, although this strategy may succeed to some extent, its practical use is limited, since running all sources of false information and fake news dry is virtually impossible. A second option is to make users of information more autonomous by teaching them how to detect fake news and how to assess the credibility of sources of information (cf., e.g., Meyer et al. in this volume). This may be a more sustainable strategy. Still, even being able to correctly identify biases or false information does not guarantee that *accurate* pieces of information are used in a way that increases knowledge: personal cognitive biases may detain a person from incorporating information in their web of beliefs, and prior assumptions may lead a person to ignore relevant evidence instead of using it to revise their beliefs (cf. Knauff in this volume).

This paper explores to what extent certain limitations on behalf of learners can impede or hinder positive learning (PL), even when the learner is presented with unbiased information. The corresponding research question is: assuming an ideal learning environment, what can still go wrong, due to limitations of the learner? Such limitations are also likely to take effect under non-ideal learning environments, so the results are relevant in practical contexts, as well. More generally, this will provide hints as to how the ability for PL can be fostered by helping learners to overcome their cognitive limitations.

A more fundamental question behind this approach is how the concept of PL can be defined (cf. Zlatkin-Troitschanskaia et al. 2017) and under what conditions a learning experience should be deemed successful. Success is a normative notion, and Zlatkin-Troitschanskaia et al. (2017) explicitly characterize PL as a normative concept, without specifying particular norms. Hence, a more specific definition of PL must make the assumed norms explicit (see section 2).

Being capable of PL entails that one follows these norms; in other words, following these norms is *necessary* for PL. But is it also *sufficient* for PL? If not, which factors can still lead to the acquisition and sustainment of *false beliefs*, and to what extent can they be influenced by education? These are among the main questions dealt with in this paper.

One result of the discussion will be that following certain epistemic norms (see section 3) is not sufficient for PL. Also an "ideal reasoner" who satisfies these norms perfectly can fail to acquire *true beliefs*, even when presented with unbiased information (see section 4). The reason is that prior beliefs and false assumptions about the structure of the domain about which the learner gains information can impede PL. This raises the question of how severe and common such biases are among learners and how they can be attenuated by education (see section 5).

The main contribution of this paper is to show how to usefully narrow the notion of PL down by focusing on the norms in accordance with which learners should seek, acquire, and use information. This approach reveals theoretical obstacles to learning the ability for PL and may serve as a basis for research on the empirical obstacles and challenges surrounding PL (cf. Zlatkin-Troitschanskaia et al. 2017). As I will point out in section 5, this has a threefold relevance to PL, PLATO, and the prospects of a "practical philosophy of mind":

(i)   A narrow focus on basic epistemic norms, which highlights the common ground between different theoretical approaches to belief formation, enables a first substantial working definition of PL (see section 5.1 A working definition of positive learning).

(ii) The working definition can directly be applied within the diverse parts of the PLATO program (cf. Zlatkin-Troitschanskaia et al. 2017). This not only helps integrate different research areas, but also enables further developments of the concept of PL itself, based on the goals of the involved disciplines and their individual scientific demands (see sections 5.2 Relevance to PLATO and 5.3).

(iii) Practical philosophy focuses on normative aspects of human action. While the relevant type of action typically involves interaction between human agents, contemporary philosophy of mind is also concerned with *mental* actions (such as volitional attention, see Metzinger 2017), which are central in the age of information. The concept of PL can play a key role in weaving these different threads together, thus developing a practical philosophy of mind (see section 5.3).

2 Desiderata for a definition of Positive Learning derived from the Ethics of Belief and Bayesian Inference

As a first characterization, we can say that PL is the acquisition of "new warranted knowledge", in line with moral, epistemic, and other norms (cf. Zlatkin-Troitschanskaia et al. 2017, p. 2).[1] This characterization provides a rough description of what PL is about. Here, I provide a list of three desiderata that a more specific definition of PL must satisfy.

*   Desideratum 1: (*Epistemicity*) PL is a concept involving epistemic norms. These norms should be made explicit and motivated.
*   Desideratum 2: (*Flexibility*) PL is the central common thread of the diverse research areas comprised by PLATO (cf. Zlatkin-Troitschanskaia et al. 2017). Hence, a working definition of PL should be general enough as to be applicable in different areas and admit of further, domain-specific refinements.
*   Desideratum 3: (*Empirical Tractability*) PL is not just a research target, but primarily an educational goal. Hence, a working definition of PL must not be too restrictive; it must be possible to achieve PL in practice. To what extent it can be achieved in practice is a question that must be empirically tractable.

It should be noted that the list of desiderata does not include any reference to moral norms. Furthermore, it might seem that a flexible working definition of PL would be too unsubstantial to be useful. In what follows, I will draw on the field of the *ethics of belief* (EoB; see Chignell 2017) and on theoretical work on *Bayesian inference* to show which theoretical challenges even an account of PL that seeks to satisfy the above list of desiderata must face. Since these challenges are not trivial, it would be premature to provide a more demanding list of desiderata. However, desideratum 2 also acknowledges the need for more specific definitions of PL, and I will suggest below (section 5.3) in which directions such further steps may be taken.

EoB discusses epistemic, prudential, moral, and other norms relevant to belief-formation. In particular, EoB is concerned with the question whether epistem-

---

1   This characterization is similar to the characterization offered by the PLATO draft proposal (Zlatkin-Troitschanskaia et al. 2017, p. 2). While the characterization given therein does not explicitly refer to epistemic or other norms, I take it that "warranted knowledge" is the result of a method of belief acquisition that fulfills certain epistemic norms, and which thereby results not just in knowledge, but *warranted* knowledge.

ic and other values can generate *moral* norms.[2] Here are two examples of relevant questions:

> "Is it ever or always morally wrong (or epistemically irrational, or practically im-
> prudent) to hold a belief on insufficient evidence? Is it ever or always morally right
> (or epistemically rational, or practically prudent) to believe on the basis of sufficient
> evidence, or to withhold belief in the perceived absence of it?" (Chignell 2017, sec-
> tion "Introduction").

At least *prima facie*, it seems that PL should involve epistemically rational, practically prudent, and morally right ways of belief formation. Therefore, EoB can
inspire specifications of the norms in terms of which PL can be defined. At the
same time, EoB is highly relevant because it points to controversial issues regarding particular norms, as well as to potential conflicts between different types of
norms (see section 3).[3] Based on such findings, I will suggest that the concept of PL
be (at least preliminarily) defined using *epistemic* norms only. This already raises
theoretical and empirical questions: The question of whether and how non-epistemic norms can be incorporated in an account of PL will remain a challenge for
future research.

Bayesian reasoning is, as I show below (section 4), a formal method that is in
line with basic epistemic norms.[4] Hence, it can be regarded as a model of "ideal
reasoning", in the sense that it provably satisfies these norms in a rational way (cf.
Knauff in this volume). The motivation for using a model of "ideal reasoning",
instead of just investigating the reasoning deficits of human beings empirically,
is twofold. First, such models can be (and are) used as a benchmark for empirical
research (see Griffiths and Tenenbaum 2006, Geisler and Ringach 2009, Oaksford

---

2   The *locus classicus* for the debate is the paper *The ethics of belief* by William Kingdon
     Clifford (1999[1877]).

3   A problem I will ignore for the most part of this paper is that the epistemic status
     of norms is difficult, to say the least: the question whether normative sentences or
     propositions can even be true or false is a controversial issue, especially when it comes
     to moral claims (for an introduction, see van Roojen 2016). For the purposes of this
     paper, I will remain neutral regarding this issue. In other words, I am bracketing the
     question whether there are moral facts or moral properties; instead, I am focusing on
     questions of the following form: if this or that norm is assumed, what consequences
     does that have (for the notion of PL)?

4   Though, of course, not the only one. However, since it is a well-studied method,
     important results can be used to investigate the limits of an "ideal reasoner" (see
     section 4).

and Chater 2009, Chater et al. 2010). Second, any limitations that an ideal reasoner has when it comes to the ability for PL will likely also be displayed by *all* human beings. In other words, the limitations exposed by investigating an idealized model can be expected to point to fundamental impediments of (human) reasoners. This makes investigating the size and severity of their effects on learning and decision making especially relevant. One of the most fundamental limitations revealed by this approach is, as Feldman (2016, p. 24) puts it, that "[h]umans, like any observer, inherently cannot distinguish their own *models* of reality from reality itself."

3   Three basic epistemic norms for Positive Learning

As long as a model of reality works, it does not matter for the agent whether it is a "true" model, or whether that question even makes sense. However, when intelligent beings interact, individual preferences typically clash and being able to influence or secretly manipulating the models of others becomes advantageous. The generation and spreading of fake news and biased information may be the evolutionarily most recent incarnation of this strategy. In fact, even believing one's self-generated false information may be the product of an adaptive ability, namely the ability for self-deception (for the hypothesis that self-deception is an adaptive ability, see Trivers 2000; von Hippel and Trivers 2011; for a recent model of self-deception see Pliushch 2017). Therefore, self-deception may constitute a *practically prudent* strategy. However, this does not mean that it recommends itself as a deliberate method for conscious belief formation, since it involves believing against evidence to the contrary, which seems to render it *epistemically irrational* (or even morally blameworthy).

The more general point illustrated by the example of self-deception is that different values that may be regarded as relevant to belief formation can be in conflict with each other. This constitutes a challenge for specific accounts of PL, since a definition of PL should not involve norms that lead to contradictions. As a result, a lesson to learn from EoB is that a working definition of PL should, at least preliminarily, be restricted to epistemic norms, in order to avoid such theoretical conflicts and to reduce the complexity of an account of PL (cf. Zlatkin-Troitschanskaia et al. 2017).

To give another example of a conflict created by different types of norms in belief formation: Misbeliefs such as *positive illusions* can have prudential value (see McKay and Dennett 2009). Positive illusions are *false beliefs* that depict a (future) state of affairs in an overly positive way. Here are some examples:

"People tend to underestimate how long a project will take to complete and how much it will cost. Most of us predict deriving greater pleasure from a vacation than we subsequently do, and we anticipate encountering more positive events in an upcoming month (such as receiving a gift or enjoying a movie) than we end up experiencing [...]. Across many different methods and domains, studies consistently report that a large majority of the population (about 80% according to most estimates) display an optimism bias". (Sharot 2011b, pp. R941-R942).

Some positive illusions may systematically promote well-being and mental health (McKay and Dennett 2009; Sharot 2011b, p. R944; cf. also Dormann et al. in this volume). This suggests that there is a *prima facie* prudential reason to maintain such misbeliefs. The general structure of a *prudential norm* derived from this can be formulated as follows: If the belief that *p* is likely to make a prudential end *E* obtain, then *p* should be believed (unless there are other reasons not to believe that *p*; for more details see Chignell 2017, section 2.2, and the references cited therein).

In the case of a beneficial misbelief that *p*, there is a reason not to believe that *p*, viz. that *p* is false, and the subject may be aware that *p* is likely to be false. This raises the question of how to balance prudential values (e.g., health, well-being) with epistemic values (e.g., empirical adequacy). There are at least two ways in which this question can be approached: a domain-general and a domain-specific way. As a first option, one can determine to what extent a certain type of beneficial misbelief is shared by large parts of a population (as we have seen, positive illusions fall within this category). Then one can investigate the causes and effects of that type of beneficial misbelief and determine whether they might interfere with general learning capacities in undesirable ways. As a second option, one can determine whether certain beneficial misbeliefs impede learning in a specific domain. For instance, when it comes to time management or risk assessment, positive illusions are likely to be detrimental. Consequently, teaching the ability for PL in such domains is likely to profit from discounting the associated prudential values. I will return to these general considerations in section 5.

A first result we obtain from these considerations is that different types of value that are relevant to belief formation can be in conflict with each other. However, the extent to which PL is negatively affected by this is difficult to assess without focusing on specific learning domains. Hence, it would be premature to recommend that certain types of value should always be prioritized over others. Still, at least preliminarily restricting an account of PL to epistemic norms can help reduce the complexity of the discussion and establish a foundation from which to develop more specific concepts of PL (perhaps in different ways, depending on the specific learning domain in which that notion is to be applied).

With this in mind, we can now provide a tentative definition of an "ideal reason-er" (IR), i.e., a reasoner (hopefully) able to achieve PL. An IR should form beliefs in accordance with three basic epistemic norms: (1) *Evidentialism*, (2) *Degrees of Plausibility*, and (3) *Non-Arbitrary Updates*. This set of norms is basic in the sense that it can be regarded as a least common denominator.

(1) An IR should not ignore or dismiss any *relevant evidence*. This is, roughly, what van Inwagen has called „Clifford's Other Principle" (1996, p. 145). This norm is important to avoid dogmatism.

(2) In the presence of *uncertainty*, an IR should *assign degrees of plausibility* to propositions. This norm is important to avoid hasty conclusions when the re-liability of a source of information is uncertain. In particular, it also means that one should not be completely certain that *p* if the evidence for the proposition *p* is uncertain.

(3) In the light of new information, an IR should *update degrees of plausibility non-arbitrarily*. This norm is important to prevent that marginal changes in the information base lead to global belief revision. A stronger version defended, for example, by John Locke is that degrees of plausibility should be *proportional* to the strength of the evidence (1836[1690], p. 533).

These three norms serve, for the purposes of this paper, as a lose definition of an IR. In section 5.1A working definition of positive learning , I will draw on these norms to provide a first working definition of PL. A more rigorous (and slightly more specific) definition can be given by considering how these epistemic norms can be analyzed formally. By investigating the limitations of such a rigorously de-fined IR, we can reveal principled obstacles to achieving PL (see the following sec-tion). Against the backdrop of such conceptual considerations, existing empirical data can help determine to what extent subjects are able to approximate an IR and which open questions need to be investigated to make progress on this question.

4   On the virtues and limitations of Bayesian reasoning

In his posthumously published monograph *Probabilitiy. The Logic of Science*, Jaynes (2003) provides an intriguing foundation for probability (which is slightly more general than set-theoretic probability, based on the *Kolmogorov axioms*). Starting with three "general desiderata on rational inference" (Jaynes 2003, pp. 17-19), Jaynes shows that "there is only one set of mathematical operations for manipulating plausibilities which has all these properties." (Jaynes 2003, p. 19). In effect, the derived set of mathematical operations are in accord with the axioms of probability, and, simplifying a little, we can say that the only formal method that satisfies the desiderata is Bayesian inference. Crucially, the desiderata are highly similar to the three basic epistemic norms listed in the previous section (however, they are slightly more specific).

The first desideratum is that degrees of plausibilities be represented by real numbers. This is more specific than the norm called *Degrees of Plausibility* above, because it is possible to represent degrees of plausibility other than by real numbers.[5] However, the differences between the resulting theories are rather subtle and can be neglected for the purposes of this paper.[6]

The second desideratum is *"Qualitative correspondence with common sense"* (Jaynes 2003, p. 18). By "common sense", Jaynes actually refers to an idealized version of common sense[7], which is important, since common sense is inflicted with a host of biases (for a survey, see Friedman 2017). An example of what Jaynes has in mind is the following rule: if new information increases the plausibility of A, but does not change the plausibility of B, then the joint plausibility of A and B cannot decrease. In general, belief updates should be non-arbitrarily related to changes in the available evidence.

The finally desideratum is consistency. Jaynes (2003, p. 19) spells it out as follows (the robot mentioned by Jaynes in the following quotation is basically what I am calling an IR in this paper):

"(IIIa) *If a conclusion can be reasoned out in more than one way, then every possible way must lead to the same result.* (1.39a)
(IIIb) *The robot always takes into account all of the evidence it has relevant to a question. It does not arbitrarily ignore some of the information, basing its conclusions only on what remains. In other words, the robot is completely nonideological.* (1.39b)

---

5   Examples include Spohn's (2012) ranking theory, AGM belief revision (Alchourrón et al. 2014), and fuzzy logic. I am grateful to Markus Knauff for hinting me at this (cf. in this volume).

6   Does it even matter which way of formally capturing the three basic norms is chosen? There are, e. g., many similarities between Spohn's ranking theory and probability theory. However, it is problematic to identify "S believes that p" with "S assigns probability greater than r to p", because this leads to the notorious Lottery paradox (see Spohn 2009, section 3).

7   "Our topic is the *normative principles of logic*, and not the principles of psychology or neurophysiology. To emphasize this, instead of asking, 'How can we build a mathematical model of human common sense?' let us ask, 'How could we build a machine which would carry out useful plausible reasoning, following clearly defined principles expressing an *idealized common sense*?'" (Jaynes 2003, p. 8; italic emphasis added).

(IIIc) *The robot always represents equivalent states of knowledge by equivalent plausibility assignments. That is, if in two problems the robot's state of knowledge is the same (except perhaps for the labeling of the propositions), then it must assign the same plausibilities in both. (1.39c)"*

Of these sub-desiderata, (IIIb) is most relevant here, because it entails the epistemic norm called *Evidentialism* in the previous section. Since the three basic epistemic norms are entailed by Jaynes's desiderata, Jaynes's "robot" is a (slightly stricter) version of the IR we are investigating in this paper. Hence, any shortcomings and limitations of Jaynes's robot will also be shared by our IR (unless they follow from the more specific restrictions imposed by the desiderata). The fact that the robot performs Bayesian inference means we can draw on the respective literature to discover what those limitations are.

There are at least three limitations that are relevant in the context of PL: (1) potentially biased priors, (2) no guaranteed convergence to truth, (3) no guaranteed compliance with non-epistemic norms. The third limitation is not surprising, since it is an in-built limitation: we explicitly defined "ideal reasoning" with respect to epistemic norms only. In the following I will explain the (1) and (2) limitations:

(1) The first limitation refers to the fact that Bayesian inference always requires prior assumptions, which may be biased and hence can affect the result of the inference in a negative way (i.e., PL can fail to be achieved, even if the information considered is itself unbiased). Ideally, false prior assumptions will, eventually, be "washed out" by continuously updating one's belief in accordance with reliable evidence. However, this process may take too long to be feasible in practice, and some biases may be too rigid to be corrected by learning (for more on this, see Talbott 2016, section 6.2). The relevance of this problem will become clear below, where we consider empirical results on cognitive biases and prejudices: some biases are general and may have been adaptive in our evolutionary past, but may be dangerous in certain contexts (see Johnson and Fowler 2011, p. 320). Hence, it will be important to explore whether and how such biases can be attenuated or overcome.

(2) A second limitation is that Bayesian inference is non-monotonic, so a previous conclusion can be revised in the light of new evidence. In particular, this also means that more evidence does not necessarily bring a Bayesian reasoner "closer

to the truth"[8], even if there is nothing wrong with the evidence (see Feldman 2016, pp. 14-15). A relevant illustration of this point can be found in a paper by Michael Oppenheimer et al. on "negative learning" in climate science (Oppenheimer et al. 2008). Using a model of a hypothetical climate system, the authors show how Bayesian learning can fail, even in the long run, to correctly infer the equilibrium climate sensitivity[9] of the system, if there are subtle errors in the structural assumptions made about the system. These structural errors are not "washed out" over time. Consequently, estimates of climate sensitivity derived during Bayesian learning can converge to a false value (which may engender a treacherous confidence). Furthermore, in the context of climate change, both over- and underestimating the equilibrium climate sensitivity is costly (in fact, overestimating climate sensitivity may be more costly, because it can lead one to underestimate the increase in global warming, see Oppenheimer et al. 2008, pp. 165-166). Especially important here is that, as the authors point out, one source of negative learning can be overconfidence (albeit not the only one). This overconfidence can even be strengthened by a (seemingly) reliable model, which models certain parameters with high certainty. This is relevant because overconfidence is a widespread, robust and potentially dangerous cognitive bias.

But how can such a cognitive bias exist if it can be dangerous? A model by Johnson and Fowler (2011, p. 317) suggests that "there can be material rewards for holding incorrect beliefs about one's own capability". The hypothesis supported by this model is that "overconfidence can actually be advantageous on average (even if costly at times), because it boosts ambition, morale, resolve, persistence or the credibility of bluffing". (ibid.). Hence, overconfidence is another example of a positive illusion that can be systematically beneficial for us. Furthermore, the results on climate change models by Oppenheimer suggest that the limitations of IRs identified above can even mutually reinforce each other: false assumptions about a given domain can lead to false conclusions, and a tendency to overestimate one's own reasoning abilities, or the coherence of one's web of belief, can lead to overconfidence in the conclusion of one's reasoning processes.

---

8   Measuring "distance from truth" is not possible in real-world situations. However, in model situation, not only data (evidence) but also the hidden causes of those data are known (they are specified by the model). Hence, it can be determined whether a certain method, such as Bayesian learning, converges on a true representation of the model system or not (cf. also Oppenheimer et al. 2008, p. 157).

9   The *equilibrium climate sensitivity* of a system is "the equilibrium temperature change from a doubling of carbon dioxide concentrations" and it "captures the response of geophysical feedbacks on temperature that reduce or amplify the effect of the change in radiative forcing" (Oppenheimer, p. 164).

Having discussed some principled limitations of an IR, we can now determine what additional obstacles to achieving PL are created by the fact that human reasoning can only be regarded as an approximation to ideal reasoning. In other words, while an IR satisfies the three basic epistemic norms defined in section 3 perfectly, human reasoners will tend to violate these norms in certain ways.

The most prevalent departure from ideal reasoning probably consists in a violation of the first basic epistemic norm, i.e., *Evidentialism*. On the one hand, limited time and limited cognitive capacity will always prevent us from taking all relevant evidence into account. On the other hand, and more importantly, we have a tendency to treat available evidence in a biased way:

> "Humans integrate information into self-relevant beliefs asymmetrically based on the desirability of the information at hand. [...] For self-relevant beliefs, where people are motivated to hold positive views, a valence-dependent asymmetry in how people use favorable and unfavorable information results in positively biased views, such as unrealistic optimism (Sharot et al. 2011) and the illusion of superiority (Korn et al. 2012). Although such views are biased, they are not necessarily suboptimal. The positive effects of these illusionary beliefs on our affective state (Loewenstein 2006; Parker and Brunnermeier 2004; Bracha and Brown 2012), health (Taylor et al. 2000), and motivation (Varki 2009; Bénabou and Tirole 2002) may be adaptive, on balance (see Sharot 2011b, Sharot 2011a, for reviews)". (Sharot and Garrett 2016, p. 31; *citation style adapted*).

Interestingly, as the authors point out in the quotation, this biased way of treating evidence seems to favor prudential values over epistemic values. In fact, it may be one of the mechanisms underlying the generation and maintenance of positive illusions. Hence, rather than focusing on particular beneficial misbeliefs, it may be more effective to focus on this general cognitive bias and to make learners aware of it. Being aware of the possibility that one is treating available evidence in a subjectively biased way may enable one to reach more careful conclusions in contexts in which it is especially important to remain open-minded.

Another bias, overconfidence, has already been mentioned above. We can describe overconfidence as a violation of the second and third basic epistemic norms, *Degrees of Plausibility* and *Non-Arbitrary Updates*. If one firmly holds the belief that p, although the evidence for it is uncertain, we can say that one fails to assign a degree of plausibility to it (because one is absolutely certain[10]). Alternatively, if

---

10   Which is, an extreme case of a plausibility. However, in the definition of *Degrees of Plausibility*, I explicitly stated that one should not be completely confident in the presence of uncertainty.

one becomes increasingly confident that p, although the evidence does not support this change in the assigned degree of plausibility, one is violating the third basic epistemic norm. Again, it may be especially important to make learners aware of this cognitive bias, and to investigate in which domains it can fail to have beneficial effects. This is suggested by the results of Johnson's and Fowler's (2011) model:

> "We predict that where the value of a prize sufficiently exceeds the costs of competing, overconfidence will be particularly prevalent in some very important domains that have inherently high levels of uncertainty, including international relations (where events are complex and distant and involve foreign cultures and languages), rare or unpredictable phenomena (such as natural disasters and climate change), novel or complex technologies (such as the Internet bubble and modern financial instruments) and new and untested leaders, allies and enemies. Although overconfidence may have been adaptive in our past, and may still be adaptive in some settings today, it seems that we are likely to become overconfident in precisely the most dangerous of situations". (Johnson and Fowler 2011, p. 319).

Since these are only predictions, empirical research on the prevalence and negative effects of cognitive biases such as overconfidence is especially pressing. This also highlights how important even the three basic epistemic norms can be when it comes to domains that matter to society or humanity as a whole.

5   Conclusion

5.1   A working definition of Positive Learning

We saw that grounding an account of PL on EoB is desirable, but difficult because of controversial issues regarding the relevant norms on belief-formation: How many and which types value are relevant to PL? How can different types of value be balanced, and how can conflicts between different norms be resolved? Does the concept of PL presuppose that norms have truth values?

In response to these problems, and to reduce the complexity of the discussion, I suggested to preliminarily restrict an account of PL to three basic epistemic norms: *Evidentialism*, *Degrees of Plausibility*, and *Non-Arbitrary Updates*. We can now formulate a working definition of PL, based on these three norms.

Working definition of PL: Positive learning is the acquisition of new, justified[11] true beliefs, where the belief-formation involved is in line with the following three basic epistemic norms.

* *Evidentialism:* The epistemic subject should not ignore or dismiss any relevant evidence.
* *Degrees of Plausibility:* If the evidence for a proposition p is uncertain, the subject should assign a degree of plausibility to p that reflects this uncertainty.
* *Non-Arbitrary Updates:* When the subject gains new information, the subject should update degrees of plausibility non-arbitrarily.

Does this working definition satisfy the desiderata formulated in section 2? The definition fulfills desideratum 1 (Epistemicity), because it makes the involved epistemic norms explicit. It is a flexible definition (desideratum 2, Flexibility), because it leaves it open what evidence should be regarded as *relevant* and which ways of updating degrees of plausibility qualify as being *non-arbitrary*. Still, this does not make the definition empty, because, as we have seen, there is at least one way of formulating the three basic epistemic norms rigorously (Jayne's desiderata), and this also shows that Bayesian reasoning can be regarded as ideal reasoning, in the sense that it satisfies slightly more specific versions of the three basic epistemic norms. What is more, this also shows that the working definition is empirically tractable (desideratum 3), because failures resulting from imperfect (qualitative) approximations to Bayesian inference provide a clue to empirical obstacles to achieving (and teaching the ability for) PL in practice.

5.2   Relevance to PLATO

Clarifying the significance and impact of such obstacles is important to the PLATO program as a whole, because it shows that even "ideal reasoning" does not guarantee approximating truth, since the priors and structural assumptions of a Bayesian model can always be biased. These are important theoretical obstacles to achieving PL.

Empirically, approximating "ideal reasoning" is hampered by subjective valences and cognitive biases (which can generate positive misbeliefs that may in

---

11   That the acquired beliefs be justified is already an epistemic norm. Here, I regard the term as a placeholder, to be replaced by more specific definitions of PL (see also section 5.3). Note that satisfying the three epistemic norms included here will in many cases already lead to the acquisition of justified beliefs, broadly construed.

some contexts be dangerous). In short, teaching rational inference and making students aware of epistemic values does not make them capable of avoiding negative learning – at least not necessarily.

Undoubtedly, there are many contexts in which cognitive biases and adaptive misbeliefs do not play a significant role, or can even enhance learning. For instance, students may be more motivated to reach a learning goal (understanding a complex theory, learning a language, writing a term paper, etc.) if they have a positive illusion about their own learning ability (e.g., regarding the anticipated energy they will have to invest to complete the task). In such contexts, prudential norms could be part of a definition of PL.

However, there are also contexts in which the goal of learning can only be defined indirectly. For instance, when students are asked to discuss and envisage possible solutions to socially relevant problems, there will not be a single viable or "correct" solution, and arguments for or against a particular solution may create a feeling of uncertainty. Furthermore, complex and difficult tasks may require a high frustration tolerance. In such situations, positive illusions regarding one's own abilities may be difficult or impossible to maintain, and including prudential norms in a definition of PL may be less useful. Instead, the question to what extent students can be taught to become tolerant against negative effects of negative affective states becomes relevant, and competencies that support such a tolerance might be included in a definition of PL.

In short, empirical results regarding the causes and effects of cognitive biases and systematic misbeliefs are not only relevant to determine practical limitations of learners (i.e., to investigate to what extent learners can approximate an IR and thereby gain the ability for PL); in addition, empirical results are also relevant for developing more specific definitions of PL: the severity of negative effects of cognitive biases in different domains can, for example, help determine whether epistemic or prudential values should gain a larger weight in certain contexts, and, consequently, in domain-specific definitions of PL.

5.3   Suggestions for future research

The discussion in this paper suggests various relevant directions for future research. Here, I provide a tentative agenda with four potential projects that aim to further develop the concept of PL.

Project 1: Domain-specific definitions of PL

Domain-specific definitions of PL can by developed by discounting or emphasizing the theoretical obstacles to achieving PL, depending on which of these obstacles are relevant within that domain. Two general questions that need to be answered are the following:

1. To what extent, and in which learning contexts, can cognitive biases and (positive) illusions be dangerous and should therefore be reduced or overcome?
2. To what extent, and in which learning contexts, can cognitive biases and (positive) illusions be conducive to achieving a certain goal and should, therefore, be tolerated or even fostered?

The answers to these questions are likely to depend on the particular bias and context considered. Hence, it may also be useful to incorporate different epistemic, prudential, or other norms in domain-specific definitions of PL.

A further option to develop more specific versions of PL is to focus on the three basic epistemic norms and adapt them to individual learning domains. In particular, this would include specifying what type of evidence counts as relevant in that domain (thus making the first epistemic norm, *Evidentialism*, more specific).

Project 2: Epistemic justification in the age of information

The working definition of PL proposed in this paper remains silent on the question what it takes for a belief to be justified. This is not too problematic, because the three basic epistemic norms can at least be regarded as necessary conditions on the acquisition of justified beliefs. However, in the age of information, new challenges arise for the concept of justification (cf. Miller and Record 2013): Is it sufficient to know that a reliable source on the Internet contains a reason for the belief that p, or is it necessary to have a more direct access to the knowledge base for that belief? Given that many online sources are not reliable, and given that Internet users tend to offload memories to the Internet (Ward 2013), does this mean that technology amplifies cognitive biases and causes users to systematically violate the three basic epistemic norms?

Project 3: Extending the scope of PL to unconscious mental processes

Belief formation is not only guided by conscious reasoning processes, but, as we saw above, also by unconscious, potentially biased internal processes and states (cf. Zlatkin-Troitschanskaia et al. 2017). Some of these internal states may be systematic, but beneficial, misrepresentations (Wiese 2016), which raises the question how, for instance, the prudential value of unconscious mental states should be balanced with the epistemic value of conscious beliefs.

This suggests that a wider concept of PL could target changes in mental states and processes other than beliefs and conscious reasoning. Research conducted within the influential framework of predictive processing (see Clark 2016; Hohwy 2013; Wiese and Metzinger 2017) shows how diverse mental phenomena can be accounted for by positing neurophysiologically plausible computational processes that approximate Bayesian inference. In fact, it hast recently been argued that these processes can literally be regarded as inferences (see Kiefer 2017), so it makes sense to investigate which epistemic norms are satisfied by them and how deviances from these norms may lead to our cognitive biases and (positive) illusions.

Project 4: Moral norms and PL

There are at least two ways in which moral norms can be used to enrich the concept of PL. A first option would be to argue that certain methods of belief formation are morally praiseworthy (or blameworthy; see section 2). A second, and possibly more relevant, option would be to argue that certain ways of *using* and *distributing* information are morally praiseworthy (or blameworthy). Here, basic moral values, such as fairness, distributive justice, or epistemic virtues (e.g., intellectual courage and caution, or demureness and openness to new ideas and information) could be investigated.

The four potential research projects outlined here can all be regarded as contributions to a "practical philosophy of mind": reasoning and belief-formation are mental actions for which the concept of PL seeks to provide regulations. These regulations are needed to cope with new challenges in the age of information. If we want to tap the full potential of technological progress, and master its risks, we will also have to master our own minds.

Acknowledgments

I am highly grateful to the organizers and participants of the PLATO conference (June 2017) for their valuable input and feedback. Special thanks go to Thomas Metzinger for providing extremely helpful comments on a draft of this paper.

Bibliography

Alchourrón, C. E., Gärdenfors, P., & Makinson, D. (2014). On the logic of theory change: Partial meet contraction and revision functions. *Journal of Symbolic Logic, 50*(2), 510-530. doi:10.2307/2274239

Bénabou, R., & Tirole, J. (2002). Self-confidence and personal motivation. *The Quarterly Journal of Economics, 117*(3), 871-915. doi:10.1162/003355302760193913

Bracha, A., & Brown, D. J. (2012). Affective decision making: A theory of optimism bias. *Games and Economic Behavior, 75*(1), 67-80. doi:10.1016/j.geb.2011.11.004

Chater, N., Oaksford, M., Hahn, U., & Heit, E. (2010). Bayesian models of cognition. *Wiley Interdisciplinary Reviews: Cognitive Science, 1*(6), 811-823. doi:10.1002/wcs.79

Chignell, A. (2017). The ethics of belief. In E. N. Zalta (Ed.), *The Stanford Encyclopedia of Philosophy* (Spring 2017 ed.). Stanford University: The Metaphysics Research Lab. https://plato.stanford.edu/archives/spr2017/entries/ethics-belief/. Accessed: 27 July 2017.

Clark, A. (2016). Surfing Uncertainty. New York, NY: Oxford University Press.

Clifford, W. K. (1999[1877]). The ethics of belief. In T. J. Madigan (Ed.), *The ethics of belief and other essays* (pp. 70-96). Amherst, NY: Prometheus Books.

Feldman, J. (2016). What Are the "True" Statistics of the Environment? *Cognitive Science*, 1-33. doi:10.1111/cogs.12444

Friedman, H. H. (2017). *Cognitive Biases that Interfere with Critical Thinking and Scientific Reasoning: A Course Module.* Social Science Research Network (SSRN). https://ssrn.com/abstract=2958800. Accessed: 27 July 2017.

Geisler, W. S., & Ringach, D. (2009). Natural Systems Analysis. *Visual Neuroscience, 26*(1), 1-3. doi:10.1017/S0952523808081005

Griffiths, T. L., & Tenenbaum, J. B. (2006). Optimal Predictions in Everyday Cognition. *Psychological Science, 17*(9), 767773. doi:10.1111/j.1467-9280.2006.01780.x

Hohwy, J. (2013). *The predictive mind.* Oxford, England: Oxford University Press.

Jaynes, E. T. (2003). *Probability theory. The logic of science.* Cambridge, England: Cambridge University Press.

Johnson, D. D. P., & Fowler, J. H. (2011). The evolution of overconfidence. *Nature, 477*(7364), 317-320. doi:10.1038/nature10384

Kiefer, A. (2017). Literal Perceptual Inference. In T. Metzinger & W. Wiese (Eds.), *Philosophy and Predictive Processing.* Frankfurt am Main, Germany: MIND Group. doi:10.15502/9783958573185

Korn, C. W., Prehn, K., Park, S. Q., Walter, H., & Heekeren, H. R. (2012). Positively Biased Processing of Self-Relevant Social Feedback. *The Journal of Neuroscience, 32*(47), 16832-16844. doi:10.1523/jneurosci.3016-12.2012

Locke, J. (1836[1690]). *An essay concerning human understanding* (27. ed.). London, England: Tegg and Son.

Loewenstein, G. (2006). The Pleasures and Pains of Information. *Science, 312*(5774), 704-706. doi:10.1126/science.1128388

McKay, R. T., & Dennett, D. C. (2009). The evolution of misbelief. *Behavioral and Brain Sciences, 32*(06), 493. doi:10.1017/S0140525X09990975

Metzinger, T. K. (2017). The Problem of Mental Action. In T. K. Metzinger & W. Wiese (Eds.), *Philosophy and Predictive Processing.* Frankfurt am Main, Germany: MIND Group. doi: 10.15502/9783958573208

Miller, B., & Record, I. (2013). Justified Belief in a Digital Age: On the Epistemic Implications of Secret Internet Technologies. *Episteme, 10*(02), 117-134. doi:10.1017/epi.2013.11

Oaksford, M., & Chater, N. (2009). Precis of Bayesian rationality: The probabilistic approach to human reasoning. *Behavioral and Brain Sciences, 32*(1), 69-84; discussion 85-120. doi:10.1017/S0140525X09000284

Oppenheimer, M., O'Neill, B. C., & Webster, M. (2008). Negative learning. *Climatic Change, 89*(1), 155-172. doi:10.1007/s10584-008-9405-1

Parker, J. A., & Brunnermeier, M. K. (2004). *Optimal Expectations.* NBER Working Paper No. w10707. Social Science Research Network (SSRN). https://ssrn.com/abstract=583705-. Accessed: 27 July 2017.

Pliushch, I. (2017). The Overtone Model of Self-Deception. In T. K. Metzinger & W. Wiese (Eds.), *Philosophy and Predictive Processing.* Frankfurt am Main, Germany: MIND Group. doi: 10.15502/9783958573222

Sharot, T. (2011a). *The Optimism Bias.* New York, NY: Pantheon Books.

Sharot, T. (2011b). The optimism bias. *Current Biology, 21*(23), R941-R945. doi:10.1016/j.cub.2011.10.030

Sharot, T., & Garrett, N. (2016). Forming Beliefs: Why Valence Matters. *Trends in Cognitive Sciences, 20*(1), 25-33. doi:10.1016/j.tics.2015.11.002

Sharot, T., Korn, C. W., & Dolan, R. J. (2011). How unrealistic optimism is maintained in the face of reality. *Nature Neuroscience, 14*(11), 1475-1479. doi:10.1038/nn.2949

Spohn, W. (2009). A Survey of Ranking Theory. In F. Huber & C. Schmidt-Petri (Eds.), *Degrees of Belief* (pp. 185-228). Dordrecht, Netherlands: Springer.

Spohn, W. (2012). The laws of belief: Ranking theory and its philosophical applications. Oxford, England: Oxford University Press.

Talbott, W. (2016). Bayesian Epistemology. In E. N. Zalta (Ed.), *The Stanford Encyclopedia of Philosophy* (Winter 2016 ed.). Stanford, CA: Metaphysics Research Lab at Stanford University. https://plato.stanford.edu/archives/win2016/entries/epistemology-bayesian/. Accessed: 27 July 2017.

Taylor, S. E., Kemeny, M. E., Reed, G. M., Bower, J. E., & Gruenewald, T. L. (2000). Psychological resources, positive illusions, and health. *American psychologist, 55*(1), 99-109. doi:10.1037/0003-066X.55.1.99

Trivers, R. (2000). The Elements of a Scientific Theory of Self-Deception. *Annals of the New York Academy of Sciences, 907*(1), 114-131. doi:10.1111/j.1749-6632.2000.tb06619.x

van Inwagen, P. (1996). It is wrong, everywhere, always, and for anyone, to believe anything upon insufficient evidence. In J. Jordan & D. Howard-Snyder (Eds.), *Faith, Freedom, and Rationality* (pp. 137-153). Lanham, MD: Rowman & Littlefield.

van Roojen, M. (2016). Moral Cognitivism vs. Non-Cognitivism. In E. N. Zalta (Ed.), *The Stanford Encyclopedia of Philosophy* (Winter 2016 ed.). Standford, CA: Metaphysics Research Lab at Stanford University. https://plato.stanford.edu/archives/win2016/entries/moral-cognitivism/. Accessed: 27 July 2017.

Varki, A. (2009). Human uniqueness and the denial of death. *Nature, 460*(7256), 684-684.

von Hippel, W., & Trivers, R. (2011). The evolution and psychology of self-deception. *Behavioral and Brain Sciences, 34*(1), 1-16. doi:10.1017/S0140525X10001354

Ward, A. F. (2013). Supernormal: How the Internet Is Changing Our Memories and Our Minds. *Psychological Inquiry, 24*(4), 341-348. doi:10.1080/1047840X.2013.850148

Wiese, W. (2016). Action Is Enabled by Systematic Misrepresentations. *Erkenntnis, 1-20.* doi:10.1007/s10670-016-9867-x

Wiese, W., & Metzinger, T. K. (2017). Vanilla PP for Philosophers: A Primer on Predictive
Processing. In T. K. Metzinger & W. Wiese (Eds.), *Philosophy and Predictive Processing*. Frankfurt am Main, Germany: MIND Group. doi:10.15502/9783958573024

Zlatkin-Troitschanskaia et al. (2017). *Positive Learning in the Age of Information*. Unpublished Manuscript, Draft Proposal Cluster of Excellence, Johannes Gutenberg University
Mainz.

A Model of Positive and Negative Learning

Learning Demands and Resources, Learning Engagement, Critical Thinking, and Fake News Detection

Christian Dormann, Eva Demerouti, and Arnold Bakker

Abstract

This chapter proposes a model of positive and negative learning (PNL model). We use the term negative learning when stress among students occurs, and when knowledge and abilities are not properly developed. We use the term positive learning if motivation is high and active learning occurs. The PNL model proposes that (a) learning-related demands and resources contribute to learning engagement and burnout, (b) that learning engagement improves critical thinking, which (c) should enhance students' abilities to detect fake news. Two studies demonstrate the validity of the learning engagement and burnout constructs, and learning-related demands and resources as possible antecedents. Also, critical thinking mediates the effect of learning engagement on fake news detection. Still, 30.30% of the students believed more in fake news than in real news. We discuss implications of the PNL model for the design of learning conditions.

Keywords

Positive Learning; Negative Learning; Stress; Motivation; Critical Thinking; Fake News; Learning Demands; Learning Resources.

1   Positive and Negative Learning

The media frequently report on university students' stress, decreasing motivation, reduced performance, increased turnover, or diminishing competencies to transfer to their jobs what they have learned (e.g., Forbes 2013). Whilst in most Western countries there has been little debate that education is the key to future societal development and economic success, these adverse developments are coupled with tendencies of politicians to discredit research evidence (e.g., The Guardian 2017) and prefer "*alternative facts*" (NBC News 2017), for example, misrepresenting the scientific evidence that shows the atmosphere of the earth is warming (Weaver 2017). This is unfortunate because research delivers the evidence that constitutes the core of curricular contents at universities, and if politicians question the validity of curricular contents, students possibly reduce their engagement in their studies even more.

Media reports on students' attitudes are substantiated by research evidence. Students' believes in the meaningfulness of their studies are indeed undermined, cynicism could increase, and students feel frequently stressed (Herbst et al. 2016). In their review and meta-analysis of stress interventions among students, Regehr, Glancy and Pitts (2013, p. 7) concluded that "[...] *that approximately half of the university students report moderate levels of stress-related mental health concerns, including anxiety and depression,*" The prevalence of clinically relevant levels of depression was estimated to be as high as 30.6% (Ibrahim et al. 2013). Further, we shall expect graduates to know the most important research evidence, but frequently they do not (e.g., Rynes et al. 2002), and evidence-based decisions are rarely made in practice (e.g., Briner 2007).

When undesirable learning outcomes occur, we use the term *negative learning* (see Zlatkin-Troitschanskaia et al. 2017). In particular, when negative states such as exhaustion and cynicism occur, we use the term *learning burnout*. Positive antitheses to negative learning and learning burnout are being vigorous, dedicated, and fully absorbed while studying. Such states constitute what we term *learning engagement*, which is part of *positive learning* (cf. Zlatkin-Troitschanskaia et al. in this volume). We propose a *P*ositive and *N*egative *L*earning model (PNL model). The PNL model describes a process according to which study-related demands (e.g., time pressure, self-control demands) and resources (e.g., socially supportive teachers, self-efficacy) are antecedents of learning engagement and learning burnout, which impact on students' active learning (e.g., critical thinking). Critical thinking, in turn, is proposed to impact on students' media literacy (e.g., Trilling and Fadel 2009), including the ability to distinguish between "*fake news*" and real news.

The present chapter presents two studies. Study 1 establishes the factorial validity of the (state) learning engagement concept, and it further presents discriminant validity with regard to (state) learning burnout. In addition, Study 1 investigates self-control demands and self-efficacy as possible antecedents of learning engagement and learning burnout. Study 2 presents further evidence for the factorial validity of the (trait) learning engagement concept. Study 2 also tests a part of the proposed PNL model in terms of a mediation model, according to which critical thinking mediates the effect of learning engagement on the ability to distinguish between fake news and real news.[12]

1.1 Learning engagement and learning burnout

Engagement is a broad concept. In the literature, the term engagement has been used with reference to a huge variety of multidimensional constructs and experiences, including affects, cognitions, and behaviors. In the educational literature (e.g., Fredricks et al. 2004) the term engagement is particularly used to focus on positive outcomes of studying. This involves, among others, the completion of studies, study performance, and achievements (e.g., Eccles and Wang 2012). In many instances, two major components of engagement are identified (e.g., Finn and Zimmer 2012; Finn 1989). The emotional component comprises of feelings of belonging and valuing, interest and joy. The behavioral component involves participation in and commitment to activities related to the class, school or university, task performance and persistence in studying. However, existing conceptualizations of engagement are relatively heterogeneous: "[...] *at times, it seemed as though the terms student engagement and school engagement, were being used rather loosely to mean everything that is good about an individual's relationship with his or her school.*" (Eccles and Wang 2012, p. 137).

A more coherent stream of the engagement concept can be found in the literature on work engagement (Bakker and Demerouti 2017; Demerouti et al. 2001; Kahn 1990; Macey and Schneider 2008). The concept of work engagement (cf. Bakker and Demerouti 2017) has been developed as a conceptual counterpart to job burnout. Although some authors view burnout and engagement as opposite

---

12   Acknowledgement: We are grateful to *Dennis Bierbaum, Andreas Bornscheuer, Esra Demirci, Anne Förster, David Gläser, Sabrina Henrich, Tobias Knecht, Pia Kömpf, Fabian Kreckel, Sarah Obermann, Isabell Staufenbiel, Philipp Stein, Patrick Maximilian Weber, Celina Willems, Sandra Wintermeyer, Maria Wortmann,* and *Sandra Christina Zender* for their support in developing the fake news items, the item to measure critical thinking, and for collecting the data of Study 2.

sides of a single dimension (e.g., Maslach et al. 2001), most scholars today agree that engagement and burnout are distinct albeit related constructs.

The concept of work engagement has been demonstrated to comprise three dimensions. It is regarded as *"a positive, fulfilling, work-related state of mind that is characterized by vigor, dedication, and absorption"* (Schaufeli et al. 2002, p. 74). Vigor comprises aspects such as feeling energized, vital, strong, and persevering. Dedication includes being enthusiastic about the job, finding it useful, meaningful, and inspiring, and being proud of it. Absorption is characterized by being fully immersed in the job, forgetting about time and everything else, and feeling happy while working.

In a similar vein, job burnout is also characterized by three dimensions. *"Burnout is a syndrome of emotional exhaustion, depersonalization, and reduced personal accomplishment that can occur among individuals who do 'people work' of some kind"* (Maslach and Jackson 1986, p. 1). Although initially thought to result from "people" work, it is now widely accepted that any kind of overtaxing activity could lead to burnout. When surveying the general population, the term depersonalization is usually replaced by "cynicism", which reflects an indifferent or distant attitude towards the tasks that one has to perform. Emotional exhaustion is replaced by "exhaustion", which now refers to fatigue irrespective of its cause. Finally, personal accomplishment is replaced by "lack of professional efficacy", which encompasses both social and non-social aspects of task performance (cf. Schaufeli and Buunk 2003).

Work engagement has been characterized by using a variety of time perspectives ranging from trait concepts (comprising stable positive views of life and work), to state and state-like concepts (e.g., feelings of energy or absorption; e.g., Schaufeli and Bakker 2004; Macey and Schneider 2008). Sonnentag, Dormann and Demerouti (2010) have delineated how contrary to the standard view of engagement as a trait-like concept, state work engagement can be conceptualized. Sonnentag et al. (2010) claimed that there is, however, still a lack of empirical evidence regarding the construct validity of the state engagement concept. Venz, Pundt, and Sonnentag (2017) recently demonstrated the factorial validity of state work engagement, but the validity of the state learning engagement construct is not yet unknown.

In the present study, we aim at establishing the construct validity of state learning engagement (Study 1) and trait learning engagement (Study 2). We therefore investigate the factor structure of nine items that cover the three proposed dimensions of engagement. We further investigate the convergent and discriminant validity with regard to state study burnout (Study 1). Thus, our first three hypotheses were:

H1: There is a three-factor structure underlying the items for measuring state learning engagement (Study 1).

H2: There is a three-factor structure underlying the items for measuring state learning burnout (Study 1).

H3: The state learning construct is valid, that is, it has convergent and discriminant validity with regard to state learning burnout (Study 1).

Whereas our Study 1 applied state-like measures that refer to experiences made in the preceding week, our Study 2 used trait-like measures that addressed what students experience or what they do in general. Therefore, we used Study 2 to establish the factorial validity of the trait learning engagement concept. Our fourth hypothesis, thus, was:

H4: There is a three-factor structure underlying the items for measuring trait learning engagement (Study 2).

1.2   Development of learning engagement and learning burnout

To explain the development and consequences of engagement and burnout, the job demands-resources model (JDR model; Bakker and Demerouti 2017) provides a coherent framework. The JDR model extended the job demands-control model (Karasek 1979; Karasek 1998; Karasek and Theorell 1990) by including a broader range of variables that may impact on stress and motivational processes, and by mainly focusing on burnout as a stress outcome and on engagement as a motivational outcome.

According to the JDR model, engagement results from the combination of high work demands (e.g., complex tasks) with high job resources (e.g., high autonomy). In Karasek's (1998) terms, this reflects the 'active learning' hypothesis. Through appropriate resources, demands people can efficiently cope with the demands, and learning and mastery result (e.g., Taris et al. 2003). In the absence of any demands, there is a lack of activation, which may even result in a loss of previously acquired skills. Karasek (1998, p. 34) termed this particular loss *"negative learning"*, but in the current chapter we propose an extended negative learning concept.

According to our extended view, another aspect of negative learning occurs in the absence of resources. Demands can then not adequately be coped with, and burnout and other stress symptoms develop. Although the JDR model particularly emphasizes the importance of situational, that is, work-related demands and resources, it also recognizes person-related demands (e.g., too high self-set goals) and resources (e.g., self-efficacy). Noteworthy is that in addition to possible positive main effects of resources and negative effects of demands, the combination of demands and resources determines whether burnout or engagement develop (i.e., a moderation effect).

Similar to the JDR model (Bakker and Demerouti 2017), our PNL model proposes that demands reduce learning engagement and resources increase learning engagement. For learning burnout, we expected effects of opposite sign. In general, the PNL model also proposes that resources moderate the effects of demands on engagement and on burnout, but our sample size was only small (see below) and lacks statistical power for detecting such effects (Klein and Mossbrugger 2000). Thus, our (directional) hypotheses were:

H5: Learning-related self-control demands reduce learning engagement (H5a) and increase learning burnout (H5b; Study 1).

H6: Learning-related self-efficacy increases learning engagement (H6a) and reduces learning burnout (H6b; Study 1).

According to the JDR model and its antecedent models such as the demand control model (Karasek 1979), demands hamper and resources foster active learning and growth. This is more likely achieved if high demands are coupled with high resources. Our PNL model proposes that active learning is indeed achieved through a process, in which increased engagement and reduced burnout are important mediating variables. Since in neither of our two studies all three concepts (demands/resources, engagement/burnout, and active learning) were measured simultaneously, we could not test this proposition in the present studies. However, Study 2 addressed both trait engagement and active learning in terms of critical thinking. Thus, our next hypothesis was:

H7: Trait learning-engagement increases critical thinking (Study2).

Critical thinking has been regarded as one core abilities underlying media literacy (Maksl et al. 2014; Silverblatt 2008). The concept of media literacy is based on the supposition that information presented in the media is frequently incomplete, sometimes ambiguous, inaccurate or even wrong (Maksl et al. 2014; Thoman and Jolls 2004). Students' media literacy in general and their critical thinking abilities in particular should enable them to cope with information-related uncertainties. This also includes information presented in news media (Maksl et al. 2014). Critically thinking and reflecting information presented in news media should also improve peoples' ability to identify fake news, which we regard as a critical ability in the 21st century. Thus, our final two hypotheses were:

H8: Critical thinking improves identification of fake news (Study 2).

H9: Learning-engagement indirectly improves identification of fake news via critical thinking (Study 2).

Figure 1 summarizes the PNL model. It consists of three groups of concepts. Learning-related demands and resources trigger positive and negative learning processes, which eventually result in desirable or undesirable learning outcomes. The concepts shown in circles are the particular ones used in the present studies; they could be replaced by other variables representing the three groups of concepts. The dotted arrows shown in the left part of Figure 1 represent the moderating effects proposed by the PNL model; as noted earlier, they were not tested in the present studies.

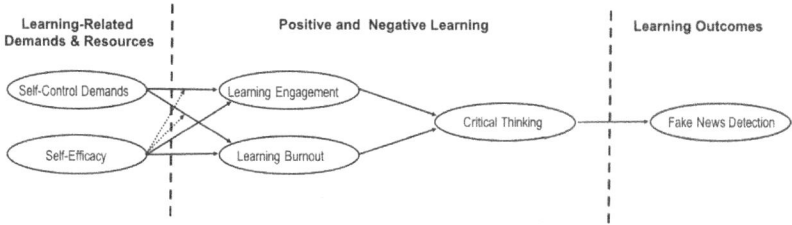

Fig. 1   The Positive and Negative Learning (PNL) Model

2   Study 1

2.1   Sample and design

Data were gathered from overall $N = 68$ students participating in an introductory lecture to business education during the winter term 2016. Participation was voluntary and no course credit was given. Most students were in their first two semesters (72.2%). Of the participants, 57.4% were female. On average, participants were 23.74 years old ($SD = 3.69$).

Data was gathered at the end of a weekly introductory lecture to business education during the last three weeks in 2016. Participation rate was roughly 80% of all course attendants during the first wave of data collection (Time 0; $N = 68$). Participation rate then dropped to $N = 18$ at the third wave.

2.2 Measures

2.2.1 State study engagement

State study engagement was measured using nine items from the Utrecht Work Engagement Scale (UWES; Schaufeli et al. 2006). Item wording was changed to address participants' study-related experiences during the preceding week (e.g., "Summarizing the last week, I felt bursting with energy during my studies") instead of the experiences made at work during the past in general (e.g., "At my work, I feel bursting with energy"). Vigor (V), dedication (D), and absorption (A) were measured with three items, respectively. Responses were made on a 7-point scale ranging from 1 = *never* to 7 = *always*. The item stem was "Summarizing the last week", which was followed by the experiences listed in Table 1 in the Results Section.

2.2.2 State study burnout

State study burnout was measured using seven items from the Maslach Burnout Inventory – General Survey (cf. Maslach et al. 2008). Item wording was changed to address participants' study-related experiences during the preceding week as described earlier for study engagement. Exhaustion (E) was measured with three items. Cynicism (C) and lack of professional efficacy (P) were measured with two items, respectively. Responses were made on a 7-point scale ranging from 1 = *never* to 7 = *always*. The item stem was "Summarizing the last week", which was followed by the experiences listed in Table 2 in the Section 2.3.

2.2.3 State self-control demands

To measure state self-control demands, we used an adaption of scales developed by Neubach and Schmidt (2006; see also Diestel and Schmidt 2011). These scales measure in how far individuals have to (a) apply impulse control during learning, (b) overcome inner obstacles while learning, and (c) resist distractions while learning. Theoretically, all different acts of self-control should draw on a single limited resource called self-control capacity, and consecutive exertion of self-control causes this single source to deplete (cf. Muraven and Baumeister 2000). Then, for example, dedication oneself to a task becomes more difficult and exhaustion is another likely consequence.

For each of the three dimensions of self-control demands, we used three items that were collapsed into a nine-item scale. Responses for each item were made on a 5-point scale ranging from 1 = *does not apply at all* to 5 = *does fully apply*. Cronbach's alpha was .91 across all waves.

2.2.4   State self-efficacy

State self-efficacy was measured using an adaptation of scales developed by Schwarzer and Jerusalem (1999). We used four items that assessed whether participants found ways to overcome inner resistances, whether they experienced little difficulties to achieve their goals and objectives, whether they could handle upcoming problems by themselves, and whether they approached difficulties in a relaxed manner because they knew about their abilities. All items referred to the preceding week. Responses for each item were made on a 5-point scale ranging from 1 = *does not apply at all* to 5 = *does fully apply*. Cronbach's alpha was .77 across all waves.

2.3   Results

2.3.1   Construct validity of state learning engagement

Because of the decline in participation rate and the low ratio of parameters to participants, we did not conduct a (multi-level) confirmatory factor analyses. Rather, we conducted an exploratory factor analysis of Time 0 data only (i.e., from the first wave of observation). An initial exploratory factor analysis of the state study engagement yield two factors with eigenvalues larger than 1.0, however, the eigenvalue of the third factors was only slightly below 1.0. Hence, a three-factor solution was computed. The results are shown in Table 1.

Tab. 1   Factor Loadings (oblique rotation) of the State Study Engagement Items (Time 0)

	I	II	III
I felt strong and vigorous during my studies (V)		.83	
I felt bursting with energy during my studies (V)		.63	
I could continue studying for very long periods at a time (V)		.57	
I was immersed in my studies (A)	.50		.66
I forgot everything else around me during my studies (A)			.58
Time flew when I was studying (A)			.52
I found the studies that I did full of meaning and purpose (D)	.88		
I was enthusiastic about my studies (D)	.83		
My studies inspired me (D)	.63		

Note: Factor loadings below .40 in absolute value are not shown for clarity.

Table 1 shows that, in terms of largest factor loadings, the three-factor structure fully confirmed. Only the "immersed" item, which was supposed to reflect absorption, had a substantial cross-loading on the dedication factor. However, this cross-loading was smaller than the main loading. The second factor (vigor) fully reflected expectations. Thus, although the eigenvalue of the third factor was slightly below 1.0, our H1 (Is there a three-factor structure underlying the items for measuring state learning engagement (Study 1)?), was confirmed.

To assess the variance within (across Time 0 to Time 2) and between individuals, ICC(1) (James 1982) were computed for vigor (ICC = .68), dedication (ICC = .64), and absorption (ICC = .60). This indicated that most variance of learning engagement was between participants.

Next, we factor analyzed Time 0 state study burnout items. As before, an initial exploratory factor analysis of the state study burnout yield two factors with eigenvalues larger than 1.0. However, again, the eigenvalue of the third factor was only slightly below 1.0. Hence, again, a three-factor solution was computed. The results are shown in Table 2.

Tab. 2 Factor Loadings (oblique rotation) of the State Study Burnout Items (Time 0)

	I	II	III
I felt burned out from my studies (E)	.77		
I felt emotionally drained from my studies (E)	.74		
Studying for so long was really a strain for me (E)	.70		
I have become less enthusiastic about my studies (C)		.80	
I have become more cynical about my studies (C)		.74	
I have accomplished many worthwhile things during my studies (P)			.80
In my opinion, I was a good student (P)			.68

Note: Factor loadings below .40 in absolute value are not shown for clarity.

Table 2 shows that the state study burnout items exhibited the expected three-factor structure. No substantial cross-loading were observed. Thus, our H2, was confirmed, too.

To assess the variance within (across Time 0 to Time 2) and between individuals, ICC(1) (James 1982) were computed for exhaustion (ICC = .67), cynicism (ICC = .74), and lack of professional efficacy (ICC = .65). This indicated that most variance of learning burnout was between participants.

In the next step, we explored the relations between states of study engagement and states of study burnout. The correlations (and the means, standard deviations, and Cronbach's alphas) are shown in Table 3.

Tab. 3 Descriptive Statistics of State Study Engagement and State Study Burnout (Time 0)

		M	SD	1	2	3	4	5	6
1	Vigor	3.09	1.08	.81					
2	Dedication	4.03	1.17	.61	.69				
3	Absorption	3.51	1.11	.56	.55	.88			
4	Exhaustion	3.84	1.23	-.33	-.38	-.29	.82		
5	Cynicism	3.36	1.58	-.44	-.59	-.51	.59	.85	
6	Reduced Personal Efficacy	4.57	1.56	-.65	-.36	-.31	.18	.35	.72

Note: All correlations significant except exhaustion with reduced personal efficacy ($p > .18$). Cronbach's alphas in the diagonal.

To begin with, reliabilities were generally acceptable despite the small number of items. Only for state study dedication Cronbach's alpha was smaller than the generally recommended level of .70 (e.g., Nunally 1978).

The correlations suggest that the state study engagement scales had convergent correlations; they correlated among each other in the range from .55 to .61. For state study burnout, convergent correlations were considerably lower, and the correlation of cynicism with reduced personal efficacy ($r = .18$) failed to become significant.

The relations among engagement and burnout scales suggest that discriminant validity might not always been given. Vigor, which correlated with the remaining engagement scales not higher than .61 (dedication), correlated with the burnout scale 'lack of professional efficacy' with $r = -.65$. Similarly, dedication was highly correlated with the burnout scale 'cynicism' with $r = -.59$. For absorption, correlations with burnout scales were somewhat smaller ($-.29 > r > -.51$). Thus, our H3 was fully confirmed in terms of the convergent validity, and was partly confirmed in terms of discriminant validity.

2.3.2 Antecedents of state learning engagement and state learning burnout

Our first two hypotheses proposed learning-related self-control demands to reduce learning engagement and to increase learning burnout (H5, Study 1) and learning-related self-efficacy to increase learning engagement and to decrease learning burnout (H6, Study 1). As noted earlier, ICCs of learning engagement and learning burnout were substantial. Therefore, we used multilevel modeling with Mplus (Muthén and Muthén 1998-2015).

As recommended by Zhang, Zyphur and Preacher (2009) we decomposed our Level 1 variables into within-individual and between-individual components; we did so by including both individuals' actual ratings and individuals' mean ratings simultaneously within our model. This procedure allows us to test relationships between Level 1 variables simultaneously on both levels and thus avoids potential problems of conflated within-level and between-level relationships (Zhang et al. 2009; Preacher et al. 2010). To eliminate possible confounding effects of unmeasured traits, within-variables were centered at the persons' mean levels. Between-variables were grand mean centered.

The results of the multilevel analysis of self-control demands and self-efficacy as antecedents of learning engagement and learning burnout are shown in Figure 2. To reduce the number of parameters to be estimated, we did not analyze all three symptoms of burnout and engagement separately. Rather, we used a latent variable for each of the two constructs. The top part of Figure 2 shows the results within individuals (Level 1), and the bottom part show the results between individuals (Level 2).

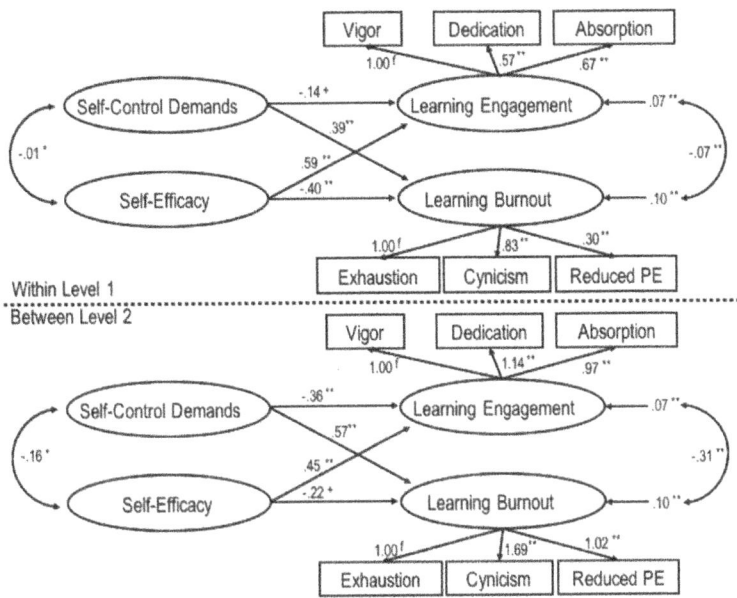

Fig. 2 Unstandardized results of the multilevel analysis of self-control demands and self-efficacy as antecedents of learning engagement and learning burnout (f = fixed parameter, **: $p < .01$, *: $p < .05$, +: $p < .10$, one-tailed; error variances of observed indicators are not shown for clarity)

The results displayed in Figure 2 show that our hypotheses were confirmed. Learning-related self-control demands had a negative relation with learning engagement (H5a) at the between level, and a tendency for such an effect at the within level. Further, learning-related self-control demands had a positive relation with learning burnout (H5b) at both levels. For self-efficacy as a resource all signs were reversed, as expected. Self-efficacy had significant positive relations with learning engagement (H6a) and significant negative relations with learning burnout (H6b) at both levels.

2.4   Discussion of Study 1

Study 1 aimed at providing first evidence of the validity of the state learning engagement construct. Validity should be established in terms of factorial validity, convergent and discriminant validity with regard to learning burnout, and criterion-related validity with regard to theoretically meaningful antecedents, that is, learning-related demands and resources.

The factor solution was almost as expected. Although the third factor had an eigenvalue slightly below 1.0, the three-factor solution confirmed the three factors state vigor, dedication, and absorption. The convergent validities among the three scales were also as expected, but divergent validities with regard to state learning burnout were not fully convincing. Delineated from the JDR model (Bakker and Demerouti 2017), we proposed that learning-related self-control demands should increase learning burnout and decrease learning engagement, which was also confirmed. Self-efficacy as a personal resource had the reversed effect, as expected.

Although Study 1 yielded the evidence we expected, there are some limitations. First, sample size was rather low and not at all representative, so generalizations cannot be validly made and replications and extensions are needed. Second, low sample size was also a problem because it prevented a valid test of the interactions between demands and resources as implied by the JDR model. Third, deriving causal conclusions is difficult, although diary study designs are more internally valid than cross sectional designs. The diary design enabled us to control personality influences (unobserved heterogeneity) by person mean centering the variables at the within level. However, reversed causation is still a possible alternative. For example, students with high levels of burnout might feel less self-efficacious and might report more self-control demands.

To summarize, the evidence obtained in Study 1 suggests state learning engagement and state learning burnout to be valid indicators of positive and negative learning, respectively. Although we used not more than three items to measure each dimension and future studies shall establish reliabilities and validities of the full UWES scales, reliabilities were satisfactory. Learning related demands and resources were theoretically expected and empirically found to precede state learning engagement and state learning burnout, which further support their validity.

Study 2 was used to further validate the concept of learning engagement. Factorial validity was determined for (trait) learning engagement, which was also proposed to increase critical thinking and the ability to identify fake news.

3   Study 2

3.1   Sample and design

Data were gathered from overall $N = 134$ students of various disciplines, who were approached by business education students of a research-oriented class, which was supervised by the first author of this chapter. Participation was voluntary. Almost two thirds (65.7%) of the participating students were female. Most students were enrolled in a bachelor program (51.5%), and 41% were enrolled in a master program. The remaining ones already had a degree comparable to a master (e.g., a German "Staatsexamen" or a German "Diplom"). On average, participants were 25.29 years old ($SD = 4.35$).

Data collection took place during spring 2017. No information about participation rate is available. Each student of the research-oriented class had to collect data from at least seven other students who were not members of the class. Students of various disciplines were approached mainly on campus.

3.2   Measures

3.2.1   Trait study engagement

Trait study engagement was measured using nine items from the Utrecht Work Engagement Scale (UWES; Schaufeli and Bakker 2003). Item wording kept to address participants' study-related experiences in general (e.g., "In general, I felt bursting with energy during my studies") As in Study 1, vigor (V), dedication (D), and absorption (A) were measured with three items, respectively. Responses were made on a 7-point scale ranging from $1 = never$ to $7 = always$.

3.2.2   Critical thinking

The items to assess students' levels of critical thinking were developed according to the skills and sub-skills of critical thinking identified by Facione (1990).

> According to Facione, *"we understand critical thinking to be purposeful, self-regulatory judgment which results in interpretation, analysis, evaluation, and inference, as well as explanation of the evidential, conceptual, methodological, criteriological, or contextual considerations upon which that judgment is based"* (p. 2).

The sub-skills of critical thinking were identified by Facione (1990) using the Delphi method, in which experts from various disciplines participated in six rounds of questions to achieve a consensus. The consensus list of critical thinking skills comprised of six skills (sub-skills in parentheses): interpretation (categorization, decoding significance, clarifying meaning), analysis (examining ideas, detecting arguments, analyzing arguments), evaluation (assessing claims, assessing arguments), inference (querying evidence, conjecturing alternatives, drawing conclusions), explanation (stating results, justifying procedures, presenting arguments), and self-regulation (self-examination, self-correction).

Tab. 4 Items Used to Measure Critical Thinking

Do you separate the different information in news?
Do you recognize different aims of the news?
Do you put the news in context with the current events of the day?
Do you evaluate the trustworthiness of news while reading?
Do you check the background of the used arguments?
Do you search for further background information while dealing with a text?
Do you have clear positions/views?

A set of items covering all sub-skills was beyond the scope of the present study. By consensus, we identified the skills that were most likely to be relevant for fake news detection. We then developed items for these sub-skills. To reduce the "bandwidth" and increase "fidelity" (e.g., Hogan and Roberts 1996) regarding the focal outcome variable, most items explicitly referred to critically dealing with information "in the news". Finally, we reduced the items to a set of nine to limit the burden for participants. These items are shown in Table 4. The questionnaire also included a short introduction to these questions: *"In the following we are interested in how you deal with new information or news when you are spontaneously exposed to them. Suppose, you listen to news on the radio or you see news on TV or the Internet. When responding to the questions below, please think about what you **typically** do. We are not so much interested in whether you are able to do so. Rather, we are interested in what you **normally** do."*

All items had to be answered on a four-point scale ranging from 1 (= *never or almost never*) to 4 (= *always or almost always*). An explanatory factor analysis revealed a clear bend in the scree plot after the first factor. Thus, we computed a single scale, which had a Cronbach's alpha of .77.

3.2.3   Fake News Detection Test (FNDT)

Together with the students of the research-oriented class, a Fake News Detection Test (FNDT) was developed. Different groups of students developed 22 fake news items overall. Some of these items included real news, mostly taken from the last 6 months. Fake news items were developed by altering real news to different extents. In some instances, only the headline was changed (e.g., "Turkish president

Erdogan re-installed Capital Punishment" – the real news was that Erdogan aimed at conducting a referendum accordingly). In other instances, the content of the news was massively changed (e.g., German finance minister Schäuble is competing against IMF managing director Lagarde with his proposal for a debt cut for Greece – the real news was that Schäuble was a strong opponent against a debt cut). From the initial set of 22 items, we chose 12 that were included in the final questionnaire.

	Debt Cut for Greece
	Wolfgang Schäuble (CDU) is competing against IMF Managing Director Christine Lagarde. After a long debate, the Eurozone finance ministers and the International Monetary Fund (IMF) were able to agree on the proposal by Wolfgang Schäuble, a debt cut for Greece. The exact agreement should now be concluded at the next meeting on 15 June, said Eurogroup president Jeroen Dijsselbloem after the end of the consultations. We are already "very close" to a solution. This hinted German Federal Minister of Finance, Wolfgang Schäuble (CDU), who had previously pledged clear commitments by the Europeans to debt relief for Athens. Chancellor Angela Merkel also welcomes the unity of the European Monetary Union and thus sets a clear sign for pro-Europe ahead of the next German Bundestag election in 2017.

	Not at all	Almost not	Almost	Absolutely
F3.4 Are you convinced the content of this news is fully correct?	☐1	☐2	☐3	☐4

Fig. 3   Example item of the Fake News Detection Test
Note: The picture shown in the left part of the original item was replaced by a photo taken by the authors, and the 'ZDF' and 'heute' icons were replaced by similar symbols due to copyright reasons.

All items were presented in a similar fashion, as it is shown in Figure 3. There was a picture on the left side, presented together with some information of the reporting news media (in this instance it was the daily news "heute" of the largest German television company ZDF, which is a public company). Below there were four questions, of which only the most important one is shown in Figure 3. Participants were required to indicate whether they believe the news is "fully correct". We used "fully correct" so that even small changes to real news ideally would have required a "not at all" response. The other three questions (not shown) were: "Have you been dealing with the content of the news before?" (news familiarity), "How much does the news touches you emotionally?" (news emotionality), and "In how far does the content of the news impacts on your everyday life?" (news relevance).

Response scales were as shown in Figure 3 and identical to all four questions. Participants' responses to the three items not shown in Figure 2 were used as control variables in subsequent analyses.

Table 5 lists all verbatim Items (in German) of the FNDT. They are in the same order as used in Study 2. The last column indicates whether the respective item was fake or real.

Tab. 5 Title and German Verbatim Wording of the Items Used in the Fake News Detection Test (FNDT)

Item	Title	Text	Real (R) / Fake (F)
F1	Anerken-nungsquote	In den ersten vier Monaten 2016 wurden mehr als 90 Prozent der Asylanträge positiv beschieden – diese Anerkennungsquote ist in den vergangenen Monaten deutlich gestiegen, weil der Anteil der Flüchtlinge aus Bürgerkriegsländern wie Syrien steigt. Für sie lag die Gesamtschutzquote im Asylverfahren 2015 bei mehr als ein Prozent, für Afghanen hingegen nur bei knapp 50 Prozent, für Migranten aus den Westbalkanstaaten betrug die Anerkennungsquote weniger als ein Prozent. Der Chef des Bundesgrenzschutzes, Frank Jürgens Weise, schätzt, dass insgesamt 55 Prozent der rund 1,2 Millionen Menschen, die seit 2013 als Asylsuchende nach Deutschland gekommen sind, eine Bleibeberechtigung bekommen haben.	F
F3	Schulden-schnitt für Griechenland	Wolfgang Schäuble (CDU) setzt sich gegen IWF Chefin Christine Lagarde durch. Nach einer langen Debatte konnten sich die Finanzminister der Euro-Staaten und der Internationale Währungsfonds (IWF) nun auf den Vorschlag von Wolfgang Schäuble, ein Schuldenschnitt für Griechenland, einigen. Die genaue Vereinbarung solle nun beim nächsten Treffen am 15. Juni beschlossen werden, sagte Eurogruppen-Chef Jeroen Dijsselbloem nach Ende der Beratungen. Man sei einer Lösung bereits „sehr nahe". Dies ließ der Bundesfinanzminister Wolfgang Schäuble (CDU), der sich zuvor auf eindeutige Zusagen der Europäer zu Schuldenerleichterungen für Athen gepocht hat, durchblicken. Auch Bundeskanzlerin Angela Merkel begrüßt die Geschlossenheit der Europäischen Währungsunion und setzt damit vor der kommenden Bundestagswahl 2017 ein klares Zeichen Pro-Europa.	F

Tab. 5 (continued)

Item	Title	Text	Real (R) / Fake (F)
F10	Donald Trump beim Besuch der Holocaust-Gedenkstätte Yad Vashem in Jerusalem	Ein deutsch-israelischer Historiker hat den Eintrag des amerikanischen Präsidenten Donald Trump in das Gästebuch der Holocaust-Gedenkstätte Yad Vashem in Jerusalem kritisiert. Trump hatte am Dienstag geschrieben: „Es ist eine Ehre, mit all meinen Freunden hier zu sein – so fantastisch + werde nie vergessen."	R
F7	828 Asylanträge: Schutzquote für türkische Asylbewerber deutlich gestiegen	Der Anteil der türkischen Asylsuchenden, die in Deutschland Schutz bekommen, ist im April sprunghaft gestiegen. Das Bundesamt für Migration und Flüchtlinge entschied im April über 828 Asylanträge von Türken und gewährte 28 Prozent von ihnen Schutz. Das geht aus der Antwort des Innenministeriums auf eine schriftliche Frage der Linken hervor. Im Vormonat hatte die Quote bei 8,7 Prozent gelegen, im Schnitt von Januar bis März bei 7,5 Prozent. Am 16. April hatte sich eine knappe Mehrheit der Türken in einem Referendum für Verfassungsänderungen ausgesprochen, die dem Präsidenten Recep Tayyip Erdogan deutlich mehr Macht geben. Ob es einen Zusammenhang zwischen der gestiegenen Schutzquote und dem Referendum gibt, geht aus der Antwort nicht hervor.	R
F11	Der türkische Präsident Erdogan führt die Todesstrafe wieder ein	In 13 Wahllokalen - die meisten davon in Konsulaten - fand die Abstimmung statt: Zwischen dem 27. März und dem 9. April votierten hunderttausende Türken in Deutschland mehrheitlich für das von Staatschef Recep Tayyip Erdogan angestrebte Präsidialsystem. Der Schreck darüber, dass die Wähler von deutschem Boden aus für ein autoritäres System votierten, war danach groß. Und schon bald könnte es in der Türkei ein weiteres Referendum geben. Erdogan hat angekündigt, die Todesstrafe wiedereinzuführen.	F
F18	Trump bietet Ausreisewilligen kostenlose One-Way Tickets nach Afrika und Mexiko an	„Nach meinem Wahlsieg habe ich von vielen Anhängern des liberalen Flügels vernommen, dass sie nicht mehr im größten Land der Welt leben möchten. Nun, jetzt ist es an der Zeit zu handeln. Ich persönlich werde Flugtickets nach Mexiko oder in ein afrikanisches Land bezahlen, für alle die, die die USA verlassen wollen. Wir wollen euch hier nicht haben. Geht und macht Amerika wieder großartig."	F

Tab. 5 (continued)

Item	Title	Text	Real (R) / Fake (F)
F9	Bildung hängt in Berlin vom Migrationshintergrund ab	Das Amt für Statistik Berlin-Brandenburg hat den aktuellen Mikrozensus herausgegeben. Die meisten Migranten kommen aus Syrien. Wenn es um Bildungsabschlüsse geht, gibt es zwischen Berlinern mit und ohne Migrationshintergrund einen Unterschied. So verfügen 3 Prozent der Migranten zwischen 18 und 30 Jahren über das Abitur. Bei gleichaltrigen Hauptstädtern ohne Migrationshintergrund liegt dieser Wert mit 53 Prozent deutlich höher. Das geht aus den neuesten Erhebungen des Mikrozensus hervor, der vom Amt für Statistik Berlin-Brandenburg herausgegeben wird. Die größte Migrantengruppe in Berlin bilden aus Syrien stammende Menschen: Ihre Zahl wird mit 1.231.000 angegeben. Danach kommen 80.000 Berliner mit polnischem Migrationshintergrund und 52.000 Personen russischer Herkunft.	F
F23	Europas Regeln gelten nicht für Internet-Monopolisten	Obwohl Facebook bei der Übernahme des Kurznachrichtendiensts WhatsApp nicht die Wahrheit gesagt hat, muss der Konzern keine Strafe fürchten. Nach einer Pressemitteilung der EU Kommission könne man das amerikanische Unternehmen nicht belangen, da sein Hauptsitz nicht in der Europäischen Union liegt.	F
F12	KMK-Chefin für stärkere Nutzung privater Smartphones in der Schule	Berlin (dpa) – Die Vorsitzende der Kultusministerkonferenz (KMK), Claudia Bogedan, hat sich für eine stärkere Nutzung privater Smartphones im Unterricht ausgesprochen. „Alle besitzen ein Smartphone, warum sollen wir sie dann nicht auch in der Schule einsetzen?", sagte die Bremer Bildungssenatorin der „Rheinischen Post". „Natürlich nicht zum Spielen und zur Ablenkung, sondern um es sinnvoll zu nutzen." Medien sollten künftig in allen Fächern flächendeckend eine Rolle spielen. Die Senatorin legt heute mit ihren Kollegen aus den anderen Ländern die Digitalstrategie der Kultusministerkonferenz vor.	R

Tab. 5 (continued)

Item	Title	Text	Real (R) / Fake (F)
F19	Deutschland braucht einen Grenzzaun	Der Vorsitzende der Linkspartei „Die Linke", Jörg Meuthen, fordert in der Diskussion um die Sicherung der deutschen Grenzen den Bau eines Grenzzauns. Meuthen erklärte: „Die illegale Einwanderung nach Deutschland, vor allem über die Grenze zu Frankreich, findet weiter jeden Tag ungebrochen statt. Um das zu verhindern, müssen die Grenzübergänge wirksam kontrolliert und Menschen, die keine Einreiseberechtigung haben, abgewiesen werden. Das kann aber nur funktionieren, wenn gleichzeitig der Übertritt über die grüne Grenze wirksam verhindert.	F
F20	MAD ermittelt angeblich wegen Aufrufs zum Putsch	Der Militärische Abschirmdienst (MAD) ermittelt wegen angeblichen Putsch-Plänen. Ein Stabsoffizier soll im Zuge des Falls Franco A. davon gesprochen haben. Ein Stabsoffizier soll bei einem Lehrgang gesagt haben: „Ich habe es so satt, dass 200.000 Soldaten unter Generalverdacht gestellt werden, wegen zwei Verrückten. Die Ministerin ist bei mir unten durch, das muss man ansprechen oder putschen".	R
F22	SPD will Geringverdiener entlasten	Hilfen für kleine und mittlere Einkommen, kostenlose Kitas, Änderungen beim Spitzensteuersatz: Die Sozialdemokraten umreißen ihr Konzept zur Bundestagswahl – ohne besonders genau zu werden.	R

3.3   Results

3.3.1   Construct validity of trait learning engagement

Like in Study 1, we performed an explanatory factor analysis of the trait learning engagement items. Like in Study 1, an initial factor analysis revealed that the third factor had an eigenvalue only slightly below 1.0. Thus, again, we extracted three factors.

Tab. 6 Factor Loadings (oblique rotation) of the Trait Study Engagement Items

	I	II	III
My studies inspire me (D)	.89		
I am enthusiastic about my studies (D)	.76		
I find the studies full of meaning and purpose (D)	.71		
I am immersed in my studies (A)	.65		
I forget everything else around me during my studies (A)		.94	
I can continue studying for very long periods at a time (V)		.61	
Time flies when I am studying (A)		.48	
I feel strong and vigorous during my studies (V)			.88
I feel bursting with energy during my studies (V)			.59

Note: Factor loadings below .40 in absolute value are not shown for clarity.

The rotated factor solution is presented in Table 6. The first factor mainly reflected dedication, but one item that was expected to measure absorption also loaded on this factor. The second factor mainly reflected absorption, but one item that was expected to measure vigor also loaded on this factor. The third factor clearly reflected vigor. Thus, overall, the evidence for a three-factor trait engagement construct in Study 2 was not as clear as it was for state learning engagement in Study 1. Thus, H4 was only partly supported. Nevertheless, we decided to compute the three trait learning engagement scales according to the theoretical classification of the items because only two out of the nine items loaded on the 'wrong' factor. Cronbach's alphas were .73 for vigor, .83 for dedication, and .56 for absorption. The correlations among the three scales were of similar size as those for state engagement ($r = .54$ for vigor and dedication, $r = .68$ for vigor and absorption, and $r = .53$ for dedication and absorption).

3.3.2 Psychometric properties of the Fake News Detection Test (FNDT)

We expected to achieve a reliable FNDT score by recoding the fake news and then sum the recoded responses to the fake news and the responses to the real news. However, an item analyses revealed that all items had positive item total correlations *without* recoding; participants either tend to believe or disbelieve all news irrespective if they were fake news or real news. Therefore, we computed a Fake News Score (FNS; seven items, Cronbach's alpha = .77), a Real News Score (RNS; five items, Cronbach's alpha = .60), and the difference RNS – FNS (ΔRF), which represents participants' sensitivities to distinguish fake news from real news. The correlations of RNS and FNS was r = -.15. The reliability of the difference scale was .74 using the equation provided by Peter, Churchill and Brown (1993).

Mean level of ΔRF was positive and M = .30, and the standard deviation was SD = .62. Thus, students believed slightly more that the real news were fully correct than the fake news, on average. However, the standard deviation was relatively large compared to the mean, implying that there was a substantial proportion of students who believed more in the fake news than the real news. In fact, these were 30.30% of the participants.

3.3.3   News familiarity, emotionality, and relevance

Fake news familiarity (7 items, alpha = .77), real news familiarity (5 items, alpha = .63), fake news emotionality (7 items, alpha = .79), real news emotionality (5 items, alpha = .65), fake news relevance (7 items, alpha = .76), and real news relevance (5 items, alpha = .59) scales were computed. They served as control variables in regression analyses.

3.3.4   The mediating effect of critical thinking between trait learning engagement and the ability to identify fake news

Our hypotheses proposed trait learning-engagement to increase critical thinking (H7), and critical thinking to improve identification of fake news (H8) as well as to mediate the effect of trait learning engagement on fake news identification (H9). We tested these hypotheses using the process procedure by Hayes (2014) in SPSS. We performed the analyses three times for each of the three-trait engagement dimension because process cannot handle multiple 'independent' variables simultaneously. However, in each analysis the respective two other engagement facets were entered as covariates together with all other control variables (age, gender, and fake and real news familiarity, emotionality, and relevance). The results are shown in Table 7.

The top panel of Table 7 shows the results of the regression of the difference between the real news scores and fake news scores (ΔRF) on trait vigor as independent variable. Among the control variables, participants gender and familiarity with the real news items had significant effects. Males performed better than females and greater familiarity with the real news positively impacted on ΔRF. There was also a tendency to perform better if the real news had emotionally affected participants. As expected, critical thinking had a positive and significant effect on ΔRF, which confirmed H8. However, vigor did neither directly nor indirectly (via critical thinking) impact on ΔRF, which contradicted H9. This was due to a nonsignificant effect of vigor on critical thinking (Beta = .00, SE = .05, $p > .99$; not shown in Table 7), which contradicted H7.

The middle panel of Table 7 shows the results of the respective analysis with dedication as independent variable, in which vigor replaced dedication as control variable. For the constant, all control variables, and the mediating variable, the results were identical to the top panel and are, therefore, not shown again. Dedication as independent variable had no significant direct effect, but, as expected, indirectly affected ΔRF via critical thinking. The direct effect of dedication on critical thinking was also significant (Beta = .15, SE = .04, $p < .01$; not shown in Table 7). Thus, for dedication, H7 and H9 were confirmed.

The bottom panel of Table 7 shows the results of the respective analysis with absorption as independent variable. Absorption as independent variable had no significant direct effect, no significant indirect effect, and did not significant impact on critical thinking (Beta = -.03, SE = .05, $p > .53$; not shown in Table 7). Thus, for absorption, H7 and H9 were not confirmed.

To summarize, H7 was confirmed because critical thinking significantly and positively impacted on ΔRF. H8 and H9 were confirmed for dedication only, but neither for vigor nor for absorption.

Tab. 7 Results of Mediation (Process) Analyses of ΔRF on Vigor (top panel), Dedication (middle panel), and Absorption (bottom panel) via Critical Thinking (Mediator)

	Coeff.	SE	T	P
Independent Variable: Vigor				
Constant	-.55	.52	1.08	.28
Control Variables				
Dedication	-.07	.06	-1.24	.22
Absorption	.06	.07	.92	.36
Age	-.00	.01	-.03	.97
Gender	-.24	.12	-2.05	.04*
Fake News Familiarity	-.21	.14	-1.53	.13
Real News Familiarity	.30	.13	2.34	.02*
Fake News Relevance	-.06	.18	-.31	.76
Real News Relevance	-.04	.19	-.21	.83
Fake News Emotionality	-.19	.17	-1.12	.27
Real News Emotionality	.37	.20	1.84	.07
Mediating Variable				
Critical Thinking	.28	.12	2.25	.01**

Tab. 7   (continued)

	Coeff.	SE	T	P
Independent Variable				
direct effect	.05	.07	.67	.50
indirect effect via critical thinking	.00	.02	[-.03; .03]	
Independent Variable: Dedication				
Constant	*all identical to top panel*			
Control Variables				
Mediating Variable				
Critical Thinking				
Independent Variable				
direct effect	-.07	.06	-1.24	.22
indirect effect via critical thinking	.04	.02	[.01; .09]**	
Independent Variable: Absorption				
Constant	*all identical to top panel*			
Control Variables				
Mediating Variable				
Critical Thinking				
Independent Variable				
direct effect	.06	.07	.92	.36
indirect effect via critical thinking	-.01	.02	[-.04; .01]	

Note: Gender (1 = male, 2 = female). Control variables were tested with two-tailed probability. Mediating and independent variables were tested with one-tailed probability. **: $p < .01$; *: $p < .05$. The process procedure does provide confidence intervals [shown in brackets] but no probability levels for indirect effects.

3.4   Discussion of Study 2

Study 2 aimed at testing parts of the proposed framework model, according to which combinations of learning-related demands and resources could cause negative learning (e.g., learning burnout) and positive learning (e.g., learning engagement). Learning engagement was further proposed to lead to active learning (e.g., critical thinking), which should enhance students' media literacy (e.g., distinguishing between fake news and real news). In particular, Study 2 aimed at testing whether learning engagement has a mediating effect on the ability to distinguish real news from fake news, and whether this effect is mediated via critical thinking. Further, Study 2 investigated the factorial validity of trait learning engagement.

Like for state learning engagement, the factor structure of trait learning engagement comprised of three factors, although the third factor had an eigenvalue slightly below 1.0. Also, two out of nine items had cross loadings that exceeded their loadings on their expected factor. Nevertheless, the three three-item scales were sufficiently reliable except for absorption (alpha = .56), which had the highest reliability in Study 1. We have to leave it to future studies to analyze if the full absorption scale of the UWES has higher reliability.

Study 2 applied two further scales, that we developed to test the proposed mediating mechanism. The first scale measured critical thinking about news. The items were based on the theoretical classification by Facione (1990), but to reduce the burden, we could use only seven items in Study 2. The scale had sufficient reliability (alpha = .77).

The other scale we developed was the FNDT. The FNDT comprised five real news items and seven fake news items, which were created by changing the content of real news. Interestingly, all items had positive total correlations; students tend to either believe or disbelieve all news. Therefore, we used the difference between the real news agreement score minus the fake news agreement score, which reflects students' abilities to distinguish between real news and fake news. The difference scale had sufficient reliability (.74).

Evidence for the proposed mediated relation was found for the dedication facet of learning engagement, whereas we found no such effect for vigor and absorption. This could have been due to the lower reliabilities of vigor and absorption, or due to collinearity of the three engagements scales, which correlated among each other not lower than $r = .53$.

A limitation of Study 2 is the cross-sectional design and the sole use of self-report measures, which prevent validly deriving causal conclusions. We nevertheless believe that a causal interpretation is likely. The FNDT and its ΔRF scale were performance tests, which are unlikely to be biased in favor of our hypotheses. Several possible third variables were statistically controlled, including the participants' familiarity, emotionality, and relevance with the content of the news. There could be unmeasured third variables that impact on the ΔRF as well as critical thinking, for example, general mental ability. However, we believe that general mental ability exerts its influence on ΔRF via critical thinking, rather than via variables unrelated to students' abilities to think critically. We also believe that critical thinking is a cause rather than a consequence of ΔRF. Although it could be reasoned that students' responses to the critical thinking items were based on their cognitions while dealing with fake news, we should note that the fake FNDT was at the end of the questionnaire. Thus, responding to the FNDT is unlikely to have impacted on the responses to the critical thinking items.

To summarize, Study 2 provided further evidence of the (trait) learning engagement concept, it showed that a newly developed critical thinking scale was reliable, and it developed a FNDT, which yielded a satisfactory reliable ΔRF scale. Study 2 also showed that being fully dedicated while learning is related to students' levels of critical thinking, which then helps them distinguishing between real news and fake news.

4 Conclusions

High levels of stress among university students, low levels of students' motivation, and little transfer of knowledge, skills and abilities after entering the labor market are frequently reported in the media, and this is in line with extant research evidence (e.g., Forbes 2013; Herbst et al. 2016). In the present chapter, we introduced the term negative learning when stress occurs and knowledge, skills and abilities are not developed or even diminish. Contrary, we used the term positive learning if student motivation is high and active learning takes place. Based on the JDR model (Bakker and Demerouti 2017) we proposed the PNL model of positive and negative learning. According to the PNL model, learning-related demands and resources contribute to learning engagement and learning burnout. Following conceptualizations of job burnout (Maslach et al. 2001), learning burnout was assumed to consist of the three factors exhaustion, cynicism, and reduced efficiency. Following conceptualizations of work engagement (Schaufeli et al. 2002), learning engagement was assumed to consist of the three factors vigor, dedication, and absorption. Learning engagement was further proposed to lead to active learning as characterized by critical thinking, which should enhance students' abilities to distinguish between real news and fake news.

The present chapter reported results from two studies, which aimed at testing part of the proposed process model and at testing the validity of the state engagement construct. The factorial validity of state learning engagement in Study 1 was very clear, whereas there were two cross loadings in the factor solution of trait learning engagement in Study 2. State study burnout also showed the expected three-dimensional structure in Study 1. Both state learning engagement and state study burnout had good convergent validities in Study 1, but their discriminant validity was not fully convincing because there were substantial correlations between state engagement and state burnout. These correlations were larger than usually found in studies using trait-like measures in the working population. Although it might be possible that students and employees have different experiences that could explain the differences in correlational patterns, we rather believe that it is the measurement of both concepts as states in our Study 1, which makes the differences. Like positive affectitiv and negative affectitiv as personality traits are mainly uncorrelated, having positive and negative emotions at the same time occurs rather rarely. Similarly, experiencing study engagement and study burnout during the same week is less likely, too. Unfortunately, we could not investigate the discriminant validity of their trait counterparts because trait burnout was not measured in Study 2. Nevertheless, future studies should use the full set of UWES items to the learning context and further examine their validity as traits and as states.

Study 2 further tested if critically thinking about news mediates between learning engagement and the ability to identify fake news. This mediation was confirmed for dedication. Being a dedicated learner means being enthusiastic about one's studies, finding learning useful, meaningful, and inspiring, and being proud of it. Our results suggest that being dedicated learners makes students more critical when it comes to evaluating information in the news, which eventually improves their ability to distinguish real news from fake news.

Sadly, as many as almost one third of our sample (30.30%) believed more in fake news than in real news. We believe this figure is high enough to become concerned because fake news have recently been made responsible for a variety of problematic developments. For example, fake news have increasingly be used by opposing parties during elections (e.g., Polage 2012), and studies confirmed that exposure to fake news during election campaigns impact on recipients' perceptions of the candidates (e.g., Moy et al. 2006; Young 2006). Impacts of fake news on the economy have already become apparent, too. The fake tweet on April, 23th, 2013 claiming an attack on the White House caused the stock exchange to go wild (Leinwand Leger et al. 2013). Similar effects can be assumed in a variety of other areas, such as the labor market (e.g., attractiveness of organizations as employers), attitudes towards refugees, foreigners, or ethnic minorities (e.g., bias in estimating their involvement in crimes; e.g., Oberwittler and Höfer 2006), or consumer issues (e.g., rejecting certain products or brands). These are poor developments because decisions of correctly informed citizens contribute best to the overall societal development. We applaud all technological attempts and political regulations (see e.g., Ciampaglia in this volume) to reduce the number and impact of fake news on people, but we believe the best protection are well-educated people themselves. As our results show, critical thinking provides good guard.

The full PNL model goes beyond our finding that critical thinking improves identification of fake news. It also predicts how this could be achieved, namely by making people engaged and active learners and by preventing learning burnout. Further, the PNL model also proposes that too high or too many demands and too low or too few resources cause problems. Although we were not able to test for the proposed moderating effects of resources, the PNL model suggests that positive learning is achieved and negative learning is avoided if high (but not too high) demands are coupled with qualitatively and quantitatively appropriate resources. Qualitatively appropriate resources are those that "match" the demands (cf. de Jonge and Dormann 2006). In our study, we considered self-efficacy believes to match self-regulation demands. For example, recall that self-efficacy items asked whether students find ways to overcome inner resistances or whether they experience little difficulties to achieve their goals and objectives. On the one hand, this should help students to cope with the potential stressfulness of self-regulation demands. Recall that self-regulation demands address, for example, the demand to overcome inner obstacles while learning or to resist distractions while learning. On the other hand, a good combination of self-regulation demands with self-efficacy should lead to active learning and growth, including engagement and the ability to think critically.

The PNL model and its parent models such as the JDR model (Bakker and Demerouti 2017) or the demand control model (Karasek 1979) allow derivation of a variety of potentially stressful demands and helpful resources, which could be identified in the learning content (e.g., too complex tasks; excellent textbooks), the learning environment (e.g., poorly motivated teachers, highly supportive teachers), and in the learner (e.g., performance orientation, mastery orientation). It is possibly too early to use the PNL model as a base for designing better study conditions. However, we believe the first results presented in this chapter represent a promising starting point.

Bibliography

Bakker, A. B., & Demerouti, E. (2017). Job demands–resources theory: Taking stock and looking forward. *Journal of Occupational Health Psychology, 22,* 273-285.

Briner, R. B. (2007). Is HRM evidence-based and does it matter? Institute of Employment Studies Opinion Paper OP6.

Demerouti, E., Bakker, A. B., Nachreiner, F., & Schaufeli, W. B. (2001). The job demands resources model of burnout. *Journal of Applied Psychology, 86,* 499–512.

Diestel, S., & Schmidt, K.-H. (2011). Costs of simultaneous coping with emotional dissonance and self-control demands at work: Results from two German samples. *Journal of Applied Psychology, 96,* 643–653.

Eccles, J., & Wang, M.-T. (2012). Part I commentary: So what is student engagement anyway. In S. L. Christenson (Ed.), *Handbook of Research on Student Engagement* (pp. 133-145). New York, NY: Springer.

Facione, P. A. (1990). *Critical Thinking: A Statement of Expert Consensus for Purposes of Educational Assessment and Instruction*. Millbrae: The California Academic Press.

Finn, J. (1989). Withdrawing from school. *Review of Educational Research 59*(2), 117–42.

Finn, J. D., & Zimmer, K. S. (2012). Student engagement: What is it? Why does it matter? In S. L. Chistenson, A. L. Reschly & C. Wylie (Eds.), *Research on student engagement* (pp. 97-131). New York, NY: Springer.

Forbes (2013). Motivation Matters: 40% Of High School Students Chronically Disengaged From School. https://www.forbes.com/sites/ jamesmarshallcrotty/2013/03/13/ motivation-matters-40-of-high-school-students-chronically-disengaged-from-school/#4b3c93 5e6594. Accessed: 13 March 2017.

Fredricks, J. A., Blumenfeld, P. C., & Paris, A. H. (2004). School engagement: Potential of the concept, state of the evidence. *Review of Educational Research, 74*, 59-109.

Hayes, A. F. (2014). *Comparing conditional effects in moderated multiple regression: Implementation using PROCESS for SPSS and SAS*. White paper downloadable from www. processmacro.org.

Herbst, U., Voeth, M., Eidhoff, A. T., Müller, M., & Stief, S. (2016). *Studierendenstress in Deutschland – eine empirische Untersuchung [Stress among students in Germany - an empirical investigation]*. Berlin: AOK Bundesverband.

Hogan, J., & Roberts, B. W. (1996). Issues and non-issues in the fidelity-bandwidth trade-off. *Journal of Organizational Behavior, 17*, 627–637.

Ibrahim, A. K., Kelly, S. J., Adams, C. E., & Glazebrook, C. (2013). A systematic review of studies of depression prevalence in university students. *Journal of psychiatric research, 47*(3), 391-400.

James, L. R. (1982). Aggregation bias in estimates of perceptual agreement. *Journal of Applied Psychology, 67*, 219-229.

Jonge, J. de, & Dormann, C. (2006). Job demands, job resources and psychological well-being: A longitudinal test of the triple match principle. *Journal of Applied Psychology, 91*, 1359-1374.

Kahn, W. A. (1990). Psychological conditions of personal engagement and disengagement at work. *Academy of Management Journal, 33*, 692-724.

Karasek, R. A. (1979). Job demands, job decision latitude and mental strain: Implications for job redesign. *Administrative Science Quarterly, 24*, 385-408.

Karasek, R. A. (1998). Demand-Control Model: A social, emotional, and physiological approach to stress risk and active behaviour development. In J. M. Stellmann (Ed.), *Encyclopaedia of Occupational Health and Safety* (4th ed., p. 34). Geneva, Switzerland: International Labour Office.Karasek, R. A., & Theorell, T. (1990). *Healthy Work: Stress, Productivity, and the Reconstruction of Working Life*. New York, NY: Basic Books.

Klein, A., & Moosbrugger, H. (2000). Maximum likelihood estimation of latent interaction effects with the LMS method. *Psychometrika, 65*, 457-474.

Leinwand Leger, D., Shell, A., & Goldbacher, R (2013). *AP Twitter feed hacked; no attack at White House*. USA TODAY. 1:29 p.m. ET April 23; Updated 8:19 p.m. ET April 23. https://www.usatoday.com/story/theoval/2013/04/23/obama-carney-associated-press-hac k-white-house/2106757/. Accessed: March, 18th, 2017

Macey, W. H., & Schneider, B. (2008). The meaning of employee engagement. *Industrial and Organizational Psychology: Perspectives on Science and Practice, 1*, 3-30.

Maksl, A., Ashley, S., & Craft, S. (2014). Measuring news media literacy. *Journal of Media Literacy Education, 6 (3)*, 29 – 45.

Maslach, C., & Jackson, S.E. (1986). *MBI: Maslach Burnout Inventory* (Manual Research Edition). Palo Alto, CA: Consulting Psychologists.

Maslach, C., Schaufeli, W.B., & Leiter, M.P. (2001). Burnout. *Annual Review of Psychology, 52*, 397-422.

Maslach, C., Leiter, M., & Schaufeli, W. B. (2008). Measuring burnout. In C. L. Cooper & S. Cartwright (Eds.), *The Oxford handbook of organizational well-being* (pp. 86–108). Oxford, England: Oxford University Press.

Moy, P., Xenos, M. A., & Hess, V. K. (2006). Priming effects of late-night comedy. *International Journal of Public Opinion Research, 18*, 198-210.

Muraven, M., & Baumeister, R. F. (2000). Self-regulation and depletion of limited resources: Does self-control resemble a muscle? *Psychological Bulletin, 126*, 147-259.

Muthén, L. K., & Muthén, B. O. (1998-2015). *Mplus User's Guide* (7th ed.). Los Angeles, CA: Muthén & Muthén.

NBC News (2017). Conway: Press secretary gave "alternative facts". http://www.nbcnews.com/meet-the-press/video/conway-press-secretary-gave-alternative-facts-860142147643. Accessed: 31 July 2017.

Neubach, B., & Schmidt, K.-H. (2006). Beanspruchungswirkungen von Selbstkontrollanforderungen und Kontrollmöglichkeiten bei der Arbeit [Effects of self-control demands and job control on occupational strain]. *Zeitschrift für Psychologie, 214*, 150 –160.

Nunally, J.C. (1978). *Psychometric Theory*. New York, NY: McGraw-Hill.

Oberwittler, D., & Höfer, S. (2006). Crime and justice in Germany: An analysis of recent trends and research. *European Journal of Criminology, 2*, 465-508.

Peter, J. P., Churchill, G. A., & Brown, T. J. (1993). Caution in the use of difference scores in consumer research. *Journal of Consumer Research, 19*, 655-662.

Polage, D. C. (2012). Making up history: False memories of fake news stories. *Europe's Journal of Psychology, 8*, 245-250.

Preacher, K.J., Zyphur, M.J., & Zhang, Z. (2010). A general multilevel SEM framework for assessing multilevel mediation. *Psychological Methods, 15*, 209-233.

Regehr, C., Glancy, D., & Pitts, A. (2013). Interventions to reduce stress in university students: a review and meta-analysis. *Journal of Affective Disorders, 148*(1), 1-11. doi: 10.1016/j.jad.2012.11.026.

Rynes, S. L., Colbert, A. E., & Brown, K. G. (2002). HR professionals' beliefs about effective human resource practices: Correspondence between research and practice. *Human Resource Management, 41* (2), 149–174.

Schaufeli, W.B., Salanova, M., González-Romá, V., & Bakker, A.B (2002). The measurement of engagement and burnout: A two sample confirmatory factor analytic approach. *Journal of Happiness Studies, 3*, 71-92.

Schaufeli, W. B., & Bakker, A. B. (2004). The Utrecht Work Engagement Scale (UWES): Preliminary Manual. Occupational Health Psychology Unit, Utrecht University, Utrecht, the Netherlands.

Schaufeli, W. B., & Buunk, B. O. (2003). Burnout: An overview of 25 years of research and theorizing. In M. J. Schabracq, J. A. M. Winnubst & C. L. Cooper (Eds.), *The Handbook of Work and Health Psychology* (pp. 383-425). Chichester, England: Wiley.

Schaufeli, W. B., Bakker, A., & Salanova, M. (2006). The measurement of work engagement with a short questionnaire: A cross-national study. *Educational and Psychological Measurement, 66*, 701-716.

Schwarzer, R. & Jerusalem, M. (Eds.) (1999). Skalen zur Erfassung von Lehrer- und Schülermerkmalen. Dokumentation der psychometrischen Verfahren im Rahmen der Wissenschaftlichen Begleitung des Modellversuchs Selbstwirksame Schulen. [Scales for measuring characteristics of teachers and students. Documentation of the psychometric procedures used in the scientific consultation of the project self-efficacious schools]. Berlin: Freie Universität Berlin.

Silverblatt, A. (2008). *Media literacy: Keys to interpreting media messages* (3rd ed.). Westport, CT: Praeger.

Sonnentag, S., Dormann, C., & Demerouti, E. (2010). Not all days are created equal: The concept of state engagement. In A. Bakker & M. Leiter (Eds.), *Work engagement: A handbook of essential theory and research* (pp. 25-38). New York, NY: Psychology Press.

Taris, T. W., Kompier, M. A., de Lange, A. H., Schaufeli, W. B., & Schreurs, P. J. G. (2003). Learning new behaviour patterns: A longitudinal test of Karasek's active learning hypothesis among Dutch teachers. *Work & Stress, 17,* 1-20.

The Guardian (2017). The climate change battle dividing Trump's America. https://www.theguardian.com/science/2017/mar/18/the-scientists-taking-the-fight-to-trump-climate-change-epa. Accessed: 18 March 2017.

Thoman, E., & Jolls, T. (2004). Media literacy — A national priority for a changing world. *American Behavioral Scientist, 48,* 18-29.

Trilling, B., & Fadel, C. (2009). *1st century skills: Learning for life in our times.* San Francisco, CA: Jossey-Bass.

Venz, L., Pundt, A., & Sonnentag, S. (2017). What matters for work engagement? A diary study on resources and the benefits of selective optimization with compensation for state work engagement. *Journal of Organizational Behavior, 28 June 2017,* 1-13. doi:10.1002/job.2207

Weaver, S. (2017). Scott Pruitt's misleading senate testimony – Will "alternative science" replace real science at EPA? http://blogs.edf.org/climate411/2017/02/08/scott-pruitts-misleading-senate-testimony-will-alternative-science-replace-real-science-at-epa/. Accessed: 31 July 2017.

Young, D. G. (2006). Late-night comedy and the salience of the candidates' caricatured traits in the 2000 election. *Mass Communication and Society, 9,* 339-366.

Zhang, Z., Zyphur, M.J., & Preacher, J. K. (2009). Testing multilevel mediation using hierarchical linear models. *Organizational Research Methods, 12,* 695-719.

Zlatkin-Troitschanskaia et al. (2017). Positive Learning in the Age of Information. Draft Proposal Cluster of Excellence. Johannes Gutenberg University Mainz (Unpublished Manuscript).

Reconciling Morality and Rationality

Positive Learning in the Moral Domain

Gerhard Minnameier

Abstract

Morality and (economic) rationality are often understood as juxtaposed: a moral course of action would not be economically beneficial and vice versa. The paper reveals why this view, although common, is premature. In particular it delivers a game-theoretic analysis of moral problems and solutions and explains how moral principles function as what economists call "institutions". If this is the core of morality, there is no conflict between morality and (economic) rationality, properly understood. However, institutions always go with suitable sanctions (positive and/or negative), an aspect frequently overlooked in the moral camp. This has important consequences for positive learning in the moral domain, in particular with respect to fostering morality and rationality.

Keywords

Game Theory; Institution Economics; Moral Functioning; Moral Judgement; Moral Motivation; Moral Principles; Prisoners' Dilemma; Rational Choice; Situation-Specificity.

1   Introduction

Like any other kind of motivated behaviour, moral action should be rational in the sense that it is effective and efficient. In the case of morality, it often happens that well-intentioned behaviour produces evil results, and in this sense, especially if one can, or could, know this, moral action can be irrational. More generally, moral rationality is about how we can best live up to our moral concerns and convictions. In this sense, there seems to be neither a conflict between morality and rationality, nor between ethics and economics.

However, morality and rationality are often juxtaposed, so that economic rationality and moral rationality seem to exclude each other. This is true, in particular, when economists say that defection is the dominant strategy in a one-shot prisoners' dilemma (PD), while in the moral camp defection is taken as an indication of low moral motivation. People with high moral motivation should withstand the incentives of the game and cooperate (see Nunner-Winkler 2007). In fact, Nunner-Winkler uses the PD as an instrument to measure moral motivation. Hence, it seems one can *either* be moral (and cooperate) *or* economically rational (and defect).

If this were true, it would entail a fundamental conflict that pervades much of our daily lives. It would cast us into permanent internal conflict, since we would have to live with a fundamental trade-off between being rational and economically wise, on the one hand, and being morally responsible, on the other hand. Moreover, the resulting and, as it seems, inescapable schizophrenia would be part and parcel of modern humankind, and it would constitute a real and serious dilemma for business and economics education (see Beck et al. 1996).

I am using the subjunctive here, because I think this view is entirely wrong and is the result of fundamental misconceptions of both morality and (economic) rationality. The paper intends to set this straight and correct the picture with a few general strokes. First, I shall explain how morality and rationality can be reconciled from a decision-theoretic point of view (section 0). Next, morality will be analysed in terms of game theory, which reveals aspects of morality that are not only immensely important, but also frequently overlooked (section 0). In section 0, moral principles are explicated as institutions and illustrated with a few examples. Finally, section 0 concludes, highlights educational ramifications and desiderata for future research.

Altogether, the present approach paves the way for positive learning in the moral domain. It explains how "rational morality" works and how it can be successfully implemented in human interaction. Thus, reconciling morality and rationality means to allow for "learning that fosters students' ability to become mentally autonomous, morally sensitive and responsible citizens (MMR) capable of making ethical, evidence-based, and rational decisions (EER)" (Zlatkin-Troitschanskaia 2017, p. 13), where these two objectives are neither incompatible, nor unattainable.

2 Morality in action – a decision-theoretic view

Part of the problem arises from a false understanding of moral functioning and action. We typically understand morality in the sense of personal values or principles relating to others' legitimate claims, how their welfare is affected by our actions and how we can coordinate them with our own legitimate claims. Turiel (2006, p. 10), for instance, defines morality in terms of prescriptive judgments "about welfare, justice, and rights [...] that involve concern with dignity, worth, freedom, and treatment of persons".

Thus, the moral person is thought to have acquired certain moral principles and expected to live according to those values. Moreover, it seems not to suffice simply to know what is just and morally appropriate, because it is generally believed that one may be well equipped to judge morally, yet fail to act morally. This is known as the "judgment-action gap" (Walker 2004).

According to the classical four component model, moral functioning comprises the following (Rest 1984, p. 27):

1. "To interpret the situation in terms of how one's actions affect the welfare of others",
2. "To formulate what a moral course of action would be; to identify the moral ideal in a specific situation",
3. "To select among competing value outcomes of ideals the one to act on; deciding whether or not to try to fulfill one's moral ideal", and
4. "To execute and implement what one intends to do."

These components have later been called "moral sensitivity" (1), "moral judgment" (2), "moral motivation" (3), and "moral character" (4) (Rest et al. 1999, p. 101).

Moral motivation (MM) captures the idea that above and beyond merely knowing what a moral course of action would be, it has to be important to the self to live up to moral standards, in particular when morality stands against personal benefits and one consequently has to decide whether to forego these for the sake of morality or not. This is what the above definition of MM tells us. However, this definition is inconsistent, for the conflict between personal interests or inclinations, and other-regarding motives or precincts is the very topic of morality and calls for a moral judgement of its own. Any moral principle has to mediate between self-regarding and other-regarding aspects of a choice. Hence, MM cannot be separate from moral judgement. The answer to the question that the above definition of MM poses requires a moral judgment (see Minnameier 2010). Moreover, on what should moral motivation depend if not an underlying moral judgement? If MM were detached from it, it could not be distinguished from any other kind of motivation.

These reasons render MM suspect. However, there is yet another problem in connection with how proponents of MM measure it. Nunner-Winkler (2007) uses the prisoners' dilemma (PD) to determine whether people have high or (too) low MM. Figure 1 illustrates the PD (to be precise, this is the one-shot PD, because it can also be played repeatedly).

	D	C
C	*1, 4*	*3, 3*
D	*2, 2*	*4, 1*

Fig. 1   The prisoners' dilemma

The PD is a very significant model, since it models competition in a market economy, but also other important situations like cheating in exams, shirking in group work, and many more. The payoffs in the matrix just have an abstract meaning and only exemplify the basic structure. The players make a simultaneous choice between two alternative strategies: cooperate (C) or defect (D). For instance, in the economic context business people have an inclination to cooperate and form a cartel of one sort or another. This would allow them to increase their profits (to the detriment of the consumer who would have to pay higher prices or do with a lower innovation rate). So, both players (i.e., business people) could benefit from cooperation (3, 3). However, if competition in the market economy works the way it should, each of them would have an incentive to breach the compact in order to attract more customers (4, 1). Even though this seems rational from the point of view of the individual businessman, it takes the players to a situation in which the payoffs are (2, 2), since in effect both of them would defect.

The intuitive reaction is to say that they had better cooperate. A closer look, however, reveals that this is not so easy, since it is irrational (at least economically irrational). The main insight is that an agent does not have to know what the other player chooses. In either case, defection is better. If the other chooses C, C yields 3 while D yields 4. If the other chooses D, C yields 1 while D yields 2. Hence, there is no risk and no exception; D is always beneficial from the point of view of one single agent.

For Nunner-Winkler and her conception of MM, things look different. The morally motivated agents should not choose in such a selfish way and stick to the idea, that mutual cooperation would be best for the group. Hence, playing C indicates high MM, on Nunner-Winkler's account. And this, if true, creates a serious predicament, at least for economic education or the education of professionals in general who have to be trained to cope with competitive environments of all sorts, since MM would make them economically incompetent and vice versa.

However, modeling moral agency in this way has three systematic drawbacks. One is that the distinction between moral judgements and prudential judgements becomes blurred. If moral principles are taken as some kind of personal values, it is hard, if not impossible, to distinguish them from non-moral values. One might object that moral values, in contrast to other values, are typically understood as "other-regarding". However, we could not possibly discern truly moral motives (for the sake of the other) from self-interested motives for honour or self-regard, or even some pathological orientation like self-humiliation. What's more, whatever the deeper reason for a moral orientation or virtue may be, it always remains a personal value or a set of personal values of the individual in question. Therefore, acting according to this kind of principle would necessarily and by definition be in the agent's proper self-interest. Hence, the convergence with prudential judgements.

The *second* drawback is that the final decision whether to follow or not to follow a certain moral principle appears as one of how important it is *for the agent* to follow this course of action, given the restrictions. It is from this point of view that advocates of moral motivation have argued that it just had to be high enough to outweigh what is perceived as a non-moral course of action. However, this amounts to just compensating the negative weight of restrictions by the positive weight of moral motivation and, again, turns the problem into prudential question (because high moral motivation would just be a kind of a second-order moral preference).

Above and beyond the mere decision-theoretic view, the *third* problem is that individuals with low moral motivation can benefit from those with high moral motivation. In the PD they can reap the fruit that the ones with high moral motivation leave them (or even *offer* them). If somebody consistently cooperates in the PD, this is tantamount to an invitation to defect. So, what would be won? And would it be realistic to hope that the good role model one gives would finally be copied? Certainly not.

In the section 0, morality will be analysed in terms of game theory, which opens up an entirely different perspective on the problem. However, even in the decision-theoretic context, where moral principles are taken as fundamental moral preferences, the problem of MM can be solved, if we extend our notion of moral judgement. In particular, moral judgment can be conceived to consist of three separate, yet closely related, inferences, namely *abduction, deduction and induction* (Minnameier 2012; 2013; 2016). MM can be reinterpreted in this framework and thus incorporated into the broader notion of moral judgement, and moral judgement, in turn, can be incorporated into suitable understanding of rational choice, i.e., a reason-based theory of rational choice (Dietrich and List 2013).

3   Morality in interaction – a game-theoretic view

Let us consider a simple game that resembles the PD. It is called "hawk and dove" (HD), in which the players compete for a certain resource of value v, i.e., some territory, and where the players have the following two strategies: The first is to play "hawk" (H), which means to fight until one either wins the territory or is injured and has to retreat (the cost of injury is denoted c). The second is to play "dove" (D), which means to display hostility, but retreat before sustaining injury. The payoffs of the four strategy profiles are shown in Fig. 2a. Let $v = 20, c = 40$, and let us further assume that both combatants have equal strength, so that there is a 50 percent chance of winning for each of them. Fig. 2b shows the resulting payoffs.

	H	D			H	D
D	$0, v$	$v/2, v/2$		D	$0, 20$	$10, 10$
H	$(v-c)/2, (v-c)/2$	$v, 0$		H	$-10, -10$	$20, 0$

| a | b |

Fig. 2 The hawk-and-dove game with (a) the payoffs in general form and (b) the payoffs if $v = 20, c = 40$

Unlike the PD, HD does not have a stable pure strategy Nash equilibrium. There are two pure strategy Nash equilibria (H, D and D, H) which, however, are asymmetric. On top of these, there is a symmetric equilibrium in mixed strategies, in which each player chooses H and D with probability $p = .5$. In this case, each player earns an expected payoff of 5. However, similar to the PD, this symmetric mixed strategy Nash equilibrium is Pareto-inefficient, because both players end up with 5, when 10 would have been possible.

Fortunately, there is a way out – not within the game, but by augmenting the game and thereby changing it. Imagine some choreographer who issues a new rule, and let us call this the "property" rule (P). This new rule turns HD into a new game ("hawk-dove-property", or HDP). Rule P introduces a new strategy P that the players can choose, namely: "When first at the resource, play H, otherwise play D." This is a realistic and common rule which is used, for example, when people compete for seats on trains, parking spaces, spots for sunbathing on the beach, etc. Furthermore, it is also common for people when they come in second or so, that they still try to impose themselves in case the other party might be too gentle and compliant. Therefore, it seems quite realistic that such an agent plays D rather than backing out right away.

If we apply this new rule to augment the original game, and if we further assume equal chances to be the first (or second) at the resource, we obtain the following payoff matrix (see Fig. 3). For reasons of simplicity this contains only the row-player's payoffs.

	H	D	P
P	$(v-c)/4$	$3v/4$	$v/2$
D	0	$v/2$	$v/4$
H	$(v-c)/2$	v	$3v/4 - c/4$

a

	H	D	P
P	-5	15	10
D	0	10	5
H	-10	20	5

b

Fig. 3 The hawk-dove-property game with the payoffs (a) in general form and (b) if $v = 20, c = 40$

This "property rule" is a very simple and basic rule. In its simplest form it is probably the first moral rule that children acquire, when they learn that they have to respect others' property or devise rules how to use commons like the toys in a nursery school. Here, it is common that the (temporary) right of use is allocated according to the "first come, first served" principle.

We have assumed that a "choreographer" issued the new rule. However, the players themselves might invent the rule, once they realise the predicament in which they have manoeuvred themselves collectively (in terms of the symmetric, but Pareto-inefficient mixed strategy Nash equilibrium of the original game).

As we have seen, the move from HD to HDP changes the game quite fundamentally. We can analyse what happens in the context of a differentiation of types of games originally introduced by Schelling (1960, pp. 83-89); he starts by defining the two extremes of pure conflict and pure coordination games and then defines a third type that combines both extremes, which he calls "mixed-motive games".

The PD and HD are of the latter type. They are characterized by the fact that the Pareto-superior strategy profile is not a Nash equilibrium, so that the players typically end up in some inferior Nash equilibrium. In a coordination game, the Pareto-efficient strategy is a Nash equilibrium, so that coordination is typically achieved by conventions that are self-enforcing. For instance, no punishment is needed to make people drive their cars on the left in the UK and on the right on the continent. These conventions sustain themselves, because nobody has an incentive to deviate from them (except perhaps people who are about to commit suicide). Finally, a zero-sum game has no Nash equilibrium, because a fixed sum is to be divided, so that each agent would prefer to have more, while the other one would prefer not give anything away. In other words, one can only win, if the other loses. The so-called "dictator game" is an example in case.

The PD as a mixed-motive game has four different outcomes: win-win, win-lose, lose-win, lose-lose, where the latter is the Nash-equilibrium. Here, it is possible, in principle, that both players win by cooperating. Unfortunately, this is not a Nash equilibrium. However, this situation can be changed, if we augment the game by allowing for communication which allows the players to promise each other not to defect and agree suitable sanctions in case one of them might breach the contract.

Such sanctions (e.g., the prospect of revenge) would discount the value of unilateral defection. If, for instance, the payoff of four is discounted in this way by 3 units, then we have the following three outcomes: 1, 1 (C, D or D, C), 2, 2 (D, D), and 3, 3 (C, C). In other words, the implementation of this rule has effectively turned the original *mixed-motive game* into a *coordination game*.

---

4   Moral principles as institutions

As we have seen in section 0, agents can overcome the restrictions of typical co-operation games. When they succeed, they play so-called "correlated equilibria" instead of Nash equilibria. The correlated equilibrium is a concept that captures human interaction much better than that of a Nash equilibrium (Gintis 2014, p. 142). It has been introduced by Aumann (1987), but since it goes beyond the framework of classical game theory, it has been largely neglected (Gintis 2014, p. 47). As already mentioned above, playing a correlated equilibrium requires that the original game be changed by the introduction of a new rule; and it has been shown that this move turns a mixed-motive game into coordination game, in which the

Pareto-superior strategy profile (the correlated equilibrium of the original game) is a Nash equilibrium.

From this understanding it is only a small, but crucial, step to consider moral principles as solutions concepts for mixed-motive games that work just in the way explicated above. This means that we understand moral principles as institutions which introduce new rules together with appropriate (positive and/or negative) sanctions. In other words, moral principles are to be understood as "institutions" in the sense of "rules of the game" which transform the initial games. In the course of such a transformation, the initial game is turned into a new one at a higher order; and this new game governs the original one (see also Binmore 2010; 2011).

This takes us to quite a different understanding of morality, compared to Turiel's definition (see above). Haidt (2012, p. 270), for instance, understands morality in terms of "interlocking sets of values, virtues, norms, practices, identities, institutions, technologies, and evolved psychological mechanisms that work together to suppress or regulate self-interest and make cooperative societies possible". Admittedly, the multifarious aspects combined in this definition, to my mind, blur or obscure the very core of morality. However, the definition explicitly states "institutions" and the aim to "make cooperative societies possible." This marks perhaps but a small difference in words compared with Turiel's definition, but it changes the meaning of morality quite fundamentally. To wit, we no longer speak of personal values of the agent, but of rules of a (moral) game, and this involves that the players at least understand this game. Relating to the rational-choice-theoretical terminology of preferences and restrictions, moral principles do not translate into personal preferences for certain outcomes, but into preferences for certain (moral) games. The content of these preferences can, accordingly, only be actualised, if the other player(s) are able and motivated to play this game.

In the following, I will explain and illustrate four very simple moral principles in their function as institutions. In this context, I will also show how specific problems arise within these moral frames of reference, i.e., how new problems are encountered that constitute new mixed-motive games (at a higher level) and how these problems are solved by inventing higher order moral principles that, again, turn these mixed-motive games into coordination games. Whereas economists generally speak of "social norms" without explicating the inner structure of each norm and the overall system of norms, the presented approach can do the job.

It has been shown above how agents can overcome a Hobbesian state of nature, in which, according to the "law of Nature (...) every man has right to everything" (1651/2001, p. 65 [Chap. 15, §2]), but which results in a "war of every one against every one" (1651/2001, p. 59 [Chap. 14, §4]). HD illustrates this situation, and HDP, which includes the property rule, describes the solution. In the most basic form, coordination according to the property rule is governed by sympathetic role taking, i.e., first of all, one has to learn how it feels for the other, when things are taken away, based on one's own experiences of being deprived of something. The property rule allows us to coordinate these perspectives and at the same time create value for all players as the interaction is orderly and peaceful.

Now, considering Fig. 2 once again, it is obvious that against a player who chooses P, P is the best response. (P, P) is a Nash equilibrium and, therefore, a stable stationary state in repeated interaction. However, what happens if the column-player is a kind of a "moral saint" who would always yield to others and act in a dovish way? We see that against D, P is no longer the best response, because the row-player can improve his payoff by choosing H. In other words, the "moral saint" clearly *corrupts morality* by virtually *inviting* the row-player to leave the path and move from P to H.

By the same token, we can now discard the idea of high *moral motivation* according to Nunner-Winkler (see above), since MM would not only be futile, but do a disservice to morality. In fact, it would only make the "morally motivated" agent feel superior (and therefore probably good), but apart from this it would corrupt morality. Obviously, this is only true in PD-like situations, i.e., in some kind of mixed-motive game. However, these are the very situations to which morality (of any kind) applies.

This reveals the importance of sanctions. In everyday life we are probably not aware of this, because we do not use negative sanctions, and we do not have to use them, if coordination works just fine. However, we use positive sanctions all the time by signalling respect for the other's property and by returning signs of approval. For instance, this often happens in the context of formal and informal priority rules in traffic.

Let us now turn to the (second-order) problems that arise based on the simple property rule. As long as everyone has theirs, everything is fine. However, if one has a certain kind of resource the other is deprived of, there is a problem. For instance, if you want two bake a cake, but have forgotten to buy flour, you would not get anywhere with what you have. In such circumstances our neighbours would normally share some of their flour with us to help us out, and we would share with them in similar circumstance.

The *sharing norm* helps us overcome this problem, and if there is only one indivisible resource, the equivalent is the *turn-taking norm*. Again, whenever this kind of interaction works, it is accompanied by positive sanctions in the form of saying "thank you" and "you are welcome". In case, someone does not want to share, we generally issue signals indicating dislike or anger.

Yet, another problem arises, however, when the agents are not on a par in some relevant respect, so that sharing cannot or should not work reciprocally. For instance, when we donate something for poor people or those suffering from natural catastrophes, we do not expect anything in return, neither now nor later. This illustrates a difference in neediness and a case in which the general ethics of *care* becomes relevant. In this sense, we also expect parents to care for their children, older siblings for the younger ones, and superiors for their subordinates. Another relevant difference might be one of *deservingness*. If several people work together on a common project, the ones who have put in most effort should get a bigger share of the overall pie than the lazier ones. In contrast to the simple (equal) sharing norm, this norm incorporates *equitable sharing*.

What has been expounded so far, are three moral principles that build on each other in the sense of developmental stages an in the sense of a more and more complex order of moral games. These three moral principles all rely on sympathy and benevolent (or even altruistic) relationships. Therefore, one can always benefit from helping others or letting them have theirs, because of the pleasure to contribute to others' happiness and the enjoyment of affiliation. However, there are also true conflicts of interest, in which helping others may be fatal. Consider, for example, the situation of a couple of graduates applying for jobs, over which they (have to) compete. Here, they may even feel a lot of sympathy for each other; yet, they clearly are competitors. In such a conflict of interest the agents have to follow the rule that everybody has their own interests to pursue, or in a proverb: *"Near is my shirt, but nearer is my skin"*. This does not equivalent with selfishness, because one also respects that others do the same, in fact, have to do the same.

Furthermore, in some cases one can mitigate the conflict by throwing dice or so. In this case, the winner is determined in a fair and easy way. However, it still is a conflict of interest and it still involves respect for the winner and for the procedure. Thus, *respect* is the currency, in which the sanctions are valued in conflicts of interest. This also applies to the following to stages (which I will not expound in detail), in which, first, a conflict of interest creates a dilemma on the social level (as in the PD, where the morality of contract helps us solve this problem), and in which, second, the so-called Golden Rule is employed to respect others' interests, where those others have nothing to offer in a deal.

Altogether, I have mentioned six moral stages and the respective principles that form two triads, one based in a context of sympathy, the other in a context of conflicting interests. In the context of sympathy, the sanctions are issued in terms of *like* and *dislike*. In the context of conflicting interests, the sanctions are issued in terms of *respect* and *disrespect*. Apart from these sanctions that relate directly to the content of the specific moral principle, an extended form of punishment is possible. It applies in situations, in which the other is either unwilling or unable to "play by the rules" of this game. In such a case, one can always punish by moving one stage down to play the lower level game. For instance, if someone fails to share with me, I would stop sharing at some point, which means that I move down to the game in which only the simple property rule applies and where everybody stays with what they have.

5   Conclusions and educational ramifications

It has been known for a long time, that people's moral judgement and action is usually situation-specific, i.e., changes from situation to situation (see, e.g., Beck et al. 2002; Krebs and Denton 2005; Rai and Fiske 2011). As a phenomenon, this is well-established. However, as far as I know it has never been explained in a systematic way, apart from the flawed explanations based on moral motivation, and apart from an earlier approach by Beck (2008; see also Beck et al. 1999, 2002), on which the present one builds up to some extent. The theory I have set forth is able to explain consistently and coherently, how situation-specific moral functioning really works. At the same time, it reconciles morality and rationality (or economics and ethics, for that matter).

The latter point is especially important in the educational context, because it removes the dilemma discussed in the introduction between teaching for rationality or for morality. If morality is properly understood, morality and economics are not opposites, but complements. There are other important educational ramifications: In particular, the approach reveals that good-heartedness, perhaps paired with high "moral motivation", is not only not enough for sound moral action, but can even be entirely wrong. The reason is that people who always yield to others violate the rules and thus "invite" their counterparts to act self-interestedly. Rather than victimizing themselves, moral agents should, therefore, focus on getting others (back) on the path of virtue, so that morality is implemented on the social level.

Furthermore, agents would have (1) to know (or develop) moral principles, (2) to understand specific moral situations (i.e., the respective moral conflicts), (3) to understand the specific moral restrictions the situations pose and the affordances pose they offer, and (4) to know moral sanctioning mechanisms (positive and negative) and be able to use them proficiently.

It has been shown in Minnameier et al. (2016) that this approach explains differences between economists and non-economists when playing a PD, and that the economists' choices may be driven by the restrictive circumstances rather than merely self-interest, as has been suggested in previous research (Marwell and

Ames 1981; Carter and Irons 1991; Selten and Ockenfels 1998; Ruske and Suttner 2012).

Future empirical research based on this approach will have to reveal the moral orientations and the moral functioning of adolescents and young adults in various professions and training programmes. We will have to know what they learn in the moral domain, how they learn or are trained, how they cope with the challenges they face, and whether their orientations and coping strategies are appropriate or not. Based on this research general and professional moral education could be reconceived and developed systematically and in terms of positive learning. In particular, the education I have in mind would make people become aware of the opportunities and restrictions the certain situations present, of moral principles as solutions to specific problems of cooperation, and of the ways in which these can be successfully implemented. This is equivalent to the ideals of MMR and EER mentioned in the introduction (cf. Zlatkin-Troitschanskaia et al. 2017).

On the theoretic level, we would have to reconsider morality and ethics from a philosophy of science perspective (cf. Wiese in this volume). Classical game theory can be used descriptively (to explain what happens) and technologically (to determine what a rational choice would be). Institution economics, in contrast, is normative and goes beyond classical game theory in that it explains how dilemmas that are described in game theory can be overcome. I have associated morality with this branch of economics. However, it is quite a different project, and a different normative question, to determine what is just from an objective point of view, independent from how to implement this in some kind of interaction. For instance, it is one thing to argue that mutual cooperation would be the best outcome in a PD, and it is another to implement institutions that allow us to attain this. In this sense, we can distinguish the – truly or narrowly *ethical* – question of determining what is just from an outside point of view, from the *moral* question of actually establishing justice from the point of view of an agent who has to interact with other agents. There is a lot of potential for systematic interdisciplinary research, if we achieve to differentiate and integrate these disciplinary (and subdisciplinary) perspectives – in the context of the "positive learning" framework and beyond.

Bibliography

Aumann, R. J. (1987). Correlated equilibrium and an expression of Bayesian rationality. *Econometrica, 55*, 1-18.

Beck, K. (2008). Moral judgment in economic situations – Towards systemic ethics. In F. Oser & W. Veugelers (Eds.), *Getting involved: Global citizenship development and sources of moral values* (pp. 359-370). Rotterdam, Netherlands: Sense.

Beck, K., Brütting, B., Lüdecke-Plümer, S., Minnameier, G., Schirmer, U., & Schmid, S. N. (1996). Zur Entwicklung moralischer Urteilskompetenz in der kaufmännischen Erstausbildung – Empirische Befunde und praktische Probleme. In K. Beck & H. Heid (Eds.), *Lehr-Lern-Prozesse in der kaufmännischen Erstausbildung – Wissenserwerb, Motivierungsgeschehen und Handlungskompetenzen. Zeitschrift für Berufs- und Wirtschaftspädagogik, Beiheft, 13,* 187-205. Stuttgart, Germany: Steiner.

Beck, K., Heinrichs, K., Minnameier, G., & Parche-Kawik, K. (1999). Homogeneity of moral judgement? – Apprentices solving business conflicts. *Journal of Moral Education, 28,* 429-443.

Beck, K., Dransfeld, A., Minnameier, G., & Wuttke, E. (2002). Autonomy in heterogeneity? Development of moral judgement behaviour during business education. In K. Beck (Eds.), *Teaching-learning processes in vocational education - Foundations of modern training programmes* (p. 87-119). Frankfurt am Main: Lang.Binmore, K. (2010). Game theory and institutions. *Journal of Comparative Economics, 38,* 245-252.

Binmore, K. (2011). *Natural justice.* New York, NY: Oxford University Press.

Carter, J. R., & Irons, M. (1991). Are economists different, and if so, why? Journal of Economic Perspectives 5: 171–177.

Dietrich, F., & List, D. (2013). A reason-based theory of rational choice. *Noûs 47,* 104-134.

Gintis, H. (2014). *The bounds of reason: Game theory and the unification of the behavioral sciences* (revised ed.). Princeton, NJ: Princeton University Press.

Haidt, J. (2012). *The righteous mind: Why good people are divided by religion and politics.* New York, NY: Pantheon Books.

Hobbes, T. (1651/2001). *Leviathan.* South Bend, IN: Infomotions.

Krebs, D. L., & Denton, K. (2005). Toward a more pragmatic approach to morality: A critical evaluation of Kohlberg's model. *Psychological Review, 112,* 629-649.

Marwell, G., & Ames, R. (1981). Economists free ride, does anyone else? *Journal of Public Economics, 15,* 295–310.

Minnameier, G. (2010). The Problem of Moral Motivation and the Happy Victimizer Phenomenon – Killing two birds with one stone. *New Directions for Child and Adolescent Development 129,* 55-75.

Minnameier, G. (2012). A cognitive approach to the 'happy victimiser'. *Journal of Moral Education 41,* 491-508.

Minnameier, G. (2013). Deontic and responsibility judgments: An inferential analysis. In F. Oser, K. Heinrichs & T. Lovat (Eds.), *Handbook of moral motivation: Theories, models, applications* (pp. 69-82). Rotterdam, Netherlands: Sense.

Minnameier, G. (2016). Rationalität und Moralität – Zum systematischen Ort der Moral im Kontext von Präferenzen und Restriktionen. *Zeitschrift für Wirtschafts- und Unternehmensethik 17,* 259-285.

Minnameier, G., Heinrichs, K., & Kirschbaum, F. (2016). Sozialkompetenz als Moralkompetenz – Theoretische und empirische Analysen. *Zeitschrift für Berufs- und Wirtschaftspädagogik, 112,* 636-666.

Nunner-Winkler, G. (2007). Development of moral motivation from childhood to early adulthood. *Journal of Moral Education, 36,* 399–414.

Rai, T. S., & Fiske, A. P. (2011). Moral psychology is relationship regulation: Moral motives for unity, hierarchy, equality, and proportionality. *Psychological Review, 118,* 57-75.

Rest, J. R. (1984). The major components of morality. In W. M. Kurtinez & J. L. Gewirtz (Eds.), *Morality, moral behavior, and moral development* (pp. 24-38). New York, NY: Wiley.

Rest, J., Narvaez, D., Bebeau, M. J., & Thoma, S. J. (1999). *Postconventional moral thinking: A neo-Kohlbergian approach*. Mahwah, NJ: Lawrence Erlbaum Associates.

Ruske, R., & Suttner, J. (2012). Wie (un-)fair sind Ökonomen? – Neue empirische Evidenz zur Marktbewertung und Rationalität. *ORDO: Jahrbuch für die Ordnung von Wirtschaft und Gesellschaft, 63*, 179–194.

Schelling, T. C. (1960). *The strategy of conflict*. London, England: Oxford University Press.

Selten, R., & Ockenfels, A. (1998). An experimental solidarity game. *Journal of Economic Behavior & Organization, 34*, 517-539.

Turiel, E. (2006). Thought, emotions, and social interactional processes of moral development. In M. Killen & J. G. Smetana (Eds.), *Handbook of moral development* (pp. 7-35). Mahwah, NJ: Erlbaum.

Walker, L. (2004). Gus in the gap: Bridging the judgment-action gap in moral functioning. In D. K. Lapsley & D. Narvaez (Eds.), *Moral development, self, and identity* (pp. 1-20). Mahwah, NJ: Erlbaum.

Zlatkin-Troitschanskaia et al. (2017). *Positive Learning in the Age of Information*. Unpublished Manuscript, Draft Proposal Cluster of Excellence, Johannes Gutenberg University Mainz.

Positive Learning Through Negative Learning

The Wonderful Burden of PLATO

Fritz Oser

Abstract

Based on the concept of Negative Knowledge and on a proposed transformational model, I will try to present a central but controversial idea about the value of Negative Learning (NL). Thus, in I will propose a solution to the problem, which at a first sight does not seem obvious at all. The idea is that NL must be used to understand and protect the content of PL. Then, I try to apply this solution to the PLATO project. To conclude, after a critical review of the PLATO research work, I will outline and recognize certain generalizations of the transformational concept.

Keywords

Negative Knowledge; PLATO; Positive Learning; Negative Learning; Transformation.

1   Introduction

The extremely comprehensive project PLATO (*Positive Learning in the Age of informaTiOn*) deals with the concept of positive (and negative) learning (Zlatkin-Troitschanskaia et al. 2017). It starts with the assumption that media-based information is often

> "biased, false, deliberately inaccurate, conflicting, unverified, preselected, and algorithmically obscure. This information is morally and/or ethically problematic and collides with fundamental values of democratic and humanistic societies. When Internet users are unable to recognize biased or false information, are misguided by it, and use it as a basis to generate knowledge, *negative learning (NL)* occurs" (Zlatkin-Troitschanskaia et al. 2017, p. 3).

The question PLATO deals with is how to prevent biased or false information, how to protect students, researchers and teachers from it, and how to ward catastrophic consequences of such disturbing epistemic concepts. We ask: Is this a valid question? Can we imagine a different way, namely, for example, that instead of preventing something from falsehood a transformation of it to rightness could be initiated and in this way the negative be used to produce the positive?

Before I propose some thoughts on the three papers, I will discuss (1) Dormann, Demerouti, and Bakker (in this volume), *Learning engagement: An important facet of positive learning*; (2) Minnameier (in this volume), *How to be both moral and professional*; and (3) Wiese (in this volume), *On some conceptual and empirical obstacles to teaching the ability for positive learning*, I will try to present this central but controversial idea about a fully positive value of NL. Consequently, in this text, I will first propose a solution to the problem of negativity. Then, I will try to apply this solution to the three papers presented here. To conclude, I wish to generate and recognize certain generalizations of the presented concept.

2   The concept of Negative Knowledge

How should we react to and deal with biased, false, unverified and ethically problematic information? From the theory of Negative Knowledge (Oser and Spychiger 2005) we know that (in many cases) the negative secures the positive. Knowing what is not true makes what is true more obvious. Wittgenstein (1968) in the Tractatus refers to the fact (freely reported) that if you want to understand what is true, you must understand the opposite. The false helps to produce the right. It gives security to adequate thinking. Knowing the false also <u>protects</u> the right. Knowing the false also <u>prevents us</u> from using or even doing it. Thus, if we want to understand justice, we must experience injustice (Tugendhat 1984). If we want to understand caring behavior, we must experience uncaring behavior. If we want to support PL, we must use NL (transformation model). For the construct of the truth, the opposite, the untruth, is needed. To keep a theory alive, its falsification is required (Heid 2015).

A practical application of this contrafactual concept is what I call the Trump-Effect. Politicians and educators have always wanted to stimulate political discourse, political reflection and even political participation in adolescents, young adults and in courses called general education. But they did not succeed. Since Trump has been elected and has been reacting to current developments with irrational statements and deeds, in restaurants, schools, families, at workplaces, everywhere people discuss political issues, political values and political traditions. If one had asked one year ago about the Climate Contract of Paris, most people wouldn't have known what it was. After Trump's rejection of that contract, even fourth graders now know what it is about. Many begin to understand the endangered relationship between nations and cultures. And Trump's controversial twittering brings former political enemies together for the sake of an open society. Thus, to produce inaccurate and even "fake" behavior can be helpful against a political Sleeping Beauty or at least efficient for producing Negative Knowledge (see below).

Can we, thus, say that in these cases the goals justify the means? Of course, 'not', but as Zlatkin-Troitschanskaia et al. (2017) remarks, it is a fact that false, broken, immoral and biased information surrounds us. I would like to show how NL does not lead to Negative Knowledge, that there are positive functions of NL, that studies on failure show how humans "rise from the ashes" (Yamakawa et al. 2013) and why scientists often avoid bringing together PL and NL. To understand Positive Knowledge, we need to deal with its opposite.

In the realm of error psychology, the construct of Negative Knowledge and its function plays a central role (Oser 2015). Negative Knowledge refers to negative events stored in the episodic memory, mistake experiences, accidents, failure events, error consequences, fake news, all these relate to processes, strategies, concepts that are inaccurate, inadequate, or ineffective. Knowledge about such issues is Negative Knowledge. Thus, Negative Knowledge is a construct dealing with remembering errors, our own ones and the ones of others. It produces consciousness on how something does not work (as opposed to how it works), which strategies do not lead to the solution of complicated problems (as opposed to those that do) and why we disagree in certain contexts (as opposed to why we agree). Negative Knowledge refers to remembering specific experiences, things, processes or strategies that are inaccurate, inadequate or ineffective. Negative Knowledge leads subjects to remember the consequences with respect to shame, guilt and punishment. The functions of Negative Knowledge are to provide protection from making the mistake again, to organize the world and to draw boundaries, to constitute contrasts and orientation achievements, to provide security and certainty, to allow socalled opposite transfer, to cause changes in behaviour, to develop alarm functions with respect to almost-mistakes etc.

3   The value of Negative Learning

A substantial question is how we can use NL to produce a positive outcome. One example is the so-called performance test concept (Shavelson, Zlatkin-Troitschanskaia, and Mariño 2018). In a performance test situation, persons do not just remember knowledge or produce a belief or decide on a multiple choice task, they rather solve a complex problem using or not using available positive or negative information and search for a solution which is not necessarily right but at least adequate from its functional perspective. Here is an example: In an intervention study for preventing students from entrepreneurial failure - in 2010, 37,682 firms were launched in the small country of Switzerland; 6,204 of them went officially bankrupt, a 23% increase compared to the previous year – we wanted to know if students from the intervention group would be able to "save a struggling firm" through a concrete case analysis and problem-solving process (pre-posttest comparison). In the following, I merely want to demonstrate how we presented unreliable versus reliable and useful (relevant) versus not useful (irrelevant) information in this performance test, and how we were wondering how students use both. The point is that we – instead of keeping students away from "biased, false, deliberately inaccurate, conflicting, unverified, preselected, and algorithmically obscure" information we used it for finding out the opposite, the reliable and relevant, the true and unbiased one. One of the stories we used went like this:

> *A young firm produces a lifestyle drink that is distributed by a major retail chain. In the story, the founders decided against self-distribution in bars, cafes and so on and instead committed to exclusively supplying a retail chain for three years with their lifestyle drink. Sales started well and the founders bought a new bottling plant financed by a bank loan.*

After students had to find out possible weaknesses of the situation, it got more difficult:

The retail chain wants to withdraw from the contract due to damaging circumstances. "Cola" threatened the retail chain that it would stop supplying its products if the retail chain did not stop selling the young company's lifestyle drink.

The students, after first having looked for possible solutions for the situation, were now – and this is the central part of the test - given information pieces like from street-papers, comments of "experts", letters of colleagues, stories, e-mails, concepts from Google, recommendations of specialists etc. They had to use all these information parts – some of which were not reliable or relevant - to solve the situation. In other words, they first had to make a decision (see Table 1 as an example).

Tab. 1 Example of information pieces that have to be judged as reliable/non-reliable, relevant/non-relevant

	Reliable		Relevant	
	yes	no	yes	no
Letter to the editor published in a newspaper		X		X
Advertisement of a new energy drink		X		X
Mail from a friend		X	X	
Discussion a team-meeting		X	X	
www document / information about potential dangers of energy drinks	X			X
Public invitation / young entrepreneurs' prize	X		X	
Letter from a lawyer	X		X	

After this preparation work, students had to find a solution, which includes strong evaluation and shows real competence for saving this firm. After the basic awareness of a problem and the respective use of a lot of positive and negative information, the students did their best to solve the problem and evaluate the findings on the basis of expert solutions that we present at the end of the study.

Therefore, in this study, we seek as a principle instead of avoiding NK to use "biased, false, deliberately inaccurate, conflicting, unverified, preselected, and algorithmically obscure" information in order to find a serious and sustainable solution, the truth with respect to a theory and the grounded function of a serious concept. We have to support students in being cautious, doubtful, critical and sensitive, but also courageous to search and defend the opposite, the right, morally settled and the effectively evidenced.

There are hidden pitfalls and problems within this concept. Three of them are presented: (1) All academic fields have different truth and different falseness. For medical issues, biased information is different than for historical issues. Medical practitioners and scientists need to collect wrong information differently and to learn from it differently than historians. (2) To open up to "biased, false, deliberately inaccurate, conflicting, unverified, preselected, and algorithmically obscure" information is often connected with shame, disturbed self-efficacy and a feeling of helplessness. We have to deal with such reactions with regard to all sorts of produced or used or defended or critically disturbed falseness. (3) To use false information for understanding and producing the right one is never an obvious process. As in the Trump example, nobody could ever have preconceived what happened after his election. We must consider that fake news hurt the normal love for truth. As Frankfurt (2006) mentioned, we have to question how and why humans love the truth, but need to discover this love in every situation and within every generation in a new way.

4   Discussion: A transformation concept

Dormann, Demerouti and Bakker (in this volume) speak about positive learning (PL) in using the concept *of work engagement* as a fulfilling, production-related state of mind. They work out a motivational concept with a two-sided construct, engagement items and burnout items. The authors predict that engagement prevents *emotional exhaustion*, burnout and similar (disengagement) on one hand and on the other hand leads to PL. Critical thinking is seen as a means for guarding against fake news in its psychological and emotional dimension. Here is an important question because the basic tenet of this prediction is not clear. I do accept that work engagement prevents burnout, but I cannot see how it leads to PL. There is a lack of a transformation model. We can imagine that high work engagement leads to high "biased, false, deliberately inaccurate, conflicting, unverified, preselected, and algorithmically obscure" information. It needs something else to guarantee that comparisons are made, that NL is mirrored somehow from solid evidence-based and critically reflected knowledge. Nevertheless we learn on which consequences NL can have.

Minnameier (in this volume) states that people engaged in economics have to use moral principles, understand specific moral situations, understand specific moral restrictions, know moral sanctioning in the face of PL, *and in the face of NL*. He demonstrates logically how moral falseness can be produced. From high interest is how we coordinate truthfulness with social bounding (moral dimension).

There are two questions: One problem is that the Prisoner Dilemma is in itself a moral problem, namely to promise each other to hide the truth and thus to produce a priori a lie. Second, it seems that there is a different logic regarding economical gain and moral justification. Sometimes these two logics overlap and sometimes not. To find out about these different rationalities we need to use Negative Knowledge. But this should be developed further.

Wiese (in this volume) draws attention to the teaching of rational inferences. He shows that the ideal reasoner, even using Bayes-optimal inferences, cannot avoid reaching false conclusions. That is why he proposes that knowing about general cognitive and emotional biases, and being shown how they affect one's own reasoning in some domains, can motivate students to avoid such biases more generally. And this is exactly what we mean: Here is a proposition to use "biased, false, deliberately inaccurate, conflicting, unverified, preselected, and algorithmically obscure information" to make students aware that the right can only be seen in front of the false. This is a different view on distinguishing cases of PL from cases of NL, and question *to what extent PL can be taught to students (didactical, philosophical dimension)* through making the negative visible. Wiese states that neither is ignoring evidence morally wrong nor can just ignoring misbeliefs help to go further. Both aspects must come together.

Behind these papers there is good scientific, theoretical and empirical work. Nevertheless, not all of these scientists really confront us with how to transform NL into PL, or better, how to use NL for producing PL. We need a transformation concept - like Wiese demonstrates – where people remember the wrongness of the false in order to produce and protect the right. We need examples where we see that working trough biased or false information leads to the right, the truth and the morally well settled. In this way, the truth becomes more transparent and more solid than it would be without negativity. This message also includes a warning: Don't hide, don't prevent, don't flee, don't avoid, don't side-track NL, but go through and remember.

5   Conclusion

To transform a knowledge piece on how things do not work into a knowledge piece on how they work means to parallel and to compare its information bases in a certain way. This comparison process has to be accompanied by a value judgment. In addition, we must guarantee that both the wrong and the right are kept alive. This allows that the function of the wrong is to protect and secure the right. To do this systematically would be the wonderful burden of PLATO.

Bibliography

Frankfurt, H. G. (2006). *On truth*. New York: Knopf.

Heid, H. (2015). Über Relevanz und Funktion des Fehlerkriteriums. In: M. Gartmeier, H. Gruber, T. Hascher & H. Heid (Hrsg.), *Fehler. Ihre Funktionen im Kontext individueller und gesellschaftlicher Entwicklung* (S. 33-52). Münster: Waxmann.

Oser, F. (2015). „Und eine neue Welt…". Funktionen des Negativen Wissens. Oder: Wenn Fehler Früchte tragen. In: M. Gartmeier, H. Gruber, T. Hascher & H. Heid (Hrsg.), *Fehler. Ihe Funktionen im Kontext individueller und gesellschaftlicher Entwicklung* (S. 71-92). Münster: Waxmann.

Oser, F. & Spychiger, M. (2005). *Lernen ist schmerzhaft. Zur Theorie des Negativen Wissens und zur Praxis der Fehlerkultur.* Weinheim/Basel: Beltz.

Shavelson, R. J., Troitschanskaia, O., & Mariño, J. P. (2018). International performance assessment of learning in higher education (iPAL)—Research and Development. In: O. Zlatkin-Troitschanskaia, H. A. Pant, M. Toepper, C. Lautenbach & C. Kuhn (Eds.), *Assessment of Learning Outcomes in Higher Education – Cross-national Comparisons and Perspectives.* Wiesbaden: Springer.

Tugendhat, E. (1984). *Probleme der Ethik*. Ditzingen: Reclam.

Wittgenstein, L. (1963). Tractatus logico-philosophicus. Frankfurt: Suhrkamp.

Yamakawa, Y. Peng, M. W. & Deeds D. L. (2013). Riaing from the ashes: Cognitive determinants of venture growth after entrepreneurial failure. In: *Entrepreneurship Theory and Practice*. (p. 1-52) DOI: 10.1111/etap.12047

Zlatkin-Troitschanskaia et al. (2017). *Positive Learning in the Age of Information*. Draft Proposal Cluster of Excellence. Johannes Gutenberg University Mainz (Unpublished Manuscript).

Part V
Learning with Information and Communication Technology: Impact and Risk Evaluation

Deeply Sensing Learners for Better Assistance

Towards Distribution of Learning Experiences

Koichi Kise

Abstract

Most of the current e-learning systems rely on shallow sensing of learners such as achievement tests and log of usage of e-learning systems. This poses a limitation to know internal states of learners such as confidence and the level of knowledge. To solve this problem, we propose to employ deeper sensing by using eye trackers, EOG, EEG, motion and physiological sensors. As tasks, we consider English learning. The sensing technologies described in this paper includes low level estimations (the number of read words, the period of reading), document type recognition and identification of read words, as well as high level estimations about confidence of answers, the English ability in terms of TOEIC scores and unknown words encountered while reading English documents. Such functionality helps learners and teachers to know the internal states and will be used to describe learning experiences to be shared by other learners.

Keywords

Confidence; Document Type Recognition; E-learning; English Ability Estimation; EOG; Eye-tracker; Lerner Sensing; Read Word Identification; Reading Detection; TOEIC Score Estimation; Unknown Word; Wordometer.

1   Objectives

"The eyes have one language everywhere." This is an English proverb that tells you the potential of analyzing behaviors. Even in the case that it is difficult to presume what people think and feel from their words, it may be possible to estimate them by watching eye movements. In the context of learning, such analysis of behaviors enables us to know more about internal states of learners. Experienced teachers are always doing such analysis for providing students better and personalized assistance, though there exists a limit on the number of students taken care by a single teacher.

One way to remove the limit is to employ information technologies (IT) to help teachers and learners. IT can sense learners to estimate their internal states, which are then sent to learners and teachers. Up to now, a lot of efforts have been made to realize e-learning systems with such functionality. Most of them sense learners through achievement tests and logs of the system usage. Achievement tests are direct way to know the level of understanding but have limitations on its density: not all items can be tested so that achievement tests are sparse in terms of coverage. Logs are dense but indirect to know internal states. For example, if a learner stops working on a learning material, it is difficult to know its reason. It may be because it is either too difficult, or boring. In this sense, we call such traditional sensing "shallow sensing."

For assistance closer to the level of human teachers, we suppose it is necessary to sense learners in deeper ways. If it is possible for us to monitor the level of knowledge densely, learners do not miss their weak points. In addition to sense the level of knowledge, other internal states such as concentration and boredom can be of help to guide learners. As targets for sensing, we can consider eye movements obtained by eye trackers, movements of other body parts such as a head and a hand, physiological signals such as skin temperature, heart rate, etc., as shown in Figure 1.

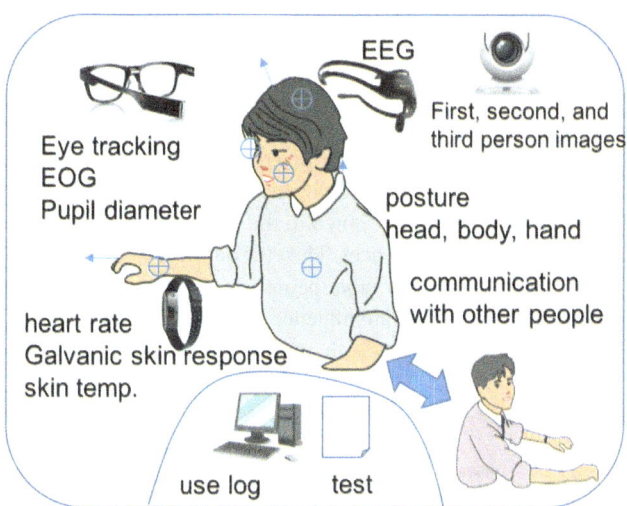

Fig. 1 Deep Sensing

Based on the above notion of "deep sensing", we have just launched a project called "experiential supplements" for achieving personalized learning assistance. The final goal of the project is to establish a way to sense, record, modify and apply experiences of learning. The underlying notion of this process is as follows. In many cases, difficulty a learner is facing has already been experienced and solved by other learners. Thus, sharing such experiences is a reasonable way to assist learners. In order to improve the acceptability of other persons' experiences, we employ "modify" process before "apply" to a learner. Recorded experiences are modified to the form called "experiential supplements" for effective, and easier intake to change learners' internal states and behaviors.

In this paper, we mainly focus on the sensing part in the whole project. In Section 2, we explain the overall framework of "experiential supplements". In Section 3, tasks and methods we have already developed are explained. Section 4 summaries this paper.

2   Framework

The notion of experiential supplements can be understood by analogy with production of medicine as shown the upper part of Figure 2. Materials are processed to extract active ingredients, which are then mixed with additives to make it easier to take. The next step is to mold "medicine" which will be applied to a person. The case of experiential supplements is shown in the lower part. People's experiences are sensed to obtain data of experiences. Then the data are modified with additives to make it easier to be accepted by other people. As additives for experiences, we employ "cognitive biases" which can influence the attitude of the user. This allows us to generate a modified information about experiences and to prescribe them to the user.

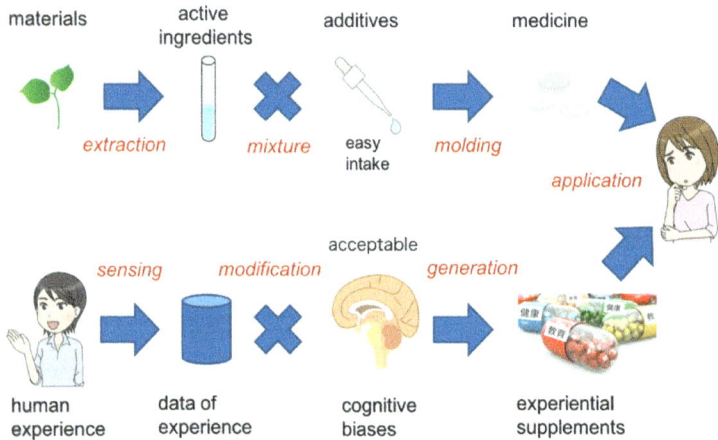

Fig. 2   Medicine and experiential supplements

Figure 3 shows the overview of our project "experiential supplements." The purpose of this project is to develop a platform for changing people's behavior in an effective way by applying people's experiences. The underlying notion is that in many cases the problem a user encountered has already been experienced and solved by others. As the application fields of experiential supplements, we have the following three: learning, health care and sports/entertainment. As compared to learning, which is mainly cognitive activities, sports/entertainment is mostly physical activities, and health care is the mixture of both depending on the type of health we focus.

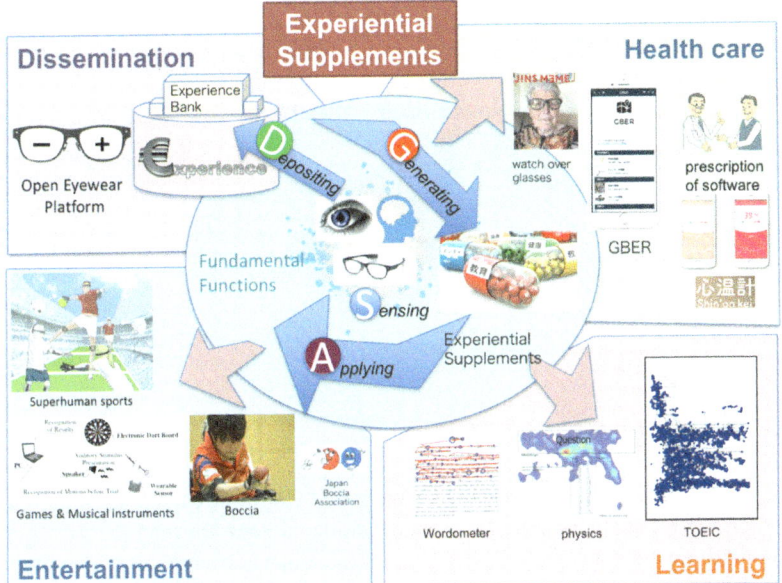

Fig. 3 Overview of experiential supplements

3 Tasks and methods

In this section, we focus on the sensing in the field of learning and describe some examples of tasks and methods we have already developed. The tasks we consider here is to assist English learning from low to high levels as shown in Figure 4. Since all of the tasks are about reading, which have been well studied in relation to eye movements (Liversedge et al. 2011; Rayner 1998; Rayner et al. 2012; Van Gompel et al. 2007), we employ eye trackers as a main sensor.

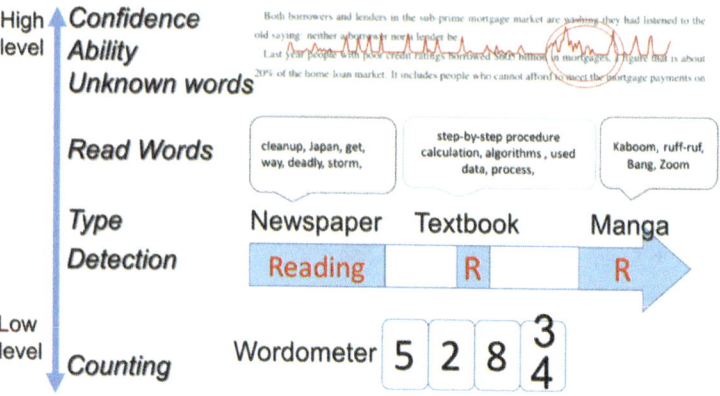

Fig. 4 Levels of tasks

3.1   Wordometer

We start with a low level sensing of quantity. The most fundamental task is "wordometer" which measures how many words the user has read (Kunze et al. 2015). We intend to build it as a step counter (pedometer) of our knowledge life.

The wordometer has been implemented using one of the following three devices: JINS MEME, mobile and stationary eye tracker. JINS MEME is commercial glasses with EOG (electrooculography), accelerometer and gyroscope as shown in Figure 5. With this device, we are able to detect eye movement, blinks and head motion. As eye trackers, we employ a mobile eye tracker (SMI Eye Tracking Glass (ETG)) and a stationary eye tracker (Tobii Eye X).

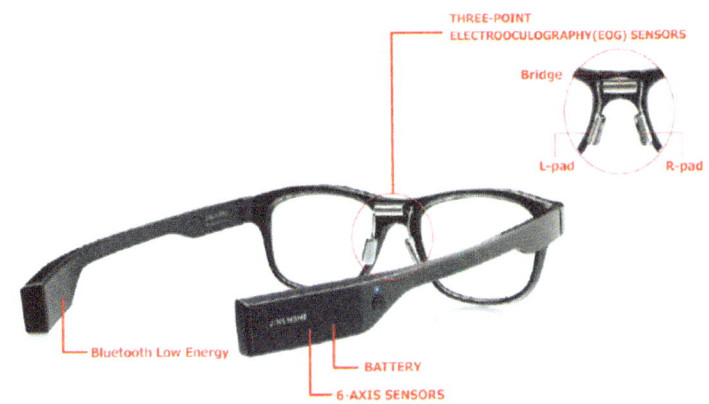

Fig. 5 JINS MEME

We have several versions of wordometers depending on which device to use. However, the basic computation is shared as follows. The task of estimating the number of read words is formalized as a regression problem. Taking features of sensor outputs as input, we apply support vector regression to estimate the number of words. First, raw eye gaze data are transformed into a sequence of saccades and fixations (Buschner and Dengel 2009). Then some features such as the number of detected line breaks, and the number of fixations are calculated. The line break is detected as a large backward (right to left) movement of eyes.

The error of estimation depends on the device to use, setup of the experiments and the amount of text to read. The setup indicates whether the learning by support vector regression is either user dependent or independent, as well as document dependent or independent. Generally speaking, the error ranges from 3% to 14 %, which is comparable to that of pedometers.

We expect that, as pedometers motivate people to walk more and continue to walk, the same can happen to users of wordometers. We are now trying to prove it experimentally with a larger scale user study.

3.2   Reading detection

Another basic function in terms of quantity is reading detection, which means to estimate the period of reading among daily activities. The reading behavior is characterized by periodical eye movement: a sequence of small forward saccades (from left to right) followed by a large backward saccade (from right to left; line break).

As devices, we have employed either JINS MEME or SMI ETG. Unlike the case of wordometer, the method for each device is quite different.

Here, we explain the case with SMI ETG: We employ eye movement features such as average and variance of saccade length, the sum and the average of fixation time, etc. After user independent learning of SVM to classify activities into either reading or others, the F-measure 90% has been obtained from the experiment with 10 people doing 50 to 80 minutes activities half of which are reading.

3.3   Document type recognition

In order to know more about the above statistics of the amount and the period of reading, document type recognition which classifies read documents into several types such as newspaper, textbook, and magazine is applied. We have employed one of the following two devices: an electroencephalograph (EEG) device called Emotiv, and SMI ETG.

In the following, we describe the case with SMI ETG to make the document type recognition user independent (Shiga et al. 2016). Figure 6 shows an image from the scene camera on ETG with image feature points. Taking into account both eye gaze features and image features obtained from the scene camera, we have achieved the accuracy of 85% of the classification from the experiment with 8 participants.

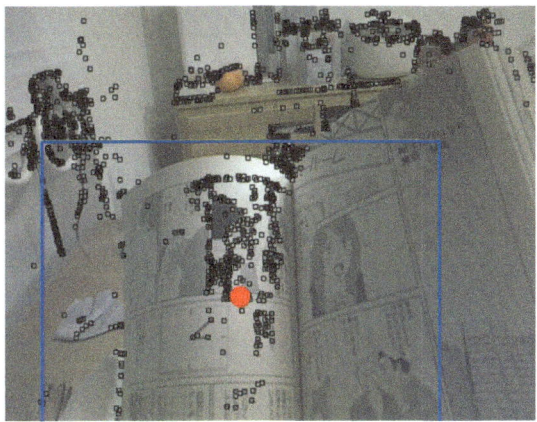

Fig. 6   Scene camera image of SMI ETG and image feature points

3.4   Read word identification

We can consider further quantification of learning activities through reading by identifying the read words. This allows us to build a Bag-of-Words (BOW) model of our reading activities from which we can know the contents of learning.

We employ one of the following two eye tracking devices Tobii Eye X and SMI ETG for this purpose. Let us focus here on the case with Tobii Eye X. The main issue is how to deal with errors on the estimated fixation positions (Sanches et al. 2016). After the matching of eye gaze data to the displayed textlines, it is possible to know the start and the end of reading. This enables us to build the BOW illustrated as tag clouds shown in Figure 7 (Augereau et al. 2015).

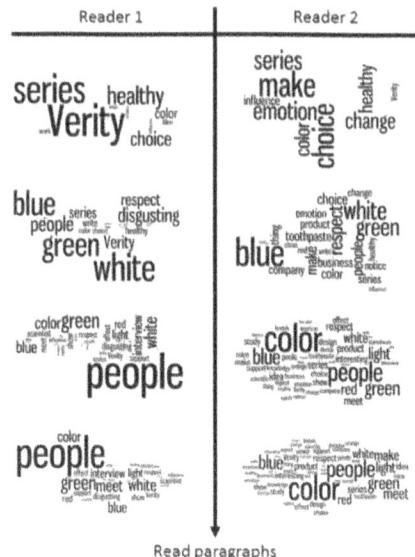

Read paragraphs

Fig. 7 Read word identification and its representation as a series of tag clouds

3.5   Confidence

It is helpful for learners if we can estimate the confidence of answers to determine which part should be reviewed. In particular, it is meaningful to find answers which are correct by chance (without confidence) and those which are incorrect with high confidence (something erroneously understood).

Although it is not easy to solve this problem in general, it is tractable if we limit the estimation to answers of multiple choice questions. This is because eye gaze for an answer with confidence is different from that without it as shown in Figure 8.

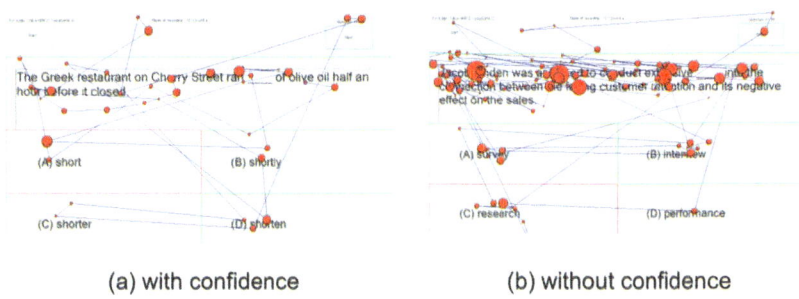

(a) with confidence   (b) without confidence

Fig. 8   Estimation of confidence using eye gaze

We have developed a method to estimate whether the answer is with confidence or not for a part of an English standardized test called TOEIC (Test of English for International Communication). In the TOEIC test, we focus on Part 5: reading section which is a sentence completion task with 4 choices to fill the blank. The SVM is employed for this purpose with gaze features as input in addition to the correctness of the answer. Based on the experiment with 11 participants and 80 questions, our method is capable of estimating the confidence with the accuracy of 90%.

3.6   English ability

The wordometer is to count the quantity of reading to encourage learners to read more. We consider that the same holds for the English ability (Augereau et al. 2016) if we can estimate it. For this purpose, we estimate the score of TOEIC, which ranges from 10 to 990. In this task, we focus on the Part 7 (passage comprehension) of the reading section. A typical format of the Part 7 includes a passage and some questions about its contents, each of which is a four-choice question.

We analyzed the eye gaze shown in Figure 9. The accuracy of estimation depends on the setting of experiments: whether learning is user independent or not, as well as document independent or not. In the easiest case, that is document dependent setting with optimal feature selection, we can estimate the score with the error of 30 points by just taking into account the eye gaze on two passages.

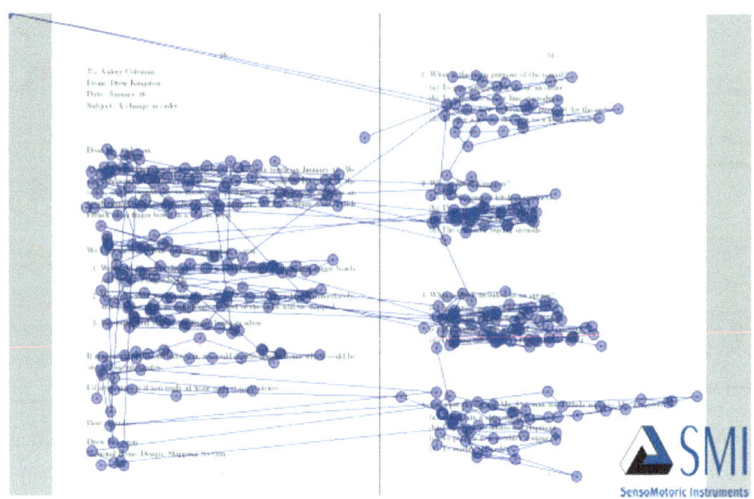

Fig. 9   Estimation of the TOEIC score based on eye gaze

3.7   Unknown words

Vocabulary building is an important task for English learners. However, it requires
a tedious task of making a list of unknown words. We have built a method that
automates it by taking as input only the gaze data while reading English text. A
deep neural network is employed to determine whether a word with the gaze is
unknown. The precision of 33% is achieved on condition that almost no unknown
words are missing (recall 99%) from the experiment with 5 participants and 16
documents.

4   Conclusion

In this paper, we summarized our results of sensing deeply learners' behaviors
using various devices including eye trackers, EOG, accelerometer, gyroscope and
EEG. The purpose of sensing is to know the internal states of learners from low
to high levels.

   As we mentioned in Section 2, sensing is just the first step towards sharing
learning experiences. It is required to build methods to describe and share the
experiences in the form called "supplements" to change learners' behavior and to
facilitate "positive" learning (see, e.g., also Ishimaru et al. in this volume).

Bibliography

Augereau, O., Fujiyoshi, H., & Kise, K. (2016). *Towards an Automated Estimation of English Skill via TOEIC Score Based on Reading Analysis.* 23rd International Conference on Pattern Recognition (ICPR) (pp. 1285–1290). doi:10.1109/ICPR.2016.7899814.

Augereau, O., Kise, K., & Hoshika, K. (2015). *A Proposal of a Document Image Reading-life Log Based on Document Image Retrieval and Eyetracking.* 13th International Conference on Document Analysis and Recognition (ICDAR) (pp. 246–250). doi:10.1109/ICDAR.2015.7333761

Buscher, G., & Dengel, A. (2009). Gaze-based filtering of relevant document segments. Workshop WSSP held in conjunction with WWW2009, Madrid, Spain.

Kunze, K., Masai, K., Inami, M., Sacakli, Ö., Liwicki, M., Dengel, A., Ishimaru, S., & Kise, K. (2015). Quantifying Reading Habits – Counting How Many Words You Read. In K. Mase, M. Langheinrich & D. Gatica-Perez (General Chairs), *Proceedings of the 2015 ACM International Joint Conference on Pervasive and Ubiquitous Computing* (pp. 87–96). New York: ACM. doi:10.1145/2750858.2804278.

Liversedge, S. P., Gilchrist, I. D., & Everling, S. (Eds.) (2011). *The Oxford Handbook of Eye Movements, Part 6: Eye Movement Control During Reading.* Oxford: Oxford University Press.

Rayner, K. (1998). Eye movements in reading and information processing: 20 years of research. *Psychological bulletin, 124*(3), 372–422.

Rayner, K., Pollatsek, A, Ashby, J., & Clifton Jr., C. (2012). *Psychology of Reading* (2nd ed.). New York: Psychology Press.

Sanches, C. L., Augereau, O., & Kise, K. (2016). Vertical Error Correction of Eye Trackers in Nonrestrictive Reading Condition. *IPSJ Transactions on Computer Vision and Applications, 8*(7). doi:10.1186/s41074-016-0008-x.

Shiga, Y., Utsumi, Y., Iwamura, M., Kunze, K., & Kise, K. (2016). Automatic Document Type Classification Using Eye Movements and Egocentric Images. *Trans. IEICE (D), J99-D*(9), 950–958 [in Japanese].

Van Gompel, R. P. G., Fischer, M. H., Murray, W. S., & Hill, R. L. (Eds.) (2007). *Eye Movements: A Window on Mind and Brain.* Amsterdam: Elsevier.

Augmented Learning on Anticipating Textbooks with Eye Tracking

Shoya Ishimaru, Syed Saqib Bukhari, Carina Heisel, Nicolas Großmann, Pascal Klein, Jochen Kuhn, and Andreas Dengel

Abstract

This paper demonstrates how eye tracking technologies can understand providers to realize a personalized learning. Although curiosity is an important factor for learning, textbooks have been static and constant among various learners. The motivation of our work is to develop a digital textbook which displays contents dynamically based on students' interests. As interest is a positive predictor of learning, we hypothesize that students' learning and understanding will improve when they are presented information which is in line with their current cognitive state. As the first step, we investigate students' reading behaviors with an eye tracker, and propose attention and comprehension prediction approaches. These methods were evaluated on a dataset including eight participants' readings on a learning material in Physics. We classified participants' comprehension levels into three classes, novice, intermediate, and expert, indicating significant differences in reading behavior and solving tasks.

Keywords

Attention; Augmented Text; Comprehension; Didactics; Eye Tracking; Learning; Reading Behavior; Physics.

1   Objective

Curiosity is an important factor for learning. Every human has a different way of learning based on individual speed and preferences. However, teaching activity has been, traditionally, static and consistent among various learners. We assume that the system which provides individualized information for each learner based on their interests can foster positive learning (cf. Zlatkin-Troitschanskaia et al. 2017). This paper demonstrates how technologies can provide such kind of personalized learning. Since textbook has played an important role in learning and education, we propose the concept of "Anticipating Textbook," which displays the information need based on gaze, i.e. using eye tracking devices to measure visual attention and employ them for vivid interaction with textual information. In order to develop the system, it is necessary to predict the timing when learners have or lose their interest on the content in real time. If, for instance, learners are overwhelmed by difficult learning content misconceptions may occur, and the system intervenes (e.g., showing illustrative videos, switching to less complex representations, etc.); if readers need additional data, instructional support or more advanced information, the anticipating textbook reacts accordingly by presenting this kind of information. It is estimated that about 80% of all knowledge stored in memory is captured via the eyes (Murphy 2016). Gaze can be interpreted as a proxy for the user's attention, and eye movements are known to be usually tightly coupled with cognitive processes in the brain, so that a great deal about those processes can be observed using eye tracking (Dengel 2016). We propose attention and comprehension prediction approaches by measuring students' reading behaviours. The objectives of this paper are to present 1) the concept of the anticipating textbook and 2) attention and comprehension prediction methods while reading.

2   Theoretical framework

Tracking eye movements on text has a long history. In first experiments conducted during the 19th century, subjects reading text were monitored with the simplest means and the findings were basically of descriptive nature. Javal (1878), Landolt (1881) and Lamare (1892) were among the first to conduct eye tracking studies on text (Wade and Tatler 2009). While early experiments were of rather descriptive nature and provided early evidence that the eye moves in a series of jerks (i.e., saccades) while reading, the second half of the 20th century started to focus on cognitive aspects. Especially during the last thirty years the available tracking methods improved dramatically and with the availability of remote eye tracking devices and a computer-based evaluation of eye movements there was a remarkable increase in insights into the human perception and reading process (Rayner 1998, p. 372). Sophisticated experiments could be performed with gaze-contingent stimuli, based on the subject's eye movements and behavior. Furthermore, the first truly interactive eye tracking applications were implemented (e.g., Bolt 1990) in which eye tracking was used for entertainment applications. However, the real-time usage of gaze on text, for the sake of education and training or information provision, has not explicitly been considered for a long time. The first application focusing on that aspect was iDict by Hyrskykari et al. (2000). The system was implemented to provide translations on comprehension problems detected in the reader's gaze patterns. In several papers, we presented an algorithm for online reading detection based on eye tracking data (Biedert et al. 2012) and introduce an application for assisted and augmented reading called the eyeBook (Biedert et al. 2010). The idea behind the eyeBook is to create an interactive and entertaining reading experience and to help the reader to better understand the text and what is behind. Eye tracking systems observe which text parts are currently being read by the user not only on the screen but also on paper (Kunze et al. 2013, Ishimaru et al. 2016, and Toyama et al. 2013).

Considering the above work around eye tracking, we apply the approach of augmented text to educational textbook. Figure 1 shows a concept sketch of the anticipating textbook. The system recognizes a student's cognitive state (e.g., attention, interest, comprehension) using several sensors including an eye tracker. Then the system changes the content or the layout dynamically to improve a student's motivation and understanding. For example, playing a video instead of showing a static picture should attract students' interest. Since students prefer different representations depending on their skill level (cf. Klein et al. in this volume), the system displays the adapted representation based on cognitive state analysis. If the system tracks the level of understanding while reading, it can pick up or generate tasks a student should solve to correct his/her misunderstanding.

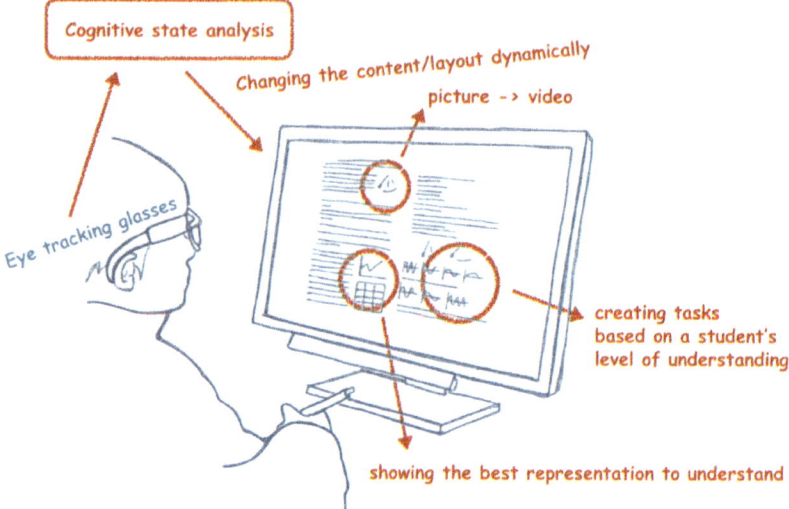

Fig. 1   The concept sketch of the anticipating textbook

3   Methods

In order to implement the anticipating textbook, we start from investigating students' cognitive states while reading a textbook. In following, this paper presents our attention and comprehension extraction methods. As preprocessing, raw data from eye tracking glasses are converted to gaze points on a document with a projection function based on SIFT features (Lowe 1999) and classified into fixations and saccades (Buscher et al. 2008).

3.1   The AOI based attention extraction

We divide a text beforehand based on the roll (e.g., the introduction, definitions, applications on the document shown in Figure 2) then focus on the period of time needed to read the content to obtain knowledge. Thus, for each area a sum of fixation durations is calculated, which is divided by the size of area to be normalized.

3.2 The AOI based comprehension prediction

We apply a support vector machine (SVM) to predict students' comprehension. On the basis of AOI based fixation duration described as above, each duration in AOIs are calculated as features. From the document in Figure 2, for example, three features (durations on the introduction, definition, and application) are used. Since this method requires a student's reading behavior from the beginning to the end of a document, it can only be applied as an offline analysis.

3.3 The subsequence based comprehension prediction

On the other hands, an online analysis is required in order to change the content dynamically while reading. Therefore, we also investigate whether a subsequence (e.g., 1 minute of reading) is enough useful to predict students' comprehension. In this approach, we calculate four features (mean and standard deviation of fixation durations and saccade lengths) in a subsequence and apply SVM based classification.

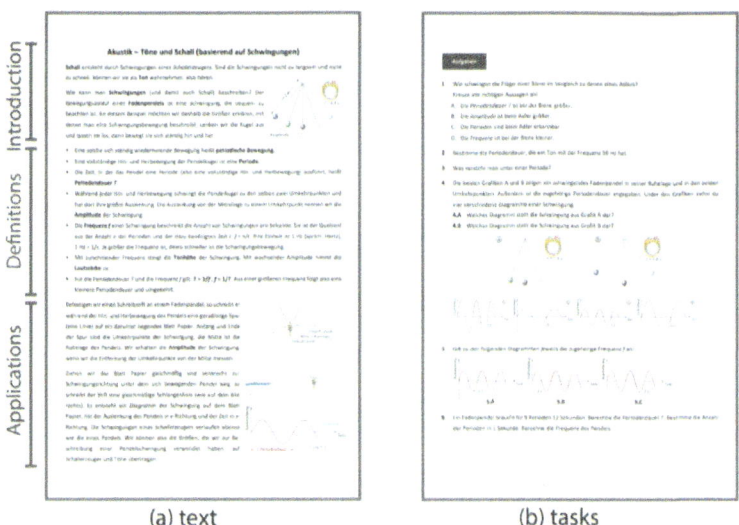

(a) text   (b) tasks

Fig. 2 A document with text and tasks in physics

These two figures are in one page on a display (text on the left and tasks on the right) during the experiment.

4   Data sources and the experimental design

We asked 8 participants to wear eye-tracking glasses, to read a physics textbook and to solve respective exercises as shown in Figure 3. The participants were 6-grade students at a German high school (11 or 12 years old). The document we prepared is "Basic Phenomena in Acoustics" (cf. Figure 2). It consists of four parts: the introduction, itemized definitions, applications, and related tasks. Only an explanation of about the content (the left page in Figure 2) was displayed at first. After participants understood the content, they could make tasks appear by pressing a key. They could go back to read the content to help them in their solving tasks. In this paper, we define these two steps as "reading" and "solving."

Fig. 3   An overview of the experiment
A participant is solving questions on a display with wearing SMI Mobile Eye Tracking Glasses 2.

To evaluate whether our proposed method works with different eye tracking devices, two types of eye tracking glasses were used during the experiment. We used *Tobii Pro Glasses 2* with five participants (*a*, *b*, *d*, *e*, *f*). The glasses record eye gaze at a sampling frequency 100 Hz and a scene video at 25 Hz. We applied one-point calibration with a marker before starting each recording. The data of the other three participants (*c*, *g*, *h*) were recorded with *SMI Eye Tracking Glasses 2*. The glasses record eye gaze at a sampling frequency 60 Hz and a scene video at 30 Hz. We apply three-point calibration with this device.

For evaluations of the comprehension prediction methods, training and testing dataset was created by leave-one-subject-out. All data from one participant are used for testing and data from other participants are used for training.

5 Results and discussion

5.1 The attention extraction

Table 1 shows percentages of time participants paid attentions for the introduction, definitions, and the applications on the document. We calculated the percentage depending on each situation while reading a text and solving tasks. The data in Table 1 is sorted by the number of correct answers. We categorized 8 participants to 3 comprehension levels based on their scores: novice (the score is 4 or less), intermediate (the score is 5), and expert (the score is 6 or more).

Tab. 1 Percentages of time participants paid attentions

Participant	Score (out of 14)	Expertise	Attentions while reading [%]			Attentions while solving [%]		
			Intro.	Def.	Appl.	Intro.	Def.	Appl.
a	3	Novice	14	49	37	13	59	28
b	4	Novice	17	43	40	17	48	35
c	5	Intermediate	7	51	42	4	44	52
d	5	Intermediate	31	41	28	21	49	30
e	5	Intermediate	23	37	40	27	40	33
f	6	Expert	16	47	37	12	60	28
g	7	Expert	34	50	16	25	56	19
h	7	Expert	28	64	8	22	70	8

By calculating mean values for each comprehension level, it has become obvious that students with high-level comprehension do not pay attention to the applications part while both reading and solving tasks compared to other levels (cf. Figure 4 and Figure 5). They understand that the applications part is useful for understanding the content, yet there is not much information that can be used as hints for solving tasks. They preferred to read definitions part because there are direct hints (principles, formulas, etc.). Intermediates and novices spend much time to paying attention to the application part while both reading and solving.

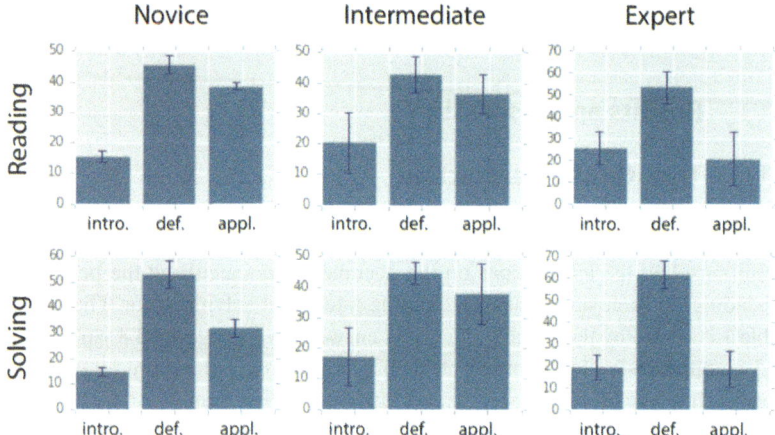

Fig. 4   Histograms of the time students paid attentions [%]
Error bars represent standard deviations.

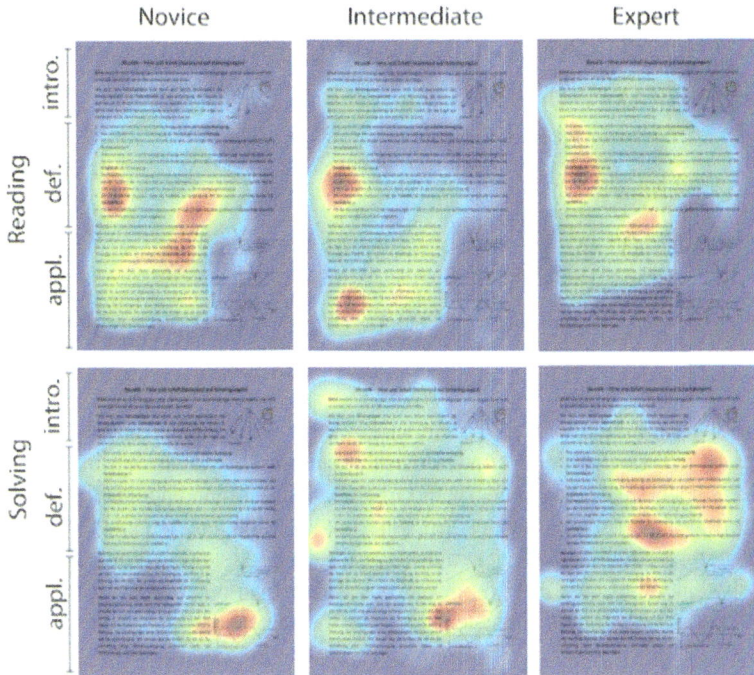

Fig. 5   Fixation duration based heat maps while a student is reading the text and solving tasks

5.2   The comprehension predictions

By using the categories (novice, intermediate, and expert) as ground truth, we estimated participants' completions. Figure 6 and Figure 7 represent confusion matrices of the estimation results. The AOI based approach succeeded to estimate all completions of participants. The estimation accuracy of the subsequences based approach was 70%.

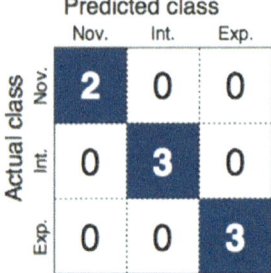
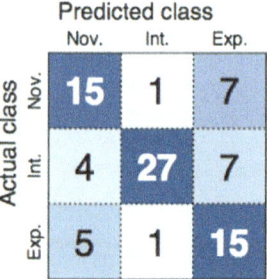

Fig. 6   The AOI based prediction result   **Fig. 7**   The subsequence based prediction result

Figure 8 shows all participants' feature plot in subsequences based approach. The higher the participant's completion is, the larger mean saccade length is measured. Novice students read a textbook with large fixation duration and small saccade length, and intermediate students read with small fixation duration and large saccade length. It cleared that novice students read a textbook slowly with small steps. The distribution of data plot from experts is larger than others. Expert students sometimes skip their eyes on the text, focus on the content they are interested in.

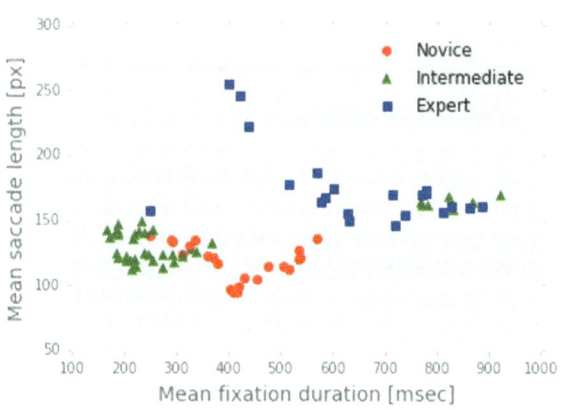

Fig. 8   Feature representation of all participants' data in subsequences based approach
          Each dot represents a data segment of one minute

6   Scientific significance of the study

In this paper, we present an initial method to extract students' attention by using gaze data. By applying the approach to activities including reading a text and solving tasks, it is revealed that reading behavior is related to students' comprehension. Expert students, for example, tend to pay attention on definition part to understand the content. In a next step, this information can be used to foster positive learning, for example, by giving visual cues to novice or intermediate students to identify relevant text passages for problem-solving. We also predicted students' completion (ground truth was calculated by the score of tasks) with two approaches. One is attentions on AOI based, and the other is features from gaze subsequence based prediction. The former one works better than the later one, but it requires the recording of reading from beginning to end. We found that features from a window of gaze data in one minute can enough classify students' completion into three classes with 70% accuracy. These results serves as a basis for on-line classification of learning states which can be used in a follow-up study to automatically address individual learning groups with tailored content.

Bibliography

Biedert, R., Buscher, G., & Dengel, A. (2010). The eyebook – using eye tracking to enhance the reading experience. *Informatik-Spektrum, 33*(3), 272–281.

Biedert, R., Hees, J., Dengel, A., & Buscher, G. (2012). A robust realtime reading-skimming classifier. In S. N. Spencer (Ed.), *Proceedings of the 2012 Symposium on Eye Tracking Research and Applications* (pp. 123–130). Santa Barbara, CA: ACM.

Bolt, R. A., & Starker, I. (1990). A gaze-responsive self-disclosing display. In J. C. Chew & J. Whiteside (Eds.), *Proceedings of the SIGCHI Conference on Human Factors in Computing Systems* (pp. 3–10). New York: ACM. doi:10.1145/97243.97245

Buscher, G., Dengel, A., & van Elst, L. (2008). Eye movements as implicit relevance feedback. In M. Czerwinski & A. Lund (General Chairs), *CHI' 08 Extended Abstracts on Human Factors in Computing Systems* (pp. 2991–2996). New York: ACM.

Dengel, A. (2016). Digital co-creation and augmented learning. In L. Uden, I-H. Ting & M. Santos-Trigo (Eds.), *Proceedings of the 11th International Knowledge Management in Organizations Conference on the changing face of Knowledge Management Impacting Society* (Art. No. 3). New York: ACM. doi:10.1145/2925995.2926052

Hyrskykari, A., Majaranta, P., Aaltonen, A., & Räihä, K.-J. (2000). Design issues of iDICT: a gaze-assisted translation aid. In A. T. Duchowski (Chairman), *Proceedings of the 2000 Symposium on Eye Tracking Research and Applications* (pp. 9–14). New York: ACM.

Ishimaru, S., Kunze, K., Kise, K., & Dengel, A. (2016). The wordometer 2.0: estimating the number of words you read in real life using commercial EOG glasses. In P. Lukowicz & A. Krüger (General Chairs), *Proceedings of the 2016 ACM International Joint Conference on Pervasive and Ubiquitous Computing: Adjunct* (pp. 293–296). New York: ACM.

Kunze, K., Kawaichi, H., Yoshimura, K., & Kise, K. (2013). The wordometer – estimating the number of words read using document image retrieval and mobile eye tracking. *2013 12th International Conference on Document Analysis and Recognition*, 25–29.

Lowe D. G. (1999). Object recognition from local scale-invariant features. In IEEE (Ed.), *The proceedings of the seventh IEEE international conference on computer vision* (pp. 1150–1157). IEEE Computer Society. doi:10.1109/ICCV.1999.790410

Murphy R. (2016). Learning-related vision problems. Allaboutvision.com. http://www.allaboutvision.com/parents/learning.htm. Accessed: 12 August 2017.

Rayner, K. (1998). Eye movements in reading and information processing: 20 years of research. *Psychological bulletin, 124*(3), 372–422.

Toyama, T., Suzuki, W., Dengel, A., & Kise, K. (2013). User attention oriented augmented reality on documents with document dependent dynamic overlay. *In IEEE (Ed.), 2013 IEEE International Symposium on Mixed and Augmented Reality - Arts, Media, and Humanities (ISMAR-AMH 2013)* (pp. 299–300). Institute of Electrical and Electronics Engineers.

Wade, N. J., & Tatler, B. W. (2009). Did javal measure eye movements during reading? *Journal of Eye Movement Research, 2(5)*, 1–7.

Zlatkin-Troitschanskaia et al. (2017). *Positive Learning in the Age of Information*. Unpublished Manuscript, Draft Proposal Cluster of Excellence, Johannes Gutenberg University Mainz.

The Potential of the Internet of Things for Supporting Learning and Training in the Digital Age

Miloš Kravčík, Carsten Ullrich, and Christoph Igel

Abstract

The rapid progress in the development of information and communication technologies opens new opportunities in education, which go hand in hand with new risks that may be difficult to foresee. Our aim here is to focus mainly on the Internet of Things and related technologies, in order to investigate how they can improve this field. We claim a proper analysis and interpretation of the big educational data can enable more precise personalization and adaptation of learning and training experiences, in order to make them more effective, efficient and attractive. Nevertheless, it will require new approaches to implement novel tools and services for more effective knowledge acquisition, deeper learning and skill training, which can take place in authentic settings and stimulate motivation of learners.

Keywords

Internet of Things; Personalization; Adaptation; Learning; Training; Augmented Reality; Wearables; Learning Nuggets; Nudges; Blockchain.

1   Introduction

Development of humans is highly influenced by the tools and media they use (cf., e.g., Maurer et al. in this issue). Neuroplasticity research has shown that our experiences change our brains throughout our life course (Doidge 2007), which means that people can always learn and acquire new knowledge and skills. The Internet together with other information and communication technologies (ICT) have a huge impact on the behaviour of people (Carr 2011), which includes also serious issues, like a loss of concentration abilities or problems with critical thinking and deep learning (cf. Zlatkin-Troitschanskaia et al. 2017). Every medium develops some cognitive skills at the expense of others (Greenfield 2009). Whether a tool helps or harms depends on the individual abilities and the way of its usage. Moreover, the long-term effects can differ diametrically from the short-term ones and may be very difficult to predict (cf., e.g., Knauff in this volume). These are risks that should not be ignored, and we must analyse them and try to understand their consequences, in order to avoid the potential harm that can be caused to humans. This requires monitoring of a long-term technological impact on users and assessment of possible risks (as a part of the PLATO program, cf. Zlatkin-Troitschanskaia et al. 2017).

On the other side, the unique opportunities offered by new ICT (like the Internet of Things, wearables and augmented reality) are extremely tempting for researchers and developers in the field of Technology Enhance Learning (TEL). A proper analysis and interpretation of the big data in education can help us better understand the effectiveness and efficiency of learning experiences, as well as individualize and optimize them. In addition, long-term effects of ICT on learning can be monitored, which should help also in cultivation of so important metacognitive skills, like self-regulation, self-monitoring and self-reflection (cf., e.g., Meyer in this volume). These skills are crucial in dealing with cognitive biases of humans, which are often misused against them. On the other hand, there is a big challenge to exploit these biases for the benefit of the learner. This would be a significant achievement in TEL. In the time when lifelong learning becomes unavoidable, cultivation of learning skills is crucial. But learning requires effort and energy from the learner, therefore stimulation of a natural curiosity, dealing with uncertainty, as well as development of the art of doubting and critical thinking have to be part of this process.

Another important aspect is the authenticity of learning embedded in other processes, like work (cf. Shavelson in this volume). This directly influences motivation and consequently efficiency of the learning and training experience, leading not only to acquisition of new knowledge, but also to cultivation of specific target skills. This is of crucial importance in the time when such paradigmatic change takes place like the transition towards Industry 4.0 (Wahlster 2014).[1]

2   The Internet of Things

The Internet of Things (IoT) is "a global infrastructure for the information society, enabling advanced services by interconnecting (physical and virtual) things based on existing and evolving interoperable information and communication technologies" (ITU 2012). IoT can improve authenticity of learning experiences, raising the motivation of participants, which has a crucial impact on the efficiency of the learning process. Better personalization and adaptivity of learning can be informed by the information collected through a rich palette of available sensors, like those for environment analysis, for home automation and manufacturing, as well as bio-sensors. It brings a potential for a new quality of personalized learning experiences, based on a better understanding of the users, their current status (including attention, emotions and affects) as well as their context. It also opens new horizons for design and implementation of novel virtual learning environments. Together with wearable technologies (WT) and augmented reality (AR) they can substantially enhance the usage of human senses in order to learn, to acquire new knowledge and train new skills.

From a technical perspective, IoT consists of objects that are identifiable, able to communicate and to interact (Miorandi et al. 2012). Identifiable means that objects have a unique digital identifier – *Electronic Product Code* (EPC), which is typically broadcast using *Radio-Frequency Identification* (RFID) technology, a very basic way of communication. Further communication, i.e. sending and receiving data to other objects, is enabled by various wireless technologies, realizing the step from single things to a network of things. The objects are not passive, but use sensors to collect information about their environment, and actors to trigger actions. On top of the hardware, software layers enable applications. IoT middleware provides a common way to access heterogeneous IoT devices, and simplifies the development of IoT applications. The technical challenges of IoT are not yet solved and its diverse areas are subject of active research. Nevertheless, IoT technology

---

1   This brings new challenges for professional development, with a direct inclusion of employees in its planning and realization. Lifelong competence development is important for various reasons. Companies need to identify their competence gaps and fill them efficiently. Employees can have their own aspirations regarding their lifelong professional development and plan them accordingly. Moreover, there is also the interest of the whole society to reduce the unemployment rate.

has matured sufficiently to be commercialized and to be used as enabler for research, including educational one.

Early work on IoT for education focuses mostly on using RFID for recognizing an object and presenting a list of information items or activities for that object (e.g., Broll et al. 2009), later extended to include social interaction on objects (e.g., Yu et al. 2011). Research on using the full IoT potential for learning is still in an early stage, with previous work sketching challenges and opportunities and describing architectures (Thomas et al. 2012, Atif et al. 2015), and there is still a significant gap of knowledge when it comes to research that goes beyond the technological perspective.

3   Big educational data

A plethora of sensors together with log files generated by e-learning platforms contribute to the big educational data, which represents a huge amount of information on the performed learning processes. To analyse and understand this data properly is a real challenge for researchers, developers, and users as well. As mentioned above, the gap between the technological and pedagogical perspective is essential (cf. Zlatkin-Troitschanskaia et al. 2017). Nevertheless, certain research fields help to overcome it, providing a base to build on.

Educational Data Mining (EDM) aims at automatically extracting meaning from large repositories of data related to learning activities, using computational methods for discovering data patterns. This may enable for instance identification of effective learning paths for a particular user as well as activities associated with better grades. Romero and Ventura (2010) list the most typical tasks in the educational environment that have been resolved through EDM techniques: analysis and visualization of data, providing feedback for supporting instructors, recommendations for students, predicting student performance, student modeling, detecting undesirable student behaviours, grouping students, social network analysis, developing concept maps, constructing courseware, as well as planning and scheduling.

Learning Analytics (LA) aims to improve the overall effectiveness of the learning experience, providing relevant alerts and predictions. Its use can be divided into five stages (Pardo 2014): collect, analyze, predict, act, and refine. It is crucial to enable various degrees of privacy and data security, to allow different levels of integration, depending on special preferences of individuals and other bodies, like companies (Kravčík et al. 2016a). Visualization of observable data on the learner's behaviour can even provide feedback about their non-observable cognitive and metacognitive learning activities (Nussbaumer et al. 2012). A major aspiration related to LA is to measure learning not only in formal, but also in informal environments.

4   Personalized and adaptive learning

As mentioned earlier, the big educational data is an important source of information that is available for individualized learning. The descriptions of the domain can be adjusted for a particular user in the current context, according to the chosen pedagogical methodology and preferred adaptation strategies. To overcome related technological and conceptual differences, semantic interoperability between heterogeneous information resources and services needs to be achieved (Aroyo et al. 2006). Modern context-aware and ubiquitous ICT allows for *smart learning*, providing the learner with the right support, depending on the current context and personalized to the individual needs, which are determined also from the learner's behaviour. Hence, smart learning requires an appropriate fusion of education and technology (Li et al. 2016).

4.1   User and context modeling

Personalization of a learning experience must take into account the information about the user, especially the learning objective (like target competences) and personal preferences. These inform the selection of an appropriate pedagogical approach, in order to make the learning process effective, efficient, and attractive. The actual contextual constraints lead to adaptations considering the current environment as well as available objects.

Santos et al. (2016) identified several issues in personalization of learning experiences, like effective detection and management of contextual and personal data of the learners, including also their affective status. This should lead to better understanding of the person, processing information from various resources (e.g., wearables with physiological and context sensors) and related big data. It is also important to harmonize different learning objectives, like short- and long-term ones, according to the learner's preferences. As these preferences can change quickly, available sensors can help significantly in the recognition of such alterations. High-dimensional data collected from sensors can be utilized to infer contextual preferences based directly on the individual's behavior (Unger et al. 2017). But the learners, and sometimes also others who are involved (e.g., teachers, tutor, parents), should know what information the machine collected about them. An

Open Learner Model makes a machines' representation of the learner available as an important means of support for learning (Bull and Kay 2010).

There was a lack of support for user modeling to harness and manage personal data gathered from IoT. The IoTum user modeling framework (Kummerfeld and Kay 2017) aims to fill this gap. It makes it easy for IoT application developers to use as well as to achieve light-weight, flexible, powerful, reactive user modeling that is accountable, transparent and scrutable (Kay and Kummerfeld 2012). Other approaches deal with elicitation of human cognitive styles (Raptis et al. 2017), affective states (Sawyer et al. 2017), as well as modeling psychomotor activities (Santos and Eddy 2017).

4.2   Adaptive learning and training

Each type of education should be based on a sound pedagogical methodology, which takes into account the learners with their aims, abilities, and preferences, but also the subject domain and the contextual settings. A suitable instructional design stimulates the motivation of participants as well as makes the learning experience effective and efficient. Nevertheless, each learning design can be specified only to a certain degree of detail and then it must be adapted to concrete settings, which can dynamically change over time. This run-time adaptation has to reflect the status and behaviour of learners, keeping them ideally in the *flow* status with their full attention and concentration on their tasks, avoiding frustration from too high demands on one side as well as boredom from trivial activities on the other.

Cultivation of *metacognitive skills* is a big challenge, as they have a direct impact on the individual's quality of life and are essential for lifelong learning. In this context, the effectiveness of education can be improved by the application of *Self-Regulated Learning* (SRL) (cf., e.g., Dormann et al. in this issue). For this purpose, the employed technologies should support an individualised approach as well as a right balance between the learner's freedom and guidance, in order to stimulate motivation, while considering also the effectiveness and efficiency of the learning experience. Moreover, useful assistive services have to be *open* and take into account the available technology and learning culture of learners. At the same time, they should be *responsive*, providing the right mix of adaptivity and recommendations of available options, in order to facilitate various degrees of guidance and freedom (Nussbaumer et al. 2014). Effective support for SRL must integrate advice in the form of personalized nudges (alerts that can be easily avoided) and reflection facilities in a suitable way (Kravčík and Klamma 2014). In any educational setting proper *awareness* and *reflection* services provide valuable feedback for participants and can cultivate their metacognitive skills. The challenge is to interpret the data collected in the learning process meaningfully and present them in an understandable form. To support this by useful technology, its designers and developers have to incorporate knowledge from various fields, including education, psychology, neuroscience and informatics (Kravčík et al. 2017).

Training of skills just from texts and pictures is usually difficult, therefore more dynamic and interactive media are required here, which is crucial for workplace learning. In order to demonstrate a particular skill, operation, or action, the challenge is to find relevant information segments in a vast amount of multimedia resources for a particular objective, context and user. Personalization and adaptive techniques applied on annotated video data may be a good direction in facilitating informal learning at the workplace (Kravčík et al. 2016b). Another promising alternative is offered by AR and WT towards smart ambient learning (Koren and Klamma 2015). Real-time automated feedback can be provided by a combination of wearable, voice-analysis, and motion-sensing technologies when people practice nonverbal communication skills for public speaking (Schneider et al. 2016). This outlines new ways of assessment, based on the direct monitoring of the human behaviour in the authentic settings and providing either a real-time feedback or an analysis of the performance over a certain time. Motor skill learning is an area where WT and user modeling can be synergistically combined for providing support (Dias Pereira dos Santos et al. 2017). Moreover, new opportunities for immersive procedural training open up, like capturing and re-enactment of expert performance, enabling immersive, in-situ, and intuitive learning (Guest et al. 2017).

A crucial limitation of the available adaptation and recommendation services is usually a lack of their understandability and scrutability, which is a typical problem when Artificial Intelligence (AI) techniques like Deep Learning are employed (de Bra 2017). For learning purposes such machine made decisions should be explainable by rules or evidence, in order to raise the trust of users. Generally, a loss of control stimulates negative feelings of users, therefore also clear and manageable privacy policies are required (Colbeck 2017).

5   APPsist system

To demonstrate intelligent adaptive learning technology that paves the way towards Industry 4.0, we introduce the APPsist system, which represents the first general applicable service-oriented architecture, with company specific specializations. Its smart services include user- centered support of qualification and training of employee, as well as user-adaptive context-based support, exploiting formalized expert knowledge.

APPsist is an example of how data collected from sensors is used for knowledge acquisition and assistance. The goal was to develop a new generation of mobile, context-sensitive and intelligent-adaptive assistance systems for knowledge and action support in smart production. The researchers and developers focused on the skills and competences of the staff and attempts to compensate for any skills that may be lacking with respect to performing tasks at the workplace – action support. In addition, knowledge-support services facilitate the continuous expansion of staff expertise through the acquisition of knowledge and skills in relation to production, product, and process. Here, the aim was to promote the professional development of the staff so that they can gradually start to perform more demanding tasks and serve as a counterbalance to the demographic change and the shortage of skilled workers. This support includes the setup and operation of a manufacturing unit in the production process, as well as the preventive maintenance, maintenance, and troubleshooting.

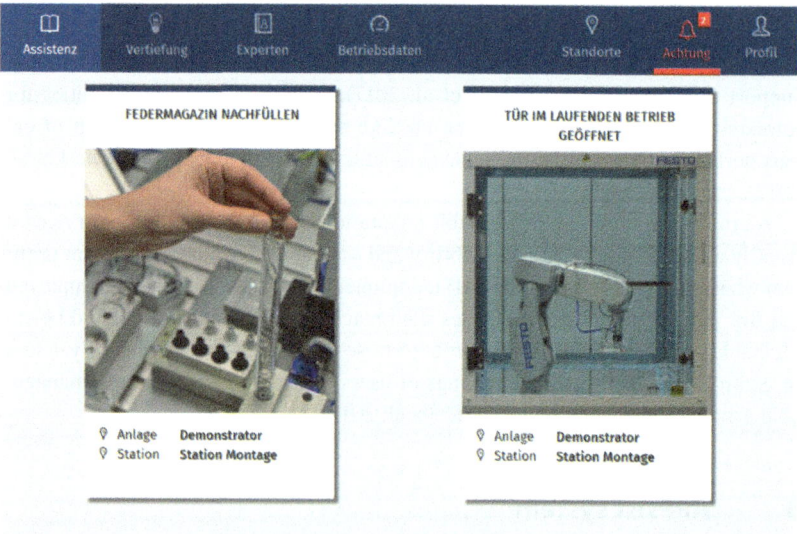

Fig. 1   Screenshot showing recommended work procedures

The solution offers both assistance and knowledge services for employees. These software components provide specific types of support: assistance services assist in solving a current problem, while knowledge services support the transfer of knowledge, it means the achievement of individual medium- and long-term development goals (Ullrich et al. 2015). Such assistance during a particular activity may mean step-by-step instructions or superimposition of information in the field of vision through AR. Contextual recommendations include suitable work activities, but also information relevant in the current context, for example, from manuals.

The current state of the art is represented by service architectures whose functionality results from the interplay of a large number of services. Each of the services thereby implements a specific, independent functionality and makes these available for other services. The APPsist system is based on a service-oriented architecture (Ullrich et al. 2015) that can be applied and connected to an existing machine park. It uses the available sensor data, which serves to monitor and control the production process, to interpret the activities of human operators interacting with the machines and to offer suggestions of what activities to perform. For instance, when APPsist detects a machine state that corresponds to a problem, it checks which maintenance activities can solve the problem and which operators are allowed to perform the maintenance activity. Using a mobile application, it then offers relevant content (instruction manuals, background information) and maintenance procedures to the operators. So APPsist can offer personalized learning and training experiences leading towards acquisition of the target knowledge or skill, recommending appropriate work procedures, but also suitable learning content. This support takes into account the development goals of the workers as well as their performed work activities.

In the context of using IoT for learning and training in manufacturing it is relevant that APPsist puts machine sensor data into relation with activities of the human operators and uses it to interpret whether the operator' actions were correct or incorrect (Ullrich et al. 2016). Thus, actions performed in the "analogue" world become digitally available, and usable for analysis, interpretation and reaction. With the ongoing digitization of spaces through the IoT technology, the amount of data becoming available for digital processing will further increase. Further research is required to investigate how such data can be used for learning and training, but examples such as APPsist show that this is possible.

6   Perspectives and conclusion

Nowadays, the necessity of re-qualification due to new challenges at the workplace meets with the strong need to cultivate critical thinking, in order to resist the systematic manipulation of individual opinions and mental models, exploiting cognitive biases of humans. In these circumstances the traditional push models of education typical for formal learning, which are based on transmission of knowledge that exists prior to the execution of the learning process, very often do not suffice. Instead, novel pull models of informal learning are required, which facilitate creation of knowledge during the execution of the learning process (Naeve et al. 2008). From various perspectives and interpretations of a certain event or entity the learner can create his or her own understanding, with a certain degree of uncertainty. In this process trust in the knowledge resources plays an important role and can be permanently updated. One of the most important competences becomes the ability to ask the right question.

Industry 4.0 brings many challenges and demands to improve informal learning, especially directly at the workplace. This should open new opportunities for retraining and upskilling of employees. Generally, learning offers should be based not only on individual preferences of users, but also on the effectiveness and efficiency of the learning and training experience, considering also the current context, including learner's emotional status and attention. New sensors and IoT offer more alternatives for collection and analysis of the big data acquired in formal, informal and workplace learning processes. They can enable a better recognition of learner's objectives, preferences and context, which should lead to a more precise personalization and adaptation of learning experiences. Their effectiveness and efficiency can be improved by WT and AR, which should lead to novel training methods, cultivating required competences. What can be interesting in the workplace and informal learning context is a combination of learning nuggets and nudges, which means enhancing micro-learning offers (nuggets) with suitable recommendations (nudges). While the former typically represent small segments of content, the later can be useful in driving learning processes.

IoT is decentralized, connecting autonomous devices directly to one another. Compared to the traditional top-down models it represents an alternative, which can provide greater privacy and security, but trust is a crucial issue here. The *blockchain* technology (Tapscott and Tapscott 2016) is critical for the IoT, as it allows devices to autonomously execute digital contracts and function as self-maintaining, self-servicing devices. This new paradigm delegates the trust at the object level, allowing animation and personalization of the physical world. Moreover, it provides novel refined facilities for users to control their privacy and protect their data. The blockchain technology has the potential to disrupt various areas and education is one of them. There are several opportunities how to do it (Tapscott and Tapscott 2017) and from our perspective the most crucial one is a new education, replacing the prevalent broadcast model with preparation for lifelong learning (cf. Gardner in this volume). This includes all competences relevant for a knowledge worker, including critical thinking, problem solving, collaboration, and communication.

IoT can strongly contribute to the collection of a huge amount of data on various artefacts, their relationships and people interacting with them. The challenge is to analyse and interpret this data properly, generating meaningful knowledge about the context and about individual users. Based on this, suitable learning and training experiences can be designed and provided to humans. Moreover, IoT enables new opportunities how these experiences can be personalized and adapted to the current context automatically. It means encoding educational instructions as well as personalization and adaptation strategies directly in IoT, which can be seen as a virtual (parallel) machine. This requires new programming approaches in this field. But whatever we do, we need to control and monitor the delegation of certain decision making activities to machines, in order to observe their long-term impact and to minimize related risks.

Bibliography

Aroyo, L., Dolog, P., Houben, G. J., Kravčík, M., Naeve, A., Nilsson, M., & Wild, F. (2006). Interoperability in personalized adaptive learning. *Journal of Educational Technology & Society, 9*(2), 4–18.

Atif, Y., Mathew, S. S., & Lakas, A. (2015) Building a smart campus to support ubiquitous learning. *Journal of Ambient Intelligence and Humanized Computing, 6*(2), 223–238.

Broll, G., Rukzio, E., Paolucci, M., Wagner, M., Schmidt, A., & Hussmann, H. (2009). PERCI: Pervasive Service Interaction with the Internet of Things. *IEEE Internet Computing, 13*(6), 74–81.

Bull, S., & Kay, J. (2010). Open Learner Models. In R. Nkambou, J. Bourdeau & R. Mizoguchi (Eds.), *Advances in Intelligent Tutoring Systems* (pp. 301–322). Berlin: Springer.

Carr, N. (2011). *The shallows: What the Internet is doing to our brains*. New York: Norton.

Colbeck, J. (2017). I'll be Watching You: Policing the Line between Personalization and Privacy. *Proceedings of the 25th Conference on User Modeling, Adaptation and Personalization* (p. 2). ACM.

De Bra, P. (2017). After Twenty-Five Years of User Modeling and Adaptation… What Makes us UMAP? *Proceedings of the 25th Conference on User Modeling, Adaptation and Personalization* (p. 1). ACM.

Dias Pereira dos Santos, A., Yacef, K., & Martinez-Maldonado, R. (2017). Let's Dance: How to Build a User Model for Dance Students Using Wearable Technology. In *Proceedings of the 25th Conference on User Modeling, Adaptation and Personalization* (pp. 183–191). ACM.

Doidge, N. (2007). *The brain that changes itself: Stories of personal triumph from the frontiers of brain science.* New York: Penguin.

Greenfield, P. M. (2009). Technology and informal education: What is taught, what is learned. *Science, 323*(5910), 69–71.

Guest, W., Wild, F., Vovk, A., Fominykh, M., Limbu, B., Klemke, R., Sharma, P., Karjalainen, J., Smith, C., Rasool, J., Aswat, S., Helin, K., Di Mitri, D., & Schneider, J. (2017). Affordances for Capturing and Re-enacting Expert Performance with Wearables. In *Proceedings of the 12th European Conference for Technology-Enhanced Learning (EC-TEL).* Springer.

ITU (International Telecommunication Union). (2012). Internet of Things Global Standards Initiative. Retrieved from http://www.itu.int/en/ITU-T/gsi/iot/Pages/default.aspx 19 May 2017.

Kay, J., & Kummerfeld, B. (2012). Creating personalized systems that people can scrutinize and control: Drivers, principles and experience. *ACM Transactions on Interactive Intelligent Systems (TiiS), 2*(4), 24.

Koren, I., & Klamma, R. (2015). Smart Ambient Learning with Physical Artifacts Using Wearable Technologies. In D. Preuveneers (Ed.), *Workshop Proceedings of the 11th International Conference on Intelligent Environments* (pp. 325–332). IOS

Kravčík, M., & Klamma, R. (2014). Self-Regulated Learning Nudges. In *Proceedings of the First International Workshop on Decision Making and Recommender Systems* (DMRS2014) (pp. 52–54). CEUR Vol. 1278.

Kravčík, M., Mikroyannidis, A., Pammer, V., Prilla, M., & Ullmann, T. D. (2017). Editorial. In Awareness and Reflection in Technology Enhanced Learning [Special issue], *International Journal of Technology Enhanced Learning, 9*(2), (pp. 99–102). Inderscience.

Kravčík, M., Neulinger, K., & Klamma, R. (2016a). Data analysis of workplace learning with BOOST. In *Proceedings of the Workshop on Learning Analytics for Workplace and Professional Learning (LA for work).* In conjunction with the 6th International Learning Analytics and Knowledge Conference, Edinburgh, UK (pp. 25–29).

Kravčík, M., Nicolaescu P., Siddiqui A., & Klamma R. (2016b) Adaptive Video Techniques for Informal Learning Support in Workplace Environments. In T. T. Wu, R. Gennari, Y. M. Huang, H. Xie & Y. Cao (Eds.), *Emerging Technologies for Education: First International Symposium, SETE 2016, Held in Conjunction with ICWL 2016, Rome, Italy, October 26-29, 2016, Revised Selected Papers* (pp. 533–543). Cham: Springer.

Kummerfeld, B., & Kay, J. (2017). User Modeling for the Internet of Things. In *Proceedings of the 25th Conference on User Modeling, Adaptation and Personalization* (pp. 367–368). ACM.

Li, Y., Chang, M., Kravčík, M., Popescu, E., Huang, R., & Chen, N. S. (2016). *State-of-the-Art and Future Directions of Smart Learning.* Singapore: Springer.

Miorandi, D., Sicari, S., Pellegrini, F. D., & Chlamtac, I. (2012). Internet of things: Vision, applications and research challenges. *Ad Hoc Networks, 10,* 1497–1516.

Naeve, A., Yli-Luoma, P., Kravcik, M., & Lytras, M. D. (2008). A modelling approach to study learning processes with a focus on knowledge creation. *International Journal of Technology Enhanced Learning, 1*(1-2), 1–34

Nussbaumer, A., Scheffel, M., Niemann, K., Kravčík, M., & Albert, D. (2012). Detecting and reflecting learning activities in Personal Learning Environments. In *Proc. of the 2nd Workshop on Awareness and Reflection in Technology-Enhanced Learning (artel12) at European Conference for Technology-Enhanced Learning* (pp. 125–131). CEUR Vol. 931.

Nussbaumer, A., Kravčík, M., Renzel, D., Klamma, R., Berthold, M., & Albert, D. (2014). A Framework for Facilitating Self-Regulation in Responsive Open Learning Environments. *arXiv preprint arXiv:1407.5891.*

Pardo, A. (2014). Designing Learning Analytics Experiences. In J. Larusson & B. White (Eds.), *Learning Analytics*. New York, NY: Springer.

Raptis, G. E., Katsini, C., Belk, M., Fidas, C., Samaras, G., & Avouris, N. (2017). Using Eye Gaze Data and Visual Activities to Infer Human Cognitive Styles: Method and Feasibility Studies. In *Proceedings of the 25th Conference on User Modeling, Adaptation and Personalization* (pp. 164–173). ACM.

Romero, C., & Ventura, S. (2010) Educational data mining: a review of the state of the art. *IEEE Transactions on Systems, Man, and Cybernetics, Part C (Applications and Reviews), 40*(6), 601–618.

Santos, O. C., & Eddy, M. (2017). Modeling Psychomotor Activity: Current Approaches and Open Issues. In *Enhanced Proceedings of the 25th Conference on User Modeling, Adaptation and Personalization* (pp. 305–310). ACM.

Santos, O. C., Kravčík, M., & Boticario, J. G. (2016). Preface to Special Issue on User Modelling to Support Personalization in Enhanced Educational Settings. *International Journal of Artificial Intelligence in Education, 26*(3), 809–820.

Sawyer, R., Smith, A., Rowe, J., Azevedo, R., & Lester, J. (2017). Enhancing Student Models in Game-based Learning with Facial Expression Recognition. In *Proceedings of the 25th Conference on User Modeling, Adaptation and Personalization* (pp. 192–201). ACM.

Schneider, J., Börner, D., van Rosmalen, P., & Specht, M. (2016). Can you help me with my pitch? Studying a tool for real-time automated feedback. *IEEE Transactions on Learning Technologies, 9*(4), 318–327.

Tapscott, D., & Tapscott, A. (2016). *Blockchain Revolution: How the Technology Behind Bitcoin Is Changing Money, Business, and the World*. New York: Penguin.

Tapscott, D., & Tapscott, A. (2017). *The Blockchain Revolution & Higher Education. Educause Review, 52*(2), 11–24.

Thomas, A., Shah, H., Moore, P., Rayson, P., Wilcox, A., Osman, K., Evans, C., Chapman, C., Athwal, C., While, D., Pham, H., & Mount, S. (2012). E-Education 3.0: Challenges and Opportunities for the Future of iCampuses. In *Proceedings of the Sixth International Conference on Complex, Intelligent, and Software Intensive Systems* (pp. 953–958). IEEE.

Ullrich, C., Aust, M., Dietrich, M., Herbig, N., Igel, C., Kreggenfeld, N., Prinz, C., Raber, F., Schwantzer, S., & Sulzmann, F. (2016). APPsist Statusbericht: Realisierung einer Plattform für Assistenz-und Wissensdienste für die Industrie 4.0. In *Proceedings of DeLFI Workshop* (pp. 174–180). CEUR Vol. 1669.

Ullrich, C., Aust, M., Kreggenfeld, N., Kahl, D., Prinz, C., & Schwantzer, S. (2015). Assistance- and knowledge-services for smart production. In *Proceedings of the 15th International Conference on Knowledge Technologies and Data-driven Business* (pp. 40). ACM.

Unger, M., Shapira, B., Rokach, L., & Bar, A. (2017). Inferring Contextual Preferences Using Deep Auto-Encoding. In *Proceedings of the 25th Conference on User Modeling, Adaptation and Personalization* (pp. 221–229). ACM.

Wahlster, W. (2014). Semantic Technologies for Mass Customization. In W. Wahlster, H.-J. Grallert, S. Wess, H. Friedrich & T. Widenka, T. (Eds.), *Towards the internet of ser-vices. The THESEUS research program* (pp. 3–13). Cham: Springer.

Yu, Z., Liang, Y., Xu, B., Yang, Y., & Guo, B. (2011). Towards a Smart Campus with Mobile Social Networking. In *Proceedings of the International Conference on Internet of Things and 4th International Conference on Cyber, Physical and Social Computing* (pp. 162–169). IEEE.

Zlatkin-Troitschanskaia et al. (2017). *Positive Learning in the Age of Information*. Unpublished Manuscript, Draft Proposal Cluster of Excellence, Johannes Gutenberg University Mainz.

The Digital Misinformation Pipeline

Proposal for a Research Agenda

Giovanni Luca Ciampaglia

Abstract

Digital misinformation poses a major risk to society and thrives on cognitive, social, and algorithmic biases. As social media become engulfed in rumor, hoaxes, and fake news, a "research pipeline" for the detection, monitoring, and checking of digital misinformation is needed. This chapter gives a brief introductory survey to the main research on these topics. The problem of digital misinformation does not lie squarely within a single discipline; instead, it is informed by research in several areas. An integrated research agenda devoted to the implementation of these tools should take into account a wide range of perspectives.

Keywords

Digital Misinformation; Echo Chambers; Fact Checking; Social Bots; Algorithmic Bias; Computational Social Science; Knowledge Networks; Social Media.

1 Introduction

The Internet, and social media in particular, form the infrastructure upon which takes place the exchange of information of the modern marketplace of ideas. With its endless cycle of production and consumption of information, social media let us spend our finite attention in exchange for news, information, and knowledge. The laws of this exchange are starting to be discovered (Ciampaglia et al. 2015a), thanks in part to the growing availability of data on collective phenomena (Lazer et at. 2009), but together with the promise for a better understanding of collective human behavior come novel risks that pose fundamental challenges to social media, and society at large. The risk is the massive, uncontrolled, and oftentimes systematic spread of untrustworthy content.

Digital misinformation spreads on social media under many guises. There are rumors, hoaxes, conspiracy theories, propaganda, and, more recently, fake news. While it is hard to attribute the spread of misinformation to the outcome of specific events, like the recent presidential elections in the US, a successful attempt at misinforming the public has been in one instance able to manipulate the stock market (Ferrara et al. 2016). In more widespread cases, like the diffusion of anti-vaccine sentiment through large swaths of society, misinformation has been directly associated to the resurgence of measles (Hotez 2016).

Misinformation thrives on social media due to a complex mix of cognitive, social, and algorithmic biases. We rely upon social media and other algorithmic systems like search engines to filter the large volume of information stimuli that, on a daily basis, the modern media ecosystem generates. Without a way to filter and to make sense of all this content, we would be left in a state of perpetual information overload (Nematzadeh et al. 2016; Qiu et al. 2017).

Algorithmic biases play a role in the selection of content that we see on social media. Currently, content is ranked and filtered based on a number of signals that include social recommendations, popularity, and emotional triggers rather than trustworthiness and quality. Giving priority to what is popular can have counter-intuitive effects on the quality of a cultural market (Salganik et al 2006), though in principle popularity may foster quality (Nematzadeh et al. 2017) and it has been observed empirically that search engines do not bias the quality of information we find through them (Fortunato et al. 2006). In practice, however, when it comes to social media many of these algorithmic choices are made with the intention of maximizing user engagement.

Algorithmic biases may also compound with social and cognitive ones. According to the principle of homophily, we naturally tend to interact with those who are similar to us or who hold beliefs close similar to ours. This shapes the structure of the social network creating distinctive groups (McPherson et al. 2001). While the Internet had been heralded as a way to bring universal access to multiple viewpoints, prior work has shown that polarization and ideological segregation are present in online conversations too (Conover et al. 2011; Conover et al. 2012; Adamic and Glance 2005). When it comes to social media, ideological segregation results in isolated and homogeneous communities often referred to as "echo chambers." Inside these communities, confirmation bias and other cognitive distortions are amplified, while the critical thinking necessary to fact-check claims is bypassed.

What causes echo chambers? Beyond the homophily naturally observed in social networks, echo chambers may be an unintended consequence of the mechanisms governing online interactions. Theoretical models explain the emergence of echo chambers via our tendencies to be influenced by what we see and to cut ties to those with whom we disagree.

As a result of echo chambers, worldviews are biased and people are vulnerable to manipulation. This potential for widespread manipulation offers fertile grounds to digital propaganda, astroturf, and information operations (Weedon and Stamos 2017). Growing evidence shows that a key factor in the success of information is the presence of large hosts of automated accounts whose goal is to amplify specific pieces of misinformation. These amplifiers are often referred to as social bots (Ferrara et al. 2016).

What to do? Professional journalism, guided by ethical principles of trustworthiness and integrity has been for decades the answer to episodes of rampant misinformation, like yellow journalism. Digital misinformation, however, spreads too quickly and across too many pieces of content for journalists to keep up with it. For example, analysis of Twitter shares has shown that there is a lag of approximately 13 hours between when fake news peaks and the subsequent verification starts to spread (Shao et al. 2016). While this span may seem relatively short, social media have been shown to be able to disseminate content orders of magnitude faster (Sakaki et al. 2010).

Because content spreads too quickly for journalists to react on time, one possibility could be to curb the creation of misinformation directly at the source by banning producers and spreaders of misinformation. This solution is, however, not desirable for two reasons. First, censorship is ethically problematic as it could potentially lead to a chilling effect for the freedom of expression and speech among Internet users. Second, it is relatively easy to create new domains on the Internet, as well as new identities on social media, a considerable advantage for any actor set on spreading misinformation.

Thus, even assuming that ethical concerns can be addressed in a satisfactory way, approaches of this kind could have only limited impact in curbing the production of misinformation.

In summary, both the volume and rate at which misinformation spreads nowadays on social media is beyond what journalists and the general public can do to control it. Tools and algorithms are needed to address the problem of digital misinformation, taking into account its specific features and the complex mix of biases and actors involved in its spread. In the following, I propose an agenda for research aimed at achieving the goal of a general reduction of the propagation of digital misinformation.

2   The digital misinformation pipeline

Because misinformation is a form of digital content like any other it is useful to think in terms of the life-cycle of digital content on the Internet and to identify various stages at which one can address the problem of misinformation.

1. **Production.** The first stage is the creation of misinformation content. Defining and detecting misinformation is an active area of research, that has been recently surveyed by various authors (Conroy et al. 2015; Wu et al. 2016; Joshi and Carman 2016). Challenges include the detection of instances of misinformation in dynamic streams of messages and documents. This is a hard task, as misinformation, like other forms of deception may feature hyperbole, irony, sarcasm, and other language nuances that algorithms have a hard time detecting. Common datasets like CREDBANK (Mitra and Gilbert 2015), the Observatory on Social Media (Davis et al. 2016), and Hoaxy (Shao et al. 2016; Shao et al. 2017) could help in this area as they may form a standard benchmark for comparing results across common tasks. Finally, at this stage it is also worth understanding the ecosystem of misinformation producers and their incentives in the production of deceiving content (Starbird 2017).

2. **Diffusion.** The second stage is the spreading proper. Though specific patterns differ, it is useful to distinguish an early phase and an aftermath. By simple measures of collective attention such as the number of shares or retweets, information diffusion is known to be extremely heterogeneous, in part due to two phenomena: the heavy-tail structure of the network, and the competition between multiple pieces of content (Weng et al. 2012). Therefore, there is a need for tools to model these types of information diffusion processes, and to predict the long-term spread of content. Some work has borrowed ideas from computa-

tional epidemiology to do so (Tambuscio et al. 2016). More importantly, it has been shown that the early signals of engagement can offer accurate predictors of the long-term of a piece of content (Szabo and Huberman 2010). Therefore, in principle it could be possible to reduce the current gap to allow journalists to act in a more reactive manner.

A number of systems are already implementing some of these ideas and providing resources on which to build upon. The TwitterTrails system monitors the propagation of rumors and provides indicators of the likelihood that a claim is false based on the characteristic signature of its diffusion (Takis Metaxas 2015). The Hoaxy system allows users to search and explore a vast database of fake news claims and related fact-checking (Shao et al. 2016; Shao et al. 2017). The News Tracer™ system, an industrial system developed at Thomson Reuters, allows reporters to assess individuals tweets in terms of reliability and credibility of its source (Lin et al. 2015).

3. **Verification.** The last stage is the peak and aftermath of the diffusion of misinformation. Presently, it is at this stage that journalists enter the stage and start doing their job of fact-checking those claims that have surfaced on social media. Human fact checkers could benefit enormously from automation at different stages of the process, which includes newsgathering, verification, report production, and dissemination. A number of research and industrial systems are already addressing some of these aspects. The ClaimBuster project, for example, extracts check-worthy in US presidential debates and other speeches (Hassan et al. 2017).

Semantic Web technologies could be also of tremendous aid in automating at least some aspects of fact-checking. With the advent of modern large-scale knowledge bases like Wikidata or the Google Knowledge Graph, the semantic information contained in the Web is in fact becoming more structured. Knowledge bases could be used to support computational tools to automate news verification. There are currently a number of approaches that are focusing on checking very simple relational statements of the form subject-predicate-object. These approaches are predicated on the idea that knowledge bases can be represented as a graph, and advocate the use of a range of graph mining techniques to extract the latent knowledge contained in them (Ciampaglia et al. 2015b; Shiralkar et al. 2017a; Shiralkar et al. 2017b; Shi and Weninger 2016). Obviously, real instances of misinformation are much more complex and nuanced than simple predicate statement, and one challenge will be to incorporate advances in other fields of artificial intelligence, like sentiment analysis and natural language processing.

3   Discussion

Digital misinformation poses major societal and global risks (Howell 2013). While the major social media platforms are acting to cut some of the most obvious financial incentives behind the production of questionable content, to counter digital misinformation we must develop new solutions that take into account the mix of biases that produces echo chambers, and the presence of manipulation and computational propaganda.

The proposed research agenda uses the metaphor of a pipeline to identify the various stages at which research and development is needed to address the problem of digital misinformation. This choice is not casual since, like in any pipeline, bottlenecks at any stage can reduce the overall success of the endeavor. This is a particularly pressing issue for the last stage, the one devoted to improving the current state of fact checking. The first two stages are concerned with closing the gap between the production of misinformation and its verification by improving methods and techniques to define and detect instances of viral misinformation in their early stage of diffusion. The rationale is that, in order to reduce the overall exposition of the population to digital misinformation, the best use of the limited resources in the newsroom is to prioritize efforts towards viral claims. But in most newsroom fact-checking is still carried out manually, often with painstaking dedication. This means that unless we improve the speed of fact-checking, any achievement in earlier stages of the pipeline would likely have little or no impact on the diffusion of digital misinformation.

This is not the first time that we see efforts to control the spread of rumors. During World War II, rumor clinics were set up in the US to debunk gossip and other forms of rumors that could have potentially hampered the morale of the population in the wartime effort. In fact, those very same rumor clinics enabled the first psychological studies on rumors and misinformation (Knapp 1944). Obviously, no single modern version of the rumor clinic will be able to clear social media of all its misinformation. But we stand to benefit from any coordinated efforts between academic research, journalism, and the tech industry that, like the ones proposed here, aim to understand and address the rampant phenomenon of digital misinformation.

Bibliography

Adamic, L. A., & Glance, N. (2005). The political blogosphere and the 2004 US election: divided they blog. In *Proceedings of the 3rd international workshop on Link discovery* (pp. 36–43). ACM.

Ciampaglia, G. L., Flammini, A., & Menczer, F. (2015a). The production of information in the attention economy. *Scientific Reports, 5*(9452). doi:10.1038/srep09452

Ciampaglia, G. L., Shiralkar, P., Rocha, L. M., Bollen, J., Menczer, F., & Flammini. A. (2015b). Computational fact checking from knowledge networks. *PLoS ONE, 10*(6), e0128193.

Conover, M., Ratkiewicz, J., Francisco, M., Gonçalves, B., Flammini, A., & Menczer, F. (2011). Political polarization on Twitter. In *Proc. 5th International AAAI Conference on Weblogs and Social Media (ICWSM)*.

Conover, M. D., Gonçalves, B., Flammini, A., & Menczer, F. (2012). Partisan asymmetries in online political activity. *EPJ Data Science, 1*(1), 6.

Conroy, N. J., Rubin, V. L., & Chen, Y. (2015). Automatic deception detection: Methods for finding fake news. *Proceedings of the Association for Information Science and Technology, 52*(1), 1–4.

Davis, C. A., Ciampaglia, G. L., Aiello, L. M., Chung, K., Conover, M. D., Ferrara, E., Flammini, A., Fox, G. C., Gao, X., Gonçalves, B., Grabowicz, P. A., Hong, K., Hui, P.-M., McCaulay, S., McKelvey, K., Meiss, M. R., Patil, S., Kankanamalage, C. P., Pentchev, V., Qiu, J., Ratkiewicz, J., Rudnick, A., Serrette, B., Shiralkar, P., Varol, O., Weng, L., Wu, T.-L., Younge, A. J., & Menczer, F. (2016). OSoMe: the IUNI observatory on social media. *PeerJ Computer Science, 2*(e87). doi: https://doi.org/10.7717/peerj-cs.87

Ferrara, E., Varol, O., Davis, C., Menczer, F., & Flammini, A. (2016). The rise of social bots. *Comm. ACM, 59*(7), 96–104.

Fortunato, S., Flammini, A., Menczer, F., & Vespignani, A. (2006). Topical interests and the mitigation of search engine bias. *Proceedings of the National Academy of Sciences, 103*(34), 12684–12689.

Hassan, N., Arslan, F., Li, C., & Tremayne, M. (2017). Toward automated fact-checking: Detecting check-worthy factual claims by ClaimBuster. In *Proceedings of the 23rd ACM SIGKDD International Conference on Knowledge Discovery and Data Mining*, KDD '17, (pp. 1803–1812). New York, NY, USA: ACM.

Hotez, P. J. (2016). Texas and its measles epidemics. *PLOS Medicine, 13*(10),1–5.

Howell, L. (2013). *Global Risks 2013*, chapter Digital Wildfires in a Hyperconnected World (pp.23–27). World Economic Forum, 2013. [Online; accessed 19-August-2015].

Joshi, A., Bhattacharyya, P., & Carman, M. J. (2016). Automatic Sarcasm Detection: A Survey. *ArXiv e-prints*.

Knapp, R. H. (1944). A psychology of rumor. *Public opinion quarterly, 8*(1), 22–37.

Lazer, D., Pentland, A., Adamic, L., Aral, S., Barabási, A.-L., Brewer, D., Christakis, N., Contractor, N., Fowler, J., Gutmann, M., Jebara, T., King, G., Macy, M., Roy, D., & Van Alstyne, M. (2009). Computational social science. *Science, 323*(5915), 721–723.

Liu, X., Nourbakhsh, A., Li, Q., Fang, R., & Shah, S. (2015). Real-time rumor debunking on Twitter. In *Proceedings of the 24th ACM International on Conference on Information and Knowledge Management*, CIKM '15 (pp. 1867–1870). New York, NY, USA. ACM.

McPherson, M., Smith-Lovin, L., & Cook, J. M. (2001). Birds of a feather: Homophily in social networks. *Annual review of sociology, 27*(1), 415–444.

Takis Metaxas, P., Finn, S., & Mustafaraj, E. (2015). Using TwitterTrails.com to investigate rumor propagation. In *Proceedings of the 18th ACM Conference Companion on Computer Supported Cooperative Work & Social Computing*, CSCW'15 Companion (pp. 69–72). New York, USA: ACM.

Mitra, T., & Gilbert, E. (2015). CREDBANK: A large-scale social media corpus with associated credibility annotations. In *Proceedings of the International AAAI Conference on Web and Social Media*.

Nematzadeh, A., Ciampaglia, G. L., Ahn, Y.-Y., & Flammini. A. (2016). From conversation to cacophony: Information overload and collective communication in Twitch. *ArXiv e-prints*.

Nematzadeh, A., Ciampaglia, G. L., Menczer, F., & Flammini, A. (2017). How algorithmic popularity bias hinders or promotes quality. *ArXiv e-prints*.

Qiu, X., Oliveira, D. F. M., Sahami Shirazi, A., Flammini, A., & Menczer, F. (2017). Limited individual attention and online virality of low-quality information. *Nature Human Behavior, 1*(0132). doi: 10.1038/s41562-017-0132

Sakaki, T., Okazaki, M., & Matsuo, Y. (2010). Earthquake shakes Twitter users: real-time event detection by social sensors. In *Proceedings of the 19th international conference on World Wide Web* (pp. 851–860). ACM.

Salganik, M. J., Sheridan Dodds, P., & Watts, D. J. (2006). Experimental study of inequality and unpredictability in an artificial cultural market. *Science, 311*(5762), 854–856.

Shao, C., Ciampaglia, G. L., Flammini, A., & Menczer, F. (2016). Hoaxy: A platform for tracking online misinformation. In *Proceedings of the 25th International Conference Companion on World Wide Web*, WWW '16 Companion (pp. 745–750). International World Wide Web Conferences Steering Committee.

Shao, C., Ciampaglia, G. L., Varol, O., Flammini, A., & Menczer, F. (2017). The spread of fake news by social bots. *ArXiv e-prints*.

Shi, B., & Weninger, T. (2016). Discriminative predicate path mining for fact checking in knowledge graphs. *Knowledge-Based Systems, 104*, 123–133. doi:10.1016/j.knosys.2016.04.015

Shiralkar, P., Avram, M., Ciampaglia, G. L., Menczer, F., & Flammini, A. (2017a). Relsifter: Scoring triples from typelike relations. In *Proceedings of WSDM Cup 2017*.

Shiralkar, P., Flammini, A., Menczer, F., & Ciampaglia, G. L. (2017b). Finding streams in knowledge graphs to support fact checking. In *Proceedings of the 2017 IEEE 17th International Conference on Data Mining*.

Starbird, K. (2017). Examining the alternative media ecosystem through the production of alternative narratives of mass shooting events on Twitter. In *Proceedings of the International AAAI Conference on Web and Social Media* (pp. 230–239). Palo Alto, California: AAAI Press.

Szabo, G. & Huberman, B. A. (2010). Predicting the popularity of online content. *Communications of the ACM, 53*(8), 80–88. doi:10.1145/1787234.1787254

Tambuscio, M., Oliveira, D. F. M., Ciampaglia, G. L., & Ruffo, G. (2016). Network segregation in a model of misinformation and fact checking. *ArXiv e-prints*.

Weedon, J., Nuland, W., & Stamos, A. (2017). *Information operations and facebook*. Retrieved from https://fbnewsroomus.files.wordpress.com/2017/04/facebook-and-information-operations-v1.pdf.

Weng, L., Flammini, A., Vespignani, A., & Menczer, F. (2012). Competition among memes in a world with limited attention. *Scientific Reports, 2*(335). doi:10.1038/srep00335

Wu, L., Morstatter, F., Hu, X., & Liu, H. (2017). Minning Misinformation in Social Media. In M. T. Thai, W. Wu & H. X. (Eds.), *Big Data in Complex and Social Networks* (pp. 123–152). Boca Raton, FL: CRC Press.

Contributors

Bakker, Arnold Institute of Psychology, Faculty of Social Sciences, Erasmus University Rotterdam, Postbus 1738, 3000 DR Rotterdam, the Netherlands
Email: bakker@fsw.eur.nl

Banerjee, Mita Department of English and Linguistics, Johannes Gutenberg University Mainz, Jakob-Welder-Weg 18, 55128 Mainz, Germany
E-Mail: mita.banerjee@uni-mainz.de

Berliner, David Mary Lou Fulton Teachers College, Arizona State University, Tempe, AZ 85287, USA
E-Mail: berliner@asu.edu

Bisang, Walter Department of English and Linguistics, Johannes Gutenberg University Mainz, Jakob-Welder-Weg 18, 55128 Mainz, Germany
E-Mail: wbisang@uni-mainz.de

Breakstone, Joel Stanford History Education Group, Stanford University, 485 Lausen Mall, Stanford, CA 94305, USA
E-Mail: breakstone@stanford.edu

Bukhari, Syed Saqib German Research Center for Artificial Intelligence (DFKI), Trippstadter Straße 122, 67663 Kaiserslautern, Germany
E-Mail: saqib.bukhari@dfki.de

Ciampaglia, Giovanni Luca Network Science Institute, Indiana University Bloomington, 1001 Sr 45/46, Bloomington, IN 47408, USA
E-Mail: gciampag@indiana.edu

Coyle, Do   School of Education, University of Aberdeen, MacRobert Building, 4th Floor, King's College, Aberdeen, AB24 5UA, Scotland
E-Mail: do.coyle@abdn.ac.uk

Cress, Ulrike   Leibniz Knowledge Media Research Center, Schleichstraße 6, 72076 Tübingen, Germany
E-Mail: u.cress@iwm-tuebingen.de

Demerouti, Eva   Department Industrial Engineering & Innovation Sciences, University of Technology Eindhoven, P.O. Box 513, 5600 MB Eindhoven, the Netherlands
E-Mail: E.Demerouti@tue.nl

Dengel, Andreas   German Research Center for Artificial Intelligence (DFKI), Smart Data & Knowledge Services, Trippstadter Straße 122, 67663 Kaiserslautern, Germany
E-Mail: Andreas.Dengel@dfki.de

Dormann, Christian   Department of Business and Economics Education, Johannes Gutenberg University Mainz, Jakob Welder-Weg 9, 55099 Mainz, Germany
E-Mail: lsDormann@uni-mainz.de

Gardner, Howard   Harvard Graduate School of Education, Harvard University, 13 Appian Way, Cambridge, MA 02138, USA
E-Mail: hgasst@gse.harvard.edu

Großmann, Nicolas   Faculty of Physics, University of Kaiserslautern, Erwin-Schroedinger-Str. 46 - 523, 67663 Kaiserslautern, Germany
E-Mail: grossmann@physik.uni-kl.de

Hansen-Schirra, Silvia   Language, Culture and Translation Science, Johannes Gutenberg University Mainz, An der Hochschule 2, 76726 Germersheim, Germany
E-Mail: hansenss@uni-mainz.de

Heisel, Carina   Faculty of Physics, University of Kaiserslautern, Erwin-Schroedinger-Str. 46, 67663 Kaiserslautern, Germany
E-Mail: heisel@physik.uni-kl.de

Hemati, Wahed   Text Technology Lab, Goethe-University Frankfurt am Main, Robert-Mayer-Straße 10, 60325 Frankfurt am Main, Germany
E-Mail: prg2.wahed@ki.informatik.uni-frankfurt.de

Hoffer, Michael   Goethe Center for Scientific Computing (G-CSC), Goethe-University Frankfurt am Main, Kettenhofweg 139, 60325 Frankfurt am Main, Germany
E-Mail: michael.hoffer@gcsc.uni-frankfurt.de

Hofmann, Sascha   Language, Culture and Translation Science, Johannes Gutenberg University Mainz, An der Hochschule 2, 76726 Germersheim, Germany
E-Mail: s.hofmann@uni-mainz.de

Igel, Christoph   German Research Center for Artificial Intelligence (DFKI), Educational Technology Lab, Alt-Moabit 91c, 10559 Berlin, Germany
E-Mail: christoph.igel@dfki.de

Imhof, Margarete   Department of Psychology in Educational Science, Johannes Gutenberg University Mainz, Binger Str. 14-16, 55122 Mainz, Germany
E-Mail: imhof@uni-mainz.de

Ishimaru, Shoya   German Research Center for Artificial Intelligence (DFKI), Trippstadter Straße 122, 67663 Kaiserslautern, Germany
E-Mail: Shoya.Ishimaru@dfki.de

Jabs, Robert   Goethe Center for Scientific Computing (G-CSC), Goethe-University Frankfurt am Main, Kettenhofweg 139, 60325 Frankfurt am Main, Germany
E-Mail: quasnt@googlemail.com

Kelly, Spencer D.   Department of Psychology and the Center for Language and Brain, Colgate University, 13 Oak Drive, Hamilton, NY, 13346, USA
E-Mail: skelly@colgate.edu

Kircher, Tilo   Department of Psychiatry and Psychotherapy, Philipps-University Marburg, Rudolf-Bultmann-Straße 8, 35039 Marburg, Germany
Email: kircher@med.uni-marburg.de

Kise, Koichi   Department of Computer Science and Intelligent Systems, Osaka Prefecture University, Gakuencho, Naka, Sakai, Osaka, 599-8531, Japan kise@cs.osakafu-u.ac.jp

Klein, Pascal   Department of Physics, Physics Education Research Group, University of Kaiserslautern, Erwin-Schroedinger-Str. 46, 67663 Kaiserslautern, Germany E-Mail: pklein@physik.uni-kl.de

Knauff, Markus   Department of Psychology, Justus Liebig University Giessen, Otto-Behaghel-Strasse 10F, 35394 Giessen, Germany E-Mail: markus.knauff@psychol.uni-giessen.de

Koretz, Daniel   Harvard Graduate School of Education, Harvard University, 6 Appian Way, Cambridge, MA 02138, USA Email: daniel_koretz@gse.harvard.edu

Kosslyn, Stephen M.   Minerva Schools at KGI, 1145 Market St, San Francisco, CA 94103, USA E-Mail: skosslyn@minerva.kgi.edu

Kravčík, Miloš   German Research Center for Artificial Intelligence (DFKI), Educational Technology Lab, Alt-Moabit 91c, 10559 Berlin, Germany E-Mail: milos.kravcik@dfki.de

Kuhn, Jochen   Department of Physics, Physics Education Research Group, University of Kaiserslautern, Erwin-Schroedinger-Str. 46, 67663 Kaiserslautern, Germany E-Mail: kuhn@physik.uni-kl.de

Lücking, Andy   Faculty of Computer Science and Mathematics, Goethe-University Frankfurt am Main, Robert-Mayer-Straße 10, 60325 Frankfurt am Main, Germany E-Mail: luecking@em.uni-frankfurt.de

Maurer, Marcus   Institut of Journalism and Communication Studies, Johannes Gutenberg University Mainz, Jakob-Welder-Weg 12, 55128 Mainz, Germany E-Mail: mmaurer@uni-mainz.de

McGrew, Sarah Stanford History Education Group, Stanford University, 485 Lausen Mall, Stanford, CA 94305, USA
E-Mail: smcgrew@stanford.edu

Mehler, Alexander Computer Science and Mathematics Department, Goethe-University Frankfurt am Main, Robert-Mayer-Straße 10, 60325 Frankfurt am Main, Germany
E-Mail: mehler@em.uni-frankfurt.de

Meyer, Oliver Department of English and Linguistics, Johannes Gutenberg University Mainz, Jakob-Welder Weg 18, 55128 Mainz, Germany
E-Mail: omeyer@uni-mainz.de

Minnameier, Gerhard Department of Economic Education, Goethe-University Frankfurt am Main, Theodor-W.-Adorno-Platz 4, 60629 Frankfurt am Main, Germany
E-Mail: minnameier@econ.uni-frankfurt.de

Molerov, Dimitri Department of Education Studies, Humboldt-Universität zu Berlin, Geschwister-Scholl-Straße 7, 10117 Berlin, Germany
E-Mail: molerov@hu-berlin.de

Nägel, Arne Goethe Center for Scientific Computing (G-CSC), Goethe-University Frankfurt am Main, Kettelhofweg 139, 60325 Frankfurt am Main, Germany
E-Mail: arne.naegel@gcsc.uni-mainz.de

Nagels, Arne Department of English and Linguistics, Johannes Gutenberg University Mainz, Jakob-Welder-Weg 18, 55128 Mainz, Germany
E-mail: anagels@uni-mainz.de

Nitzke, Jean Language, Culture and Translation Science, Johannes Gutenberg University Mainz, An der Hochschule 2, 76711 Germersheim, Germany
E-Mail: nitzke@uni-mainz.de

Oeberst, Aileen Department of Social and Legal Psychology, Johannes Gutenberg University Mainz, Binger Str. 14-16, 55122 Mainz, Germany
E-Mail: aoeberst@uni-mainz.de

Ortega, Teresa   Stanford History Education Group, Stanford University, 485 Lausen Mall, Stanford, CA 94305, USA
E-Mail: teortega@stanford.edu

Oser, Fritz   Department of Educational Science, University of Fribourg, Rue R.-A. de Faucigny 2, 1700 Freiburg, Switzerland
E-Mail: fritz.oser@unifr.ch

Quiring, Oliver   Institute of Journalism and Communication Studies, Johannes Gutenberg University Mainz, Jakob-Welder-Weg 12, 55128 Mainz, Germany
E-Mail: sekretariat-quiring@uni-mainz.de

Schemer, Christian   Institute of Journalism and Communication Studies, Johannes Gutenberg University Mainz, Jakob-Welder-Weg 12, 55128 Mainz, Germany
E-Mail: schemer@uni-mainz.de

Schmidt, Susanne   Department of Business and Economics Education, Johannes Gutenberg University Mainz, Jakob-Welder-Weg 9, 55128 Mainz
E-Mail: susanne.schmidt@uni-mainz.de

Shavelson, Richard J.   Stanford Graduate School of Education, Stanford University, 485 Lasuen Mall, Stanford, CA 94305-3096, USA
E-Mail: richs@stanford.edu

Straube, Benjamin   Department of Psychiatry and Psychotherapy, Philipps-University Marburg, Rudolf-Bultmann-Straße 8, 35039 Marburg, Germany
E-Mail: Benjamin.Straube@med.uni-marburg.de

Ullrich, Carsten   German Research Center for Artificial Intelligence (DFKI), Educational Technology Lab, Alt-Moabit 91c, 10559 Berlin, Germany
E-Mail: carten.ullrich@dfki.de

Vreeze, Jort de   Leibniz Knowledge Media Research Center, Schleichstraße 6, 72076 Tübingen, Germany
E-Mail: j.devreeze@iwm-tuebingen.de

Wiese, Wanja   Theoretical Philosophy, Johannes Gutenberg University Mainz, 55099 Mainz, Germany
E-Mail: wawiese@uni-mainz.de

Wineburg, Sam   Stanford Graduate School of Education, Stanford University, 485 Lasuen Mall, Stanford, CA 94305-3096, USA
E-Mail: wineburg@stanford.edu

Wittum, Gabriel   Goethe Center for Scientific Computing (G-CSC), Goethe-University Frankfurt am Main, Kettenhofweg 139, 60325 Frankfurt am Main, Germany
E-Mail: wittum@techsim.org

Zlatkin-Troitschanskaia, Olga   Department of Business and Economics Education, Johannes Gutenberg University Mainz, Jakob Welder-Weg 9, 55099 Mainz, Germany
E-Mail: lstroitschanskaia@uni-mainz.de

The manufacturer's authorised representative in the EU is Springer
Nature Customer Service Centre GmbH, Europaplatz 3, 69115 Heidelberg,
Germany. If you have any concerns regarding our products, please
contact ProductSafety@springernature.com

Printed and bound by CPI Group (UK) Ltd, Croydon, CR0 4YY
30/04/2026
02100217-0001